IMPRINT

PROJECT MANAGEMENT
Florian Kobler, Cologne

COLLABORATION
Harriet Graham, Turin
Inga Hallsson, Cologne

PRODUCTION
Frauke Kaiser, Cologne

DESIGN
Sense/Net Art Direction
Andy Disl and
Birgit Eichwede, Cologne
www.sense-net.de

GERMAN TRANSLATION
Kristina Brigitta Köper, Berlin

FRENCH TRANSLATION
Claire Debard, Freiburg

© VG BILD-KUNST
Bonn 2012, for the works of
Benoît Cornette, Odile Decq,
Jean Nouvel, and Ben van
Berkel

PRINTED IN ITALY
ISBN 978–3–8365–3440–6

© 2012 TASCHEN GMBH
Hohenzollernring 53
D–50672 Cologne
www.taschen.com

ARCHITECTURE NOW!
EAT SHOP DRINK

Architektur heute! ESSEN SHOPPEN TRINKEN
L'architecture d'aujourd'hui ! MANGER BOIRE ACHETER

Philip Jodidio

TASCHEN

CONTENTS

INTRODUCTION

TO EAT, TO DRINK, PERCHANCE TO SHOP

"Some people maintain that design is not art," says Tokujin Yoshioka. "I imagine that for such people 'art' is an alluring but supremely frightening thing. People often ask me the difference between design and art. Ancient beings had no concept of design, yet there was art and music. Why do people listen to music? The answer probably lies within that question. If all designs were simple and practical, there would be no richness to life or the desires of the heart. Our lives are imbued with things like moving music, evocative cinema, uncontrollable feelings of love, and an appreciation for the mysteries of the natural world." Though it is true that Tokujin Yoshioka's vision of design often transports viewers into a realm where the intangible seems to take form, it may also be true that design, and architecture are brought closer to their pure essence when they are employed to the benefit of ephemeral pursuits… *Eat Shop Drink* is the name of this volume and it concerns restaurants, stores, and bars. By definition, such spaces must glorify transience, either following or leading the fashions of the moment. As in all disciplines, some creators, usually very few, make art out of transience, and find the permanent soul of the ephemeral, which might ultimately be called life. "We are living in the age when design overflows," continues Tokujin Yoshioka. "In such an age, I have pondered on expressing something that does not have form or design. In other words, it is something that transcends the general idea of form and design, and provokes emotion. It is not about dealing with forms or making minimal forms, but about designing what gets us right into the work, lifts up our spirits. I would like to design something that moves even myself. In recent years, I am challenging myself to incorporate formless elements that appeal to our heart—such as new ideas, colors, scents—and to design an emotion itself. One of them is a phenomenon called 'light;' another one is something that you cannot see, and yet another is something that has unlimited forms because it transforms its appearance."

REVELERS UNDER THE CHERRY BLOSSOMS

The Japanese art of woodblock printing as it was practiced between the 17th and 20th centuries bears the name of *Ukiyo-e*, meaning "images of the floating world." This is an evanescent world of fleeting beauty where cherry blossoms or maple leaves are expressions of nature that surpass any art. In *Ukiyo-e*, contemporary Japanese society encountered ancient Buddhist ideas of impermanence with an insouciance seen in the *hanami* or *yozakura*, where revelers sit beneath the cherry trees and drink. Though some famous chefs and fashion designers prefer to ensconce their art in the architecture of permanence, most moments of eating, shopping, and drinking are potentially festive and generally ephemeral. So, too, then are the majority of the recent realizations selected for this book. And yet, eating, drinking, and shopping (for essentials?) are permanent needs, more basic than almost any other source of architectural design and construction. This dichotomy is actually a very positive point for the development of architecture. Since shops and bars are often inserted into existing spaces, or can be on a very small scale, clients may well accept to commission younger architects or designers, as can be seen in a number of the projects published here. Where substantial experience is often demanded for large newly built structures, a refurbishment or an interior design commission is within the reach of young, talented architects, one reason for the choice of the subject of this book. Tokujin Yoshioka's work as seen

1
Tokujin Yoshioka, "The Invisibles,"
Milan, Italy, 14–19 April, 2010

here in fact has more to do with installation art than with the actual creation of points of sale or consumption, yet the principle is the same for any truly gifted creator, to approach the "pure essence" of architecture and design when they are applied to ephemeral pursuits. Restaurants, bars, and shops are also places where disciplines come together, where art can meet architecture and design.

WHAT COLOR IS YOUR RGB?

In fact, a number of the projects featured here are based on little more than the "light" that the Japanese designer refers to. Nightclubs are particularly well adapted to the intrusion of light as an architectural or even emotional presence. The Brazilian designer Muti Randolph has, in fact, made a career of bringing light and sound together into a single space. His D-Edge 2.0 (São Paulo, Brazil, 2009–10, page 300) is an expansion on the earlier D-Edge (2003) club next to the same location. Randolph states: "The space is determined by the light, and the light is determined by the music. The main idea is to show the relation of music and space through lighting, using software that analyzes the sound and makes the light change accordingly." Light effects have long been a part of nightclubs and dance locations in particular, but the advent of the bright RGB devices, and in particular LED arrays, has transformed and multiplied the potential for computer-driven displays that can generate an infinite variety of color effects. In the case of D-Edge 2.0, the music itself, linked by computer to the lighting system, defines the ambiance of the space to an extent that almost obviates the need for any architecture beyond a basic protective shell.

The young Spanish group 2G Arquitectos has worked in a similar vein for their Nébula or Lightcloud club in Almendralejo (Badajoz, Spain, 2009–10, page 50). The designers speak of a "fog of light and music," of a "cloud of light." Inserted into an existing space, the Nébula does nothing less than to envelop dancers with "strokes of light and sound."

Tokujin Yoshioka expressed his own ideas on potential "invisibility" in an installation for the furniture manufacturer Kartell on the occasion of the 2010 Milan Furniture Fair. The designer had previously explored the concept of invisibility for his work with such pieces as Waterfall (Tokyo, Japan, 2006), a private bar featuring a 4.2-meter-long block of optical glass, or his 2002 "Chair that disappears in the rain." In the case of Kartell, he sought to create a chair made out of acrylics so thin that a seated person would appear to "float in the air." The presentation of these chairs was complemented by the "Snowflake" installation made up of a large number of transparent plastic "prism" sticks. Suspended in the air, these prisms naturally changed their appearance with the slightest movement, greeting visitors into an installation as close to being truly ephemeral as possible.

UP IN THE ALPS

Given the very nature of restaurants, bars, and boutiques, it is the lot of their designers or architects to make use in most cases of an existing shell or space. There are a few purpose-designed buildings in this book, but these can be examined after more common and less

2
2G, *Nébula, Almendralejo, Badajoz, Spain, 2009–10*

"permanent" examples. The young Swiss architects Ambroise Bonvin and Claudia Bétrisey (of Actescollectifs) have begun the transformation of a former restaurant and gondola station located above Crans-Montana at an altitude of 2112 meters above sea level (Chetzeron Restaurant, Crans-Montana, Switzerland, 2008–09, page 56). For the moment, Chetzeron is a stylish restaurant with spectacular views of the Rhone Valley and the chain of 4000-meter mountains opposite leading to the Matterhorn. Using stones found in neighboring fields, the architects gave their structure a rough stone cladding and above all a Minérgie (the Swiss equivalent of LEED) classification because of the building's low energy use and minimal carbon footprint. Bonvin and Bétrisey will now undertake the second phase of this project that will convert the adjoining gondola station into a 15-room boutique hotel. Given the reticence of Swiss authorities to accept any new hotels at altitudes above 2000 meters, the authorization process took a great deal of time and effort for the architects and owners of the building. Their clever reuse of an existing building, making it into a fashionable destination, is a testimony to the talent of these young architects.

PHANTOM OF THE OPERA

The Mendini Restaurant in Groningen (Groninger Museum, Groningen, the Netherlands, 2010, page 88) represents an entirely different type of reuse of an existing space. The Groninger Museum was one of the most outstanding examples of collaboration between architects and designers when it opened in 1994. Alessandro Mendini, Philippe Starck, Michele de Lucchi, and Coop Himmelb(l)au all took part in the project. Mendini was the overall director of the scheme and also the designer of the restaurant, which has just been refurbished by Maarten Baas, a 33-year-old designer based in 's-Hertogenbosch in the Netherlands. The 258-square-meter café-restaurant features handmade benches, bar, and mirror of red clay in this simple and elegant reinterpretation of a space that might have given pause to many better-known designers.

At the age of 56, Odile Decq is emerging as one of the most significant French architects of her generation. Her MACRO Museum of Contemporary Art in Rome (Italy, 2003–10) accomplished the feat of stealing some of the limelight from Zaha Hadid with her much larger and more hyped MAXXI: National Museum of XXI Century Arts (Rome, Italy, 1998–2009). Decq's most recent realization is the Opéra Restaurant (Paris, France, 2008–11, page 158) in the Opéra Garnier. "Without mimicking the existing monument, but respecting it while affirming its truly contemporary character," as she says, her "phantom" enters the old opera building giving it new life.

On a scale much smaller than the thousand square meters of the Opéra Restaurant, Yuko Nagayama, at the age of 36, undertook a task that in a way was just as challenging as the architecture of Charles Garnier (1825–98). Formed in the office of the talented architect Jun Aoki, Nagayama has completed a number of retail designs and in this instance was asked to modernize a 45-square-meter century-old coffee house in Tokyo. Her Kayaba Coffee (Tokyo, Japan, 2009, page 278) is an exemplary case of commercial reuse. While the ground floor maintains the seating that one might expect in a coffee shop, the architect has transformed the upper level into a reading area for contemporary art books. She also demonstrates that a carefully studied architectural minimalism can be perfectly compatible with one of the older coffee shops in Tokyo, a city so completely rebuilt after earthquakes, fires, and wars that century-old structures are rare.

Elena Pérez Garrigues and Daniel Blanco Cohen of Ninom were both born in 1975. They created their firm in Madrid in 2006 "with the idea of integrating architecture with disciplines such as dance, photography, and scenery." Their CVNE Wine Hall (Haro, La Rioja, Spain, 2009, page 282) is part of a larger project (1920 square meters) but it is a new installation in an 1879 building. In response to the client's desire to create "new dynamic activities centered around wine," the architects inserted an "iron box" into the preexisting space. Stripping back the old space to its bare essentials, the architects inserted not only their box but also simple modern furnishings and spotlights. Together with a selection of old wine barrels, both the traditions of the winery and its modernity are simultaneously highlighted.

WE ARE NOT REINVENTING THE WHEEL

Where the state of the economy and perhaps a pervading conservatism seem to mark the architectural scene in the United States, there are notable exceptions. One of these is the New York firm LOT-EK, which surprisingly is run by two Italian-born architects, Ada Tolla and Giuseppe Lignano. LOT-EK has specialized in temporary installations, such as their Uniqlo Container Stores (New York, 2006) and PUMACity (Alicante, Spain, and Boston, Massachusetts, 2008). They completed the permanent APAP OpenSchool (Anyang, South Korea, 2010) using shipping containers, as they have for other projects. Taking on the limited space (47 square meters) of the Van Alen Books store located at 30 West 22nd Street in Manhattan (New York, USA, 2011, page 242), the architects installed a 4.3-meter seating platform made of 70 recycled doors. With its black façade with generous glazing, the Van Alen Books space stands out because of this amphitheater-like installation, but also because of the bright yellow used by LOT-EK for the overall interior color. Van Alen's director Olympia Kazi feels that the love of books is still strong in the digital era, and she states: "We are not reinventing the wheel, we are addressing a need." LOT-EK's use of strong graphics and bright yellow links this shop to the industrial world, where other architects have often sought to produce a rarified atmosphere for the printed word. With an inexpensive and bright approach, the architects point to the ongoing and real interest of books, obviously shared by the clients of Van Alen Books.

Makoto Tanijiri was born in Hiroshima in 1974. He has already designed more than 60 houses, but his Suppose Design Office is also active in the retail and restaurant design field. His Café Day (Shizuoka, Japan, 2010, page 346) is located in a 74-square-meter space formerly occupied by two traditional Japanese bars. His solution for the new café was anything but traditional. Taking on the urban signs that surrounded the building, and a driving school in particular, he used bright yellow tones and street markings to connect the café to its external environment. The idea of an ambiguity between interior and exterior is, of course, firmly rooted in the architectural history of Japan, which gives this whimsical realization a background that is not without interest. In a sense, by making the café a part of the parking area and road system, he has updated a very old Japanese idea.

The Aesop Saint-Honoré store in Paris (France, 2010, page 250) is located at 256 Rue Saint-Honoré near the Palais Royal in an 18th-century building. The partners of March Studio, who used no less than 3500 pieces of wood to create their installation, are even younger than most of the designers in this book. Rodney Eggleston (born in 1981) and Anne-Laure Cavigneaux (born in 1980) combined their origins and skills for the Paris store of Aesop, a Melbourne-based purveyor of products for skin, hair, and body. March Studio is located in Melbourne as well; Eggleston is Australian, while Cavigneaux is a Parisian graphic artist. Working with Victorian ash harvested in managed forests in Australia, March Studio covered all available surfaces with the wood, creating a homogeneous décor quite distinct from the stones of 18th-century Paris. It seems clear that this type of installation, involving 100 square meters of floor area, is an ideal laboratory for young talents with an open-minded client (Dennis Paphitis, the founder of Aesop). Few companies, though, would dare ask 30-year-old designers to create an entire building, particularly in the difficult economic climate of the moment.

A FARMHOUSE ON A HILL

The Brazilian architect Isay Weinfeld has long been specialized in luxurious private homes, restaurants, and retail store design. In the case of the Fasano Restaurant (Punta del Este, Uruguay, 2010–11, page 384), he made use of an old stone farmhouse to create a spectacular 390-square-meter hilltop restaurant with a view toward Maldonado. Combining the roughly stacked stones of the farmhouse and its setting with a more minimalist concrete box, the architect has inhabited a place meant for an entirely different purpose in an original and efficient way. Weinfeld had already worked for the Fasano group on a number of projects, including their spectacular hotel and restaurant in São Paulo (2001–03). Clearly the sophistication employed in an urban environment and with new structures was not to be imitated in any way near the Uruguayan coast. Isay Weinfeld nonetheless succeeded in bringing the reputation of the group into the new territory of this rugged natural setting.

NOTHING HAPPENS FOR A REASON

With the construction of new museums slowing across the world for economic reasons, but also because of a glut of existing institutions, it may be that the ephemeral pursuits of eating, shopping, and drinking have somehow been drawn closer to the arts. The idea that a product, even a culinary one, can aspire to some higher, more "permanent" values is not a new one. Recently opened cafés, bars, and shops appear, though, to have found that the participation of artists or the presence of their works also serve to elevate content beyond the purely mercantile. An interesting example of this type of collaboration is the Logomo Café (Turku, Finland, 2010–11, page 76). The firm Artek, founded in 1935 by Alvar Aalto and two associates, was the patron of this project, conceived in the context of Turku's turn as European Capital of Culture in 2011. Artek called on the German artist Tobias Rehberger to create an installation called "Nothing Happens for a Reason" in the Logomo building which served as the central venue for the events. Like some others, such as the noted American landscape architect Ken Smith, Rehberger is fascinated by military camouflage techniques. He applied some of the reasoning behind British World War Two cam-

3
*Artek, "Nothing Happens for
a Reason," Logomo Café, Turku,
Finland, 2010–11*

3

ouflage to this 230-square-meter café, where a network of superimposed lines and essentially black-and-white décor overlap and even run over the Artek furnishings. The net result is to create spatial ambiguities that render the distinction between objects and architecture difficult to discern in some instances. Though it could be qualified as decorative and surely was conceived as a temporary installation, "Nothing Happens for a Reason" demonstrates that even a café can aspire to the status of an artwork. And what if temporary things are really all that matters?

ACTION MOVIE

A more ambitious and far-reaching project is the Silencio Club in Paris (France, 2010–11, page 246), conceived by the movie director David Lynch. The director of *The Elephant Man* (1980) and *Lost Highway* (1997) amongst other cult movies, Lynch has a decided interest in art and music, but this was actually his first venture into the domain of interior design. Located in a historic 1883 building at 142 Rue Montmartre in the second arrondissement of Paris, Silencio is a large (650-square-meter) space marked by an extensive use of gold leaf and randomly scattered raw wood cladding. More than a bar, Silencio is intended as a private club where live music, movie screenings, or art events will occur. An art library is part of the scheme as well. The association of a personality such as David Lynch with an interior design project and a private club surely are sufficient to assure the initial success of Silencio. Though he was assisted in the process by Raphaël Navot and the architectural office ENIA, Lynch's own propensity to cross the boundaries that usually separate disciplines as varied as movie making and interior design sets the tone for this realization. The events that will occur in Silencio are naturally ephemeral by definition and even its design seeks out an improvisational tone in many respects. While much of contemporary art has voluntarily eschewed the monumentality and permanence implicit in the museum, it might not be surprising that a space dedicated to the night (open from 6:00 p.m. to 6:00 a.m.) would today attract the real artists of the moment.

TAKASHI AND ANISH GO SHOPPING

The architect Peter Marino may be the most fashionable and successful designer of retail spaces and high-end apartments in the world. His clients, such as Chanel or Louis Vuitton, are the best-known fashion brands of the day. It is interesting to note that these brands simultaneously seek to be contemporary and yet also to play on their "traditions" and history. What could be more natural than to bring works of art into these spaces. Marino's new Chanel SoHo store (New York, USA, 2010, page 260) is replete with purpose-designed artworks by Peter Belyi, Robert Greene, Gregor Hildebrandt, Alan Rath, and Richard Woods. Here the work of art itself takes a new turn, doing its best to help sell the products. In the Louis Vuitton New Bond Street emporium (London, UK, 2010, page 254) a different approach is taken, with real works by Richard Prince, Takashi Murakami, Gilbert & George, Anish Kapoor, Christ Ofili, and Gary Hume lighting up the 1500-square-meter space. It was speculated at a certain point that museums had replaced churches as the center of civic pride. With their funding problems and systemic overreach, museums may well be falling from their period of post–World War Two glory.

4

4
*Jean Nouvel, Le Loft Restaurant,
Hotel Stephansdom Vienna, Austria,
2006–10*

MÉLANGE DE GENRES

With all due respect to more established religions, it might be asked if, in this new era of Mammon, a visit to SoHo or Bond Street might not be as close to heaven as the average shopper can ever hope to come. The great Japanese department store chains like Seibu led the way many years ago with their integrated museums and high-profile temporary art exhibitions. Why go to a museum when you can get your culture in the store. Why go to church when all you really want is a new handbag. Since the art market has fully espoused mercantilism, it is true that art seems even more in its place with a really nice pair of shoes. Curiously, it may be the architect who comes out on top of this *mélange de genres*. Space per se is pure and materials when properly used remain noble. No criticism of Peter Marino is intended in these lines; he is, once again, the master of the moment when it comes, in particular, to retail spaces, and there is surely nothing wrong with associating the projects of Chanel and Louis Vuitton with contemporary art. Rather, it is a societal trend of considerable import that projects retail sales, architecture, and art into the same forum, all to some extent obliged to cater to the immediate needs of customers. To buy or not to buy, that is the question. The new religion is not art, but shopping.

THE CHAIN HOTELS GO ARTSY

A very different approach to associating art and architecture was taken by Jean Nouvel for his Loft Restaurant in the Stephansdom Sofitel in Vienna (Austria, 2006–10, page 290). Very much a part of the overall scheme of the building, also designed by Nouvel, the rooftop restaurant has a spectacular video ceiling designed by the Swiss artist Pipilotti Rist. Rist also intervened in the lobby or bar space lower down in the structure. With Jean Nouvel's powerful architecture, her colorful ceilings, visible from the exterior thanks to the full-height glazing of the restaurant, are part of a whole, conceived under the watchful eye of the architect. Here, although the ultimate goal is for the hotel to be a commercial success, the architect and the artist have brought the full free rein of their imagination to bear on spatial experiences. This is not quite the same as hanging a painting on a shop wall, even if the two gestures have a common goal. Nouvel and Rist have created space in which disciplines meet, a rare enough occasion in the contemporary world to be pointed out.

The association of talented architects and designers in the hotel field is an ongoing phenomenon of some significance. Architects like the German group Graft became recognized designers when they installed the very chic Hotel Q! in Berlin in 2002–04. Graft is featured in this book for other projects, but hotels such as the W Hotel in London (UK, 2010–11, page 136) certainly find quality architecture or interior décor to be an important element in their success. This design-oriented chain hotel called on Rob Wagemans and Concrete from Amsterdam for its Sweat and AWAY Spa overlooking Leicester Square, its Spice Market London restaurant, and its room designs. The Mandarin Oriental, Paris (France, 2009–11, page 216), designed by Jean-Michel Wilmotte, features the Bar 8, Sur Mesure restaurant and Camélia restaurant, all the work of Jouin Manku. Wilmotte and Patrick Jouin are amongst the best-known French designers, and their mutual creative presence in a single, luxury hotel again shows that even chain hotels are anxious to create their own mark, and to explore the upper end of design to attract

5
*Gary Card, Late Night Chameleon
Café LN-CC, London, UK, 2010*

5

a special category of clients. It might be said that boutique "design" hotels like Q! inspired large hotel groups to diversify their appearance from one location to another, now calling on the best creative talents of the moment.

THE ART OF RETAIL

Though Jean Nouvel and Pipilotti Rist are clearly at the high end of contemporary architecture and art, the rapidly moving current scene takes inspiration from figures who have made their reputation in other areas than interior design. Gary Card is a set and prop designer and a graphic and illustration artist. He has worked with such stars of the contemporary art and fashion scene as Nick Knight, Stella McCartney, and Lady Gaga. His design for LN-CC (London, UK, 2010, page 116) was his first interior design commission. The Late Night Chameleon Café is really more a fashion and bookstore than its name would imply. Its developers, John Skelton and Daniel Mitchell, project a willful mix of clothing, music, and art toward their customers, in a sense developing a retail environment that blends what they perceive to be the best of the "mainstream" and the "underground." Clearly put, there are no limits other than the taste of the owners of the brand. Gary Card plunged into this assignment with a mixture of raw wood and orange acrylic. As he says, citing the "shock and awe" artists Paul McCarthy and Jeff Koons as sources of inspiration: "It's color and the perverse that intrigues me the most, especially when the two collide." Here, the interior design participates in an original commercial concept, where nobody is trying to be anything but what they are. Card and his highly touted blog, www.garycardiology.blogspot.com, are as much in fashion as LN-CC itself—the two mix and match perfectly. When the giants of the Bauhaus dreamt of the *gesamtkunstwerk*, the total work of art, they thought of art, architecture, and design. Would the total work of art today include a fourth partner in the process, which we might glibly call the "retail concept"? Again, no disrespect is meant, quite the contrary, admiration is intended. Perhaps art and architecture are changing even faster than the creators themselves would care to admit.

MOLDING THE MOON JELLY

The very definition of art or even design in the context of restaurants, bars, and stores seems to become vague in the context of a society that has made consumerism one of its highest values. There are those who strive to use the cutting edge of technology to approach design in an artistic and yet efficient way. One of the more unusual figures of this type is Evan Douglis, who was trained as an architect at the Architectural Association in London, Cooper Union in New York, and the Harvard GSD. He worked with high-end firms like that of Tod Williams, and Agrest and Gandelsonas, as well as with the more versatile figure Emilio Ambasz, before creating his own firm in 1992, the Evan Douglis Studio, now based in Troy, New York. According to him, the "Evan Douglis Studio is an architecture and interdisciplinary design firm committed to the research and application of new self-generative systems, membrane technology, and contemporary fabrication techniques as applied to a range of projects." His Moon Jelly (Choice: Kitchens and Bakery, Brooklyn, New York, USA, 2009–10, page 170) is one of his most recently completed works. Using such sophisticated techniques as three-dimensional printing, Douglis created an astonishing ceiling that he describes as a "beautiful theatrical cloud suspended above one's head." Though it is a product of contemporary industrial methods, this ceil-

6
Francisco Mangado, Café Baluarte,
Pamplona, Navarra, Spain, 2006

6

ing appears to enfold an almost infinite number of patterns, which might for some recall the swirling stars of a painting by Van Gogh. It is, says Douglis, "an extension of our continued interest in surface intricacy, animate form, and serial distraction as a totally immersive experience in architecture today." Artists who actually imagine pieces for stores or restaurants, like Pipilotti Rist in Vienna, bring originality and creativity to a space that can well transcend any specific use of the architecture. Though trained as an architect, Evan Douglis appears to be working at the physical interface of the built and the potentially decorative. Using high technology—three-dimensional printing is just now beginning to be employed in various fields—he also explores the limits between design, architecture, and art in a meaningful way. In an otherwise functional and relatively plain space, the architect has brought the ceiling alive with its patterns but also with the custom-made chandeliers. Though obviously the thinking and the inspiration at the time were very different, it might be noted that the remarkably complex ironwork of Louis Sullivan's Carson Pirie Scott Store (now the Sullivan Center, Chicago, USA, 1904) was restored to its original glory in 2010. Long before the *tabula rasa* of Gropius, Sullivan, called the "father of modernism," famously declared that "form ever follows function." Despite the rise of industrial repetition in architecture and the modern absence of decoration, the work of Sullivan still stands out. He insisted that decoration should have a practical purpose, but it might be that the clients of Moon Jelly in Brooklyn are satisfied to merely look up and lose themselves in the meanders of patterns that draw the viewer upwards.

GLASS BOX OR CARGO SHED?

Jean Nouvel's Sofitel in Vienna does include a restaurant and a bar designed by the architect, but it might be said that these were necessary adjuncts to the overall hotel project. Though fairly rare, purpose-built structures that house retail space or bars and restaurants do provide opportunities for talented architects and designers to express themselves in these fields. The Coubertin Restaurant (Olympic Hall, Olympic Park, Munich, Germany, 2010, page 82) is in fact a refurbishment and extension project in the context of the 1972 Olympic Games site. This assignment fell quite naturally to the firm Auer+Weber+Assoziierte. Founding partners Fritz Auer and Carlo Weber worked with Behnisch & Partner until creating their own firm in 1980. The original Olympic structures were designed by Günter Behnisch working with the engineer Frei Otto. The new 500-seat restaurant is a fitting tribute to the earlier work, contrasting its rectilinear purity to the spider-web curves of the 1972 complex.

Francisco Mangado did not have quite so complex a case of historic references to deal with in his Café Baluarte (Pamplona, Navarra, Spain, 2006), though it is next to the Parliament of Navarra. The main point of reference for this minimalistic glass-box structure is Mangado's own Baluarte Auditorium and Congress Center (Pamplona, 2000–03). Calling on a modernist tradition that might be said to include the Farnsworth House (Ludwig Mies van der Rohe, Plano, Illinois, USA, 1945–51), the architect sought to give users the "sensation of being outside, protected from the weather yet able to enjoy the spatial depth of the square and the views of the surrounding architecture." Unlike the Mies house however, this glass-walled box is fully capable of opening itself to the neighboring square in good weather. There are surely good

7
UNStudio, Galleria Centercity,
Cheonan, South Korea, 2008–10

7

budgetary reasons to design a simple glass structure for such use, yet Mangado makes his Café Baluarte into a real work of architecture, not that common in any context.

An interesting combination of the reuse of existing industrial space and purpose-built construction on a contiguous site is North Wharf in Auckland by Fearon Hay (New Zealand, 2010–11, page 372). Part of the 2.5-hectare Wynyard Waterfront Development area, the architects worked on three structures, one of which is a renovated historic cargo shed. Designed for retail and entertainment activities, two new buildings flank the restored 1930s Old Red Shed warehouse. As has been the case for the rehabilitation of industrial buildings elsewhere in the world, the Auckland project retains a good deal of the original "rough" finishing of the original Old Red Shed. This dockside authenticity gives a flavor to the architecture, both old and new, that heightens the sense of place for visitors. A number of years ago, architects would have been only too happy to erase any trace of an industrial past in such circumstances, but refurbishment has increased in importance even as economic constraints have made new construction rarer. It seems clear that decisions initially made on a purely economic basis have become the grounds for aesthetic reasoning that the public readily accepts. There is a sense of authenticity that can only be conferred by time, and very contemporary architecture has absorbed this lesson, willfully integrating the old and new, making the feeling of architecture and design today more complex, more varied, and surely less "slick."

SHOPPING CENTERS GET A FAÇADE

Although high-end fashion still often seeks to occupy boutiques, a good part of retail sales is concentrated in shopping centers. Three noted architects have either completed or are working on substantial facilities of this nature that deserve note. The first to finish in this category is UNStudio with their 66 000-square-meter Galleria Centercity (Cheonan, South Korea, 2008–10, page 372). Ben van Berkel and his team have long since mastered the art of employing the computer for large-scale buildings, such as their Mercedes-Benz Museum (Stuttgart, Germany, 2003–06). Van Berkel is very interested in optical effects and, in this case, uses two layers of aluminum profiles to yield a surprising moiré effect when the building is seen from the exterior. Having successfully completed the renovation of a store in Seoul for the same retail group (Galleria, 2003), UNStudio had already proven that good design can, indeed, be a sound business investment. As is usually the case in their work, the architects have intimately linked the modern exterior appearance of the complex to its equally surprising interior, described as "a kind of spatial waterfall."

Massimiliano and Doriana Fuksas have completed such remarkable projects as the million-square-meter Fiera Milano (Rho-Pero, Milan, Italy, 2002–05) and the MyZeil Shopping Mall in Frankfurt (Germany, 2009). They have recently finished the Palatino Center (Turin, Italy, 1998–2011, page 194), a 13 000-square-meter clothing sales space. The structure features multistory prismatic pillars with embedded metal shelves, and a façade made up of no less than 60 000 glass elements and 150 000 kilograms of steel. As they did on a smaller scale

8
Rizoma Arquitetura, Botanical Shop,
Brumadinho, Minas Gerais,
Brazil, 2011

8

for the Armani group (the Armani Ginza Tower, Tokyo, Japan, 2005–07, and Emporio Armani Fifth Avenue, New York, USA, 2009), the Fuksas couple demonstrates that an intelligent use of architecture and design durably attracts attention to retail spaces. As government projects have become rarer, industries such as fashion have to a certain extent taken up the slack in creative architectural commissions. Nothing can compensate global recession, but luxury goods have proven surprisingly resistant to the gloom felt in other areas.

Another of the "big" names in contemporary architecture is working on a mixed-use complex in Düsseldorf, Germany. Kö-Bogen by Daniel Libeskind (2011–13) is a 40 000-square-meter, six-story structure that combines offices and retail space. Aside from its combination of uses, the interest of Kö-Bogen also lies in the overall concept of creating a connection between landscape and the urban environment, "permeated cuts" into the architectural forms that allow the landscape elements to "naturally blend and flow into the building space." Though he remains best known for such works as the Jewish Museum in Berlin (1989–2001), Libeskind has also completed large-scale shopping-oriented projects such as the Westside Shopping and Leisure Center (Bern, Switzerland, 2005–08) and Crystals at CityCenter (Las Vegas, Nevada, 2006–09). While an earlier generation of architects might have found that shopping centers posed too many practical problems to allow for creative designs, it can be said that both retailing and the architectural profession itself have moved on from that position. Many of the shopping complexes cited here have clear and decided architectural ambitions that are a part of the retailing concept that they embody. As cultural institutions like museums or concert halls have become rarer as clients, once again retailing is emerging as a partial alternative for first-rank architects.

CONCRETE IN THE JUNGLE
Nor should it be suggested that interesting architecture for restaurants, bars, and retail must necessarily be on a large scale. Far from the urban rush of Düsseldorf or Turin, the young architects Maria Paz (born in 1985) and Thomaz Regatos (born in 1981) of Rizoma Arquitetura have completed two small structures for the Inhotim Contemporary Art Center located 60 kilometers from the Brazilian city of Belo Horizonte. Their 320-seat Oiticica Restaurant (Brumadinho, Brazil, 2010, page 310) is a low-cost concrete-and-metal screen structure that took only three months to build. Inserted to the greatest extent possible into the existing dense vegetation, the building is naturally ventilated. Rizoma also completed a Botanical Shop for the same art center in 2011 (page 314). Meant for the sale of plants and garden utensils, and built with concrete, stone, and wood in a three-month period, this 200-square-meter building cost only $125 000. The Botanical Shop is more an open pavilion than it is a traditional building, and, like the earlier restaurant, it was built with careful attention to the existing trees on the site.

MINIMAL MEDITATION
A number of the projects in this book go beyond the usual gamut of practicality to enter into areas that are not always the province of simple shops. Two cases in Japan are of particular interest. The Zen Lounge ONO/Kyoto (Kyoto, Japan, 2003, page 230) by the talented archi-

9
Waro Kishi, Zen Lounge ONO/Kyoto,
Kyoto, Japan, 2003

tect Waro Kishi is certainly not a lounge in the usual sense, nor is it really a store like any other. It is a place where Zen Buddhist monks belonging to the Soto sect come to purchase religious vestments and altar articles, but also to come and talk. It is probably this latter function that gave rise to the unexpected name "Zen Lounge." In the Soto school of Zen, the largest of the branches of Zen Buddhism, meditation with no objects or content is practiced. Awareness of a stream of thoughts with which the meditator is not meant to interfere is a part of this process. Waro Kishi's design for the Zen Lounge, impregnated with a subtle but nearly complete minimalism, is easier to understand in the context of such meditation. It is known that Japanese architecture and design strongly influenced the emergence of modernism in Europe through such figures as Bruno Taut. Minimalism, as practiced in the West, is also clearly impregnated with Japanese thought. The difference between East and West in this instance is that while minimalism as a fashion has faded away in London or Paris, it remains present in the work of Waro Kishi here, precisely because the architect is striving to accommodate forms of thinking that are not passing whims but the result of centuries of tradition.

ODE TO NEUTRALITY

The young architect Atsushi Muroi was born in Hiroshima in 1975. He works for the firm Hakuhodo, which is the second largest advertising agency in Japan. His AND Market (Kasumigaseki, Tokyo, Japan, 2011, page 210) is a 31-square-meter space that was conceived for a smart phone retailer with no ties to the major phone operators. The parent company of the client is nonetheless NEC, "one of the world's leading providers of Internet, broadband network, and enterprise business solutions." What is interesting about the AND Market is its strong visual identity, described by Muroi as "neutral" or "achromatic," and the way in which this design fits in with the client's requirements—neutrality being symbolic of the sale of various different smart phones, without specific privilege to any operator. Atsushi Muroi states: "Our project includes concept development, brand portfolio strategy, brand name and CI/VI development, and overall brand design such as the retail shop, web site, promotional tools, and characters." Further explaining his achromatic concept, Muroi continues: "Without any heightened color, not even black or white, our design symbolizes the brand essence by depicting the balance of brightness between black and white. You cannot associate AND Market with traditional colors, since it is quite unique both in its services and brand designs." Architecture here becomes indistinguishable not only from graphic design, but also, more intriguingly, from product marketing and an overall advertising concept. Again, where the Bauhaus dreamt of a synthesis of the arts, here an architect seeks a holistic vision that unites architecture, design, graphics, and, perhaps most importantly, retail sales. In this project the architect strives not for artistic accomplishment but for commercial success—it is a testimony to his talent that the final result is spatially coherent and visually arresting.

MOMENTS OF MAGIC

Like other books in the *Architecture Now* series, *Eat Shop Drink* is a survey of very recent projects. Everything seen here was completed or begun after 2003. Much of this work was imagined and built after the beginning of the 2008 economic downturn, and this is an

10

important factor. These restaurants, stores, and bars may well, on the whole, be smaller or less expensive than similar buildings and spaces imagined for the same purposes just a few years ago. One very significant point is that the economy, even when it is in crisis, does not stop architecture—rather it transforms the shape of the present. What is less expensive need not be less inventive, and probably quite the contrary holds true in the cases selected here. The pressure to earn, and consequently to spend may well have reached new heights as both business people and clients are made to be wary about the very solidity of their economic environment. A little like an earthquake, the economic implosion that began on Wall Street has shaken certainties and surely made retailers, hoteliers, and restaurant and bar owners desirous of new models, new forms of expression. Architecture, design, and art have been brought to the fore in a broad effort to give an added, nearly intangible value to products, ranging from steaks to raincoats. In an interesting twist, hard times appear to have encouraged architects and designers to be even more intertwined than they were in the past with places to eat, shop, and drink. Like great chefs, great architects are rare, but some of those referred to in this book have, indeed, reached heights of expression that go beyond the doubts and problems of the moment. They have created a type of art that is all the more meaningful, which in these spaces—an acceptance that creativity can be ephemeral even at its best—comes together with activities that are at once fleeting and essential to life. These are the "formless elements that appeal to our heart" that Tokujin Yoshioka speaks of, moments of magic.

> Our revels now are ended. These our actors,
> As I foretold you, were all spirits and
> Are melted into air, into thin air:
> And, like the baseless fabric of this vision,
> The cloud-capp'd towers, the gorgeous palaces,
> The solemn temples, the great globe itself,
> Yea all which it inherit, shall dissolve
> And, like this insubstantial pageant faded,
> Leave not a rack behind. We are such stuff
> As dreams are made on, and our little life
> Is rounded with a sleep.
>
> *The Tempest*, Act IV, Scene 1

EINLEITUNG

ESSEN, TRINKEN, VIELLEICHT AUCH SHOPPEN

„Manche Leute glauben, Design wäre keine Kunst", weiß Tokujin Yoshioka. „Ich vermute, für diese Leute ist ‚Kunst' ein Phänomen, das faszinierend, aber auch zutiefst beängstigend ist. Ich werde oft nach dem Unterschied zwischen Design und Kunst gefragt. In der Frühzeit hatte man keinen Begriff für Design, trotzdem gab es Kunst und Musik. Warum hören Menschen Musik? Die Antwort verbirgt sich vermutlich hinter dieser Frage. Wäre jede Form von Gestaltung simpel und pragmatisch, hätte das Leben keine Vielfalt, gäbe es keine Sehnsüchte. Unser Leben ist durchdrungen von Musik, die uns bewegt, Filmen, die unsere Fantasie beflügeln, unberechenbaren Gefühlen wie der Liebe und einer Faszination für die Geheimnisse der Natur." Zweifellos gelingt es Tokujin Yoshioka, uns mit seiner Vision von Design in Gefilde zu entführen, in denen das Flüchtige greifbar scheint; doch fällt grundsätzlich auf, dass Design und Architektur ihrem ureigensten Wesen besonders nahe kommen, wo flüchtigen Gücksgefühlen nachgejagt wird. Der Band *Eat Shop Drink* widmet sich Restaurants, Läden und Bars – Orten, die per definitionem das Flüchtige feiern und neuesten Trends folgen oder sie gar setzen. Wie auf allen Gebieten gelingt es nur einigen wenigen Kreativen, das Flüchtige künstlerisch zu fassen und an den wahren, bleibenden Kern des Ephemeren – das Leben selbst – zu rühren. „Wir leben in einer Zeit des Designs im Überfluss", so Tokujin Yoshioka, „einer Zeit, in der ich darüber nachdenke, wie sich ausdrücken lässt, was keine Form und kein Design hat. Etwas, das anders gesagt über unsere landläufigen Vorstellungen von Form und Design hinausgeht und Emotionen weckt. Es geht nicht um formale Spielereien oder minimalistische Formen, sondern darum, etwas zu gestalten, das uns unmittelbar mitreißt, unseren Geist beflügelt. Nur zu gern würde ich etwas entwerfen, das mich persönlich wirklich berührt. In den vergangenen Jahren habe ich die Herausforderung gesucht, Phänomene, die keine eigentliche Form haben, uns aber zutiefst berühren – neue Ideen, Farben, Düfte –, ja, Gefühle gestalterisch umzusetzen. Eines dieser Phänomene ist das Licht, ein anderes Phänomen das Unsichtbare, wieder ein anderes jenes Etwas, das unzählige Formen annehmen kann, weil es wandelbar ist."

FEIERN UNTER KIRSCHBLÜTEN

Die japanische Holzschnittkunst zwischen dem 17. und 20. Jahrhundert wird oft unter den Begriff *ukiyo-e*, „Bilder der fließenden Welt", gefasst. Eine vergängliche Welt flüchtiger Schönheit, in der Kirschblüten oder Ahornblätter ein Ausdruck von Schönheit sind, der jede Form von Kunst weit übertrifft. Im *ukiyo-e* des damaligen Japan begegneten sich buddhistische Vorstellungen von Vergänglichkeit und eine Unbekümmertheit, wie sie etwa im *hanami* oder *yozakura* ihren Ausdruck finden, wenn Ausflügler beim Kirschblütenfest unter Kirschbäumen beim Picknick zusammensitzen. Heute hingegen sehen viele Starköche und -modedesigner ihr Schaffen gern in bleibender Architektur verewigt, und doch sind die Momente, in denen wir essen, kaufen und trinken, oft Momente, in denen wir feiern – und damit zumeist flüchtig. Entsprechendes gilt für die Mehrzahl der jüngst realisierten Projekte, die für diesen Band ausgewählt wurden. Zugleich sind Essen, Trinken und Einkaufen (zumindest das Kaufen des Notwendigen) ständige Bedürfnisse, sind grundlegendere Bedürfnisse als die meisten, die Anlass zur Gestaltung von Architektur geben. Dieser Widerspruch ist aus architektonischer Sicht höchst fruchtbar. Weil Läden und Bars oft in bestehende Bausubstanz integriert werden und mitunter recht klein sind, erwägen Auftraggeber häufiger, jüngere Architekten oder Designer zu beauftra-

11
Tokujin Yoshioka, "Twilight," Milan,
Italy, 12–17 April, 2011

gen, wie etliche der hier vorgestellten Projekte belegen. Während neue Großprojekte oft erhebliche Erfahrung voraussetzen, liegt eine Renovierung oder die Gestaltung von Innenarchitektur durchaus im Bereich des Möglichen für junge Architekturtalente, einer der Gründe für die Themenwahl dieses Bandes. Tokujin Yoshiokas vorgestellte Entwürfe haben im Grunde mehr mit Installationskunst als mit der Planung von Verkaufsstellen oder Konsum zu tun – wobei dies vermutlich für alle wirklich kreativen Köpfe gilt: Es ist der Impuls, selbst bei der Umsetzung flüchtigerer Themen das „wahre Wesen" von Architektur und Design zu suchen. Schließlich sind Restaurants, Bars und Läden auch Orte, an denen verschiedene Metiers aufeinandertreffen, an denen sich Kunst, Architektur und Design begegnen können.

WELCHE FARBE HAT DEIN RGB-SCREEN?

Einige der hier präsentierten Projekte bestehen buchstäblich aus kaum mehr als „Licht", und damit aus einem der Phänomene, von denen Tokujin Yoshioka spricht. Eine besonders dankbare Bühne für Licht als architektonische, emotionale Präsenz sind Nachtclubs. Der brasilianische Designer Muti Randolph hat die Kombination von Licht und Klang zu räumlichen Gesamtkunstwerken zu seinem Beruf gemacht. Sein Projekt D-Edge 2.0 (São Paulo, Brasilien, 2009–10, Seite 300) ist eine Fortführung und Erweiterung des früheren D-Edge Club (2003), der in unmittelbarer Nachbarschaft zum neuen Projekt liegt. „Der Raum wird vom Licht definiert", so Randolph, „das Licht wiederum von der Musik. Entscheidend ist vor allem, das Verhältnis von Musik und Raum in Licht zu übersetzen; eine Software analysiert die Musik und steuert die Lichtwechsel entsprechend." Lichteffekte sind in Nachtclubs, besonders in Dance Clubs, schon lange selbstverständlich, allerdings haben sich durch lichtintensive RGB- und LED-Installationen ganz neue Möglichkeiten für computergesteuerte Displays ergeben, auf denen sich eine endlose Palette von Farbeffekten erzeugen lässt. Bei D-Edge 2.0 definiert die an das Lichtsystem gekoppelte Musik die Stimmung im Raum – im Grunde so zentral, dass der Architektur über die Schaffung einer schützenden Raumhülle hinaus kaum noch eine Funktion zukommt.

Einen ähnlichen Ansatz verfolgte die junge spanische Gruppe 2G Arquitectos bei ihrem Nébula Club in Almendralejo (Badajoz, Spanien, 2009–10, Seite 50). Die Architekten sprechen von einem „Nebel aus Licht und Musik", einer „Wolke aus Licht". Der in einem bestehenden Gebäude untergebrachte Club taucht die Tänzer in „Licht- und Soundblitze".

Tokujin Yoshioka wiederum setzte auf der Mailänder Möbelmesse 2010 für den Möbelhersteller Kartell eigene Vorstellungen von „Unsichtbarkeit" um. Ein Konzept, mit dem sich der Designer schon früher auseinandergesetzt hatte, mit Entwürfen wie Waterfall (Tokio, 2006), einer privaten Bar mit einem 4,20 m langen Tresen aus optischem Glas oder einem „Stuhl, der im Regen verschwindet" (2002). Für Kartell entwarf er einen Stuhl aus so dünnem Acryl, dass der Eindruck entsteht, als „schwebe" die sitzende Person „in der Luft". Ergänzt wurde die Präsentation durch eine Installation *Schneeflocke* aus transparenten „Prismenstäben" aus Kunststoff. Die Prismen der hängenden Cluster changierten bei der kleinsten Bewegung und zogen die Besucher in eine denkbar ephemere Rauminstallation hinein.

HOCH IN DEN ALPEN

Bei den meisten Restaurants, Bars und Boutiquen ist es das Schicksal der Architekten oder Designer, mit gegebenen Räumlichkeiten oder Raumhullen arbeiten zu mussen. Zwar finden sich in diesem Band auch einige Neubauten, doch wollen wir uns zunächst den häufigeren, weniger „permanenten" Projekten zuwenden. Die jungen Schweizer Architekten Ambroise Bonvin und Claudia Bétrisey von Actescollectifs haben den Umbau eines ehemaligen Restaurants mit Seilbahnstation über Crans-Montana, auf einer Höhe von 2112 m ü. NN, in Angriff genommen (Restaurant Chetzeron, Crans-Montana, Schweiz, 2008–09, Seite 56). Das Chetzeron ist ein stylishes Restaurant mit spektakulärem Ausblick über das Rhônetal und das Viertausendermassiv am Matterhorn. Für die raue Steinfassade des Baus verwendeten die Architekten Feldsteine von umliegenden Feldern. Besonders hervorzuheben ist jedoch, dass der Bau dank des geringen Energiebedarfs und minimalen CO_2-Fußabdrucks ein Minergie-Zertifikat (das Schweizer Niedrigenergie-Zertifikat) erhielt. Als zweiten Bauabschnitt planen Bonvin und Bétrisey den Umbau der benachbarten Seilbahnstation zum Boutiquehotel mit 15 Zimmern. Wegen der großen Zurückhaltung schweizerischer Behörden bei der Vergabe von Baugenehmigungen für Hotelneubauten auf über 2000 m ü. NN zog sich der Genehmigungsprozess in die Länge und erforderte erhebliches Engagement der Architekten und Eigentümer. Die kluge Nutzung des bestehenden Gebäudes, dank derer es zum angesagten Ausflugsziel avancierte, ist der beste Beweis für das Talent dieser jungen Architekten.

DAS PHANTOM DER OPER

Das Mendini Restaurant im Groninger Museum (Groningen, Niederlande, 2010, Seite 88) steht für einen völlig anderen Typus von Umnutzung. 1994 war das Groninger Museum bei seiner Eröffnung ein herausragendes Beispiele für die Kooperation von Architekten und Designern. Am Projekt beteiligt waren Alessandro Mendini, Philippe Starck, Michele de Lucchi und Coop Himmelb(l)au. Mendini fungierte damals sowohl als Projektleiter als auch als Gestalter des Restaurants. Dieses wurde nun jüngst von Maarten Baas, einem 33-jährigen Designer aus 's-Hertogenbosch in den Niederlanden renoviert. Das 258 m² große Café-Restaurant ist mit handgefertigten Stühlen, einer Bar sowie Spiegeln und Leuchten aus roter Keramik ausgestattet. Baas gelang die schlichte und elegante Interpretation eines Raums, der bekanntere Designer vielleicht hätte zögern lassen.

Odile Decq zählt mit 56 Jahren zu den bedeutendsten französischen Architekten ihrer Generation. Mit ihrem MACRO – Museum für zeitgenössische Kunst in Rom (Italien, 2003–10) gelang ihr das seltene Kunststück, einen kleinen Teil des Rampenlichts für sich zu beanspruchen, in dem Zaha Hadid mit ihrem ungleich größeren und stark medial beachteten MAXXI – Nationalmuseum für Kunst des XXI. Jahrhunderts (Rom, 1998–2009) stand. Decqs jüngstes Projekt ist das Restaurant l'Opéra (Paris, 2008–11, Seite 158) in der Opéra Garnier. „Ohne das alte Baudenkmal nachzuäffen, indem man es respektiert und zugleich einen dezidiert zeitgenössischen Stil verfolgt", so Odile Decq, betrete das „Phantom" die alte Oper und verleihe dem Bau neue Dynamik.

12
Actescollectifs, Chetzeron Restaurant,
Crans-Montana, Switzerland,
2008–09

12

In wesentlich kleinerem Maßstab als das 1000 m² große Restaurant l'Opéra stellte sich die 36-jährige Yuko Nagayama einer Aufgabe, die in gewisser Weise eine ebenso große Herausforderung gewesen sein dürfte wie der respektvolle Umgang mit der Architektur von Charles Garnier (1825–98). Nagayama, geprägt durch ihre Zeit im Büro des Architekturtalents Jun Aoki, hat bereits verschiedene Ladenprojekte realisiert. Ihre Aufgabe war in diesem Fall die Modernisierung eines 45 m² großen historischen Cafés in Tokio. Ihr Entwurf für Kayaba Coffee (Tokio, 2009, Seite 278) ist ein Paradebeispiel für gewerbliche Umnutzung. Während sich im Erdgeschoss die üblichen Sitzplätze des Cafés befinden, richtete die Architektin das Obergeschoss als Leseraum für Bücher über zeitgenössische Kunst ein. Zugleich bewies sie, dass sich einfühlsamer architektonischer Minimalismus mit einem alteingesessenen Café Tokios verträgt, in einer Stadt, die nach Erdbeben, Großbränden und Kriegen so grundlegend wiederaufgebaut werden musste, dass 100-jährige Bauten eine Rarität sind.

Elena Pérez Garrigues und Daniel Blanco Cohen vom Büro Ninom, beide Jahrgang 1975, gründeten 2006 ihr Büro in Madrid, um „Architektur mit Disziplinen wie Tanz, Fotografie und Bühnenbild zu verbinden". Ihre Weinverkostungshalle für CVNE (Haro, La Rioja, Spanien, 2009, Seite 282) ist Teil eines größeren Gesamtprojekts (1920 m²) und wurde als Installation in einem Bau von 1879 realisiert. Den Wunsch des Auftraggebers aufgreifend, „neue, dynamische Aktivitäten rund um das Thema Wein" anzubieten, entschieden sich die Architekten, eine „eiserne Box" in den Altbau zu setzen. Nachdem sie den historischen Raum maximal reduziert hatten, integrierten sie nicht nur ihre „Box", sondern auch schlichtes modernes Mobiliar und Leuchten sowie eine Reihe alter Weinfässer. Eine gelungene Art und Weise, sowohl die Tradition des Weinguts als auch dessen Zeitgemäßheit zu unterstreichen.

WIR WOLLEN DAS RAD NICHT NEU ERFINDEN

Während die Architekturszene in den USA von der aktuellen Wirtschaftslage und einer eher konservativen Grundhaltung geprägt ist, gibt es erstaunlicherweise auch Firmen wie LOT-EK, geführt von Ada Tolla und Giuseppe Lignano, zwei italienischstämmigen Architekten. LOT-EK hat sich insbesondere auf temporäre Installationen spezialisiert, etwa mit den Uniqlo Container Stores (New York, 2006) oder PUMA-City (Alicante und Boston, 2008). Den permanenten Bau der APAP OpenSchool (Anyang, Südkorea, 2010) realisierte das Team aus Schiffscontainern, mit denen sie bereits bei anderen Projekten gearbeitet hatten. Die begrenzte Fläche (47 m²) des Ladengeschäfts von Van Alen Books an der 30 West 22nd Street in Manhattan (New York, 2011, Seite 242) gestalteten die Architekten, indem sie eine 4,30 m hohe Sitzplattform aus 70 recycelten Türen installierten. Die Buchhandlung Van Alen mit ihrer großzügig verglasten schwarzen Ladenfront fällt nicht nur durch die amphitheaterähnliche Installation auf, sondern auch durch das leuchtende Gelb, das LOT-EK als Farbthema für das Interieur wählte. Olympia Kazi, leitende Buchhändlerin, ist davon überzeugt, dass die Liebe zu Büchern auch im digitalen Zeitalter noch immer eine große Rolle spielt: „Wir wollen das Rad nicht neu erfinden, wir reagieren ganz einfach auf ein Bedürfnis." Durch LOT-EKs Einsatz von klarer Typografie und leuchtendem Gelb zeigt sich hier eher eine Affinität zur Industriearchitektur, während andere Architekten oft ein gehobenes Ambiente für das gedruckte Wort schaffen. Mit ihrem kostengünstigen und auffälligen Ansatz signalisieren die Architekten, dass nach wie vor ein echtes Interesse an Büchern besteht – eine Auffassung, die die Kundschaft von Van Alen Books ganz offensichtlich teilt.

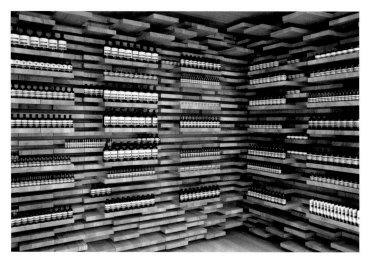

13
*March Studio, Aesop Saint-Honoré,
Paris, France, 2010*

13

Makoto Tanijiri wurde 1974 in Hiroshima geboren. Neben der Gestaltung von über 60 privaten Wohnhäusern befasst sich sein Suppose Design Office mit der Gestaltung von Läden und Restaurants. In den Räumen seines 74 m² großen Cafe Day (Shizuoka, Japan, 2010, Seite 346) befanden sich früher zwei traditionelle japanische Bars. Makoto Tanijiri greift das Umfeld des Gebäudes, insbesondere eine nahe gelegene Fahrschule auf, indem er die auffälligen Straßenmarkierungen zitiert. Durch die leuchtenden Gelbtöne und Markierungen bindet er das Café in sein Umfeld ein. Bekanntermaßen wurzelt die Mehrdeutigkeit von Innen- und Außenraum tief in der japanischen Kultur – ein nicht uninteressanter Hintergrund dieses exzentrischen Entwurfs. Indem der Designer das Café zu einem Teil von Parkplatz und Straßennetz werden lässt, aktualisiert er im Grunde eine sehr alte japanische Vorstellung.

Die Ladenräume von Aesop Saint-Honoré (Paris, 2010, Seite 250) liegen an der Rue Saint-Honoré 256, unweit des Palais Royal in einem Gebäude aus dem 18. Jahrhundert. Die beiden Partner von March Studio, noch jünger als die meisten Gestalter in diesem Band, realisierten ihre Installation mit nicht weniger als 3500 Holzelementen. Rodney Eggleston (geboren 1981) und Anne-Laure Cavigneaux (geboren 1980) vereinten ihre Kräfte auch im Hinblick auf ihre jeweilige Herkunft, als sie die Räume für Aesop, einen Kosmetikhersteller aus Melbourne, in Paris planten. March Studio hat seinen Sitz in Melbourne; Eggleston ist Australier, Cavigneaux Grafikdesignerin aus Paris. March Studio arbeitete mit Rieseneukalyptus aus nachhaltiger australischer Forstwirtschaft und verkleidete sämtliche Flächen mit Holz, sodass ein einheitliches Interieur entstand, das sich auffällig von der typischen steinernen Palette der Pariser Bauten des 18. Jahrhunderts unterscheidet. Eine Installation auf einer Fläche von 100 m² ist ein naheliegendes Experimentierfeld für junge Talente und einen offenen Auftraggeber (hier Dennis Paphitis, Gründer von Aesop). Allerdings würden es nur wenige Unternehmen wagen, 30-jährige Gestalter mit der Planung eines ganzen Gebäudes zu beauftragen, zumal im derzeit problematischen wirtschaftlichen Klima.

EIN BAUERNHAUS AUF EINEM HÜGEL

Der brasilianische Architekt Isay Weinfeld hat sich seit Langem auf gehobene private Wohnbauten, Restaurants und Ladengeschäfte spezialisiert. Für sein Fasano Restaurant (Punta del Este, Uruguay, 2010–11, Seite 380) verwandelte er ein altes, auf einem Hügel gelegenes Gehöft aus Stein in ein spektakuläres, 390 m² großes Restaurant mit Blick auf Maldonado. Der Architekt kombiniert die grobe Trockenmauer des Gehöfts und dessen Lage mit einer minimalistischen „Box" aus Beton und versteht es, einen für gänzlich andere Zwecke geplanten Bau auf originelle und effiziente Weise neu zu erobern. Weinfeld war bereits mehrfach für die Fasano-Gruppe tätig, unter anderem für ein spektakuläres Hotel und Restaurant in São Paulo (2001–03). Ohne Frage bot sich das gehobene Ambiente, das im städtischen Kontext beim Neubau Pate stand, bei diesem ländlichen Restaurant unweit der uruguayischen Küste nicht an. Dennoch gelang es Isay Weinfeld, der Gruppe auch in diesem neuen Territorium, einem naturbelassenen Standort, einen guten Ruf zu verschaffen.

NOTHING HAPPENS FOR A REASON

Vielleicht liegt es am wirtschaftlich bedingt nachlassenden Museums-Bauboom oder daran, dass es bereits eine Überfülle bestehender Institutionen gibt, dass so flüchtige Aktivitäten wie Essen, Shoppen und Trinken näher an die Kunstwelt zu rücken scheinen. Die Vorstellung, dass Produkte, selbst kulinarische Güter, nach höheren, „bleibenderen" Werten streben, ist nicht neu. Gerade die in jüngster Zeit eröffneten Cafés, Bars und Läden scheinen zu bestätigen, dass man der Beteiligung von Künstlern oder ihren Werken zuschreibt, Orte wie diese über das rein Merkantile zu heben. Ein interessantes Beispiel ist das Logomo Café (Turku, Finnland, 2010–11, Seite 76). Die Firma Artek, 1935 von Alvar Aalto und zwei Partnern gegründet, fungierte als Mäzen für dieses Projekt, das als Beitrag zur Kulturhauptstadt Turku 2011 realisiert wurde. Artek beauftragte den deutschen Künstler Tobias Rehberger mit der Installation *Nothing Happens for a Reason* (Nichts passiert aus einem Grund) für das Logomo-Gebäude, den zentralen Veranstaltungsort des Kulturhauptstadtprogramms. Wie andere Künstler, darunter auch der renommierte amerikanische Landschaftsarchitekt Ken Smith, faszinieren Rehberger Tarntechniken. Im 230 m² großen Café in Turku setzte Rehberger teilweise britische Tarntechniken aus dem Zweiten Weltkrieg ein: Ein Geflecht aus Linien im überwiegend schwarz-weiß gehaltenen Interieur überschneidet sich und läuft sogar über die Artek-Möbel hinweg. Das Ergebnis ist eine mehrdeutige räumliche Situation, die in Einzelfällen selbst die Unterscheidung von Objekten und Architektur erschweren. *Nothing Happens for a Reason* belegt trotz dekorativer Qualitäten und obwohl die Installation als temporäre Einrichtung konzipiert wurde, dass selbst ein Café den Status eines Kunstwerks beanspruchen kann. Doch was wäre, wenn das Temporäre letztlich alles wäre, was zählt?

ACTIONFILM

Ein ungleich ambitionierteres und eindrücklicheres Projekt ist der Silencio Club in Paris (2010–11, Seite 246), entworfen von David Lynch. Der Regisseur von *Der Elefantenmensch* (1980), *Lost Highway* (1997) und weiterer Kultfilme interessiert sich erklärtermaßen besonders für Kunst und Musik; dennoch war dies sein erster Ausflug auf das Gebiet der Innenarchitektur. Silencio, gelegen in einem historischen Gebäude von 1883 in der Rue Montmartre 142 im II. Arrondissement von Paris, ist ein 650 m² großer Club, der besonders durch den großzügigen Einsatz von Blattgold und die partielle Verkleidung mit unbehandeltem Holz auffällt. Mehr als eine reine Bar, wurde Silencio als Privatklub mit Livemusik, Filmvorführungen und Kunstausstellungen konzipiert. Auch eine Kunstbibliothek gehört zum Konzept. Die Assoziation mit David Lynch dürfte Silencio ohne Frage einen erfolgreichen Start bescheren. Obwohl Lynch bei der Umsetzung seiner Ideen Unterstützung von Raphaël Navot und dem Architekturbüro ENIA erhielt, ist der für ihn typische Hang, Grenzen zu überschreiten, die so verschiedene Genres wie Film oder Innenarchitektur üblicherweise trennen, deutlich zu spüren. Das Veranstaltungsprogramm des Clubs ist erwartungsgemäß offen definiert, auch das Designkonzept hat in mancherlei Hinsicht eine improvisiert Note. Da inzwischen viele zeitgenössische Künstler bewusst die Monumentalität und Permanenz des Museums als Institution meiden, überrascht es kaum, dass ein der Nacht gewidmeter Ort (der von sechs Uhr abends bis sechs Uhr morgens geöffnet ist), die wahren Künstler der Stunde anzuziehen versteht.

14

14
Concrete, W Hotel, London, UK,
2010–11

TAKASHI UND ANISH GEHEN SHOPPEN

Der international vielleicht angesagteste und erfolgreichste Architekt von Ladenräumen und gehobenen Apartments ist Peter Marino. Seine Kunden, darunter Chanel und Louis Vuitton, zahlen zu den bekanntesten Modemarken unserer Zeit. Interessant ist, dass diese Marken sowohl danach streben, zeitgemäß zu sein, als auch auf ihre „Tradition" und Geschichte verweisen. Liegt es da nicht auf der Hand, Kunst an diese Orte zu bringen? Seinen neuen Chanel SoHo Store (New York, 2010, Seite 260) stattete Marino mit einer Reihe eigens bei Peter Belyi, Robert Greene, Gregor Hildebrandt, Alan Rath und Richard Woods in Auftrag gegebener Werke aus. Hier übernimmt das Kunstwerk eine neue, nach Kräften verkaufsfördernde Funktion. In der eindrucksvollen Louis-Vuitton-Boutique an der New Bond Street (London, 2010, Seite 254) kam eine Variation dieser Strategie zum Einsatz: Hier verleihen Originalwerke von Richard Prince, Takashi Murakami, Gilbert & George, Anish Kapoor, Chris Ofili und Gary Hume der 1500-m²-Ladenfläche besonderen Glanz. Noch vor geraumer Zeit spekulierte man, heutzutage hätten Museen Kirchen als klassische städtische Vorzeigeobjekte verdrängt. Angesichts finanzieller Engpässe und systemischer Überpräsenz scheint es jedoch fast, als hätten die Museen ihre ruhmreiche Postweltkriegsära endgültig hinter sich.

MÉLANGE DE GENRES

Ohne überkommenen Religionen zu nahe treten zu wollen, muss die Frage gestattet sein, ob in unserer Ära des Mammons ein Besuch etwa in SoHo oder der Bond Street nicht dem Himmel so nahe kommt, wie es sich ein Durchschnitts-Shopper nur wünschen kann. Schon vor Jahren waren große japanische Warenhausketten wie Seibu wegweisend mit ihren integrierten Galerien und Kunstausstellungen. Warum in ein Museum gehen, wenn man Kultur auch im Kaufhaus bekommen kann? Warum in die Kirche gehen, wenn eine Handtasche doch alles ist, was man im Grunde will? Seit sich der Kunstmarkt endgültig dem Merkantilismus verschrieben hat, scheint Kunst ihren Platz umso selbstverständlicher neben einem richtig guten Paar Schuhe einzunehmen. Erstaunlicherweise ist es offenbar der Architekt, der von dieser *mélange de genres* besonders profitiert. Der Raum an sich ist rein, und Materialien, so man sie richtig einsetzt, bleiben erhaben. Dies soll nicht etwa Kritik an Peter Marino implizieren; er ist zurzeit der unangefochtene Großmeister gerade im Hinblick auf Ladenräume, und zweifellos ist nichts verkehrt daran, Chanel oder Louis Vuitton mit zeitgenössischer Kunst zu verknüpfen. Dennoch ist es ein gesellschaftlicher Trend von erheblicher Tragweite, dass Einzelhandel, Architektur und Kunst inzwischen in dieselbe Arena projiziert werden, um in gewisser Weise die Bedürfnisse von Kunden zu befriedigen. Kaufen oder nicht kaufen, das ist die Frage – die neue Religion ist nicht Kunst, sondern Shopping.

HOTELKETTEN MIT KÜNSTLERISCHEM ANSTRICH

Eine gänzlich andere Herangehensweise an Kunst und Architektur wagte Jean Nouvel mit seinem Restaurant Le Loft im Sofitel Stephansdom in Wien (2006–10, Seite 290). Das Restaurant im Dachgeschoss integriert sich formvollendet in das Gesamtkonzept des Gebäudes, ebenfalls ein Entwurf Nouvels. Hier befindet sich auch eine spektakuläre Video-Deckeninstallation der Schweizer Künstlerin Pipilotti Rist. Rist gestaltete außerdem Interventionen für die Lobby und einen Barbereich in den unteren Geschossebenen des Hotels. Im Zusammenklang

15
Evan Douglis, Moon Jelly
(Choice: Kitchens and Bakery),
Brooklyn, New York, USA, 2009–10

15

mit Nouvels eindrücklicher Architektur entsteht durch Rists farbintensive Deckeninstallationen, die dank geschosshoher Verglasung auch von außen sichtbar sind, ein Gesamtbild, das unter dem wachsamen Blick des Architekten konzipiert wurde. Obwohl es letztendlich um den kommerziellen Erfolg des Hotels geht, konnten Architekt und Künstlerin ihrer Kreativität freien Lauf lassen, um ihre Raumerlebnisse zu gestalten. Es ist durchaus nicht dasselbe, ein Bild in einer Boutique aufzuhängen, auch wenn beide Gesten dasselbe Ziel haben mögen. Nouvel und Rist haben einen Ort geschaffen, an dem es zur Begegnung verschiedener Disziplinen kommt, etwas, das in unserer Zeit selten genug ist.

Die seit einiger Zeit zu beobachtende Kooperation von Architektur- und Designtalenten in der Hotelbranche ist ein bemerkenswertes Phänomen. Architekten wie das deutsche Team von Graft wurden unter anderem durch das stilvolle Hotel Q! in Berlin (2002–04) bekannt. Auch wenn Graft in diesem Band mit anderen Projekten vertreten ist, zeigt sich beispielsweise am W Hotel in London (2010–11), dass gerade qualitätvolle Architektur und Innenarchitektur ein zentraler Aspekt des Erfolgs solcher Häuser sind. Die designorientierte Hotelkette beauftragte Rob Wagemans und Concrete aus Amsterdam mit der Gestaltung ihres Sweat and AWAY Spa mit Blick auf den Leicester Square, des Restaurants Spice Market London und der Hotelzimmer. Im Mandarin Oriental, Paris (2009–11, Seite 216), einem Entwurf von Jean-Michel Wilmotte, finden sich die von Jouin Manku gestaltete Bar 8 sowie die Restaurants Sur Mesure und Camélia. Wilmotte und Patrick Jouin zählen zu den bekanntesten französischen Architekturbüros – dass beide gemeinsam in ein und demselben Luxushotel vertreten sind, belegt, dass auch einzelne Niederlassungen von Hotelketten inzwischen großen Wert darauf legen, ein unverwechselbares Profil zu entwickeln und mit ihrem Design ein gehobenes Segment und entsprechende Kundschaft anzusprechen. Man darf wohl behaupten, dass Designhotels wie Q! die großen Hotelketten angeregt haben, ihr Auftreten von Ort zu Ort zu diversifizieren und zu diesem Zweck die besten kreativen Talente der Stunde zu engagieren.

DIE KUNST DES VERKAUFENS

Auch wenn Jean Nouvel und Pipilotti Rist zweifellos zu den Besten der zeitgenössischen Architektur und Kunst zählen, lässt sich die rasch wandelnde aktuelle Szene von Köpfen inspirieren, die ihren Namen auf anderen Gebieten als der Innenarchitektur gemacht haben. Gary Card ist Bühnenbildner und Requisiteur, Grafikdesigner und Illustrator. Er hat mit Größen der zeitgenössischen Kunst- und Modewelt gearbeitet, darunter Nick Knight, Stella McCartney und Lady Gaga. Sein Entwurf für LN-CC (London, 2010, Seite 116) war sein erster Auftrag als Innenarchitekt. Das Late Night Chameleon Café ist trotz seines Namens im Grunde eher Boutique und Buchhandlung als Café. John Skelton und Daniel Mitchell, Initiatoren des Projekts, präsentieren ihren Kunden eine eigenwillige Mischung aus Mode, Musik und Kunst – ein Ladenkontext für das Beste aus Mainstream und Underground. Außer dem Geschmack der Erfinder des Konzepts sind hier keine Grenzen gesetzt. Gary Card setzte den Auftrag mit einer gewagten Mischung aus unbehandeltem Holz und Acryl in Orange um. Als Inspiration nennt er die „Schock"-Künstler Paul McCarthy und Jeff Koons: „Was mich am meisten fasziniert, sind Farbe und das Perverse, ganz besonders, wenn beides aufeinandertrifft." Die Innenarchitektur ist hier integraler Bestandteil eines ungewöhnlichen kommerziellen Konzepts, bei dem niemand

16

vorgibt, etwas anderes zu sein, als er ist. Card und sein viel gepriesener Blog www.garycardiology.blogspot.com sind so angesagt wie LN-CC – eine geradezu geniale Kombination. Als die ganz Großen am Bauhaus vom Gesamtkunstwerk träumten, dachten sie an Kunst, Architektur und Gestaltung. Würde ein Gesamtkunstwerk heute ein viertes Element mit einschließen, das wir griffig das „Shopping-Konzept" nennen könnten? Auch dies ist nicht etwa respektlos gemeint, eher bewundernd. Vielleicht erleben Kunst und Architektur gerade einen rascheren Umbruch, als ihre Schöpfer selbst zugeben wollen.

DIE GEBURT DER OHRENQUALLE

In einer Gesellschaft, die Konsum zu einem ihrer höchsten Werte erklärt, gerät schon die grundlegende Definition von Kunst und Design – auch im Hinblick auf Restaurants, Bars und Läden – zunehmend unscharf. Doch da gibt es jene, die mit allerneusten Technologien arbeiten, um Design auf künstlerische und zugleich effiziente Weise umzusetzen. Zu den ungewöhnlicheren Vertretern dieses Ansatzes zählt Evan Douglis, studierter Architekt mit Ausbildung an der Architectural Association in London, der Cooper Union in New York sowie der Harvard GSD. Douglis arbeitete für so namhafte Büros wie Tod Williams oder Agrest & Gandelsonas und so wandelbare Gestalter wie Emilio Ambasz, bevor er 1992 sein eigenes Büro Evan Douglis Studio gründete, das inzwischen in Troy, New York, ansässig ist. Er selbst nennt sein Studio „ein Architektur- und interdisziplinäres Büro, das sich der Erforschung und Anwendung neuartiger selbstgenerativer Systeme, der Membrantechnologie und aktuellen Fertigungsmethoden verschrieben hat, die auf ein denkbar breites Spektrum an Projekten angewendet werden". Der Entwurf Moon Jelly, zu Deutsch Ohrenqualle, (Choice: Kitchens and Bakery, Brooklyn, New York, 2009–10, Seite 170) zählt zu seinen jüngst realisierten Projekten. Mit so anspruchsvollen Technologien wie 3-D-Druck realisierte Douglis eine beeindruckende Deckeninstallation, die er als „ästhetisch-dramatische, über den Köpfen der Gäste schwebende Wolke" beschreibt. Obwohl die Installation mithilfe neuester industrieller Fertigungsmethoden realisiert wurde, entfaltet sich hier eine schier unendliche Zahl von Mustern, die an die Sternenwirbel auf Gemälden Van Goghs erinnern. Der Entwurf, so Douglis, „ist eine Vertiefung unseres Interesses an komplexen Oberflächen, dynamisch-bewegten Formen und serieller Streuung, um umfassende räumliche Gesamterlebnisse in der heutigen Architektur zu realisieren". Künstler, die Arbeiten eigens für Ladenräume oder Restaurants entwickeln, wie Pipilotti Rist in Wien, verleihen dem Raum Originalität und Kreativität, die weit über den spezifischen Nutzungszweck der Architektur hinausreichen. Douglis wiederum arbeitet trotz seiner Ausbildung als Architekt an der Nahtstelle von Baulichem und potenziell Dekorativem. Mithilfe neuester Technologien – 3-D-Druck wird erst seit Kurzem in den verschiedensten Gebieten eingesetzt – gelingt es ihm, die Grenzbereiche von Design, Architektur und Kunst zu erhellen. In einem sonst funktionalen und eher schlichten Raum erweckt der Architekt die Decke dank Mustergestaltung und eigens gefertigter Lüster zum Leben. Obwohl Denken und Inspiration in früheren Zeiten zweifellos anders waren, lohnt der Hinweis auf das erstaunlich komplexe Schmiedewerk am Kaufhaus Carson Pirie Scott von Louis Sullivan (Chicago, 1904; heute Sullivan Center), das 2010 restauriert wurde und nun wieder im alten Glanz erstrahlt. Schon lange vor Gropius' berühmtem Wort von der Tabula rasa erklärte Sullivan, der auch als „Vater der Moderne" gilt, „die Form folgt immer der Funktion". Auch wenn in der Architektur industrielle Herstellungsverfahren aufkamen und die Moderne weitgehend auf das Ornament verzichtete, kommt Sullivans Werk besondere Bedeutung zu. Er beharrte darauf, dass Dekoration stets einen praktischen Nutzen haben müsse – doch vielleicht reicht es den Gästen des Moon Jelly in Brooklyn, einfach aufzuschauen und sich in den Musterschleifen zu verlieren.

GLASBOX ODER CARGOSCHUPPEN?

Obwohl zu Jean Nouvels Sofitel in Wien ein Restaurant und eine Bar gehören, die vom Architekten selbst entworfen wurden, sind dies doch zweckgebundene Zugaben des übergeordneten Bauprojekts. Als eigenständige Bauten geplante Ladenlokale, Bars oder Restaurants sind zwar relativ selten, bieten talentierten Architekten und Designern jedoch die Gelegenheit, sich auf diesem Gebiet zu profilieren. Das Coubertin Restaurant (Olympiahalle, Olympiapark München, 2010, Seite 82) ist im Grunde eine Renovierung und Erweiterung der olympischen Anlagen von 1972. Der Auftrag fiel geradezu selbstverständlich an das Büro von Auer+Weber+Assoziierte: Fritz Auer und Carlo Weber, Gründungspartner des Büros, waren bis zur Gründung der eigenen Firma 1980 bei Behnisch & Partner tätig gewesen. Günter Behnisch hatte in Zusammenarbeit mit Frei Otto die ursprünglichen olympischen Bauten geplant. Das neue Restaurant mit 500 Plätzen ist eine würdige Hommage an den älteren Komplex und steht mit seiner geradlinigen Klarheit kontrastierend neben der organischen Spinnennetzkonstruktion des Stadions von 1972.

Francisco Mangado hingegen musste sich bei seinem Café Baluarte (Pamplona, Spanien, 2006) nicht mit vergleichbar komplexen historischen Referenzen auseinandersetzen, auch wenn sein Bau in unmittelbarer Nachbarschaft zum Parlamentsgebäude der Region Narvarra liegt. Entscheidende Referenz für die minimalistische Glasbox ist vielmehr Mangados eigener Entwurf für das Auditorium und Kongresszentrum Baluarte (Pamplona, 2000–03). Bezugnehmend auf die Tradition der Moderne, in der zweifellos auch das Farnsworth House von Ludwig Mies van der Rohe steht (Plano, Illinois, USA, 1945–51), ging es dem Architekten darum, den Nutzern „das Gefühl zu geben, im Freien zu sein, geschützt vor der Witterung und doch in der Lage, die räumliche Tiefe des Platzes und den Blick auf die Bebauung in der Nachbarschaft zu genießen". Anders als bei Mies lässt sich diese Glasbox bei gutem Wetter jedoch vollständig nach außen öffnen. Sicherlich spielt auch das Budget eine Rolle, wenn man sich in solchen Fällen für eine schlichte Glaskonstruktion entscheidet, doch Mangado macht aus seinem Café Baluarte ein echtes Kunstwerk, keine Selbstverständlichkeit, ganz gleich in welchem Zusammenhang.

Eine interessante Mischung aus Umnutzung von altem Industriebestand und Neubau auf aneinandergrenzenden Grundstücken ist die North Wharf in Auckland von Fearon Hay (Neuseeland, 2010–11, Seite 188). Die drei Gebäude, darunter ein sanierter historischer Frachtschuppen, liegen im 2,5 ha großen Erschließungsgebiet Wynyard Waterfront. Die zwei für Läden und Freizeitangebote vorgesehenen Neubauten flankieren den sanierten Bau des Old Red Shed aus den 1930er-Jahren. Wie weltweit inzwischen üblich bei Industriesanierungen, wurde auch beim Projekt in Auckland darauf geachtet, den ursprünglichen „spröden" Charme des Old Red Shed beizubehalten. Die authentische Ha-

17

17
Massimiliano and Doriana Fuksas,
Palatino Center, Turin, Italy,
1998–2011

fenatmosphäre verleiht der Architektur – dem Altbau ebenso wie den Neubauten – Charakter und macht den Ort für Besucher besonders reizvoll. Noch vor wenigen Jahren hätten Architekten unter ähnlichen Umständen ohne zu zögern jede Spur der industriellen Vergangenheit getilgt, doch Sanierungen haben zunehmend an Bedeutung gewonnen, während reine Neubauten in wirtschaftlich angespannter Lage seltener werden. Augenscheinlich haben sich Entscheidungen, die ursprünglich aus wirtschaftlichen Gründen fielen, zu ästhetischen Kriterien entwickelt, denen die Öffentlichkeit durchaus aufgeschlossen gegenübersteht. Eine gewisse Form von Authentizität ist eben nur durch den Faktor Zeit zu erzielen: Die neueste zeitgenössische Architektur hat ihre Schlüsse daraus gezogen, integriert bewusst alt und neu. Im Ergebnis sind Architektur und Design heute komplexer, facettenreicher und fraglos weniger „glatt".

SHOPPINGCENTER BEKOMMEN EIN GESICHT

Während Luxusmode noch immer zumeist auf Boutiquen setzt, wird ein Großteil des Umsatzes im Einzelhandel heutzutage in Einkaufszentren gemacht. Drei namhafte Architekten haben entsprechende beachtenswerte Großprojekte realisiert oder sind mit deren Planung befasst. Als erster fertiggestellter Bau in dieser Riege ist die 66 000 m² große Galleria Centercity (Cheonan, Südkorea, 2008–10, Seite 372) von UNStudio zu nennen. Ben van Berkel und sein Team sind schon lange versiert in der computergestützten Planung von Großbauten wie etwa dem Mercedes-Benz Museum (Stuttgart, 2003–06). Van Berkels besonderes Interesse gilt optischen Effekten – in diesem Fall arbeitete er mit zwei überlagerten Ebenen aus Aluminiumprofilen, durch die ein erstaunlicher Moiréeffekt am Außenbau entsteht. Mit der früheren erfolgreichen Renovierung einer Niederlassung derselben Handelsgruppe in Seoul (Galleria, 2003) hatte UNStudio bereits den Beweis erbracht, dass gutes Design ein solides Investment für Unternehmen sein kann. Wie für das Büro typisch, verbinden die Architekten die moderne Fassade des Komplexes mit einem ebenso erstaunlichen Interieur, das sie als „eine Art räumlichen Wasserfall" beschreiben.

Massimiliano und Doriana Fuksas konnten so bemerkenswerte Projekte wie die 1 Million Quadratmeter große Fiera Milano (Rho-Pero, Mailand, 2002–05) oder das Einkaufszentrum MyZeil in Frankfurt am Main (2009) realisieren. Unlängst fertiggestellt wurde ihr Palatino Center (Turin, 1998–2011, Seite 194), ein Modezentrum mit 13 000 m² Verkaufsfläche. Highlights der Konstruktion sind geschossübergreifende Prismenpfeiler mit integrierten Querverstrebungen aus Metall und eine Fassade aus 150 000 kg Stahl und nicht weniger als 60 000 Glaselementen. Das Architektenpaar beweist, wie schon in kleinerem Maßstab bei Projekten für die Armani-Gruppe (Armani Ginza Tower, Tokio, 2005–07, und Emporio Armani Fifth Avenue, New York, 2009), dass intelligente Architektur und intelligentes Design Verkaufsflächen dauerhaft zum Anziehungspunkt machen. Seit öffentliche Aufträge seltener geworden sind, haben Branchen wie die Modewelt einen Teil des Rückgangs bei Architekturaufträgen abfangen können. Nichts kann die globale Rezession letztendlich kompensieren, doch Luxusgüter haben sich als erstaunlich unbeeindruckt von der düsteren Stimmung erwiesen, die in anderen Branchen herrscht.

18
Rizoma Arquitetura, Oiticica
Restaurant, Brumadinho, Minas
Gerais, Brazil, 2010

18

Ein anderer „großer" Name der zeitgenössischen Architektur plant derzeit einen Komplex mit gemischter Nutzung in Düsseldorf. Der Kö-Bogen von Daniel Libeskind (2011–13) ist ein 40 000 m² großer, sechsstöckiger Bau für Büro- und Gewerbeflächen. Ein weiterer interessanter Aspekt des Kö-Bogens ist neben der Mischnutzung der konzeptuelle Ansatz des Planers, eine Verbindung zwischen Landschaft und urbanem Umfeld herzustellen, etwa durch „Einschnitte", die die baulichen Strukturen „durchdringen" und dafür sorgen, dass die landschaftlichen Elemente „natürlich mit dem gebauten Raum verschmelzen und fließend in ihn übergehen". Auch wenn Libeskinds bekanntester Bau nach wie vor das Jüdische Museum in Berlin ist (1989–2001), hat er darüber hinaus Großprojekte mit gewerblicher Orientierung wie das Westside Einkaufs- und Freizeitzentrum (Bern, 2005–08) oder das Crystals im CityCenter (Las Vegas, Nevada, USA 2006–09) realisiert. Während eine frühere Generation von Architekten oft der Ansicht war, Einkaufszentren würfen zu viele praktische Probleme auf, um kreativen Gestaltungsraum zu lassen, lässt sich beobachten, dass heute weder Handel noch Architekten so denken. Viele der hier vorgestellten Shoppingkomplexe zeugen von ausgeprägten architektonischen Ambitionen, die integraler Bestandteil des Shoppingkonzepts sind, das sie verkörpern. Während kulturelle Institutionen wie Museen oder Konzertsäle inzwischen seltener als Auftraggeber in Erscheinung treten, zeichnet sich der Handel einmal mehr, zumindest teilweise, als Alternative für Architekten der ersten Liga ab.

BETON IM DSCHUNGEL

Es soll jedoch nicht der Eindruck entstehen, architektonisch interessante Restaurants, Bars und Läden müssten zwingend Großprojekte sein. Weitab des städtischen Trubels von Düsseldorf oder Turin realisierten die jungen Architekten Maria Paz (geboren 1985) und Thomaz Regatos (geboren 1981) vom Büro Rizoma Arquitetura zwei kleinere Projekte für das Institut für Zeitgenössische Kunst Inhotim 60 km außerhalb der brasilianischen Stadt Belo Horizonte. Das Restaurant Oiticica (Brumadinho, Brasilien, 2010, Seite 310) mit 320 Plätzen ist eine kostengünstige Konstruktion aus Beton und Metallschirmen, die in nur drei Monaten erbaut wurde. Das weitestgehend in die dichte Vegetation eingebettete Gebäude ist natürlich belüftet. Für dasselbe Kunstcenter baute Rizoma 2011 einen Laden im botanischen Garten (Seite 314). Die 200 m² große Ladenfläche, auf der Pflanzen und Gartenzubehör angeboten werden, konnte in dreimonatiger Bauzeit aus Beton, Stein und Holz für gerade einmal 125 000 US-Dollar errichtet werden. Der Laden ist eher offener Pavillon als traditionelles Gebäude und wurde, wie schon das Restaurant, mit besonderer Rücksicht auf den Baumbestand vor Ort geplant.

MINIMALISMUS UND MEDITATION

Einige Projekte in diesem Band sprengen die üblichen Grenzen zweckorientierter Praktikabilität und erschließen Bereiche, die sonst nicht das Terrain schlichter Läden sind. Zwei Beispiele aus Japan sind hier besonders interessant. Die Zen Lounge ONO/Kyoto (Kioto, Japan, 2003, Seite 230), ein Entwurf des fähigen Architekten Waro Kishi ist alles andere als eine Lounge im üblichen Sinne und sicherlich auch kein normales Geschäft. Mönche der zenbuddhistischen Soto-Schule kaufen hier ihre Gewänder und ihren Altarbedarf, nutzen die Lounge jedoch auch als Ort der Begegnung und des Gesprächs. Dies gab vermutlich Anlass für den eher ungewöhnlichen Namen. Die Soto-Schule des Zen, der größten Schule des Zenbuddhismus, praktiziert Meditation ohne Zweck oder Zielvorstellungen. Teil dieses Prozesses ist die Achtsamkeit für den Gedankenfluss, auf den sich der Meditierende jedoch nicht einlässt. Waro Kishis Entwurf für die Zen Lounge, der von einem subtilen, fast uneingeschränkten Minimalismus ist, lässt sich vor dem Hintergrund dieser Meditationspraxis sicher besser verstehen. Historisch gesehen hatten japanische Architektur und Gestaltung durch Persönlichkeiten wie Bruno Taut erheblichen Einfluss auf die Entstehung der Moderne in Europa. Auch der Minimalismus westlicher Couleur ist stark von japanischem Gedankengut geprägt. Einer der Unterschiede von Ost und West zeigt sich allerdings daran, dass der Minimalismus in London oder Paris als Modeerscheinung wieder verblasst ist, während er im Werk von Waro Kishi deutlich spürbar ist, gerade weil der Architekt danach strebt, einem Denken Raum zu geben, das kein kurzlebiger Trend ist, sondern die Frucht jahrhundertealter Traditionen.

ODE AN DIE NEUTRALITÄT

Der junge Architekt Atsushi Muroi wurde 1975 in Hiroshima geboren. Er arbeitet für Hakuhodo, die zweitgrößte Werbeagentur Japans. Der von ihm gestaltete AND Market (Kasumigaseki, Tokio, 2011, Seite 210) ist ein 31 m² großes Ladenlokal für einen netzunabhängigen Smartphone-Hersteller. Mutterkonzern des Unternehmens ist allerdings die Firma NEC, „einer der weltweit führenden Internet-, Broadband- und Firmennetzwerkanbieter". Interessant an Murois AND Market ist sein prägnantes Erscheinungsbild, das der Architekt als „neutral" beziehungsweise „achromatisch" beschreibt, ebenso wie die Abstimmung des Designs auf das spezifische Profil des Auftraggebers – Neutralität als Symbol für das Angebot verschiedenster Smartphones ohne Bindung an bestimmte Netzwerkanbieter. Atsushi Muroi erklärt: „Unser Projekt war ein Gesamtpaket aus Konzeptentwicklung, Markenpotfolio-Strategie, Entwicklung von Markenname, Corporate Identity und Erscheinungsbild sowie dem gesamten Branding einschließlich Filialgeschäft, Website, Werbemitteln und Typografie." Muroi geht weiter auf sein achromatisches Konzept ein: „Unser Design verzichtet auf prägnante Farben, einschließlich Schwarz und Weiß, und symbolisiert den Kern der Marke durch ein exakt austariertes Helligkeitsmittel zwischen Schwarz und Weiß. AND Market lässt sich nicht mit üblichen Farben assoziieren, schließlich sind Service und Markendesign einzigartig." Hier ist Architektur weder von Kommunikationsdesign zu unterscheiden noch, und das ist vielleicht interessanter, von Marketing und Werbekonzept. Auch hier gilt wieder: Wo das Bauhaus noch von einem Gesamtkunstwerk träumte, ist hier ein Architekt auf der Suche nach einer ganzheitlichen Vision, in der Architektur, Design, Grafik und – als entscheidender Punkt – der Einzelhandel zusammenfließen. Hier strebt der Architekt nicht nur nach künstlerischem, sondern auch nach kommerziellem Erfolg. Es zeugt von seinem Können, dass das Ergebnis räumlich schlüssig und visuell überzeugend ausfällt.

MAGISCHE MOMENTE

Wie andere Bände aus der Reihe *Architecture Now!* bietet auch *Eat Shop Drink* einen Überblick über aktuellste Projekte. Die hier vorgestellten Entwürfe wurden 2003 oder später begonnen. Ein Großteil wurde nach der Wirtschaftskrise 2008 entwickelt oder realisiert – ein ent-

19
Yuko Nagayama, Kayaba Coffee,
Tokyo, Japan, 2009

scheidender Faktor. Vermutlich sind diese Restaurants, Läden und Bars im Großen und Ganzen kleiner und kostengünstiger als vergleichbare Bauten und Räume, die noch vor wenigen Jahren geplant wurden. Entscheidend ist, dass die Wirtschaft die Architektur selbst in Krisenzeiten nicht aufhalten kann – vielmehr ist sie eine gestaltende Kraft unserer Gegenwart. Was weniger teuer ist, muss nicht weniger einfallsreich sein. Bei den hier ausgewählten Projekten ist sicherlich das Gegenteil der Fall. Der Druck, Geld zu verdienen, um es schließlich wieder auszugeben, hat in einer Zeit, in der Geschäftsleute und Kunden gleichermaßen um die Stabilität ihres wirtschaftlichen Umfelds besorgt sind, zweifellos neue Höhen erreicht. Die ökonomische Implosion, die an der Wall Street begann, hat wie ein kleines Erdbeben vermeintliche Gewissheiten erschüttert und ohne Frage dazu geführt, dass Einzelhändler, Hoteliers, Restaurant- und Barbesitzer auf der Suche nach neuen Modellen, neuen Ausdrucksformen sind. Architektur, Design und Kunst geraten zunehmend ins Blickfeld, um Produkten – vom Steak bis zum Regenmantel – zusätzlichen, schwer greifbaren Mehrwert zu geben. Es ist eine faszinierende Wendung, dass schwere Zeiten offenbar dazu geführt haben, dass Architekten und Designer heute enger als je zuvor mit Orten assoziiert werden, an denen wir essen, shoppen oder trinken. Große Architekten sind ebenso selten wie große Köche, doch manche der in diesem Band vorgestellten Planer haben in der Tat einen Grad an Ausdrucksstärke erreicht, der die Zweifel und Probleme der Gegenwart vergessen lässt. Sie schaffen eine Form von Kunst, die umso eindrücklicher ist, als sie sich mit Dingen verbindet, die ebenso flüchtig wie lebensnotwendig sind – was belegt, dass selbst kreative Sternstunden von großer Flüchtigkeit sein können. Es sind „Dinge ohne Form, die zu unserem Herzen sprechen", wie Tokujin Yoshioka formuliert, magische Momente.

> Das Fest ist jetzt zu Ende; unsre Spieler,
> Wie ich euch sagte, waren Geister, und
> Sind aufgelöst in Luft, in dünne Luft.
> Wie dieses Scheines lockrer Bau, so werden
> Die wolkenhohen Türme, die Paläste,
> Die hehren Tempel, selbst der große Ball,
> Ja, was daran nur Teil hat, untergehn
> Und, wie dies leere Schaugepräng' erblasst,
> Spurlos verschwinden. Wir sind solcher Zeug
> Wie der zu Träumen und dies kleine Leben
> Umfasst ein Schlaf.

Der Sturm, Vierter Aufzug, Erste Szene

INTRODUCTION

MANGER, BOIRE, ÉVENTUELLEMENT ACHETER

« D'aucuns affirment que le design n'est pas de l'art, dit Tokujin Yoshioka. Je suppose que pour eux, l'"art" a quelque chose d'attirant, mais aussi d'extremement angoissant. On me demande souvent la différence entre design et art. Nos ancêtres n'avaient aucune idée du design, mais connaissaient l'art et la musique. Pourquoi les gens écoutent-ils de la musique ? Poser la question est sans doute déjà y répondre. Si le design était toujours simple et pratique, la vie et les désirs du cœur n'auraient aucune richesse. Nos vies sont profondément imprégnées par des choses telles qu'une musique émouvante, un cinéma évocateur, des sentiments d'amour incontrôlés ou la perception des mystères de la nature. » De même que la vision du design de Tokujin Yoshioka transporte souvent les spectateurs dans un royaume où l'immatériel semble prendre forme, il se pourrait aussi que le design et l'architecture soient rapprochés de leur quintessence lorsqu'ils sont utilisés à des fins éphémères… Ce volume, qui porte le nom *Eat Shop Drink*, est consacré aux restaurants, magasins et bars – des lieux qui se doivent, par définition, de glorifier le transitoire, qu'ils suivent ou mènent la mode du moment. Et là comme ailleurs, des créateurs, en général très peu nombreux, font du transitoire un art et dévoilent l'âme éternelle de l'éphémère qui pourrait en fin de compte être tout simplement la vie. « Nous vivons une époque débordante de design, poursuit Tokujin Yoshioka. Dans ce contexte, j'ai voulu exprimer quelque chose qui n'a ni forme, ni design. Quelque chose qui transcende l'idée générale de forme et de design pour susciter l'émotion. Il ne s'agit pas de travailler sur les formes ou de faire des formes minimalistes, mais d'imaginer ce qui nous fait pénétrer au cœur de l'œuvre et élève nos esprits. J'aimerais créer quelque chose qui me touche moi-même. Depuis quelques années, je me mets au défi d'incorporer des éléments sans forme qui parlent à notre cœur – telles de nouvelles idées, couleurs ou senteurs – et de donner forme à une émotion. L'un de ces éléments est un phénomène appelé "lumière", un autre est invisible et un autre encore possède des formes non délimitées parce qu'il change d'apparence. »

LA FÊTE SOUS LES FLEURS DE CERISIER

L'art japonais de l'estampe gravée sur bois tel qu'il a été pratiqué entre le XVIIe et le XXe siècle porte le nom d'*ukiyo-e*, ce qui signifie « images du monde flottant ». C'est un univers évanescent de beauté fugitive dans lequel les fleurs de cerisier ou les feuilles d'érable sont des expressions de la nature qui surpassent tous les arts. Dans l'*ukiyo-e*, la société japonaise contemporaine affronte la notion bouddhiste ancestrale de l'éphémère avec une insouciance dont témoignent les fêtards qui boivent sous les cerisiers pendant les *hanami* ou *yozakura*. Si certains chefs et créateurs de mode préfèrent ancrer leur art dans une architecture faite pour durer, les moments consacrés à manger, acheter et boire sont potentiellement festifs et le plus souvent éphémères. Il en va ainsi de la plupart des réalisations récentes sélectionnées ici. Pourtant, manger, boire et acheter (l'essentiel ?) sont aussi des besoins permanents, plus élémentaires que la plupart des autres sources d'inspiration du design architectural et de la construction. Cette dichotomie constitue un élément extrêmement positif pour le développement de l'architecture. En effet, les boutiques et les bars sont souvent intégrés à des espaces existants ou sont de très petite taille, ces clients acceptent donc facilement d'en confier la réalisation à de jeunes architectes ou designers, comme en témoignent de nombreux projets

20
Tokujin Yoshioka, 132 5. Issey Miyake,
Minami-Aoyama, Tokyo, Japan, 2010

publiés ici. Alors qu'on exige souvent une expérience substantielle pour les grandes structures à construire, les rénovations ou aménagements intérieurs sont plus à la portée des jeunes architectes de talent – c'est l'une des raisons du choix de ce thème. Quant à l'œuvre de Tokujin Yoshioka présentée ici, elle est plus proche de l'installation que de la création de points de vente ou de consommation, même si le principe reste le même pour tout créateur réellement doué : approcher la « quintessence » de l'architecture et du design lorsqu'ils sont utilisés à des fins éphémères. Les restaurants, bars et magasins sont également des lieux de rencontre entre plusieurs disciplines, des lieux où l'art peut fusionner avec l'architecture et le design.

DE QUELLE COULEUR EST VOTRE RVB ?

Nombre de projets présentés sont néanmoins basés sur plus que la « lumière » à laquelle le designer japonais fait référence. Les nightcs en particulier sont des endroits parfaitement adaptés à l'intrusion de la lumière sous forme d'une présence architecturale, voire émotionnelle. Le designer brésilien Muti Randolph a ainsi fondé sa carrière sur la réunion de la lumière et du son dans un même espace – comme son D-Edge 2.0 (São Paulo, 2009–10, page 300), une extension du club D-Edge (2003). Il explique : « L'espace est déterminé par la lumière et la lumière par la musique. L'idée est de montrer la relation entre la musique et l'espace par l'éclairage, au moyen de logiciels qui analysent le son et modifient les effets lumineux en conséquence. » Les jeux de lumière font depuis longtemps partie des night-clubs et autres pistes de danse, mais l'arrivée des appareils RVB très lumineux, et notamment des consoles LED, a transformé et décuplé le potentiel des éclairages commandés par ordinateur qui peuvent générer une variété infinie de couleurs et d'effets. Dans le cas de D-Edge 2.0, la musique, reliée par ordinateur au système d'éclairage, détermine l'ambiance à un point tel qu'il exclut quasiment tout besoin d'architecture au-delà d'une coque de protection rudimentaire.

C'est aussi dans cet esprit que le jeune groupe espagnol 2G Arquitectos a travaillé son club Nébula ou « nuage d'étoiles » à Almendralejo (Badajoz, Espagne, 2009–10, page 50). Les designers parlent d'un « brouillard de lumière et de son », d'un « nuage de lumière ». Intégré à un espace existant, le Nébula ne fait rien de moins que « frapper de toutes parts les danseurs de lumière et de son ».

Tokujin Yoshioka a donné forme à ses idées de l'« invisibilité » potentielle dans une installation pour le fabricant de meubles Kartell à l'occasion du Salon du meuble de Milan 2010. Il avait déjà exploré le concept d'invisibilité avec des œuvres telles que *Cascade* (Tokyo, 2006), un bar fait d'un bloc de verre optique de 4,2 mètres de long, ou la « Chaise qui disparaît les jours de pluie » de 2002. Pour Kartell, il a voulu créer une chaise en acrylique si mince que la personne assise semble « flotter dans les airs ». La présentation du *Flocon de neige*, une installation faite d'une multitude de bâtonnets « prismatiques » en plastique transparent, accompagnait celle des chaises : suspendus en l'air, les prismes changent naturellement d'apparence au moindre mouvement et accueillent les visiteurs dans une installation la plus véritablement éphémère que possible.

EN HAUT DES ALPES

Étant donné la nature même des restaurants, bars et boutiques, de nombreux designers et architectes sont voués à tirer parti d'une enveloppe ou d'un espace existant. Si l'on trouve ici quelques bâtiments spécialement construits, ils passent après des exemples plus communs et moins « permanents ». Les jeunes architectes suisses Ambroise Bonvin et Claudia Bétrisey (Actescollectifs) ont ainsi entrepris de transformer un ancien restaurant et station de téléphérique au-dessus de Crans-Montana, à 2112 mètres d'altitude (restaurant d'altitude de Chetzeron, Crans-Montana, Suisse, 2008–09, page 56). Pour le moment, c'est uniquement un restaurant chic avec une vue fantastique sur la vallée du Rhône et la chaîne de sommets de plus de 4000 mètres qui avance vers le Cervin. À l'aide de pierres des environs, les architectes ont doté l'ensemble d'un revêtement brut et, surtout, lui ont conféré le label Minérgie (équivalent suisse du LEED) pour sa faible consommation énergétique et son empreinte carbone minimale. Bonvin et Bétrisey s'apprêtent à lancer la seconde phase du projet et transformer la station de téléphérique en une boutique hôtel de 15 chambres. En raison de la réticence des autorités suisses à autoriser les nouveaux hôtels à plus de 2000 mètres d'altitude, les architectes et les propriétaires ont dû déployer des trésors de patience et beaucoup d'efforts pour obtenir les autorisations nécessaires. La conversion astucieuse d'un bâtiment existant transformé en une destination à la mode témoigne néanmoins du talent des jeunes architectes.

LE FANTÔME DE L'OPÉRA

Le restaurant Mendini de Groningue (musée de Groningue, Pays-Bas, 2010, page 88) incarne une manière radicalement différente de réutiliser un espace existant. Le musée de Groningue, ouvert en 1994, est l'un des exemples les plus remarquables de collaboration entre architectes et designers. Alessandro Mendini, Philippe Starck, Michele de Lucchi et Coop Himmelb(l)au ont notamment participé au projet. Mendini en était le directeur général et le créateur du restaurant qui vient d'être refait par Maarten Baas, un designer de 33 ans basé à Bois-le-Duc, aux Pays-Bas. Le café-restaurant de 258 mètres carrés a été doté de bancs, d'un bar et d'un miroir d'argile rouge faits main pour la réinterprétation simple et élégante d'un espace qui aurait pu donner du fil à retordre à de nombreux designers plus connus.

À 56 ans, Odile Decq apparaît comme l'un des architectes français les plus importants de sa génération. Son Musée d'art contemporain MACRO de Rome (2003–10) lui a permis l'exploit de voler la vedette à Zaha Hadid et son Musée national des arts du XXIe siècle MAXXI (Rome, 1998–2009), pourtant beaucoup plus grand et objet d'un battage publicitaire beaucoup plus important. Sa dernière réalisation est le restaurant l'Opéra (Paris, 2008–11, page 158) à l'opéra Garnier. « Sans pasticher le monument existant, mais en le respectant tout en affirmant son caractère résolument contemporain », explique-t-elle, son « fantôme » pénètre dans le bâtiment ancien pour lui donner un nouveau souffle de vie.

21
Odile Decq Benoît Cornette,
L'Opéra Restaurant, Paris, France,
2008–11

21

À une échelle bien moindre que les mille mètres carrés de l'Opéra, Yuko Nagayama, 36 ans, a entrepris une tâche qui représente en un sens la même gageure que l'architecture de Charles Garnier (1825–98). Formée auprès de l'architecte de talent Jun Aoki, Nagayama a réalisé de nombreux commerces de détail et a reçu ici mission de moderniser un café de Tokyo de 45 mètres carrés, vieux d'un siècle. Son Kayaba Coffee (Tokyo, 2009, page 278) est un cas exemplaire de réutilisation commerciale. Si le rez-de-chaussée conserve les sièges qu'on est en droit d'attendre d'un café, l'architecte a transformé le niveau supérieur en une salle de lecture de livres d'art contemporain. Elle démontre ainsi qu'un minimalisme architectural soigneusement étudié peut parfaitement s'adapter à l'un des plus anciens cafés de Tokyo, une ville tellement reconstruite à la suite de tremblements de terre, incendies et guerres que les bâtiments de cet âge y sont rares.

Elena Pérez Garrigues et Daniel Blanco Cohen de Ninom sont nés tous les deux en 1975. Ils ont créé leur agence en 2006 à Madrid « avec l'idée d'intégrer l'architecture à des disciplines telles que la danse, la photographie et la création de décors ». Leur cave CVNE (Haro, La Rioja, Espagne, 2009, page 282) fait partie d'un projet plus important (1920 mètres carrés) mais constitue une nouvelle installation dans un bâtiment de 1879. Pour répondre au désir du client de créer « de nouvelles activités et une nouvelle dynamique autour du vin », les architectes ont inséré une « boîte en fer » dans l'espace existant qu'ils ont dépouillé jusqu'à l'essentiel, y ajoutant aussi des meubles simples et modernes et des spots. Avec un choix de fûts anciens, les traditions viticoles et sa modernité sont ainsi conjointement mises en valeur.

NOUS NE RÉINVENTONS PAS LA ROUE

Des exceptions notables existent aux États-Unis alors que la scène architecturale semble marquée par la situation économique, et peut-être par un conservatisme sous-jacent. Parmi elles, l'agence new-yorkaise LOT-EK, étonnamment dirigée par deux architectes d'origine italienne, Ada Tolla et Giuseppe Lignano, s'est spécialisé dans les installations temporaires, comme les magasins Uniqlo Container Stores (New York, 2006) et PUMACity (Alicante et Boston, 2008). Parmi leurs projets permanents, l'APAP OpenSchool (Anyang, Corée-du-Sud, 2010) est elle aussi construite à partir de containers maritimes. Pour la librairie Van Alen Books, située 30 Ouest, dans la 22e Rue de Manhattan (New York, 2011, page 242), les architectes ont relevé le défi de l'espace réduit (47 mètres carrés) et installé une plate-forme en gradins de 4,3 mètres faite de 70 portes recyclées. Avec sa façade noire au vitrage généreux, la boutique attire l'attention par l'installation qui rappelle un amphithéâtre, mais aussi à cause du jaune vif choisi par LOT-EK pour l'intérieur. La directrice de Van Alen Books, Olympia Kazi, pense en effet que l'amour des livres reste fort à l'ère numérique et déclare : « Nous ne réinventons pas la roue, nous répondons à un besoin. » Le graphisme dynamique et le jaune vif utilisés par LOT-EK rattachent le magasin au monde industriel où d'autres architectes ont souvent cherché à créer un environnement réduit pour la chose imprimée. Avec leur approche bon marché et lumineuse, les architectes soulignent l'intérêt permanent et réel pour les livres, manifestement partagé par les clients de Van Alen Books.

22

22
Suppose Design Office,
Café Day, Shizuoka, Japan, 2010

Makoto Tanijiri est né à Hiroshima en 1974. Il a déjà conçu plus de 60 maisons mais son agence Suppose Design Office est aussi très active dans le domaine du commerce de détail et de la restauration. Son Café Day (Shizuoka, Japon, 2010, page 346) occupe un espace de 74 mètres carrés qui abritait auparavant deux bars traditionnels japonais. Sa solution est cependant tout sauf traditionnelle : reprenant la signalisation urbaine qui entoure le bâtiment et une auto-école, il a utilisé un ton jaune vif et des marquages routiers pour relier le café à son environnement extérieur. Bien sûr, le concept d'ambiguïté intérieur et extérieur solidement ancré dans l'histoire architecturale japonaise donne à cette réalisation originale un arrière-plan non dénué d'intérêt. Il a, en un sens, remis à jour une notion japonaise très ancienne en intégrant le café au parking et à la route.

La boutique Aesop Saint-Honoré de Paris (2010, page 250) est située au 256 rue Saint-Honoré, près du Palais-Royal, dans un bâtiment du XVIIIe siècle. Les fondateurs de March Studio, dont l'installation compte pas moins de 3500 éléments en bois, sont plus jeunes que la plupart des designers présentés ici. Rodney Eggleston (né en 1981) et Anne-Laure Cavigneaux (née en 1980) ont réuni leurs origines et leurs talents pour la boutique parisienne d'Aesop, un fournisseur de produits pour la peau, les cheveux et les soins du corps basé à Melbourne – comme March Studio. Eggleston est australien, tandis que Cavigneaux est une graphiste parisienne. Ils ont opté pour du sorbier des oiseleurs issu de forêts gérées durablement en Australie et recouvert toute la surface disponible de bois afin de créer un décor homogène qui se distingue des pierres du Paris du XVIIIe siècle. Bien évidemment, ce type d'installation sur 100 mètres carrés de surface au sol est un laboratoire idéal pour jeunes talents et clients à l'esprit ouvert (Dennis Paphitis, fondateur d'Aesop) mais peu d'entreprises osent confier un bâtiment entier à des designers de 30 ans, surtout dans le contexte économique actuel.

UNE FERME SUR UNE COLLINE
L'architecte brésilien Isay Weinfeld est spécialisé depuis longtemps dans les demeures de luxe, les restaurants et les magasins de détail. Pour le restaurant Fasano (Punta del Este, Uruguay, 2010–11, page 384), il a tiré parti d'une vieille ferme en pierres et créé un fantastique restaurant de 390 mètres carrés en haut d'une colline avec vue sur Maldonado. En combinant les empilements bruts de pierres du cadre naturel et un coffret de béton minimaliste, l'architecte a occupé de manière originale et efficace un espace conçu pour un usage totalement différent. Weinfeld a déjà travaillé à plusieurs projets pour le groupe Fasano, notamment le spectaculaire hôtel et restaurant de São Paulo (2001–03). Si un tel raffinement dans un environnement urbain avec de nouvelles structures n'aurait su être imité dans la région côtière uruguayenne. Isay Weinfeld n'en a pas moins réussi à faire la réputation du groupe dans le territoire nouveau pour lui de ce décor naturel sauvage.

NOTHING HAPPENS FOR A REASON

Avec le ralentissement mondial dans la construction de nouveaux musées pour des raisons économiques, mais aussi à cause de la profusion des institutions existantes, les activités éphémères que sont manger, acheter et boire pourraient bien s'être rapprochées d'une certaine manière des arts. L'idée qu'un produit, même culinaire, puisse aspirer à une valorisation plus « permanente » n'est pas nouvelle mais les cafés, bars et boutiques ouverts récemment semblent avoir découvert à quel point la participation d'artistes ou la présence de leurs œuvres peut contribuer à élever le contenu au-delà de l'aspect purement mercantile. Le café Logomo (Turku, Finlande, 2010–11, page 76) est un exemple intéressant de ce type de collaboration. L'agence Artek, fondée en 1935 par Alvar Aalto et deux associés, a patronné le projet, conçu l'année où Turku a été capitale européenne de la culture (2011), et fait appel à l'artiste allemand Tobias Rehberger pour créer une installation appelée *Nothing Happens for a Reason* dans le bâtiment Logomo qui a été un lieu central des manifestations culturelles. Comme d'autres, notamment le célèbre architecte paysager américain Ken Smith, Rehberger est fasciné par les techniques de camouflage militaires. Il a appliqué certaines des théories de la Deuxième Guerre mondiale dans ce café de 230 mètres carrés où un réseau de lignes en surimpression et un décor majoritairement noir et blanc recouvrent et débordent des meubles Artek. Le résultat crée des ambiguïtés spatiales qui rendent parfois difficile de distinguer les objets de l'architecture. Bien que décoratif et certainement conçu comme une installation temporaire, *Nothing Happens for a Reason* montre que même un café peut prétendre au statut d'œuvre d'art. Et si le temporaire était tout ce qui importe ?

FILM D'ACTION

Le club parisien Silencio (2010–11, page 246), conçu par le réalisateur David Lynch, est un projet plus ambitieux et de plus grande portée. On connaît l'intérêt pour l'art et la musique de l'auteur de films cultes tels qu'*Elephant Man* (1980) et *Lost Highway* (1997), mais c'est sa première incursion dans le domaine de l'architecture d'intérieur. Situé dans un immeuble historique de 1883 au 142 rue Montmartre, dans le deuxième arrondissement, Silencio est un vaste espace (650 mètres carrés) marqué par l'utilisation de feuille d'or en abondance et d'un revêtement en bois brut disposé au hasard. Plus qu'un bar, l'endroit se veut un club privé qui accueille concerts, projections ou événements artistiques et comprend une bibliothèque d'art. L'association d'une personnalité telle que David Lynch à un projet d'architecture intérieure et un club privé suffira certainement à assurer un premier succès au Silencio. Bien qu'assisté par Raphaël Navot et l'agence d'architecture ENIA, la tendance de Lynch à transgresser les frontières qui séparent habituellement des domaines aussi variés que la réalisation de films et l'architecture d'intérieur donne le ton de cette réalisation. Les manifestations qui y seront organisées sont par définition de nature éphémère et le design même vise un caractère improvisé à plusieurs égards. Alors que l'art contemporain fuit aujourd'hui volontairement le monumental et le permanent inhérents aux musées, il ne serait pas surprenant qu'un lieu voué à la nuit (ouvert de 18 h à 6 h) attire les véritables artistes du moment.

23
*Jouin Manku, Mandarin Oriental,
Paris, Paris, France, 2009–11*

TAKASHI ET ANISH FONT DU LÈCHE-VITRINE

L'architecte Peter Marino est peut-être le designer de boutiques et d'appartements hauts de gamme le plus prisé et le plus brillant du monde. Ses clients comptent les marques les plus réputées comme Chanel ou Louis Vuitton. Il est d'ailleurs intéressant de remarquer que ces marques cherchent à la fois à se montrer contemporaines et à jouer de leurs « traditions » et histoire. Quoi de plus naturel par conséquent que d'introduire des œuvres d'art dans ces espaces ? Le nouveau magasin Chanel de Marino à SoHo (New York, 2010, page 260) regorge d'œuvres spécialement créées par Peter Belyi, Robert Greene, Gregor Hildebrandt, Alan Rath et Richard Woods. L'œuvre d'art prend ici un caractère nouveau et fait de son mieux pour aider à vendre. L'approche est différente dans le grand magasin Louis Vuitton de New Bond Street (Londres, 2010, page 254) où des œuvres de Richard Prince, Takashi Murakami, Gilbert & George, Anish Kapoor, Christ Ofili et Gary Hume illuminent l'espace de 1500 mètres carrés. On a spéculé un moment sur le remplacement des églises par les musées comme centres de la fierté civique, mais vu leurs problèmes financiers et leur démesure généralisée, ils pourraient bien perdre leur gloire de l'après-guerre.

MÉLANGE DE GENRES

Malgré tout le respect dû aux religions plus établies, on peut se demander si, à notre époque où le culte de l'argent fait tant de nouveaux adeptes, une visite à SoHo ou Bond Street ne permet pas au client moyen de se rapprocher autant du ciel qu'il ne saurait l'espérer. Les grandes chaînes japonaises de magasins comme Seibu ont ouvert la voie il y a longtemps avec leurs musées intégrés et expositions temporaires très en vue. Pourquoi aller au musée si vous pouvez vous cultiver dans un magasin ? Pourquoi aller à l'église si vous ne désirez rien d'autre qu'un nouveau sac à main ? Depuis que l'art a fusionné avec le mercantilisme, on ne saurait nier qu'il semble plus que jamais à sa place dans une très belle paire de chaussures. Curieusement, c'est parfois l'architecte qui se fait remarquer en premier dans ce mélange de genres. L'espace est en soi pureté et les différents matériaux gardent leur noblesse s'ils sont utilisés correctement. Qu'on n'y voie aucune critique de Peter Marino : il est, une fois encore, le grand homme du moment, en particulier lorsqu'il s'agit de magasins, et il n'y a certainement aucun mal à associer les projets de Chanel et Louis Vuitton à l'art contemporain. C'est plutôt une tendance sociétale significative qui propulse le commerce de détail, l'architecture et l'art sur le devant de la même scène, les obligeant à satisfaire dans une certaine mesure les besoins immédiats des clients. Acheter ou ne pas acheter, telle est la question. La nouvelle religion n'est pas l'art, mais le shopping.

LES CHAÎNES D'HÔTELS MISENT SUR L'ART

Jean Nouvel a adopté une approche très différente pour associer l'art et l'architecture dans son restaurant Le Loft du Sofitel Stephansdom à Vienne (Autriche, 2006–10, page 290). Parfaitement intégré au concept global du bâtiment, également conçu par Nouvel, le restaurant sur le toit présente un spectaculaire plafond vidéo créé par l'artiste suisse Pipilotti Rist dont on retrouve aussi la marque dans le hall ou l'espace bar, plus bas. Avec la puissante architecture de Jean Nouvel, ses plafonds colorés visibles de l'extérieur grâce au vitrage du restau-

23

rant sur toute sa hauteur, font partie intégrante d'un ensemble conçu sous l'œil vigilant de l'architecte. Malgré le succès commercial visé pour l'hôtel, l'architecte et l'artiste ont ici donné libre cours à leur imagination pour de nouvelles expériences spatiales – le geste est très différent de celui qui consiste à accrocher une peinture au mur d'une boutique, même si les deux poursuivent le même objectif. Nouvel et Rist ont créé un espace où les disciplines se rencontrent, une occasion suffisamment rare dans notre monde contemporain pour qu'on la signale.

L'association d'architectes et de designers de talent dans le domaine hôtelier est un phénomène actuel assez répandu. Des architectes comme le groupe allemand Graft ont ainsi obtenu leurs lettres de noblesse de designers avec l'aménagement de l'hôtel très chic Q! à Berlin en 2002–04. De même, l'architecture de qualité ou le décor intérieur constituent certainement des facteurs importants du succès d'établissements comme l'hôtel W de Londres (2010–11, page 136). La chaîne d'hôtels design a fait appel à Rob Wagemans et Concrete d'Amsterdam pour son spa Sweat et centre de remise en forme AWAY qui donnent sur Leicester Square, son restaurant Spice Market et le design de ses chambres. Le Mandarin Oriental, Paris (2009–11, page 216), par Jean-Michel Wilmotte, propose le Bar 8, le restaurant Sur Mesure et le Camélia, tous créés par Jouin Manku – Wilmotte et Patrick Jouin comptent parmi les designers français les plus connus et leur double présence créative dans un même hôtel de luxe montre une fois encore à quel point les chaînes hôtelières elles aussi sont soucieuses de se faire un nom et d'explorer le haut de gamme du design pour attirer une certaine catégorie de clients. On peut dire que les boutiques hôtels « design » comme Q! ont incité les grands groupes hôteliers à diversifier les apparences de leurs établissements selon les endroits, faisant appel aux créateurs les plus talentueux du moment.

L'ART DU PETIT COMMERCE

Si Jean Nouvel et Pipilotti Rist se situent clairement au plus haut niveau de l'architecture et de l'art contemporains, la scène actuelle ne cesse d'évoluer et puise son inspiration chez des artistes qui ont bâti leur réputation dans d'autres domaines que l'architecture d'intérieur. Gary Card est décorateur de théâtre et concepteur d'accessoires, graphiste et illustrateur. Il a travaillé avec des stars de l'art contemporain et de la mode telles que Nick Knight, Stella McCartney et Lady Gaga. Le LN-CC (Londres, 2010, page 116) est sa première commande d'architecture intérieure. Ce Late Night Chameleon Café est plus un magasin de mode et une librairie que son nom ne l'indique. Ses créateurs, John Skelton et Daniel Mitchell, projettent un mélange délibéré de vêtements, musique et art à l'intention de leurs clients, développant un environnement commercial qui mêle ce qu'ils perçoivent comme le meilleur des « tendances dominantes » et l'« avant-garde ». La seule limite est clairement le goût des propriétaires de la marque. Gary Card s'est lancé dans cette mission avec un mélange de bois brut et d'acrylique orange, citant les artistes *shock and awe* Paul McCarthy et Jeff Koons comme sources d'inspiration : « Je suis particulièrement attiré par le coloré et le pervers, surtout quand les deux se rencontrent. » L'architecture d'intérieur participe ici d'un concept commercial original dans lequel nul ne se veut rien d'autre que ce qu'il est. Card et son blog très racoleur www.garycardiology.blogspot.com sont autant à la mode que

24

24
*Fearon Hay, North Wharf, Auckland,
New Zealand, 2010–11*

le LN-CC – les deux se mélangent et s'harmonisent parfaitement. Lorsque les géants du Bauhaus rêvaient de la *Gesamtkunstwerk*, l'œuvre d'art totale, ils pensaient art, architecture et design. Ne devrait-elle pas aujourd'hui inclure un quatrième partenaire que l'on pourrait familière-ment appeler le « concept commercial » ? Là encore, n'y voir aucun manque de respect, c'est plutôt le contraire, l'admiration qui est visée. L'art et l'architecture changent peut-être plus vite encore que les créateurs ne l'admettent.

LE MOULAGE DE LA MÉDUSE

La définition même de l'art, ou du design pour les restaurants, bars et magasins semble perdre en précision dans une société qui a fait du consumérisme l'une de ses valeurs suprêmes. C'est dans ce contexte que s'inscrivent certains créateurs qui s'efforcent d'utiliser les technologies de pointe pour aborder le design de manière artistique et néanmoins efficace. Evan Douglis est l'un des plus étonnants. Après une formation d'architecte à l'Architectural Association de Londres, Cooper Union (New York) et Harvard GSD, il a travaillé avec des agences de renom telles que Tod Williams ou Agrest and Gandelsonas, mais aussi avec d'autres plus polyvalentes comme Emilio Ambasz, avant de créer sa société en 1992, Evan Douglis Studio, basée à Troy, New York. Pour lui, « Evan Douglis Studio est une agence d'architecture et de conception interdisciplinaire spécialisée dans la recherche et l'application de nouveaux systèmes autogénératifs, de la technologie des membranes et des techniques de production contemporaines telles qu'elles sont utilisées dans de nombreux projets. » Moon Jelly (Choice: Kitchens and Bakery, Brooklyn, New York, 2009–10, page 170) est l'une de ses dernières réalisations. À l'aide de techniques aussi sophisti-quées que l'impression 3D, Douglis a créé un surprenant plafond qu'il décrit comme « un magnifique nuage théâtral suspendu au-dessus des têtes ». Bien que produit par des méthodes industrielles modernes, il semble déployer un nombre quasi infini de motifs dont certains rappel-lent les étoiles tourbillonnantes de Van Gogh. Pour Douglis, c'est « la poursuite de notre intérêt persistant pour la complexité des surfaces, la forme animée et la distraction séquentielle sous la forme d'une expérience d'immersion totale dans l'architecture ». Les artistes qui imaginent des magasins ou restaurants, comme Pipilotti Rist à Vienne, apportent originalité et créativité à un espace parfaitement en mesure de trans-cender tout emploi spécifique de l'architecture. Malgré sa formation d'architecte, Evan Douglis semble travailler à l'interface physique entre le construit et le potentiellement décoratif. De même, il a recours à la haute technologie – l'emploi de l'impression 3D en est à ses tout pre-miers pas – pour explorer les frontières entre design, architecture et art et leur donner sens. Avec ses motifs et les lustres réalisés sur mesure, l'architecte a donné vie au plafond de cet espace sinon fonctionnel et relativement quelconque. Malgré une réflexion et une inspira-tion bien évidemment très différentes, on pourra noter dans la même veine que les ferronneries magnifiquement complexes du magasin Carson Pirie Scott (Chicago, 1904, aujourd'hui Sullivan Center) par Louis Sullivan ont été restaurées en 2010 pour retrouver leur gloire d'ori-gine. Bien avant la *tabula rasa* de Gropius, Sullivan – aussi appelé le « père du modernisme » – s'était rendu célèbre en déclarant que la « forme suit toujours la fonction » et malgré l'avancée de la répétition industrielle dans l'architecture et l'absence actuelle de décoration, ses œuvres restent des références. Il insistait sur le fait que la décoration devait avoir un but pratique, mais les clients du Moon Jelly à Brooklyn ont peut-être tout simplement plaisir à lever les yeux et se perdre dans les méandres qui attirent le regard vers le haut ?

25
Graft, Wokalicious,
Berlin, Germany, 2010–11

25

CUBE DE VERRE OU ABRI À BATEAUX ?

Si le Sofitel de Jean Nouvel à Vienne comprend un restaurant et un bar conçus par l'architecte, on a pu dire que ces ajouts étaient nécessaires au projet global. En effet, bien que plutôt rares, les structures spécialement construites pour accueillir des commerces, bars ou restaurants constituent autant d'opportunités de s'exprimer pour les architectes et designers de talent. Le restaurant Coubertin (Centre olympique, parc Olympique, Munich, 2010, page 82) n'est ainsi qu'un projet de modernisation et d'extension sur le site des Jeux de 1972. La commande a été naturellement attribuée à la société Auer+Weber+Assoziierte, dont les associés fondateurs Fritz Auer et Carlo Weber ont travaillé avec Behnisch & Partner avant de créer leur propre agence en 1980 – la structure originale avait été conçue par Günter Behnisch en collaboration avec l'ingénieur Frei Otto. Le nouveau restaurant de 500 places rend un hommage mérité au complexe de 1972, sa pureté rectiligne tranchant avec les courbes arachnéennes de ce dernier.

Francisco Mangado n'a pas été confronté à un cas si complexe de références historiques à respecter pour son Café Baluarte (Pampelune, Navarre, Espagne, 2006), malgré la proximité avec le parlement de Navarre. Le seul point de référence de son cube de verre minimaliste est le Centre des congrès et auditorium Baluarte, dont il est également l'auteur (Pampelune, 2000–03). Se réclamant d'une tradition moderniste à laquelle on pourrait inclure la maison Farnsworth (Ludwig Mies van der Rohe, Plano, Illinois, 1945–51), l'architecte a voulu donner aux utilisateurs « l'impression d'être à l'extérieur, protégés du mauvais temps mais pouvant jouir de la profondeur spatiale de la place et de la vue des réalisations architecturales environnantes ». Contrairement à la maison de Mies cependant, son cube aux parois en verre peut être entièrement ouvert sur la place avoisinante par beau temps. Les bonnes raisons budgétaires ne manquent certainement pas pour se contenter ici d'une simple structure vitrée, mais Mangado n'a pas moins fait une véritable œuvre d'architecture de son Café Baluarte, ce qui n'est pas si courant dans ce contexte.

Le projet North Wharf à Auckland par Fearon Hay (Nouvelle-Zélande, 2010–11, page 188) représente une combinaison intéressante entre la réutilisation d'un espace industriel existant et une construction dans un but précis sur un site contigu. Les architectes ont travaillé sur trois structures dans la zone de développement de 2,5 hectares du front de mer Wynyard Waterfront, dont un abri à bateaux historique rénové. Deux nouveaux bâtiments destinés à des commerces de détail et activités de loisir flanquent le hangar des années 1930 restauré, le Old Red Shed. Comme pour la remise en état de bâtiments industriels ailleurs dans le monde, le projet d'Auckland conserve en grande partie la finition « crue » d'origine de l'Old Red Shed et cette authenticité des docks donne une atmosphère à l'ensemble qui lui confère une signification accrue pour les visiteurs, qu'il s'agisse des bâtiments anciens ou nouveaux. Il y a quelques années, les architectes n'auraient été que trop heureux d'effacer toute trace de passé industriel – la rénovation a gagné en importance, de même que les contraintes budgétaires ont rendu plus rares les nouvelles constructions. Il est aujourd'hui évident que des décisions prises initialement sur une base purement économique fondent un raisonnement esthétique que le public accepte désormais sans broncher. Il existe un sens de l'authenticité que seul le temps peut conférer et l'architecture très contemporaine a retenu cette leçon qui intègre volontairement l'ancien et le nouveau de manière à rendre le sentiment pour l'architecture et le design plus complexe, plus varié et certainement moins « superficiel » que jamais.

UNE FAÇADE POUR LES CENTRES COMMERCIAUX

Si la mode haut de gamme recherche souvent les boutiques en vue, le commerce de détail est concentré pour une bonne part dans les centres commerciaux. Trois éminents architectes ont réalisé ou travaillent à des complexes de ce type qui méritent d'être mentionnés. Le premier est UNStudio et sa Galleria Centercity de 66 000 mètres carrés (Cheonan, Corée-du-Sud, 2008–10, page 372). Ben van Berkel et son équipe maîtrisent depuis longtemps l'art de l'informatique pour les bâtiments de grande envergure comme le musée Mercedes-Benz (Stuttgart, 2003–06). Van Berkel s'intéresse beaucoup aux effets d'optique et a choisi ici d'utiliser deux épaisseurs de profilés aluminium pour produire un surprenant effet extérieur moiré. Après avoir rénové avec succès un magasin à Séoul pour le même groupe (Galleria, 2003), UNStudio a déjà démontré que le design de qualité peut être un placement d'entreprise solide. Comme souvent, les architectes ont intimement lié l'aspect extérieur moderne du complexe et son intérieur tout aussi étonnant décrit comme « un genre de cascade spatiale ».

Massimiliano et Doriana Fuksas ont réalisé des projets marquants tels que les millions de mètres carrés de la Foire de Milan (Rho-Pero, Milan, 2002–05) et le centre commercial MyZeil de Francfort (2009). Ils viennent d'achever le Palatino Center (Turin, 1998–2011, page 194), un espace de vente de vêtements de 13 000 mètres carrés. La structure est marquée par des piliers prismatiques à étages aux rayonnages métalliques enchâssés et une façade composée de 60 000 morceaux de verre et 150 000 kilos d'acier. Comme ils l'ont déjà fait à moindre échelle pour le groupe Armani (tour Armani de Ginza, Tokyo, 2005–07, et magasin Emporio Armani Fifth Avenue, New York, 2009), le couple Fuksas démontre qu'un emploi intelligent de l'architecture et du design attire une attention durable sur les commerces. Les commandes d'État se font rares, mais des industries comme celles de la mode ont relancé dans une certaine mesure la création architecturale. Rien ne peut compenser la récession mondiale, mais les produits de luxe se sont avérés étonnamment résistants à la morosité ressentie dans d'autres secteurs.

Un autre des « grands » noms de l'architecture contemporaine travaille à un complexe d'usage mixte à Düsseldorf. Le Kö-Bogen par Daniel Libeskind (2011–13) est un bâtiment de 40 000 mètres carrés et six étages qui comprend à la fois des bureaux et des commerces. En plus de son usage mixte, l'intérêt du Kö-Bogen est son concept global qui crée un lien entre le paysage et l'environnement urbain au moyen d'« orifices filtres » dans les formes architecturales qui permettent aux éléments du paysage de « se mélanger naturellement et se répandre dans l'espace ». Bien qu'il reste surtout connu pour des œuvres telles que le Musée juif de Berlin (1989–2001), Libeskind a déjà réalisé des

*26
Wolfgang Kergaßner, Linde Agora,
Pullach-Höllriegelskreuth, Germany,
2006–08*

26

projets à grand échelle tournés vers le commerce tels le centre commercial et de loisirs Westside (Berne, 2005–08) et Crystals au CityCenter (Las Vegas, Nevada, 2006–09). En effet, si une génération précédente d'architectes aurait trouvé que les centres commerciaux posent trop de problèmes pratiques pour permettre un design créatif, on peut dire que le commerce autant que la profession d'architecte ont changé de position. Beaucoup des centres commerciaux cités présentent des ambitions architecturales claires et arrêtées qui font partie intégrante du concept de commerce qu'ils incarnent. Avec la raréfaction des commandes d'établissements culturels comme les musées ou salles de concerts, le commerce de détail émerge, là encore, comme une alternative pour les architectes les plus doués.

LE BÉTON DANS LA JUNGLE

On ne saurait non plus suggérer que les projets architecturaux intéressants de restaurants, bars et commerces sont forcément des projets de grande envergure. Loin de la frénésie urbaine de Düsseldorf ou Turin, les jeunes architectes Maria Paz (née en 1985) et Thomaz Regatos (né en 1981) de Rizoma Arquitetura ont réalisé deux petites structures pour le Centre d'art contemporain Inhotim, à 60 kilomètres de la ville brésilienne de Belo Horizonte. Leur restaurant Oiticica de 320 couverts (Brumadinho, Brésil, 2010, page 310) à base de panneaux en béton et métal peu onéreux a été construit en trois mois seulement. Le bâtiment, intégré le plus possible à la végétation dense qui l'entoure, est ventilé naturellement. Rizoma a également réalisé un magasin botanique pour le même Centre d'art contemporain en 2011 (page 314). Destiné à vendre des plantes et ustensiles de jardinage et construit en béton, pierres et bois en trois mois, le bâtiment de 200 mètres carrés a coûté seulement 125 000 $. Plus un pavillon ouvert qu'une construction traditionnelle, il a été réalisé, comme le restaurant, en prêtant attention aux arbres sur le site.

MÉDITATION MINIMALISTE

Plusieurs des projets qui suivent vont au-delà de la gamme pratique habituelle pour s'aventurer dans des domaines qui ne relèvent pas toujours du simple commerce. Deux exemples au Japon sont particulièrement intéressants. Le Zen Lounge ONO/Kyoto (Kyoto, 2003, page 230) du talentueux architecte Waro Kishi n'est en aucun cas un « lounge » au sens habituel du terme, ni un magasin comme un autre. C'est là que les moines bouddhistes zen de la secte Soto viennent acheter des vêtements religieux et articles d'autel, mais aussi parler. C'est sans doute cette dernière fonction qui est à l'origine du nom inattendu « Zen Lounge ». Dans l'école zen Soto, la plus importante des branches du bouddhisme zen, la méditation est pratiquée sans objet ni contenu, la conscience d'un flux de pensées que le méditateur n'est pas censé entraver fait partie du processus. Le design de Waro Kishi, marqué par un minimalisme subtil mais presque total, est plus facile à comprendre dans le contexte de ce type de méditation. On sait que l'architecture et le design nippons ont fortement influencé l'émergence du modernisme en Europe avec des noms comme Bruno Taut et le minimalisme tel qu'il est pratiqué en Occident est lui aussi clairement imprégné de la pensée japonaise. La différence entre Orient et Occident dans ce cas est que, si le minimalisme est une mode qui a passé à Londres ou

27

27 + 28
Isay Weinfeld, Fasano Restaurant,
Punta del Este, Uruguay, 2010–11

Paris, il reste présent dans l'œuvre de Waro Kishi précisément parce que l'architecte s'efforce d'adapter des formes de pensée qui ne sont pas une lubie passagère, mais le résultat de siècles de tradition.

ODE À LA NEUTRALITÉ

Le jeune architecte Atsushi Muroi est né à Hiroshima en 1975. Il travaille pour Hakuhodo, la deuxième agence de publicité du Japon. Son AND Market (Kasumigaseki, Tokyo, 2011, page 210) de 31 mètres carrés a été conçu pour un distributeur de smart phones sans lien avec les principaux opérateurs de téléphonie. La société mère du client est NEC, « l'un des principaux fournisseurs d'Internet, réseaux à large bande et solutions commerciales pour les entreprises ». L'intérêt d'AND Market vient de son identité visuelle forte, décrite par Muroi comme « neutre » ou « achromatique », et de son adéquation à la demande du client – la neutralité symbolise ici la vente de différents smart phones sans qu'aucun opérateur ne soit privilégié. Atsushi Muroi déclare : « Notre projet associe le développement conceptuel, la stratégie de porte-feuille de marque, le nom commercial et développement CI/VI et le design de marque global par le biais du commerce de détail, du site Web, des outils promotionnels et des personnages. » Il poursuit en expliquant son concept achromatique : « Sans rehausser aucune couleur, pas même le noir ou le blanc, notre design incarne l'essence même de la marque en représentant l'équilibre de clarté entre le noir et le blanc. AND Market ne peut être associé à aucune couleur traditionnelle car le concept est quasi unique, tant par ses services que par ses designs de marques. » L'architecture devient ici difficile à distinguer du graphisme, mais aussi, plus curieusement, du marketing produit et d'un concept publicitaire global. De nouveau, là où le Bauhaus rêvait d'une synthèse des arts, un architecte cherche une vision holistique qui fusionne architecture, design, graphisme et ce qui est peut-être le plus important, commerce de détail. Avec ce projet, l'architecte n'aspire pas à l'accomplissement sur le plan artistique, mais au succès commercial – le résultat final, spatialement cohérent et visuellement frappant, témoigne de son talent.

INSTANTS DE MAGIE

À l'instar d'autres livres de la série *Architecture Now!*, *Manger Acheter Boire* passe en revue des projets très récents, tous achevés ou commencés après 2003. Beaucoup ont été conçus et construits après le début de la crise économique de 2008 et c'est un facteur important : ces restaurants, magasins et bars sont sans doute, dans l'ensemble, plus petits ou moins onéreux que des constructions ou lieux similaires imaginés dans le même but il y a seulement quelques années de plus. C'est un constat significatif que l'économie, même en crise, n'arrête pas l'architecture – mais modifie plutôt la forme du présent. Être moins cher ne signifie pas être moins inventif, c'est même sans doute le contraire qui est vrai dans les exemples sélectionnés ici. La pression de l'épargne, et par conséquent de la dépense, a sans doute atteint de nouveaux sommets avec la nouvelle prudence des clients et des hommes d'affaires quant à la solidité de leur environnement économique. À la manière d'un tremblement de terre, l'implosion qui a commencé à Wall Street a secoué des certitudes et inspiré aux détaillants, hôteliers et

28

propriétaires de bars et restaurants le désir de nouveaux modèles, de nouvelles formes d'expression. L'architecture, le design et l'art ont été mis en avant dans un effort généralisé de donner une valeur ajoutée, quasi intangible, aux produits, des steaks aux imperméables. Par un tour nouveau et intéressant, les temps difficiles semblent avoir encouragé les architectes et designers à se lier plus inextricablement que jamais aux endroits où manger, acheter et boire. Comme les grands chefs, les grands architectes sont rares, mais certains de ceux présentés ici ont néanmoins atteint une hauteur d'expression qui transcende les doutes et problèmes de l'époque. Ils ont créé un genre d'art d'autant plus significatif qu'il s'accompagne dans ces espaces – c'est l'acceptation que la créativité peut être éphémère même à son meilleur niveau – d'activités à la fois fugitives et vitales. Tels sont les « éléments sans forme qui parlent à notre cœur » qu'évoque Tokujin Yoshioka, des instants de magie.

> Nos divertissements sont maintenant terminés. Comme je te l'ai dit,
> Les acteurs que tu as vus étaient tous des esprits qui
> Se sont évaporés en air, en air subtil.
> Un jour viendra que, de même que l'édifice sans base de cette vision,
> Les orgueilleuses tours, les somptueux palais,
> Les temples solennels, le globe immense lui-même,
> Avec tout ce qu'il enserre, se dissoudront,
> Et comme le spectacle substantiel qui vient de s'évanouir,
> Il n'en restera pas la trace la plus légère. Nous sommes de l'étoffe
> Dont sont faits les rêves, et notre courte existence
> Se termine par un sommeil.

La Tempête, acte IV, scène I

2 G

2G Arquitectos
C/ Federico García Lorca 48
06200 Almendralejo, Badajoz
Spain

Tel: +34 924 66 28 78
E-mail: 2g.arquitectos@gmail.com

MIGUEL ANGEL GONZÁLEZ GÓMEZ was born in Almendralejo, Spain, in 1979. He received his degree as an architect at the Superior Technical School of Architecture, University of Seville (1997–2004), a Master's degree in Interior Design from the Polytechnic University of Madrid (2007), and a Master's degree in Urbanism from Fundicotex (Professional Association for Land Use Planning, Environment, and Sustainable Development, 2007–08). His work includes the Casa E (Villafranca de los Barros, Badajoz, 2005–06); and Nébula (Almendralejo, 2009–10, published here). Work under construction includes the Casa Almendra (Almendralejo, 2008–); and the Nandos Restaurant (Almendralejo, 2011), all in Spain.

MIGUEL ANGEL GONZÁLEZ GÓMEZ wurde 1979 in Almendralejo, Spanien, geboren. Er absolvierte sein Architekturstudium an der Escuela Técnica Superior de Arquitectura der Universität Sevilla (1997–2004), erwarb einen Master in Innenarchitektur an der Polytechnischen Hochschule Madrid (2007) sowie einen Master in Stadtplanung/Fundicotex (Berufsverband für Bodennutzung, Umwelt und nachhaltige Entwicklung, 2007–08). Zu seinen Projekten zählen die Casa E (Villafranca de los Barros, Badajoz, 2005–06) und der Club Nébula (Almendralejo, 2009–10, hier vorgestellt). Derzeit im Bau sind die Casa Almendra (Almendralejo, seit 2008) sowie das Restaurant Nandos (Almendralejo, 2011), alle in Spanien.

MIGUEL ÁNGEL GONZÁLEZ GÓMEZ est né à Almendralejo, Espagne, en 1979. Il a obtenu son diplôme d'architecte à l'École technique supérieure de l'université de Séville (1997–2004), un master en architecture d'intérieur à l'Université polytechnique de Madrid (2007) et un master en urbanisme à Fundicotex (Association professionnelle de l'aménagement du territoire, de l'environnement et du développement durable, 2007–08). Ses réalisations comprennent notamment : la Casa E (Villafranca de los Barros, Badajoz, 2005–06) et la discothèque Nébula (Almendralejo, 2009–10, publiée ici). Parmi ses travaux en construction figurent la Casa Almendra (Almendralejo, 2008–) et le restaurant Nandos (Almendralejo, 2011), tous en Espagne.

NÉBULA

Almendralejo, Badajoz, Spain, 2009–10

Address: C/ Cometa, s/n. Almendralejo, Badajoz, Spain,
discotecanebula@hotmail.com, http://discotecanebula.blogspot.com. Area: 160 m². Client: Cometa Noche S.L.
Cost: €150 000. Collaboration: Juan Manuel González Gómez

The **NÉBULA** or Lightcloud is a small discotheque. The space concerned served as a bar and had been completely soundproofed, allowing the architect to carry out the new design with a considerable cost saving but requiring him to respect the existing envelope to the greatest extent possible. González calls the result an "intelligent environment of light and sound." More precisely, the intent is to create a "chameleon-like space" or a "fog of light and music"—or finally, a cloud of light. The idea of allowing light and sound to take on an architectural function is clearly a very contemporary one, mastered in this instance by this young Spanish architect. Dancers are "enveloped by strokes of light and sound."

NÉBULA (Sternnebel) ist ein kleiner Club. Die ehemalige Bar war bereits umfassend schallisoliert, weshalb der Architekt sein Projekt mit erheblicher Kostenersparnis realisieren konnte, die Raumhülle jedoch weitestgehend unverändert lassen musste. González beschreibt das Resultat als „intelligentes Umfeld aus Licht und Sound". Ihm ging es besonders darum, einen „chamäleonhaften Raum" zu schaffen, einen „Nebel aus Licht und Musik" – im Grunde eine Wolke aus Licht. Licht und Sound architektonisch zu nutzen, ist ein ausgesprochen moderner Ansatz, den der junge spanische Architekt überzeugend umsetzt. Die Tänzer tauchen in „Licht- und Soundblitze" ein.

Le **NÉBULA**, ou « nuage d'étoiles », est une petite discothèque. L'espace utilisé abritait autrefois un bar et a été entièrement insonorisé, ce qui a permis à l'architecte de refaire le design en réalisant des économies très importantes, mais lui a imposé de respecter le plus possible l'enveloppe existante. González qualifie le résultat d'« environnement intelligent de son et de lumière ». Il a en fait voulu créer un « espace-caméléon » ou un « brouillard de lumière et de son » – soit, en fin de compte, un nuage d'étoiles. L'idée de faire assumer une fonction architecturale au son et à la lumière est clairement très contemporaine, le jeune architecte espagnol s'en tire ici avec brio. Les danseurs sont « frappés de toutes parts par la lumière et le son ».

Some of the varying light effects in the bar are seen in the two images of the same space seen from opposite ends (above and right page). Drawings show the angled surfaces and patterns.

Aufnahmen des Raums aus entgegengesetzter Perspektive (oben und rechte Seite) veranschaulichen die vielfältigen Lichteffekte. Zeichnungen lassen die schiefwinkligen Flächen und Muster erkennen.

Ces deux photos des extrémités du bar prises dans le même espace (ci-dessus et page de droite) permettent de voir les différents jeux de lumière. Les plans représentent les surfaces angulaires et les motifs.

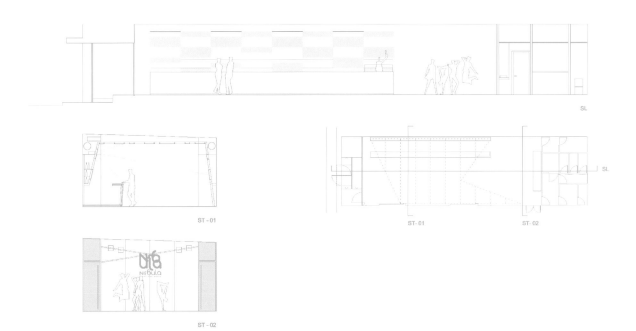

SL

ST - 01

ST - 01   ST - 02   SL

ST - 02

The lighting system allows for a very large variety of different effects, using a monochromatic approach or more varied ones.

Mithilfe des Lichtsystems lässt sich eine große Bandbreite verschiedener Effekte realisieren: monochromatische Effekte ebenso wie komplexere Kombinationen.

Le système d'éclairage permet des jeux de lumière très variés, monochromes ou plus colorés.

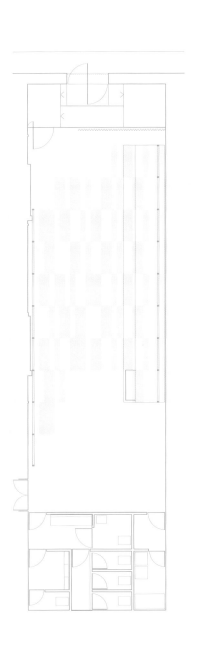

Three different photos from the same angle give an impression of the way in which visitors are enveloped by sound and light. To the left, drawings show the light panel pattern, which is irregular, as well as the overall floor plan.

Drei Ansichten aus derselben Perspektive vermitteln einen Eindruck von der Licht- und Soundlandschaft, in der sich die Clubbesucher bewegen. Links das unregelmäßige Muster der Leuchtpaneele im Kontext des Gesamtgrundrisses.

Ces trois photos prises sous le même angle donnent une idée de la manière dont les clients sont entourés de toutes parts par la lumière et le son. À gauche, plans du motif des panneaux lumineux, irrégulier comme la surface globale.

ACTESCOLLECTIFS

Actescollectifs Architectes SA
Avenue du Rothorn 2
3960 Sierre
Switzerland
Tel: +41 27 456 87 75 / Fax: +41 27 456 87 74

Rue Henri-Ruchonnet 1
1003 Lausanne
Switzerland
Tel: +41 21 323 58 55 / Fax: +41 21 323 58 50

E-mail: info@actescollectifs.ch
Web: www.actescollectifs.ch

Ambroise Bonvin was born in 1968 in Sion, Switzerland. He received his diploma as an architect from the HES, School of Architecture and Engineering in Fribourg (1989–92), and formed a first association with Claudia Bétrisey and Patrick Aumann (2000–05). Claudia Bétrisey was also born in Sion, in 1971, and she studied at the ETH (Zurich, 1990–97). Cédric Bonvin was born in Sierre in 1975 and studied architecture at the Athenaeum School (Lausanne, 1996–2001); Thomas Friberg was born in Vancouver, Canada, in 1970 and studied at the EPFL (Lausanne, 1991–97), while Pierre-Antoine Masserey was born in 1961, in Sierre, and obtained his diploma at the ETH (Zurich, 1983–88). The five created **ACTESCOLLECTIFS** together in 2009. Their work includes the cemeteries in the towns of Granges (2007) and Noës (2007); the Schweizer House (Sion, 2008–09); the renovation of the area of the town hall and railway station in Sierre (2007–13); and the Chetzeron Restaurant and Hotel (Crans-Montana, 2008–09, published here; 2nd phase underway), all in the Valais region of Switzerland.

Ambroise Bonvin wurde 1968 in Sion, Schweiz, geboren und erlangte sein Architekturdiplom an der HES – Hochschule für Technik und Architektur, Fribourg (1989–92). Ein erster Zusammenschluss erfolgte mit Claudia Bétrisey und Patrick Aumann (2000–05). Auch Claudia Bétrisey, Jahrgang 1971, wurde in Sion geboren; Studium an der ETH Zürich (1990–97). Cédric Bonvin, 1975 in Sierre geboren, studierte Architektur an der Athenaeum École d'architecture et design (Lausanne, 1996 bis 2001), während Thomas Friberg, 1970 in Vancouver, Kanada, geboren, die EPFL (Lausanne, 1991–97) besuchte. Pierre-Antoine Masserey, geboren 1961 in Sierre, schloss sein Studium an der ETH Zürich (1983–88) mit einem Diplom ab. 2009 gründeten die fünf ihr Büro **ACTESCOLLECTIFS**. Zu ihren Arbeiten zählen die Friedhöfe in Granges (2007) und Noës (2007), das Haus Schweizer (Sion, 2008–09), die Sanierung des Rathaus- und Bahnhofsviertels in Sierre (2007–13) sowie das Chetzeron Restaurant und Hotel (Crans-Montana, 2008–09, hier vorgestellt, 2. Bauabschnitt in der Planung), alle im Schweizer Kanton Wallis.

Ambroise Bonvin est né en 1968 à Sion, en Suisse. Il est diplômé en architecture de l'École d'ingénieurs et d'architectes de Fribourg HES (1989–92) et a fondé un premier collectif avec Claudia Bétrisey et Patrick Aumann (2000–05). Claudia Bétrisey est également née à Sion, en 1971, elle a fait ses études à l'ETH (Zurich, 1990–97). Cédric Bonvin est né à Sierre en 1975 et a étudié l'architecture à l'école Athenaeum (Lausanne, 1996–2001); Thomas Friberg est né à Vancouver, Canada, en 1970 et a fait ses études à l'EPFL (Lausanne, 1991–97); Pierre-Antoine Masserey est né en 1961 à Sierre et est diplômé de l'ETH (Zurich, 1983–88). Ils ont créé tous les cinq **ACTESCOLLECTIFS** en 2009. Leurs réalisations comprennent: les cimetières de Granges (2007) et Noës (2007); la maison Schweizer (Sion, 2008–09); la rénovation de la place de l'Hôtel-de-Ville et de la gare à Sierre (2007–13) et l'hôtel-restaurant de Chetzeron (Crans-Montana, 2008–09, publié ici, 2e tranche de travaux en cours), tous dans la région du Valais, en Suisse.

CHETZERON RESTAURANT

Crans-Montana, Switzerland, 2008–09

*Address: Crans-Montana (from Cry d'Err or Merbé), Switzerland,
tel: +41 27 485 08 08, fax: +41 27 485 08 09, mail@chetzeron.ch, www.chetzeron.ch. Area: 500 m²
Client: Err-Chetzeron. Cost: not disclosed*

The **CHETZERON RESTAURANT** is located at an altitude of 2112 meters above sea level in a former cable-car station. Built on the location of the prior lift restaurant during the summers of 2008 and 2009, this project is part of the overall renovation of the entire structure that is to include a small hotel too. With its glass-shielded outdoor terrace, the restaurant, which opened on December 15, 2009, offers spectacular views over the Swiss Alps and in particular of the nearby Val d'Anniviers. The architects used stone found in neighboring fields to clad the exterior of the building. The hotel rooms will be in the former garage and arrival area of the lift station on three levels. Work on this second phase of the project began in 2012. The owners of the facility have carried on a protracted legal battle to win over local authorities that were initially opposed to the creation of a new hotel on this mountain ridge site.

Das **RESTAURANT CHETZERON** liegt 2112 m ü. NN in einer ehemaligen Seilbahnstation. Das Projekt, in den Sommern 2008 und 2009 auf dem Grundstück des ehemaligen Seilbahnrestaurants realisiert, entstand im Zuge einer umfassenden Renovierung der gesamten Anlage, in deren Verlauf auch ein kleines Hotel geplant ist. Mit seiner glasgeschützten Außenterrasse bietet das am 15. Dezember 2009 eröffnete Restaurant eine spektakuläre Aussicht auf die Schweizer Alpen und das nahe gelegene Val d'Anniviers. Die Architekten nutzten Feldsteine aus der Umgebung als Verblendmaterial für die Fassade. Hotelräume sind auf drei Ebenen in der ehemaligen Garage und Ankunftshalle der Seilbahnstation geplant. Der zweite Bauabschnitt des Projekts wurde Anfang 2012 in Angriff genommen. Erst nach langwierigen juristischen Auseinandersetzungen konnten die Eigentümer die örtlichen Behörden von ihrem Hotelprojekt überzeugen, nachdem ein Neubau auf dem Gebirgskammgrundstück zunächst abgelehnt worden war.

Le **RESTAURANT D'ALTITUDE DE CHETZERON** est situé à 2112 m au-dessus du niveau de la mer, dans une ancienne station de téléphérique. Construit à l'endroit de l'ancienne cafétéria pendant les étés 2008 et 2009, le projet fait partie de la rénovation globale de l'ensemble qui prévoit aussi un petit hôtel. Avec sa terrasse vitrée, le restaurant, qui a ouvert le 15 décembre 2009, offre une vue splendide sur les Alpes suisses, et plus particulièrement le val d'Anniviers tout proche. Les architectes ont tapissé les murs extérieurs de pierres ramassées aux environs. Les chambres de l'hôtel occuperont l'ancien garage et la zone d'arrivée de la station de téléphérique sur trois niveaux. Les travaux de cette seconde phase du projet ont commencé en 2012. Les propriétaires ont dû mener une longue bataille juridique contre les autorités locales, initialement opposées à la construction d'un nouvel hôtel sur ce versant de crête.

Left, the main outdoor terrace of the restaurant. Above, a computer-generated image of the completed hotel and restaurant. Below, elevation drawings show the completed facility.

Links die Hauptterrasse des Restaurants. Oben eine computergenerierte Ansicht des Hotel- und Restaurantkomplexes nach Fertigstellung. Unten Aufrisse der Gesamtanlage.

À gauche, la principale terrasse du restaurant. Ci-dessus, une image réalisée par ordinateur de l'hôtel-restaurant achevé. Ci-dessous, des plans en élévation du complexe.

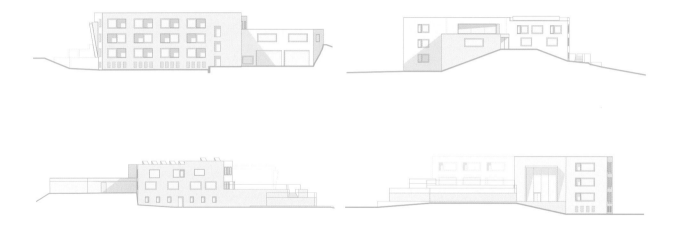

Above, a glass barrier shields outdoor clients from the cool wind.

Eine Glaswand schützt Gäste draußen vor dem Wind (oben).

Ci-dessus, des panneaux vitrés protègent les clients du vent frais à l'extérieur.

The outdoor terrace with its spectacular views of the valley of the Rhone and the Alps.

Die Terrasse mit ihrem spektakulären Blick über das Rhonetal und die Alpen.

La terrasse et sa vue splendide sur les Alpes et la vallée du Rhône.

The warm interior of the bar and restaurant contrasts with the mineral
exterior of the building. Large windows offer an ample view of the
mountains.

Das warme Interieur von Bar und
Restaurant steht in überraschendem
Kontrast zur steinernen Außenfassade
des Gebäudes. Große Fenster bieten
einen großzügigen Blick auf die Berg-
landschaft.

L'intérieur chaleureux du bar-
restaurant contraste avec l'aspect
extérieur minéral du bâtiment. De
grandes fenêtres y offrent une large
vue sur les montagnes environnantes.

Wooden cladding and furniture
emphasize the mountain atmosphere
in a convivial, modern style.

Die einladende, moderne Holzvertäfelung und -einrichtung unterstreicht
die rustikal-alpine Atmosphäre.

Le revêtement des murs et les
meubles en bois soulignent
l'ambiance montagnarde dans un
style convivial et moderne.

ALT-Q ARQUITECTURA

ALT-Q Arquitectura
C/ Trajano 44–2ºB
11002 Sevilla
Spain

Tel: +34 95 490 67 78 / Fax: +34 95 491 55 25
E-mail: alt-q@alt-q.com

ALT-Q has five principal members, of whom three are women. Francisco Márquez Pedrosa was born in Pontevedra, Spain, in 1950 and graduated as an architect from the University of Seville in 1983. María Jesús Albarreal Núñez was born in Morón de la Frontera, Spain, in 1960 and graduated from the University of Seville, in 2003. Born in Seville in 1972, Mónica González Pecci also received her architecture degree in Seville in 2003. Juan Cascales Barrio was born in Huelva, Spain, in 1972, completing his architectural education at the University of Seville in 1999. The youngest member of the team is Ana Coronado Sánchez, born in Málaga in 1982 and obtaining her degree at the same institution as her colleagues in 2009. Their work includes the Naima Jazz Café (Seville, 2006); the Zelai Bar and Restaurant (Seville, 2008, published here); and a number of as yet unbuilt projects all located in or near Seville, in Spain.

ALT Q wird von fünf Partnern geleitet, drei von ihnen sind Frauen. Francisco Márquez Pedrosa, 1950 in Pontevedra, Spanien, geboren, schloss sein Architekturstudium 1983 an der Universität Sevilla ab. María Jesús Albarreal Núñez, 1960 in Morón de la Frontera, Spanien, geboren, absolvierte sein Studium 2003 an der Universität Sevilla. Auch Mónica González Pecci, geboren 1972 in Sevilla, beendete ihr Architekturstudium 2003 in Sevilla. Juan Cascales Barrio, 1972 in Huelva, Spanien, geboren, schloss seine Ausbildung zum Architekten 1999 an der Universität Sevilla ab. Jüngstes Teammitglied ist Ana Coronado Sánchez, geboren 1982 in Málaga. Ihr Studium beendete sie 2009 an derselben Universität wie ihre Kollegen. Projekte des Büros sind u. a. das Naima Jazz Café (Sevilla, 2006), Bar und Restaurant Zelai (Sevilla, 2008, hier vorgestellt) sowie eine Reihe noch ungebauter Projekte in und um Sevilla.

ALT-Q est composé de cinq membres principaux, dont trois femmes. Francisco Márquez Pedrosa est né à Pontevedra, Espagne, en 1950 et a obtenu son diplôme d'architecte à l'université de Séville en 1983. María Jesús Albarreal Núñez, née en Espagne à Morón de la Frontera en 1960, est diplômée de l'université de Séville depuis 2003. Née à Séville en 1972, Mónica González Pecci a également obtenu son diplôme d'architecte à Séville en 2003. Juan Cascales Barrio est né à Huelva, Espagne, en 1972 et a terminé ses études d'architecture à l'université de Séville en 1999. La plus jeune de l'équipe, Ana Coronado Sánchez, est née à Málaga en 1982 et a obtenu son diplôme à la même université que ses collègues en 2009. Leurs réalisations comprennent : le café Naima Jazz (Séville, 2006) ; le bar-restaurant Zelai (Séville, 2008, publié ici) et bon nombre de projets pas encore construits, tous situés à Séville ou aux environs.

ZELAI BAR AND RESTAURANT

Seville, Spain, 2008

Address: C/ Albareda 22, 41001 Seville, Spain, +34 954 22 99 92,
www.restaurantezelai.com. Area: 166 m²
Client: María Del Carmen Alberola Morejón. Cost: €358 100

This project is located in the historic center of Seville on Albareda Street near to the Plaza Nueva. The client requested contiguous but nonetheless distinct spaces for a restaurant, bar, and gourmet shop, all within a relatively limited floor area. Placing the bar in the narrow middle section of the space, the architects create continuity by using a bamboo surface that clads the restaurant floor, runs over the restrooms, and emerges to form the roof of the working area of the bar. A sliding five-meter-long bamboo screen divides the restaurant from the bar but does not really separate the two since it is not full height. The diagonal access to the restaurant from the street creates "an outer hall that invites people" to come in. Rough wooden surfaces combine with smoother ones in a sequence that is highlighted by sophisticated lighting and a sure sense of angles and movement in the design. Whole hams hang in a shop space that lends a decidedly "organic" appearance to the whole.

Das Projekt in Sevillas historischer Altstadt liegt an der Calle Albareda, unweit der Plaza Nueva. Der Bauherr wünschte sich einen fließenden Raum mit dennoch erkennbar separaten Bereichen für Restaurant, Bar sowie einen Delikatessenverkauf auf begrenzter Grundfläche. Die Architekten platzierten die Bar im schmalen Mittelbereich des Ladenlokals. Durch eine Bambusverkleidung, die über den Boden sowie die Wand an den Kundentoiletten verläuft und schließlich als Deckenelement über dem Arbeitsbereich der Bar endet, schaffen die Planer Kontinuität. Ein 5 m breiter, nicht ganz raumhoher Schiebeparavent aus Bambus trennt Restaurant- und Barbereich. Durch seine geringere Höhe wird die Trennung jedoch nur angedeutet. Der diagonal zur Straßenfront versetzte Eingangsbereich lässt einen „Vorraum" entstehen, der „zum Eintreten einlädt". Die Raumsequenz aus unbehandeltem Holz und edleren Holzflächen wird durch aufwendige Lichtregie und das gekonnte Spiel mit Winkeln und Dynamik besonders betont. Die im Delikatessenbereich hängenden Schinken sorgen für ein entschieden rustikales Ambiente.

L'établissement est situé rue Albareda, dans le centre-ville historique de Séville, tout près de la Plaza Nueva. Le client avait exigé des espaces contigus, mais néanmoins distincts, pour le restaurant, le bar et l'épicerie fine, le tout sur une surface au sol relativement réduite. Les architectes ont placé le bar dans la partie centrale étroite et créé la continuité à l'aide d'un revêtement en bambou qui recouvre le sol du restaurant, traverse les toilettes et en ressort pour former le toit de l'espace de travail du bar. Un panneau coulissant de bambou, long de cinq mètres, divise l'espace entre restaurant et bar, mais sans les séparer complètement puisqu'il ne monte pas jusqu'au plafond. L'entrée du restaurant en diagonale par rapport à la rue crée « un hall extérieur qui invite » à entrer. Des surfaces de bois brut s'associent à d'autres plus lisses en une suite mise en valeur par un éclairage très élaboré et un design qui allie le mouvement à un sens très sûr des angles. Des jambons entiers sont suspendus dans l'espace boutique et donnent une touche « bio » à l'ensemble.

Above, the folded, angular entrance façade of the bar and restaurant. Right page, the long, narrow bar.

Oben die markant gefaltete Fassade von Bar und Restaurant. Rechts der lang gestreckte, schmale Barbereich.

Ci-dessus, l'entrée du bar-restaurant, toute en plis et angles. Page de droite, le long bar étroit.

Left, a sheltered exterior space to the rear of the establishment. Middle, a section of the bar and restaurant showing the same space to the left. Below, a sliding bamboo screen can be used to divide the space.

Links der geschützte Hinterhof. Unten ein Querschnitt von Bar und Restaurant, links im Bild der geschützte Außenbereich. Der Schiebeparavent aus Bambus (ganz unten) kann den Raum teilen.

À gauche, espace extérieur sous abri à l'arrière de l'établissement. Ci-dessous, coupe du bar-restaurant avec le même espace à gauche. En bas, un panneau coulissant de bambou peut diviser l'espace.

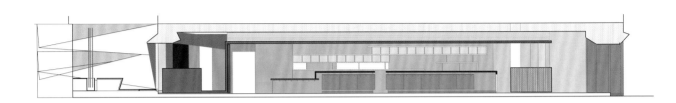

The angular appearance of the main entrance is echoed throughout the interiors. Below, plans showing the long triangular "mural" that runs through the space (in red).

Das winklige Erscheinungsbild des Haupteingangs setzt sich im gesamten Innenraum fort. Auf- und Grundrisse (unten) illustrieren den Verlauf des dreieckigen „Wandbilds" (in Rot).

L'aspect anguleux de l'entrée se retrouve à l'intérieur de l'établissement. Ci-dessous, plans avec le long « mural » triangulaire (en rouge) qui traverse l'ensemble.

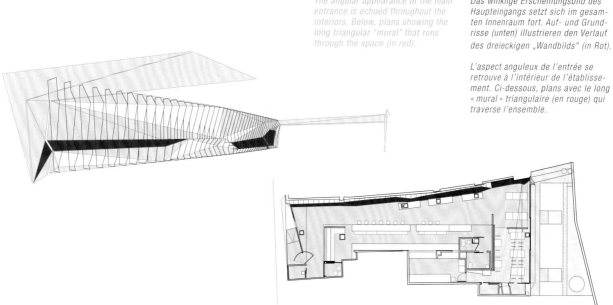

ARCHITEKTUR 6H

Architektur 6H
Kugler Eckhoff
Hasenbergsteige 12
70178 Stuttgart
Germany

Tel: +49 711 61 72 71 / Fax: +49 711 61 72 72
E-mail: sechsha@architektur-6h.de
Web: www.architektur-6h.de

WILHELM KUGLER was born in 1964 and studied at the FHT Stuttgart (1986) and the TU Delft, before obtaining his degree at the FHT Stuttgart in 1993. He was a founder of Architektur 6H in 1994, after having worked in a number of local architectural offices. **REGINALD ECKHOFF** was also born in 1964 and studied at the FHT Stuttgart, where he obtained his degree in 1991, studying the same year at the TU in Berlin and participating with Kugler in the creation of 6H. Their work includes a Showroom (Siedlungswerk, Stuttgart, 2007); the Baur-Areal Housing project including a total of 71 units (Stuttgart, 2005–09); the renovation of a historic villa (Wilhelm-Düllstr., Munich, 2010); the Jacobi Jewelry Shop (Stuttgart, 2010); and the Bleichwiese Pavilion (Backnang, 2010, published here), all in Germany.

WILHELM KUGLER, Jahrgang 1964, studierte an der FHT Stuttgart (1986) und der TU Delft, bevor er sein Studium 1993 an der FHT Stuttgart abschloss. Nach Tätigkeit in verschiedenen Büros der Region gründete er 1994 Architektur 6H. Auch **REGINALD ECKHOFF**, ebenfalls Jahrgang 1964, studierte an der FHT Stuttgart und schloss sein Studium 1991 ab. 1991 studierte er auch an der TU Berlin und gründete später mit Kugler das gemeinsame Büro 6H. Zu den Projekten des Teams zählen u. a. der Showroom Siedlungswerk (Stuttgart, 2007), das Wohnbauprojekt im Baur-Areal mit 71 Einheiten (Stuttgart, 2005–09), die Sanierung einer historischen Villa (Wilhelm-Düllstraße, München, 2010), der Juwelier Jacobi (Stuttgart, 2010) sowie der Pavillon auf der Bleichwiese (Backnang, 2010, hier vorgestellt), alle in Deutschland.

WILHELM KUGLER est né en 1964 et a fait des études à la FHT de Stuttgart (1986) et à la TU de Delft avant d'obtenir son diplôme à Stuttgart en 1993. Il a fondé Architektur 6H en 1994 après avoir travaillé dans plusieurs cabinets d'architectes locaux. **REGINALD ECKHOFF** est également né en 1964 et a aussi fait ses études à la FHT de Stuttgart où il a obtenu son diplôme en 1991, tout en étudiant à la TU de Berlin et fondant 6H avec Kugler. Leurs réalisations comptent : une salle d'expositions (Siedlungswerk, Stuttgart, 2007) ; le projet de logement Baur-Areal avec un total de 71 unités (Stuttgart, 2005–09) ; la rénovation d'une villa historique (Wilhelm-Düllstr., Munich, 2010) ; la bijouterie Jacobi (Stuttgart, 2010) et le pavillon de la Bleichwiese (Backnang, 2010, publié ici), tous en Allemagne.

BLEICHWIESE PAVILION

Backnang, Germany, 2010

Address: Annonay-Str. 2, 71522 Backnang, Germany. Area: 240 m²
Client: Gaupp Wohnungsbau GmbH. Cost: not disclosed
Collaboration: Lea-Cathrin Keim

The basic form of the structure is extremely simple and is characterized by a gray brick upper section floating over the fully glazed seating area.

Die Grundform des Baus ist denkbar schlicht. Der grau verklinkerte obere Fassadenteil scheint über dem voll verglasten Gastbereich zu schweben.

La forme de base du projet est extrêmement simple et caractérisée par une partie supérieure en briques grises qui semble flotter sur l'espace bar entièrement vitré.

Backnang is a town of about 35 000 people located 30 kilometers northeast of Stuttgart. The strict pavilion housing the coffee bar measures 14 x 14 x 7 meters and is broadly opened by a glass façade. The rough clinker-brick exterior was intentionally designed in contrast to the more refined interiors. A 7.6-meter-long exposed concrete bar and a 6.5-meter ceiling height give a decidedly generous feeling to the bar. A 4.5-meter sliding window allows the bar to be opened to the outside during warm weather. A heat pump and "thermo-active building systems" assure a high level of sustainability for the structure despite the relatively large glass surface.

Backnang ist eine Kleinstadt mit rund 35 000 Einwohnern 30 km nordöstlich von Stuttgart. Untergebracht in einem strengen, 14 x 14 x 7 m großen Pavillonbau mit großflächiger Glasfassade ist ein Café mit Bar. Die grobe Backsteinverklinkerung der Fassade wurde bewusst als Kontrast zum edleren Interieur gewählt. Ein 7,60 m langer Tresen aus Sichtbeton sowie eine Deckenhöhe von 6,50 m lassen den Raum ausgesprochen großzügig wirken. Dank einer 4,50 m breiten Glasschiebetür lässt sich die Bar bei gutem Wetter zum Außenraum öffnen. Trotz der vergleichsweise großflächigen Verglasung konnte der Bau durch eine Wärmepumpe und „thermo-aktive Bauweise" besonders nachhaltig realisiert werden.

Backnang est une ville de 35 000 habitants située à 30 km au nord-est de Stuttgart. Le pavillon de style sévère qui abrite un café mesure 14 x 14 x 7 m et est largement ouvert par une façade vitrée. L'extérieur a été volontairement conçu en brique vitrifiée brute pour contraster avec l'intérieur plus raffiné. Un bar de 7,6 m en béton apparent et une hauteur sous plafond de 6,5 m créent une impression résolument ouverte et généreuse. Une fenêtre coulissante de 4,5 m permet d'ouvrir le bar par temps chaud. Une pompe à chaleur et une « construction thermoactive » sont la garantie d'une durabilité élevée malgré la surface vitrée assez importante.

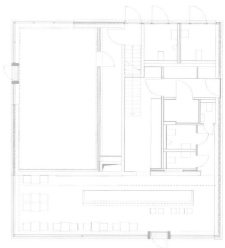

The strict lines implied by the building's exterior are developed inside,
with concrete and wood surfaces.
Color is reserved to the toilet area
(right).

Die strenge Linienführung des Außenbaus wird in den Sichtbeton- und
Holzflächen des Interieurs fortgeführt.
Farbige Akzente sind den Sanitärbe-
reichen vorbehalten (rechts).

Les lignes sévères de l'extérieur du
bâtiment se poursuivent à l'intérieur
dans les surfaces en béton et bois.
L'utilisation de la couleur est limitée
aux toilettes (à droite).

ARTEK

Artek oy ab
Lönnrotinkatu 7
00120 Helsinki
Finland

Tel: +358 505 05 40 70
E-mail: press@artek.fi
Web: www.artek.fi

ARTEK was founded in 1935 by Alvar and Aino Aalto, Maire Gullichsen, and Nils-Gustav Hahl. Having celebrated its 75th anniversary in 2010, the firm still endeavors to "build on the heritage of Alvar Aalto." The furniture of Artek does, indeed, have a relationship to Aalto's L-System, but the firm also works with such designers or architects as Shigeru Ban, Juha Leiviskä, Enzo Mari, and Tobias Rehberger, author of the installation "Nothing Happens for a Reason" in the Logomo Café (Turku, Finland, 2010–11, published here). The Artek pavilion, called The Space of Silence, was designed by Shigeru Ban for the 2007 Salone Internazionale del Mobile in Milan and for Design Miami the same year. The firm has also worked on a number of bars and restaurants, such as the Sushi + Wine Restaurant (Helsinki, Finland, 2010); the Café Cubus Ateneum (Helsinki, Finland, 2010); the Primewine Bar (Stockholm, Sweden, 2011); and the Fly Inn Restaurant, Helsinki-Vantaa Airport (Helsinki, Finland, 2011). **TOBIAS REHBERGER** was born in Esslingen am Neckar, Germany, in 1966 and studied at the Stadelschule in Frankfurt (1987–92). He received the Golden Lion award as the Best Artist at the 2009 Venice Biennale for an installation also created with Artek. According to Artek, he "is interested in the conflict between functionalism and aesthetics, and likes to question and play with the notion of art and its various strategies."

ARTEK, 1935 von Alvar und Aino Aalto, Maire Gullichsen und Nils-Gustav Hahl gegründet, konnte 2010 sein 75-jähriges Bestehen feiern. Noch heute geht es darum, „auf dem Erbe Alvar Aaltos aufzubauen". Während die Artek-Möbelsysteme in der Tat auf Aaltos L-System basieren, arbeitet das Unternehmen auch mit Designern und Architekten wie Shigeru Ban, Juha Leiviskä, Enzo Mari oder dem Künstler Tobias Rehberger, der die Installation *Nothing Happens for a Reason* für das Logomo Café (Turku, Finnland, 2010–11, hier vorgestellt) realisierte. Shigeru Ban entwarf den Artek-Pavillon, auch „The Space of Silence" genannt, für die Mailänder Möbelmesse 2007 sowie die Design Miami im selben Jahr. Artek ist zudem in verschiedenen Bars und Restaurants vertreten, darunter dem Sushi + Wine Restaurant (Helsinki, 2010), dem Café Cubus Ateneum (Helsinki, 2010), der Primewine Bar (Stockholm, 2011) und dem Fly Inn Restaurant, Flughafen Helsinki-Vantaa (Helsinki, 2011). **TOBIAS REHBERGER**, geboren 1966 in Esslingen am Neckar, studierte an der Städelschule in Frankfurt am Main (1987–92). Auf der Biennale Venedig wurde er 2009 für eine Installation, die ebenfalls in Kooperation mit Artek entstand, mit dem Goldenen Löwen ausgezeichnet. Laut Artek interessiert Rehberger „der Konflikt von Funktionalismus und Ästhetik, er hinterfragt und spielt mit dem Kunstbegriff und seinen vielfältigen Strategien".

ARTEK a été fondé en 1935 par Alvar et Aino Aalto, Maire Gullichsen et Nils-Gustav Hahl. L'entreprise, qui a célébré son 75e anniversaire en 2010, s'efforce toujours de « s'appuyer sur l'héritage d'Alvar Aalto ». Si les meubles d'Artek rappellent effectivement le système en forme de L d'Aalto, la société travaille aussi avec des designers ou architectes comme Shigeru Ban, Juha Leiviskä, Enzo Mari et Tobias Rehberger, auteur de l'installation *Nothing Happens for a Reason* au café Logomo (Turku, Finlande, 2010–11, publiée ici). Le pavillon appelé L'Espace du silence a été conçu par Shigeru Ban pour le Salon du meuble de Milan 2007 et Design Miami la même année. L'agence a aussi travaillé à plusieurs bars et restaurants, parmi lesquels : le restaurant Sushi + Wine (Helsinki, 2010) ; le Café Cubus Ateneum (Helsinki, 2010) ; le bar Primewine (Stockholm, 2011) et le restaurant Fly Inn de l'aéroport d'Helsinki-Vantaa (Helsinki, 2011). **TOBIAS REHBERGER** est né à Esslingen am Neckar, Allemagne, en 1966, et a fait ses études à la Stadelschule de Francfort (1987–92). Il a reçu le Lion d'or du meilleur artiste à la Biennale de Venise 2009 pour une installation également créée avec Artek. Selon Artek, il « s'intéresse au conflit entre fonctionnalisme et esthétique et aime remettre en question la notion d'art et ses diverses stratégies ou jouer avec ».

"NOTHING HAPPENS FOR A REASON"

Logomo Café, Turku, Finland, 2010–11

Address: n/a. Area: 230m². Client: Turku 2011 Foundation.
Cost: not disclosed. Collaboration: Florencia Colombo, Artek Studio (Architect),
Tobias Rehberger (Art Design Installation)

Tobias Rehberger states: "I like the idea of creating a visual art project which is about not seeing something," citing the way in which wartime battleships were painted to be as invisible as possible. Logomo served as the main venue for the Turku's turn as European Capital of Culture (2011), hosting more than 50 performance events as well as the café published here. The structure was used as an engineering workshop between its construction in 1876 and 2002. Counting nine subsequent extensions, Logomo offered 17 500 square meters of floor space for the events. Opened on January 16, 2011, the Logomo Café served "organic and local food." Although the installation was, indeed, based on Artek furniture, Rehberger made his own use of the objects, rendering the distinction between floors, chairs, and walls difficult to perceive along the lines of British World War Two camouflage techniques. Because of his complex vision of space and the experience of using the café, the artist refers to the café as a "comprehensive experience."

„Mir gefällt die Idee", so Tobias Rehberger, „ein primär visuelles Kunstprojekt zu entwickeln, bei dem es darum geht, etwas nicht zu sehen." Damit spielt er auf eine Camouflagetechnik an, mit der Kriegsschiffe durch spezielle Bemalung möglichst schwer erkennbar wurden. Das Kulturzentrum Logomo war zentraler Veranstaltungsort der Europäischen Kulturhauptstadt Turku 2011. Hier wurden im Rahmen des Kulturprogramms über 50 Performance-Events und auch das Café Logomo realisiert. Das Gebäude wurde von seiner Erbauung 1876 bis 2002 als Bahnwerk genutzt. Mit insgesamt neun späteren Erweiterungen bot das Kulturzentrum 17 500 m² Nutzfläche für Veranstaltungen. Im Logomo Café, das am 16. Januar 2011 öffnete, wird „Bio- und regionale Küche" angeboten. Rehberger gab der Installation aus Artek-Möbeln mit der im Zweiten Weltkrieg entwickelten britischen Tarntechnik seine unverwechselbare Handschrift: Böden, Stühlen und Wänden lassen sich nur schwer ausmachen. Der Künstler selbst beschreibt das Café wegen der komplexen Raumvision und des Erlebnisses für die Besucher als „Gesamterfahrung".

Évoquant la manière dont les cuirassés étaient peints pendant la guerre pour les rendre le plus invisible possible, Tobias Rehberger déclare : « J'aime l'idée de créer un projet qui consiste à ne pas voir quelque chose. » Le Logomo a été l'un des principaux sites en 2011, année où Turku a été capitale européenne de la culture, et plus de 50 performances y ont eu lieu, dont celle du café publiée ici. L'endroit a servi d'atelier de construction mécanique entre sa construction en 1876 et 2002. Avec neuf extensions ultérieures, ce sont 17 500 m² qui ont été mis à la disposition des artistes. Ouvert le 16 janvier 2011, le café Logomo sert des plats « biologiques et locaux ». L'installation est basée sur le mobilier d'Artek, mais Rehberger a fait une utilisation très personnelle des objets et a eu recours aux techniques de camouflage britanniques de la Deuxième Guerre mondiale pour rendre le sol, les sièges et les murs difficiles à distinguer. En raison de sa vision complexe de l'espace et de sa pratique du café, l'artiste qualifie son travail d'« expérience globale ».

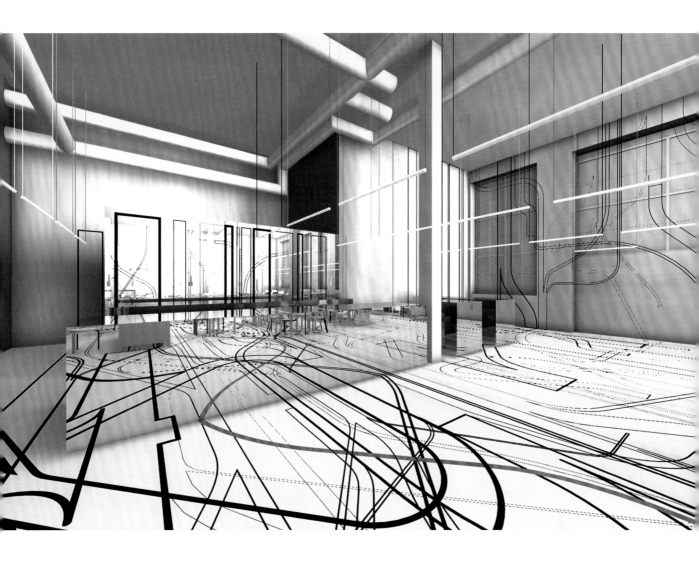

Drawings and photos show how the designer has essentially superimposed a complex line drawing on the space and its furnishings, blurring the distinction between foreground and background.

Zeichnungen und Aufnahmen zeigen die komplexe Strichzeichnung, die der Künstler über Raum und Einrichtung legt, wodurch Vorder- und Hintergrund schwer zu unterscheiden sind.

On voit sur les plans et les photos comment le designer a placé un réseau complexe de lignes en surimpression sur l'espace et son mobilier afin de rendre premier plan et arrière-plan difficiles à distinguer.

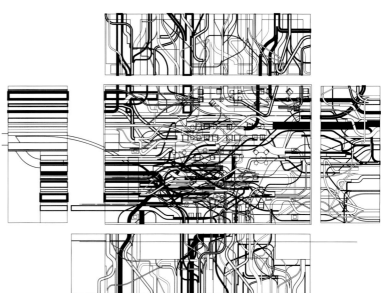

The drawing, which might resemble the plan of a transport network or a complex piping diagram, makes the usual distinction between two dimensions and three difficult to discern.

Die an einen U-Bahnplan oder ein komplexes Schaltschema erinnernde Zeichnung erschwert die Unterscheidung zwei- und dreidimensionaler Ebenen.

Le dessin, qui évoque le plan d'un réseau de transport en commun ou un schéma complexe de distribution, rend difficile la distinction habituelle entre deux et trois dimensions.

AUER+WEBER+ASSOZIIERTE

Auer+Weber+Assoziierte
Haussmannstr. 103 A
70188 Stuttgart
Germany

Tel: +49 711 268 40 40 / Fax: +49 711 26 84 04 88
E-mail: stuttgart@auer-weber.de
Web: www.auer-weber.de

FRITZ AUER, born in Tübingen, Germany, in 1933, became a Partner in the firm of Behnisch & Partner in 1966 and created Auer+Weber in 1980. **CARLO WEBER** was born in Saarbrücken, Germany, in 1934 and attended the Technische Hochschule in Stuttgart, before going to the Beaux-Arts in Paris. Like Auer, he became a Partner at Behnisch & Partner in 1966. They have worked extensively on urban renewal in Bonn, Stuttgart, and other cities. The firm, with offices in Munich and Stuttgart, currently employs 90 to 100 people and includes managing Partners Moritz Auer, Philipp Auer, Jörn Scholz, Achim Söding, and Stephan Suxdorf. They completed the Gut Siggen Seminar Building (Siggen, 2006–07); ECE Stadtgalerie, Façade (Passau, 2005–08); an office building (Altstadt-Palais, Munich, 2008); additions and alterations to the Olympic Halls (Munich, 2008); the Central Bus Terminal in Munich (2009); Buildings in Chenshan Botanical Garden (Shanghai, China, 2009); Central Facilities on the Martinsried Campus (Ludwig-Maximilians University, Munich, 2004–09); and the Coubertin Restaurant, Olympic Hall (Munich, 2010, published here). Current work includes Salle Omnisports (Antibes, France, 2012); Bielefeld University of Applied Sciences Campus (Bielefeld, 2013); House of Archaeology (Chemnitz, 2013); the extension to the Federal Ministry of Defense (Berlin, 2013); Centre Universitaire des Quais (Lyon, France, 2014); and Grandes Combes (Courchevel, France, 2014), all in Germany unless stated otherwise.

FRITZ AUER, 1933 in Tübingen geboren, wurde 1966 Partner im Büro von Behnisch & Partner und gründete 1980 Auer+Weber. **CARLO WEBER**, geboren 1934 in Saarbrücken, studierte zunächst an der Technischen Hochschule Stuttgart, anschließend an der Ecole Nationale Supérieure des Beaux-Arts in Paris. Auch er wurde 1966 Partner bei Behnisch & Partner. Auer+Weber war umfassend an Stadterneuerungsprojekten in Bonn, Stuttgart und weiteren Städten beteiligt. Die Bürogemeinschaft mit Sitz in München und Stuttgart beschäftigt derzeit 90 bis 100 Mitarbeiter, darunter die Geschäftsführer Moritz Auer, Philipp Auer, Jörn Scholz, Achim Söding und Stephan Suxdorf. Realisierte Projekte sind u. a. das Seminargebäude Gut Siggen (Siggen, 2006–07), die Fassade der ECE-Stadtgalerie (Passau, 2005–08), das Bürogebäude Altstadt-Palais (München, 2008), Erweiterung und Umbau der Olympiahalle (München, 2008), der Zentrale Omnibusbahnhof München (2009), Bauten im Botanischen Garten Chenshan (Schanghai, 2009), der Campus Martinsried (Ludwig-Maximilians-Universität, München, 2004–09) sowie das Coubertin Restaurant, Olympiahalle (München, 2010, hier vorgestellt). Zu ihren aktuellen Projekten zählen die Salle Omnisports (Antibes, Frankreich, 2012), der Campus der Fachhochschule Bielefeld (Bielefeld, 2013), das Haus der Archäologie (Chemnitz, 2013), die Erweiterung des Bundesministeriums der Verteidigung (Berlin, 2013), die Centre Universitaire des Quais (Lyon, Frankreich, 2014) und die Grandes Combes (Courchevel, Frankreich, 2014).

FRITZ AUER, né en Allemagne à Tübingen en 1933, est devenu partenaire de Behnisch & Partner en 1966 et a créé Auer+Weber en 1980. **CARLO WEBER** est né à Sarrebruck, Allemagne, en 1934 et a suivi les cours de l'Université technique de Stuttgart avant d'aller aux Beaux-Arts de Paris. Comme Auer, il est devenu partenaire de Behnisch & Partner en 1966. Ils ont beaucoup travaillé à la rénovation urbaine de Bonn, Stuttgart et d'autres villes. L'agence a des bureaux à Munich et Stuttgart, elle a 90 à 100 employés dont les associés dirigeants Moritz Auer, Philipp Auer, Jörn Scholz et Stephan Suxdorf. Ils ont réalisé : le centre de séminaires Gut Siggen (Siggen, Allemagne, 2006–07) ; la façade du centre commercial ECE Stadtgalerie (Passau, Allemagne, 2005–08) ; un immeuble de bureaux (Altstadt-Palais, Munich, 2008) ; des ajouts et modifications des Centres olympiques (Munich, 2008) ; la gare routière de Munich (2009) ; les bâtiments du jardin botanique de Chenshan (Shanghai, 2009) ; les équipements centraux du campus de Martinsried (université Ludwig-Maximilian, Munich, 2004–09) et le restaurant Coubertin du Centre olympique (Munich, 2010, publié ici). Leurs travaux actuels comprennent notamment : la salle omnisports (Antibes, 2012) ; le campus de l'Université des sciences appliquées de Bielefeld (2013) ; la Maison de l'archéologie (Chemnitz, 2013) ; l'extension du ministère fédéral de la Défense (Berlin, 2013) ; le centre universitaire des Quais (Lyon, 2014) et le site des Grandes Combes (Courchevel, 2014), tous en Allemagne sauf si précisé.

COUBERTIN RESTAURANT

Olympic Hall, Olympic Park, Munich, Germany, 2010

Address: Coubertinplatz, Olympiapark, 80809 Munich, Germany, +49 89 306 70
Area: 2540 m² (above grade), 940 m² (below grade)
Client: Stadwerke München Services GmbH. Cost: not disclosed

The contrast between the rectilinear design and the sweeping forms of the original Olympic buildings is, of course, intentional, marking a change of times without contradicting the past.

Der bewusst gewählte Kontrast des geradlinigen Entwurfs zur geschwungenen Formensprache der ursprünglichen Olympiabauten zeigt, dass sich die Zeiten geändert haben, ohne jedoch die Vergangenheit zu negieren.

Le contraste entre le design rectiligne et les larges courbes des bâtiments olympiques d'origine est, bien sûr, voulu et marque le changement d'époque sans pour autant renier le passé.

An outdoor terrace continues the design, color scheme, and spirit of the restaurant interior.

Auf der Terrasse setzen sich Design, Farbpalette und Atmosphäre des Interieurs fort.

Une terrasse reprend le design, les couleurs et l'esprit de l'intérieur du restaurant.

This restaurant is part of a modernization and extension of the 1972 structure. A new 500-seat restaurant and beer garden were created. Supply and waste facilities within the arena were also updated as were the VIP spaces, spectator terraces, press area, and the membrane ceiling of the hall, designed by Behnisch & Partner and Frei Otto. A further element of the project is the underground "Neue Kleine Olympiahalle" which can receive 4000 people. The light, airy design of the new restaurant area is a fitting complement to the more exuberant forms of the original webbed stadium and Olympiahalle design. Equally, the furnishing chosen serves to give a decidedly modern air to what might have been an exercise either in contradiction or in difficult imitation. This is an example of how modern architectural heritage can be updated and continue to remain useful well beyond its original design and purposes.

Das Restaurant mit 500 Plätzen und Biergarten entstand im Zuge der Modernisierung und Erweiterung der Olympiaanlagen von 1972. Modernisiert wurden darüber hinaus die Versorgungs- und Entsorgungseinrichtungen der Halle, der VIP-Bereich, die Zuschauertribünen, der Pressebereich sowie das von Behnisch & Partner und Frei Otto entworfene Membrandach der Halle. Ein weiteres Element ist die unterirdisch angelegte Neue Kleine Olympiahalle, die 4000 Besuchern Platz bietet. Der helle, luftige Entwurf des neuen Restaurants präsentiert sich als gelungenes Pendant zur geschwungenen Stahlnetzkonstruktion des alten Stadions und der Olympiahalle. Die Einrichtung unterstreicht das dezidiert moderne Design, das leicht in widersprüchliche Kontraste oder problematische Imitation hätte abgleiten können. Dies ist ein Beispiel dafür, wie sich das architektonische Erbe der Moderne aktualisieren lässt und Baudenkmäler ihre Funktionalität zugleich weit über ihren ursprünglichen Entwurf und Zweck hinaus wahren können.

Le restaurant fait partie de la modernisation et de l'extension de la structure de 1972. Une nouvelle salle de 500 places et un *Biergarten* ont été créés, les systèmes d'approvisionnement et de gestion des déchets du stade ont été modernisés, ainsi que les espaces VIP, les terrasses spectateurs, l'espace presse et la membrane du toit, conçue par Behnisch & Partner et Frei Otto. Parmi les autres éléments du projet, la « Neue Kleine Olympiahalle » (nouvelle petite salle olympique) souterraine peut accueillir 4000 spectateurs. Le design léger et aérien de la nouvelle salle de restaurant complète parfaitement les formes plus exubérantes du stade et centre olympique d'origine sous toile. De même, le tissu choisi permet de donner un air résolument moderne à ce qui serait sinon, soit une opposition, soit une difficile imitation. On a ici un exemple de la manière dont un héritage architectural moderne peut être remis à jour et rester utile bien au-delà de sa conception et de son objectif initiaux.

Seen at night, the open, fully glazed design takes on an almost Miesian simplicity.

Nachts gewinnt der offene, vollständig verglaste Bau geradezu Mies'sche Klarheit.

La nuit, le bâtiment ouvert entièrement vitré revêt une simplicité presque miesienne.

The cantilevered terrace can be acceded to via a ramp or the stairway seen to the right of the image above. Below, an elevation drawing seen from the same direction.

Die auskragende Terrasse wird über eine Rampe sowie eine Treppe (rechts oben im Bild) erschlossen. Unten ein Aufriss derselben Perspektive.

La terrasse en porte-à-faux est accessible par une rampe ou par l'escalier qu'on voit à droite sur la photo ci-dessus. En bas, une élévation depuis la même perspective.

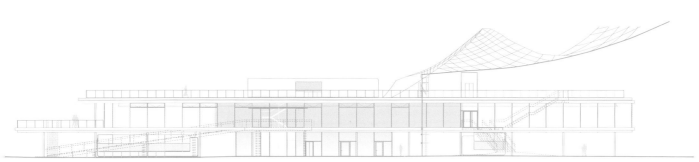

MAARTEN BAAS

Maarten Baas
Rosmalensedijk 3
5236 BD 's-Hertogenbosch (Gewande)
The Netherlands

Tel: +31 62 45 02 08
E-mail: info@maartenbaas.com
Web: www.maartenbaas.com

MAARTEN BAAS was born in Arnsberg, Germany, in 1978 but grew up in the Netherlands. He attended the Eindhoven Design Academy, graduating in 2002. He quickly created a series of works he calls Smoke, which consist in furniture he chars and then treats to again become usable. Three pieces from this series were included in the 2003 collection of Marcel Wanders for the Moooi label. His work is already included in numerous museum collections (LACMA, Indianapolis Museum of Art, etc). Baas has also worked with figures such as Ian Schrager for the promoter's Gramercy Park Hotel (New York). His 2006 works include a series called Clay Furniture, made of synthetic clay with a metal skeleton, used in the Mendini Restaurant (Groningen, the Netherlands, 2010 published here). The actual furniture was newly designed for the space and made by hand. His 2009 filmed work *Real Time* consists in filming actors who indicate the time over a 12-hour period allowing the film itself to be used as a clock. In 2009 Baas became the youngest recipient of the Designer of the Year Award. In 2011, he designed the five-meter-tall work *The Empty Chair* for Amnesty International in honor of the Chinese Nobel Peace Prize winner Liu Xiaobo, who was not allowed to attend the 2010 award ceremony.

MAARTEN BAAS wurde 1978 in Arnsberg geboren und wuchs in den Niederlanden auf. Sein Studium schloss er 2002 an der Eindhoven Design Academy ab. Bereits kurz darauf entwickelte er seine Serie Smoke: Möbelstücke, die er zunächst ansengt und anschließend so behandelt, dass sie wieder nutzbar werden. 2003 nahm Marcel Wanders drei Objekte der Serie in seine Kollektion bei Moooi auf. Baas' Entwürfe befinden sich schon jetzt in den Sammlungen verschiedener Museen (LACMA, Indianapolis Museum of Art u.a.). Darüber hinaus arbeitete er mit Persönlichkeiten wie Ian Schrager an dessen Gramercy Park Hotel (New York). 2006 entstanden Arbeiten wie die Clay Furniture, eine Möbelserie aus synthetischer Modelliermasse über einem Metallskelett. Auch im Mendini Restaurant (Groningen, Niederlande, 2010, hier vorgestellt) kamen die Clay Furniture zum Einsatz, wobei die Möbel für das Restaurant von Hand gefertigte Neuentwürfe sind. 2009 realisierte der Designer seinen Film *Real Time*, in dem Schauspieler zwölf Stunden lang die Zeit anzeigen, sodass der Film als Uhr genutzt werden kann. 2009 wurde Baas als jüngster Preisträger zum Designer of the Year ausgezeichnet. 2011 entwarf er die 5 m hohe Skulptur *The Empty Chair* für Amnesty International als Hommage an den chinesischen Friedensnobelpreisträger von 2010, Liu Xiaobo, der nicht zur Preisverleihung nach Oslo reisen durfte.

MAARTEN BAAS est né en Allemagne à Arnsberg en 1978 mais a grandi aux Pays-Bas. Il a suivi les cours de l'Académie de design d'Eindhoven dont il est diplômé depuis 2002. Il a rapidement créé une série appelée *Smoke* composée de meubles brûlés, puis vernis pour redevenir utilisables. Trois éléments en ont été intégrés en 2003 à la collection de Marcel Wanders pour le label Moooi. Ses œuvres sont déjà présentes dans les collections de nombreux musées (LACMA, Musée d'art d'Indianapolis, etc.). Baas a également travaillé avec le promoteur Ian Schrager à l'hôtel Gramercy Park (New York). En 2006, il a créé une série appelée *Clay Furniture* en argile synthétique sur armature de métal, qu'on peut notamment voir au restaurant Mendini (Groningue, Pays-Bas, 2010, publiée ici). Les meubles actuels ont été conçus spécialement et réalisés à la main. Son œuvre filmographique de 2009 *Real Time* consiste à filmer des acteurs qui indiquent l'heure pendant 12 heures, le film lui-même pouvant tenir lieu d'horloge. En 2009, Baas a été le plus jeune artiste à être élu designer de l'année. En 2011, il a créé l'œuvre haute de 5 m *The Empty Chair* pour Amnesty International en l'honneur du prix Nobel de la paix chinois Liu Xiaobo qui n'avait pas été autorisé à assister à la cérémonie de remise des prix en 2010.

MENDINI RESTAURANT

Groninger Museum, Groningen, The Netherlands, 2010

Address: Museumeiland 1, 9711 ME Groningen, The Netherlands, +31 50 3 60 36 65,
info@mendinirestaurant.nl, www.groningermuseum.nl/mendini-restaurant/home
Area: 258m². Client: Groninger Museum. Cost: €260 000

The Groninger Museum was designed in 1994 by an all-star team under the leadership of Alessandro Mendini, and including Philippe Starck, Coop Himmelb(l)au, and Michele de Lucchi. Baas made the furniture for the new café as well as the red lighting fixtures with modeled clay. During the 2010 renovation of the museum, Baas, together with Jaime Hayon and Studio Job, were commissioned to redesign the restaurant, information center, and lounge. The restaurant is used as a café for the museum public during the day and as an Italian restaurant or for private parties at night. Long benches, a red clay mirror, and the bar of the **MENDINI RESTAURANT** were also made by hand "clearly displaying the recognizable signature of Maarten Baas." With their slight color variations and distinctive character, the works of Baas give a relatively "quiet" and modest tone to the restaurant, surely more contemporary than the exuberance of Mendini's time.

Das Groninger Museum wurde 1994 mit einem Staraufgebot an Gestaltern unter Leitung von Alessandro Mendini geplant; zum Team gehörten Philippe Starck, Coop Himmelb(l)au und Michele de Lucchi. Für die Renovierung des Cafés ließ Baas Möbel sowie die roten Leuchten aus Modelliermasse fertigen. Im Zuge des Museumsumbaus erhielten Baas, Jaime Hayon und Studio Job den Auftrag, Restaurant, Informationszentrum und Lounge neu zu gestalten. Während das Restaurant tagsüber als Museumscafé genutzt wird, steht es abends als italienisches Restaurant für private Veranstaltungen zur Verfügung. Auch die langen Bänke, der rote Spiegel aus Modelliermasse und die Bar des **MENDINI RESTAURANT** wurden von Hand gefertigt und „zeigen deutlich die typische Handschrift von Maarten Baas". Durch das Farbspiel und den unverwechselbaren Charakter der Entwürfe von Maarten Baas gewinnt das Restaurant eine „ruhigere" und zurückhaltende Atmosphäre, die zweifellos zeitgemäßer ist als die Opulenz zu Mendinis Zeiten.

Le musée de Groningue a été conçu en 1994 par une équipe d'architectes de renom sous la direction d'Alessandro Mendini, avec notamment Philippe Starck, Coop Himmelb(l)au et Michele de Lucchi. Baas a réalisé les meubles du nouveau café et les luminaires rouges en argile. À la rénovation du musée de 2010, il a été chargé avec Jaime Hayon et Studio Job de refaire le design du restaurant, du centre de documentation et du salon. Le restaurant tient lieu de café pour les visiteurs du musée la journée et se transforme en restaurant italien ou privé le soir. Les longs bancs, le miroir d'argile rouge et le bar du **RESTAURANT MENDINI** ont été faits à la main et « affichent clairement la signature reconnaissable entre mille de Maarten Baas ». Avec leurs légères variations de couleurs et leur caractère spécifique, les réalisations de Baas donnent une allure plutôt « calme » et modeste au restaurant, incontestablement plus contemporaine que l'exubérance qui était de mise du temps de Mendini.

Apart from the use of some emphatic colors like fuchsia or olive green, the new design seems quite far from the original Memphis inspiration of Mendini.

Abgesehen von einigen kräftigen Farbakzenten wie Fuchsia oder Olivgrün ist das neue Design Welten von der memphisinspierten Formensprache Mendinis entfernt.

À l'exception des couleurs vives comme le fuchsia ou le vert olive, le nouveau design est en apparence très éloigné de la première inspiration Memphis de Mendini.

The basic concept is that of an efficient, "modest" dining space, with the feeling of purpose-designed furniture or lighting.

Grundprinzip des Entwurfs ist die Gestaltung eines effizienten, „bescheidenen" Gastraums mit eigens konzipiertem Mobiliar und Leuchten.

Le concept fondamental est celui d'un espace dînatoire rationnel et « modeste » avec des meubles ou luminaires spécialement conçus.

BASICHES ARCHITECTS

Basiches Architects Associates
Rua General Jardim 808, 14 andar
01223–010 São Paulo, SP
Brazil

Tel: +55 11 3129 5811
E-mail: contato@basiches.com.br
Web: www.basiches.com.br

JOSÉ RICARDO BASICHES graduated in 1997 from São Paulo University. He created Basiches Architects Associates in 1999, "acting in all segments of architecture, including interior design, from its creation and conception to its completion." **RONALDO SHINOHARA** was born in 1974 in São Paulo. He graduated from Mackenzie São Paulo University in 1997, and has worked with Basiches Architects Associates since 2005, becoming a Partner in 2010. Their completed work includes the MG House (Guarujá, 2006–08); the Ocean View House (Juquehy, 2006–09); and the Triton Store (São Paulo, 2010, published here). Two apartment projects, the Pascal Building (São Paulo, 2010) and the Unit Building (São Paulo, 2010), are both under construction, all in Brazil.

JOSÉ RICARDO BASICHES schloss sein Studium 1997 an der Universität São Paulo ab. 1999 gründete er die Bürogemeinschaft Basiches Arquitetos und arbeitet seither „auf allen Gebieten der Architektur, einschließlich Innenarchitektur, vom Entwurf über die Konzeption bis hin zur Realisierung". **RONALDO SHINOHARA** wurde 1974 in São Paulo geboren. Er schloss sein Studium 1997 an der Mackenzie Universität São Paulo ab und praktiziert seit 2005 bei Basiches Arquitetos, seit 2010 als Partner. Zu ihren realisierten Projekten zählen das MG House (Guarujá, 2006–08), das Ocean View House (Juquehy, 2006–09) und der Triton Store (São Paulo, 2010, hier vorgestellt). Zwei Apartmenthäuser, das Pascal Building (São Paulo, 2010) sowie das Unit Building (São Paulo, 2010), befinden sich im Bau (alle Projekte in Brasilien).

JOSÉ RICARDO BASICHES a obtenu son diplôme en 1997 à l'université de São Paulo. Il a créé Basiches Architects Associates en 1999, « actif dans tous les segments de l'architecture, y compris l'architecture d'intérieur, de la création et la conception à l'achèvement ». **RONALDO SHINOHARA** est né en 1974 à São Paulo. Il est diplômé de l'université Mackenzie de São Paulo en 1997 et travaille depuis 2005 avec Basiches Architects Associates – dont il est l'un des partenaires depuis 2010. Leurs réalisations comprennent : la maison MG (Guarujá, 2006–08) ; l'Ocean View House (Juquehy, 2006–09) et le magasin Triton (São Paulo, 2010, publié ici). Deux projets d'appartement, le Pascal Building (São Paulo, 2010) et l'Unit Building (São Paulo, 2010), sont en construction au Brésil.

TRITON STORE

São Paulo, São Paulo, Brazil, 2010

Address: Piso Faria Lima, Loja 3, São Paulo, SP 01489-900, Brazil, +55 11 3031 7986
Area: 228m². Client: Triton. Cost: $600 000

José Ricardo Basiches explains that he faced a double challenge working on this store located in the luxurious shopping area of Oscar Freire Street: a restricted budget and a quick time frame. Intended for the designer Tufi Duek and his Triton brand, the store is aimed at an audience that the designer calls "young and preppy." The architects inserted an inclined lining into the existing volume. A coffee area is located below street level and receives natural light due to skylights. Basiches states: "The highlights of the whole project are the mirrored inclined lining and also the modest materials employed with few variations—wood and side walls in aggregate or particle board, and also a green wall."

José Ricardo Basiches verweist auf die zweifache Herausforderung, die der Entwurf dieses Ladenlokals im gehobenen Einkaufsviertel um die Rua Oscar Freire bedeutete: ein knappes Budget sowie ein enger Zeitrahmen. Der für den Designer Tufi Duek und dessen Marke Triton konzipierte Store richtet sich an ein Publikum, das der Designer „jung und preppy" nennt. Die Architekten zogen eine geneigte Verkleidung in den bestehenden Raum ein. Unter Straßenniveau wurde ein Café eingerichtet, in das durch Oberlichter Tageslicht fällt. Basiches erklärt: „Highlights des Projekts sind die geneigte und verspiegelte Decke und die einfachen Materialien, die in nur wenigen Variationen zum Einsatz kommen – Holz und Seitenwände aus Komposit- oder Pressspanplatten sowie eine grüne Wand."

Avec ce magasin situé dans le luxueux quartier commercial de la rue Oscar Freire, José Ricardo Basiches a dû relever un double défi : un budget restreint et un délai limité. Conçu pour le designer Tufi Duek et sa marque Triton, le magasin cible un public qualifié par le créateur de « jeune et BCBG ». L'architecte a ajouté une inclinaison au volume existant, ainsi qu'un espace café sous le niveau de la rue auquel des lucarnes donnent une lumière naturelle. Basiches explique que « l'ensemble du projet est surtout porté par les plans inclinés recouverts de miroirs et les matériaux modestes utilisés sans beaucoup de variations – le bois et les parois latérales en agrégat ou panneaux de particules, avec aussi un mur vert ».

A contrast between the wooden floors and the dark walls, reflected in ceiling mirrors, makes the merchandise in the store stand out.

Der Kontrast von Holzböden und dunklen Wänden spiegelt sich in der Decke und lässt die Ware des Stores gut zur Geltung kommen.

Le contraste entre le bois du sol et les murs sombres, reflété dans les miroirs du plafond, met en valeur les produits vendus dans le magasin.

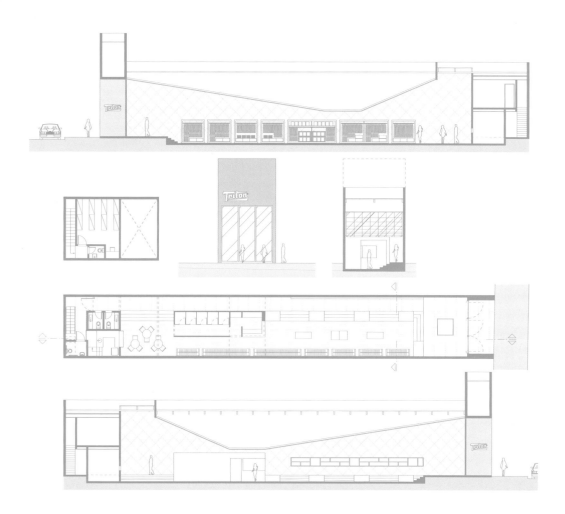

The designers make the most of the long, narrow space, alternating dark surfaces with spot lighting and mirrors. Drawings and a sketch on this page reveal the entire design.

Die Architekten nutzen den langen schmalen Raum optimal durch dunkle Flächen, Punktstrahler und Spiegel. Zeichnungen sowie eine Skizze auf dieser Seite veranschaulichen den Gesamtentwurf.

Les designers ont utilisé au mieux le long et étroit espace, faisant alterner les surfaces sombres avec les spots et miroirs. Les plans et le croquis montrent l'ensemble du projet.

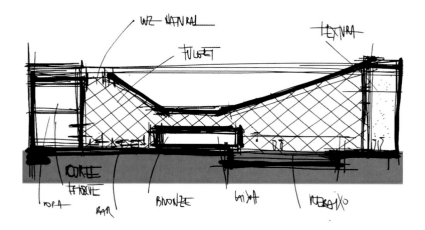

BCMF

BCMF Arquitetos
Rua Paul Pompéia 225
30330–080 Belo Horizonte, MG
Brazil

Tel/Fax: +55 31 3281 2707
E-mail: bcmf@bcmfarquitetos.com
Web: www.bcmfarquitetos.com

BCMF is an association created in 2001 by Bruno Campos, with Marcelo Fontes and Sílvio Todeschi as Partners. **BRUNO CAMPOS**, born in 1970, graduated from the Federal University of Minas Gerais (UFMG, Belo Horizonte, 1989–94), and received an M.A. in Housing and Urbanism at the Architectural Association School (London, 1997–98). He worked in the office of Weiss/Manfredi Architects, before establishing his own practice. Born in 1971, **MARCELO FONTES** also graduated from the UFMG (1990–95). **SÍLVIO TODESCHI** was born in 1968 and graduated from the UFMG in 1992. He has had his own practice since 1992, and was a collaborator of BCMF Arquitetos on several projects, before joining them as a Partner in 2010. Their work includes MOCAO (Montes Claros Stadium, 2001–03); the Deodoro Sports Complex (Shooting, Equestrian, Modern Pentathlon, Grass Hockey, and Archery) built for the Rio 2007 Pan American Games (2005–07); and they were hired by the Brazilian Olympic Committee (COB) to develop various concept studies for the Rio 2016 Candidature Bid (2008–09). More recently they have worked on the H30 Park (Favela da Serra, Belo Horizonte, 2009); the Casa Cor Bar (Belo Horizonte, 2010, published here); and are responsible for the execution of the Mineirão Stadium currently under construction, 2014 FIFA World Cup (Pampulha, Belo Horizonte, 2011–), all in Brazil.

BCMF wurde 2001 als Bürogemeinschaft von Bruno Campos gegründet, Partner sind Marcelo Fontes und Sílvio Todeschi. **BRUNO CAMPOS**, geboren 1970, schloss sein Studium an der Universidade Federal de Minas Gerais (UFMG, Belo Horizonte, 1989–94) ab und erlangte einen Master in Wohnungsbau und Stadtplanung an der Architectural Association in London (1997–98). Vor Gründung der Bürogemeinschaft war er für Weiss/Manfredi Architects tätig. Auch **MARCELO FONTES**, Jahrgang 1971, studierte an der UFMG (1990–95). **SÍLVIO TODESCHI**,1968 geboren, schloss sein Studium 1992 ebenfalls an der UFMG ab. Ab 1992 praktizierte er zunächst selbstständig und kooperierte bei mehreren Projekten mit BCMF Arquitetos, bevor er sich dem Team 2010 als Partner anschloss. Zu ihren Projekten zählen das MOCAO (Stadion Montes Claros, 2001–03), der Sportkomplex Deodoro (Schießen, Reiten, moderner Fünfkampf, Feldhockey und Bogenschießen) für die Panamerikanischen Spiele 2007 in Rio (2005–07). Im Auftrag des Brasilianischen Olympischen Komitees (COB) erarbeitete das Team verschiedene Konzeptstudien für die Bewerbung Rios für die Sommerspiele 2016 (2008–09). Jüngere Projekte sind der Park H30 (Favela da Serra, Belo Horizonte, 2009), die Casa Cor Bar (Belo Horizonte, 2010, hier vorgestellt) sowie die Bauleitung des Mineirão-Stadions für die Fußball-Weltmeisterschaft 2014 (Pampulha, Belo Horizonte, seit 2011), alle in Brasilien.

BCMF est une association créée en 2001 par Bruno Campos et ses partenaires Marcelo Fontes et Sílvio Todeschi. **BRUNO CAMPOS**, né en 1970, est diplômé de l'université fédérale de Minas Gerais (UFMG, Belo Horizonte, Brésil, 1989–94) et possède un M.A. en habitat et urbanisme de l'Architectural Association (Londres, 1997–98). Il a travaillé dans le cabinet d'architectes Weiss/Manfredi avant d'ouvrir le sien. Né en 1971, **MARCELO FONTES** est également diplômé de l'UFMG (1990–95). **SÍLVIO TODESCHI** est né en 1968 et a obtenu son diplôme à l'UFMG en 1992. Il a possédé son propre cabinet à partir de 1992 et a collaboré avec BCMF Arquitetos à plusieurs projets avant d'en devenir un partenaire en 2010. Leurs réalisations comprennent notamment le MOCAO (stade de Montes Claros, Brésil, 2001–03) et le complexe sportif de Deodoro (tir sportif, équitation, pentathlon moderne, hockey sur gazon et tir à l'arc) construit pour les Jeux panaméricains de Rio en 2007 (2005–07) ; ils ont par ailleurs été chargés par le Comité olympique brésilien (COB) de développer plusieurs études de projets pour la candidature de Rio aux Jeux olympiques de 2016 (2008–09). Plus récemment, ils ont travaillé au parc H30 (Favela da Serra, Belo Horizonte, 2009) ; au bar Casa Cor (Belo Horizonte, 2010, publié ici) et sont responsables des travaux du stade Mineirão, en construction, pour la Coupe du monde de la FIFA 2014 (Pampulha, Belo Horizonte, 2011–), tous au Brésil.

CASA COR BAR

Belo Horizonte, Minas Gerais, Brazil, 2010

Address: n/a. Area: 69m²
Client: Casa Cor / Stella Artois / Arcelor Mittal
Cost: $70 000

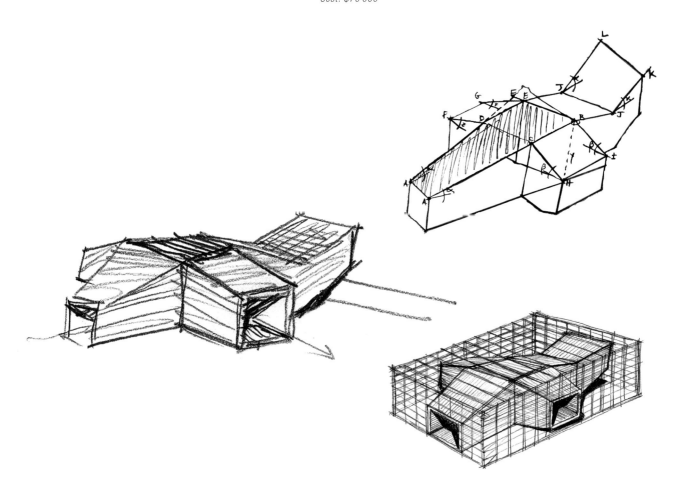

This unusual project, built in only three weeks, was implemented using a steel-frame design, and stainless-steel plate with a mirror finish inside and a matte finish on the exterior. The structure is intended to be "non-site specific," portable, and usable in different ways, but essentially it is "an informal lounge and retreat space." The architect states: "With dim lighting and some cork benches distributed at strategic points, the orange carpet floor unfolds into bleachers and stepped platforms where people can relax and admire the landscape from inside or outside. This unusual and irregular 'bolide' landed on a rooftop, in this case, but can be moved later anywhere else without losing its visual impact: a park, a plaza, a garden, or even the roof of another building."

Das ungewöhnliche Projekt wurde mit einem Stahlrahmenskelett und einer Edelstahlblechhülle realisiert, die innen verspiegelt und außen mattiert ist. Konzipiert wurde der Bau als „nicht ortsspezifisch", als transportabel und variabel nutzbar, ist im Grunde jedoch eine „entspannte Lounge, ein Ort zum Abschalten". Die Architekten erklären: „Gedämpftes Licht und eine Reihe von Korkbänken wurden an strategischen Punkten platziert; der Boden mit orange Auslegeware ist zu Tribünen und wie Treppen gestalteten Podesten ausgeformt. Hier können Gäste sitzen und die Landschaft von drinnen und draußen genießen. Der ungewöhnliche, asymmetrische ‚Bolid' ist hier auf einem Dach gelandet, lässt sich jedoch an einen beliebigen Ort versetzen, ohne an Wirkung einzubüßen: in einen Park, einen Garten oder auf das Dach eines anderen Gebäudes."

Ce projet original, construit en seulement trois semaines, a été conçu à l'aide d'une charpente en acier et de plaques en acier inoxydable au fini miroir à l'intérieur et mat à l'extérieur. La structure se veut « non rattachée à un lieu », transportable et utilisable de diverses manières, mais reste avant tout « un espace informel de détente et de retraite ». Pour l'architecte : « Avec le faible éclairage et quelques bancs en liège dispersés aux endroits stratégiques, la moquette orange se déploie sur des gradins où se détendre en admirant le paysage de l'intérieur ou de l'extérieur. Le "bolide" original et irrégulier s'est ici posé sur un toit, mais il peut être transféré n'importe où sans perdre de son impact visuel : dans un parc, sur une place, dans un jardin, ou même sur le toit d'un autre bâtiment. »

Angled but essentially tubular, the bar opens in four directions as seen in the sketches to the left, while the interior gives an impression of almost hermetic continuity.

Die schiefwinklige, schlauchförmige Bar öffnet sich in vier Richtungen, wie auf den Skizzen links zu sehen ist. Das Interieur wirkt geradezu hermetisch geschlossen.

De forme anguleuse, mais surtout tubulaire, le bar s'ouvre dans quatre directions comme on le voit sur les croquis, tandis que l'intérieur donne une impression de continuité quasi hermétique.

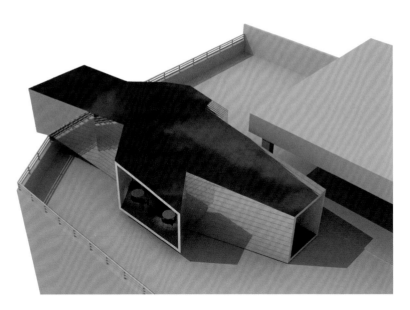

Seen in a rooftop location, the bar contrasts a cold metallic exterior with a more warmly colored interior. A drawing shows the bar with its leading edge hanging over the rooftop.

Die Bar, hier auf einem Dach, spielt mit dem Kontrast aus kaltem metallischem Außenbau und warmtonigem Innenraum. Auf der Zeichnung ist die über die Dachkante auskragende Stirnfront des Baus zu sehen.

Placé sur un toit, le bar affiche un contraste entre un extérieur métallique froid et un intérieur aux couleurs plus chaudes. Un plan le montre avec son bord accroché au toit.

At the end of a rooftop, the bar seems to be part of the garden design with its almost organic skin patterns.

Die Bar am Ende des Daches fügt sich mit ihrer fast organischen Oberflächenstruktur harmonisch in das Gartenkonzept ein.

À l'extrémité du toit, le bar semble faire partie de l'architecture du jardin avec les motifs presque organiques de son revêtement extérieur.

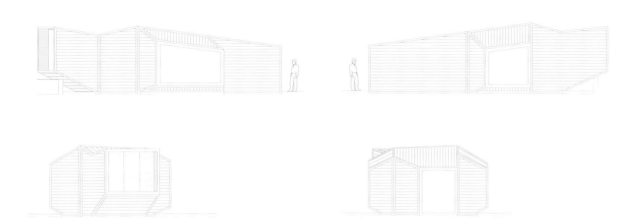

BIG

BIG
Bjarke Ingels Group
Nørrebrogade 66D, 2nd floor
2200 Copenhagen N
Denmark

Tel: +45 72 21 72 27 / Fax: +45 35 12 72 27
E-mail: big@big.dk
Web: www.big.dk

Bjarke Ingels was born in 1974 in Copenhagen, Denmark. He graduated from the Royal Academy of Arts School of Architecture (Copenhagen, 1999) and attended the ETSAB School of Architecture (Barcelona, Spain). He created his own office in 2005 under the name **BJARKE INGELS GROUP** (BIG), after having cofounded PLOT Architects in 2001 and collaborated with Rem Koolhaas at OMA (Rotterdam). In 2004 he was awarded the Golden Lion at the Venice Biennale for the Stavanger Concert House. One of his latest completed projects, the Mountain (Copenhagen, Denmark, 2006–08), has received numerous awards including the World Architecture Festival Housing Award, Forum Aid Award, and the MIPIM Residential Development Award. BIG is now led by eight Partners and has also opened an office in New York. The firm designed the Danish Expo Pavilion (Shanghai, China, 2010), whose rooftop restaurant is published here. Other recent and upcoming work includes the Superkilen Master Plan (Copenhagen, Denmark, 2011); Shenzhen International Energy Mansion (Shenzhen, China, 2013); the Danish Maritime Museum (Helsingor, Denmark, 2013); and the Faroe Islands Education Center (Thorshavn, Faroe Islands, Denmark, 2014).

Bjarke Ingels wurde 1974 in Kopenhagen geboren. Er schloss sein Studium an der Architekturfakultät der Königlichen Akademie der Künste ab (Kopenhagen, 1999) und besuchte die Architekturfakultät der ETSAB in Barcelona. 2005 gründete er sein eigenes Büro **BJARKE INGELS GROUP** (BIG), nachdem er 2001 bereits PLOT Architects mitgegründet und mit Rem Koolhaas/OMA (Rotterdam) zusammengearbeitet hatte. Für seinen Entwurf des Konzerthauses in Stavanger erhielt er 2004 auf der Biennale in Venedig den Goldenen Löwen. Eines seiner aktuellsten Projekte, Mountain (Kopenhagen, 2006–08), wurde mit zahlreichen Preisen ausgezeichnet, darunter dem World Architecture Festival Housing Award, dem Forum Aid Award und dem MIPIM Residential Development Award. BIG arbeitet inzwischen unter Leitung von acht Partnern und hat eine Dependance in New York eröffnet. Das Büro gestaltete den dänischen Pavillon für die Expo 2010 (Schanghai, 2010), dessen Dachrestaurant hier vorgestellt wird. Weitere jüngere und geplante Projekte sind u. a. der Masterplan für die Freifläche Superkilen (Kopenhagen, 2011), das Internationale Energiezentrum in Shenzhen (China, 2013), das Dänische Schifffahrtsmuseum (Helsingør, Dänemark, 2013) sowie das Bildungszentrum der Färöer-Inseln (Thorshavn, Färöer-Inseln, Dänemark, 2014).

Bjarke Ingels est né en 1974 à Copenhague. Il est diplômé de l'école d'architecture de l'Académie royale des beaux-arts (Copenhague, 1999) et a également suivi les cours de l'école d'architecture ETSAB (Barcelone). Il a ouvert son cabinet en 2005 sous le nom **BJARKE INGELS GROUP** (BIG), après avoir cofondé PLOT Architects en 2001 et collaboré avec Rem Koolhaas à OMA (Rotterdam). Il a reçu le Lion d'or 2004 à la Biennale de Venise pour la salle de concerts de Stavanger. L'un de ses derniers projets, La Montagne (Copenhague, 2006–08), a reçu plusieurs récompenses dont le prix du logement du World Architecture Festival, le prix Forum Aid et le prix MIPIM du développement résidentiel. BIG est désormais dirigé par huit partenaires et a ouvert un bureau à New York. L'agence a conçu le Pavillon danois pour l'Exposition universelle de Shanghai (Shanghai, 2010) dont le restaurant sur le toit est publié ici. Parmi leurs autres réalisations récentes et à venir, on trouve : le plan directeur du site Superkilen (Copenhague, 2011) ; la Shenzhen International Energy Mansion (Shenzhen, Chine, 2013) ; le Musée maritime danois (Elseneur, Danemark, 2013) et le Centre éducatif des îles Féroé (Thorshavn, îles Féroé, Danemark, 2014).

ROOFTOP BISTRO

Danish Expo Pavilion, Shanghai, China, 2010

Address: n/a. Area: 500 m². Client: EBST
Cost: not disclosed

BIG, designers of the Danish Pavilion at Expo 2010, had the idea of allowing visitors to "try some of the best aspects of Danish city life themselves." The building housed Hans Christian Andersen's actual *Little Mermaid*, temporarily removed from the port of Copenhagen for the occasion. A "social bench" designed by the artist Jeppe Hein wound up through the structure, leading to the **ROOFTOP BISTRO**. The architects state: "The bistro is an integral part of the pavilion experience—an exclusive yet unpretentious culinary journey through Denmark. The selection of food was based on the traditional Danish kitchen, arranged with a modern touch and with the freshest and finest ingredients commonly enjoyed in Denmark." A snaking bench linking mushroom-shaped canopies marked the rooftop space, fitting in with the image of movement chosen for the entire pavilion.

BIG, den Architekten des Dänischen Pavillons für die Expo 2010, ging es darum, den Besuchern Gelegenheit zu geben, „einige der besten Aspekte des dänischen Stadtlebens persönlich erleben zu können". Im Pavillon konnte man u. a. *Die kleine Meerjungfrau* nach dem Märchen von Hans Christian Andersen besichtigen, die man eigens für die Expo aus dem Kopenhagener Hafen nach Schanghai versetzt hatte. Eine „soziale Bank" des dänischen Künstlers Jeppe Hein folgte den Windungen des Baus hinauf zum **BISTRO AUF DEM DACH**. Die Architekten erklären: „Das Bistro ist integraler Bestandteil des Pavillonbesuchs und bietet eine exklusive, zugleich unprätentiöse kulinarische Reise durch Dänemark. Die Auswahl des Speisenangebots orientiert sich an der traditionellen dänischen Küche mit modernem Anflug und ausschließlich den frischsten und besten Zutaten, die überall in Dänemark beliebt sind." Die geschwungene Bank mit den pilzförmigen Sonnenschirmen markiert die Cafézone auf dem Dach und greift zugleich das Motiv dynamischer Bewegung auf, das sich durch den gesamten Bau zieht.

L'idée de BIG, les créateurs du Pavillon danois de l'Expo 2010, était de permettre aux visiteurs « de vivre par eux-mêmes certains des meilleurs aspects de la vie urbaine au Danemark ». Le bâtiment a accueilli la *Petite Sirène* de Hans Christian Andersen, qui a quitté temporairement le port de Copenhague pour l'occasion. Un « banc public » conçu par l'artiste Jeppe Hein s'enroule autour de l'ensemble et mène au **BISTROT SUR LE TOIT**. Pour l'architecte : « Le bistrot fait partie intégrante de l'expérience que le Pavillon propose de vivre – un voyage culinaire exclusif mais sans prétention à travers le Danemark. Le choix des mets est basé sur la cuisine traditionnelle danoise, avec une touche de modernité et les aliments les plus frais et les plus fins qu'on trouve au Danemark. » Un banc qui serpente entre des îlots-champignons marque l'espace sur le toit, parfaitement en phase avec l'idée du mouvement choisie pour le Pavillon dans son ensemble.

An aerial view shows how the visitor path winds up to the rooftop bistro of the pavilion. This page, a closer view of the outdoor seating.

Eine Luftaufnahme zeigt den sich zum Dachbistro hinaufwindenden Besucherpfad des Pavillons. Auf dieser Seite eine nähere Ansicht der Sitzgelegenheiten unter freiem Himmel.

Une vue aérienne montre le chemin qui s'enroule jusqu'au bistrot sur le toit du Pavillon. Ci-dessus, une vue plus rapprochée des sièges extérieurs.

At night the lighting makes the mush-
room- or parasol-shaped canopies
glow, rendering the space convivial
even after sunset.

*Nachts leuchten die pilzförmigen
Sonnenschirme: So bleibt das Bistro
auch abends ein beliebter Treffpunkt.*

*La nuit, les ilôts-champignons ou
parasols sont éclairés, ce qui donne
plus de convivialité à l'espace, même
après le coucher du soleil.*

A sinuous path leads visitors up, with the feeling that they are emerging into the open sky as they reach the bistro.

Erreichen die Besucher das Bistro, scheint der geschwungene Pfad weiter in den offenen Himmel zu führen.

Un sentier sinueux mène les visiteurs en haut et leur donne l'impression de pénétrer dans le vaste ciel lorsqu'ils arrivent au bistrot.

CAMPAIGN

Campaign
Unit 16 Perseverance Works
25–27 Hackney Road
London E2 8DD
UK

Tel: +44 20 32 22 08 70
E-mail: contact@campaigndesign.co.uk
Web: www.campaigndesign.co.uk

CAMPAIGN founder and Creative Director Philip Handford was born in 1972. He obtained a B.A. in Interior Architecture from Brighton University and worked with the London consultancies Imagination and Barber Osgerby, before establishing Campaign in January 2009. As he explains: "The studio is hands-on in exploring different media and methods in order to tell unique and engaging brand stories, developing integrated brand experiences through interior architecture, graphic, and interactive design." Recent projects include the Dr. Martens Pop-Up Store in Spitalfields (London, UK, 2009); a temporary installation for dunhill during New York Fashion Week (New York, USA, 2010); Foldaway, a bookshop made entirely out of cardboard for the London Festival of Architecture 2010; and Kirk Originals Flagship Store (London, 2010, published here), all in the UK unless stated otherwise.

Philip Handford, Gründer und Kreativdirektor von **CAMPAIGN**, wurde 1972 geboren. Er schloss sein Innenarchitekturstudium an der Universität Brighton mit einem B.A. ab und arbeitete für die Londoner Agenturen Imagination und Barber Osgerby, bevor er im Januar 2009 Campaign gründete. Er erklärt: „Das Studio lotet in der Praxis die verschiedensten Medien und Methoden aus, um das unverwechselbare und faszinierende Profil einer Marke zu vermitteln. Durch Innenarchitektur, Grafikdesign und interaktives Design werden ganzheitliche Markenerlebnisse entwickelt." Jüngste Projekte sind u. a. der Dr. Martens Pop-Up Store in Spitalfields (London, 2009), eine temporäre Installation für Dunhill während der New Yorker Fashion Week (New York, 2010), Foldaway, eine Buchhandlung aus Pappe für das Londoner Architekturfestival 2010, und der Flagship-Store für Kirk Originals (London, 2010, hier vorgestellt).

Le fondateur et directeur artistique de **CAMPAIGN**, Philip Handford, est né en 1972. Il est titulaire d'un B.A. en architecture d'intérieur de l'université de Brighton et a travaillé avec le cabinet-conseil londonien Imagination and Barber Osgerby avant d'ouvrir Campaign en janvier 2009. Comme il l'explique : « Le studio cherche à explorer différents médias et différentes méthodes pour raconter l'histoire de marques uniques et attachantes, développer des concepts de marques globaux en combinant l'architecture d'intérieur, le graphisme et le design interactif. » Ses projets récents comprennent : le magasin éphémère Dr. Martens de Spitalfields (Londres, 2009) ; une installation temporaire pour Dunhill pendant la Semaine de la mode de New York (2010) ; la librairie réalisée entièrement en carton Foldaway pour le festival d'architecture de Londres 2010 et le magasin-phare de Kirk Originals (Londres, 2010, publié ici), tous au Royaume-Uni, sauf mention contraire.

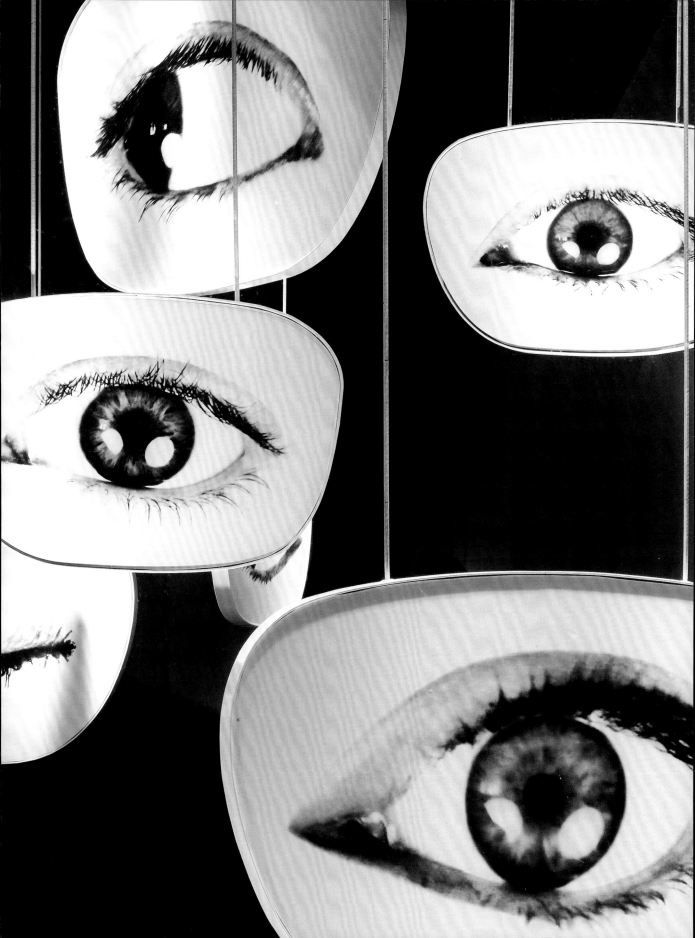

KIRK ORIGINALS FLAGSHIP STORE
London, UK, 2010

Address: 6 Conduit Street, London W1S 1XE, UK, +44 20 74 99 00 60, conduit@kirkoriginals.com,
www.kirkoriginals.com/flagship-store. Area: 65m². Client: Kirk Originals. Cost: not disclosed
Collaboration: Aaron Richardson, Ben Ayres, Tatjana Jakovicka

Campaign declares: "In stark contrast to the conventional clinical white box of traditional opticians, Campaign has created a dramatic interior for the London flagship store of global eyewear brand Kirk Originals." Winking eyes are a theme of the design, as are 187 white sculptural "heads," each wearing different eyeglass frames "as if displaying works of art." It might be said that the entire installation resembles a work of art, with one surprising element being the slightly disjointed and crowded display of the 187 eyeglass frames. The walls are painted dark blue-gray and floors are dark gray. Wall texts recall the history of the brand, while a back-wall projection "playfully reworks the Kirk Originals logo through a continual kaleidoscopic loop."

Die Designer erläutern: „Für den Londoner Flagship-Store des internationalen Brillenherstellers Kirk Originals entwickelte Campaign ein dramatisches Interieur: Ein auffälliger Kontrast zu den üblichen, klinisch weißen boxartigen Geschäftsräumen traditioneller Optiker". Motive des Entwurfs sind zum einen das zwinkernde Auge, zum anderen 187 dreidimensionale „Köpfe", die „wie eine Kunstpräsentation" verschiedene Brillengestelle tragen. Tatsächlich wirkt die gesamte Ausstattung wie ein Kunstwerk. Ein überraschendes Element sind die leicht gegeneinander versetzten, dicht an dicht präsentierten 187 Brillenmodelle. Die Wände sind in dunklem Blaugrau gehalten, die Böden dunkelgrau. Wandbeschriftungen verweisen auf die Firmengeschichte. Auf die hintere Stirnwand „wird das Kirk-Originals-Logo als kaleidoskopartige Dauerschleife spielerisch projiziert".

Selon Campaign : « En contraste fort avec les boîtes blanches aseptisées des opticiens traditionnels, nous avons créé un intérieur théâtral pour le magasin londonien de la marque mondiale de lunettes Kirk Originals. » Le design est notamment articulé autour du thème des clins d'œil, avec 187 têtes blanches sculpturales portant chacune une paire de lunettes différente « comme pour présenter une œuvre d'art ». L'installation dans son ensemble ressemble par ailleurs à une œuvre d'art, la surprise étant créée par la disposition incohérente et très serrée des 187 paires de lunettes. Les murs sont bleu gris sombre et les sols gris foncé. Des textes muraux rappellent l'histoire de la marque, tandis qu'une « version retravaillée du logo Kirk Originals » est projetée sur le mur du fond « en une boucle kaléidoscopique permanente ».

The eyes have it... With the floating eye design, Campaign immediately makes the function of this store evident while attracting visitor attention. Below, a section drawing with the wall-mounted display units.

Augen auf ... Mit dem schwebenden Augendisplay kommuniziert Campaign unzweifelhaft die Funktion des Ladens und weckt zugleich die Aufmerksamkeit der Kunden. Unten eine Schnittzeichnung mit den Wanddisplays.

Tout pour les yeux... Avec son design aux yeux en suspension, Campaign met immédiatement en évidence la fonction du magasin tout en attirant l'attention des visiteurs. Ci-dessous, un plan en coupe avec les présentoirs muraux.

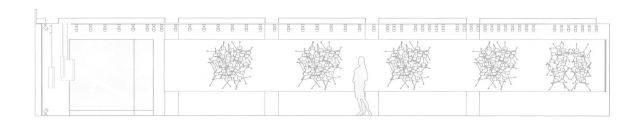

With a version of their "eye" design reduced to the size of a head, and formed in a stylized curve that fits eyeglasses, Campaign here offers an easy way to view the models on display.

Mit einer Variation ihres „Augen"-Designs, hier auf Kopfgröße reduziert und stilisiert, gelingt Campaign eine schlichte Lösung zur Präsentation der angebotenen Brillenmodelle.

Avec cette version de son design « pour yeux » réduit à la taille d'une tête, et à la forme courbe stylisée adapté aux lunettes, Campaign permet de visualiser très facilement les modèles exposés.

Below, a plan shows the wall-
mounted displays, also seen in the
photo. Black walls make the displays
stand out immediately in visual terms.

Unten ein Grundriss mit den Wanddisplays, auch im Foto darunter zu
sehen. Schwarze Wände lassen die
Displays besonders hervorstechen.

Ci-dessous, un plan avec les présentoirs muraux que l'on voit aussi sur la
photo. Les murs noirs les font nette-
ment ressortir.

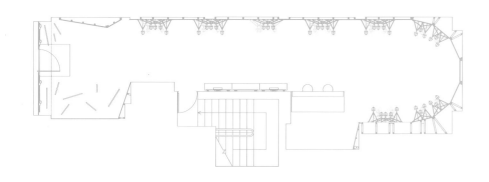

GARY CARD

Gary Card
18 Belsham Street
London E9 6NG
UK

Tel: +44 79 12 32 22 01
E-mail: garycard@gmail.com
Web: www.garycardiology.blogspot.com

GARY CARD is a set and prop designer, and a graphic and illustration artist. He has collaborated with photographers Paolo Roversi, Nick Knight, and Jacob Sutton, and stylists such as Katy Grand and Nicola Formachetti. Card has also created live installations for the windows of Stella McCartney's Bruton Street store (London, 2008). He has created pieces worn and used by Lady Gaga, has his own line of Swatches, and created illustrated children's storybook characters. He states that he seeks inspiration from the works of figures such as Paul McCarthy and Jeff Koons; photographers like Nick Knight; and directors such as David Cronenberg. "It's color and the perverse that intrigues me the most, especially when the two collide," he says. His blog, www.garycardiology.blogspot.com, was cited as one of the "10 best fashion blogs" in 2010. He has collaborated with the magazine *Dazed & Confused* for five years. His design for LN-CC (London, UK, 2010, published here) was his first interior design commission.

GARY CARD ist Bühnenbildner und Requisiteur, Grafikdesigner und Illustrator. Er hat mit Fotografen wie Paolo Roversi, Nick Knight und Jacob Sutton gearbeitet sowie mit Stylisten wie Katy Grand und Nicola Formachetti. Card realisierte außerdem Live-Installationen für die Schaufenster von Stella McCartneys Boutique an der Bruton Street (London, 2008). Von ihm stammen Entwürfe für Lady Gaga, eine eigene Uhrenlinie für Swatch und Illustrationen für Kinderbücher. Card lässt sich nach eigener Aussage von Kunstwerken von Paul McCarthy oder Jeff Koons inspirieren, von Fotografen wie Nick Knight und Regisseuren wie David Cronenberg. „Was mich am meisten fasziniert, sind Farben und das Perverse, ganz besonders, wenn beides aufeinandertrifft", so Card. Sein Blog www.garycardiology.blogspot.com wurde 2010 zu einem der „zehn besten Modeblogs" erklärt. Seit fünf Jahren arbeitet er mit dem Magazin *Dazed & Confused* zusammen. Sein Entwurf für LN-CC (London, 2010, hier vorgestellt) war sein erstes Innenarchitekturprojekt.

GARY CARD est décorateur de théâtre, concepteur d'accessoires, graphiste et illustrateur. Il a travaillé avec les photographes Paolo Roversi, Nick Knight et Jacob Sutton et des stylistes tels que Katy Grand et Nicola Formachetti. Card a également créé des installations live pour les vitrines du magasin Stella McCartney de Bruton Street (Londres, 2008). Il a créé des modèles portés et utilisés par Lady Gaga, possède sa propre ligne de Swatch et a imaginé des personnages de livres jeunesse illustrés. Il affirme trouver l'inspiration dans le travail de Paul McCarthy et Jeff Koons, de photographes comme Nick Knight et de réalisateurs comme David Cronenberg. « Je suis particulièrement attiré par le coloré et le pervers, surtout quand les deux se rencontrent », déclare-t-il. Son blog www.garycardiology.blogspot.com a été cité comme l'un des « dix meilleurs blogs de mode » en 2010. Il a collaboré au magazine *Dazed & Confused* pendant cinq ans. Le LN-CC (Londres, 2010, publié ici) est sa première commande d'architecture intérieure.

LATE NIGHT CHAMELEON CAFÉ LN-CC

London, UK, 2010

Address: 18 Shacklewell Lane, Dalston, London E8 2EZ, UK, +44 20 31 74 07 41,
appointments@ln-cc.com, www.ln-cc.com. Area: 464 m². Client: John Skelton LN-CC
Cost: not disclosed. Collaboration: Agenca Construction

LATE NIGHT CHAMELEON CAFÉ LN-CC is a London-based retail firm created by John Skelton and Daniel Mitchell. It consists in the store space in East London published here and an "online platform." Made in good part with raw wood and orange acrylic, the space is made up of three concept rooms, which as a whole "embody the LN-CC concept." One of these is an angled wooden bookshop space. The concept is described by the firm as "men's and women's wear based around unisex styling, music, books, exhibitions, and limited worldwide releases… We curate our clothing offer in a very specific way by fusing together what we believe to be the best brands within the mainline areas… with underground Japanese brands… and the best of the up-and-coming brands from all over the world… and merchandise it together." The idea of bringing together clothing, music, and art in both a physical and digital environment seems particularly well suited to the talents of the designer Gary Card.

Das Londoner Einzelhandelsunternehmen **LATE NIGHT CHAMELEON CAFÉ LN-CC** wurde von John Skelton und Daniel Mitchell gegründet. Standbeine sind der hier vorgestellte Laden im Londoner East End sowie eine „Online-Plattform". Der zu einem guten Teil aus unbehandeltem Holz und orange Acryl gestaltete Laden besteht aus drei Konzepträumen, die in ihrer Gesamtheit „das LN-CC-Konzept verkörpern". Einer der Räume wurde mit schiefwinkligen Regalen als Buchhandlung eingerichtet. Das Unternehmen versteht sich konzeptuell als Plattform für „Mode für Männer und Frauen rund um Unisex-Styling, Musik, Bücher, Ausstellungen und limitierte weltweite Releases … Unser Modeangebot wird nach ganz bestimmten Kriterien ausgewählt: Wir kombinieren die besten Mainstream-Brands … mit japanischen Underground-Labels … und den besten Newcomern weltweit … und präsentieren sie als Gesamtkonzept." Der Ansatz, Mode, Musik und Kunst zusammen in einem räumlichen und virtuellen Kontext zu präsentieren, ist bei einem Designtalent wie Gary Card besonders gut aufgehoben.

Le **LATE NIGHT CHAMELEON CAFÉ LN-CC** est une entreprise de détail basée à Londres, créée par John Skelton et Daniel Mitchell et composée de l'espace magasin, dans l'Est de Londres, publié ici, et d'une « plate-forme en ligne ». Construit majoritairement en bois brut et acrylique orange, l'endroit se compose de trois *concept rooms* qui « incarnent ensemble le concept LN-CC », notamment un espace librairie au design de bois angleux. Le concept est décrit par la société comme « des vêtements masculins et féminins dans un style unisexe, de la musique, des livres, des expositions et des sorties mondiales limitées… Nous avons une manière très particulière de composer notre offre de vêtements en associant ce que nous pensons être les meilleures marques dans les tendances dominantes… à des marques japonaises d'avant-garde… et aux meilleures des marques qui montent dans le monde entier… que nous commercialisons toutes ensemble ». L'idée d'associer vêtements, musique et art dans un environnement physique et numérique semble convenir parfaitement au talent de designer de Gary Card.

An angled orange tunnel greets
clients, seen here in sketches and
an image of the completed space.

Skizzen und eine Aufnahme der realisierten Installation zeigen den geometrischen orangefarbenen Tunnel,
der die Kunden begrüßt.

Les clients sont accueillis par un tunnel orange anguleux qu'on voit ici sur
les croquis et sur une photo de
l'espace réalisé.

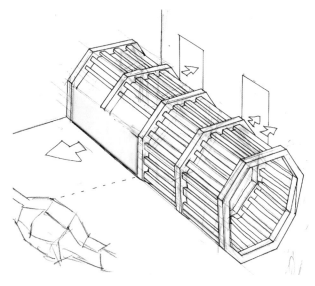

To the left, the angular bookshop space. Above, simple white display blocks show shoes or allow clothes to be hung. In keeping with the quasi-industrial spirit of LN-CC, simple hanging bulbs provide lighting.

Links die schiefwinkligen Regal-einbauten der Buchhandlung. Oben: Schuhe werden auf schlichten weißen Blockpodesten, Kleidung hängend präsentiert. Passend zum industriel-len Look wird der Store von einfachen Glühbirnen erhellt.

À gauche, l'espace librairie tout en angles. Ci-dessus, de simple blocs blancs présentent des chaussures ou servent à accrocher des vêtements. En accord avec l'ambiance presque industrielle de LN-CC, l'éclairage est assuré par de simples ampoules suspendues.

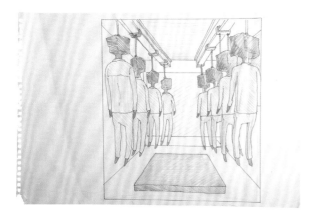

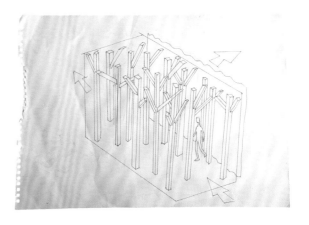

Above, sketches by Gary Card show mannequin-like forms hanging down. An open cage hanger arrangement allows clothes to be readily viewed.

Oben Skizzen von Gary Card mit stilisierten Hängepuppen. Dank einer offenen „Käfigkonstruktion" ist die präsentierte Mode leicht zugänglich.

Ci-dessus, croquis de Gary Card représentant des formes de type mannequin suspendues. Un système de cintre en forme de cage ouverte permet de voir facilement les vêtements.

DAVID CHIPPERFIELD

David Chipperfield Architects Ltd.
1A Cobham Mews
Agar Grove
London NW1 9SB
UK

David Chipperfield Architects
Gesellschaft von Architekten mbH
Joachimstr. 11
10119 Berlin
Germany

Tel: +44 207 267 94 22 / Fax: +44 207 172 67 93 47
E-mail: info@davidchipperfield.co.uk
Web: www.davidchipperfield.com

Tel: +49 30 280 17 00 / Fax: +49 30 28 01 70 15
E-mail: media@davidchipperfield.de

Born in London in 1953, **DAVID CHIPPERFIELD** obtained his Diploma in Architecture from the Architectural Association (London, 1977). He worked in the offices of Norman Foster and Richard Rogers, before establishing David Chipperfield Architects (London, 1984). The firm now has offices in London, Berlin, Milan, and Shanghai. Built work includes the River and Rowing Museum (Henley-on-Thames, UK, 1989–97); Des Moines Public Library (Des Moines, Iowa, USA, 2001–06); the Museum of Modern Literature (Marbach am Neckar, Germany, 2002–06); the America's Cup Building "Veles et Vents" (Valencia, Spain, 2005–06); the Empire Riverside Hotel (Hamburg, Germany, 2002–07); the Liangzhu Museum (Liangzhu Cultural Village, China, 2003–07); the Neues Museum (Museum Island, Berlin, Germany, 1997–2009); the City of Justice Law Courts (Barcelona, Spain, 2002–09); and the Anchorage Museum at Rasmuson Center (Anchorage, Alaska, USA, 2003–09). Recently the office has completed Museum Folkwang (Essen, Germany, 2007–10); the Kaufhaus Tyrol Department Store (Innsbruck, Austria, 2007–10, published here); the Hepworth Gallery (Wakefield, UK, 2003–11); Turner Contemporary (Margate, UK, 2006–11); and the Peek & Cloppenburg Flagship Store (Vienna, Austria, 2006–11, also published here). Underway is the Ansaldo City of Cultures (Milan, Italy, 2000–12); the expansion of the Saint Louis Art Museum (Missouri, USA, 2005–13); and the completion of the Rockbund Project (Shanghai, China, 2006–14).

Der 1953 in London geborene **DAVID CHIPPERFIELD** machte sein Diplom in Architektur an der Architectural Association in London (1977). Er arbeitete in den Büros von Norman Foster und Richard Rogers, ehe er David Chipperfield Architects gründete (London, 1984). Das Büro hat inzwischen Niederlassungen in London, Berlin, Mailand und Schanghai. Zu seinen realisierten Projekten zählen das River and Rowing Museum (Henley-on-Thames, GB, 1989–97), die Stadtbibliothek von Des Moines (Des Moines, Iowa, USA, 2001–06), das Literaturmuseum der Moderne (Marbach am Neckar, 2002–06), das America's Cup Building „Veles et Vents" (Valencia, Spanien, 2005–06), das Empire Riverside Hotel (Hamburg, 2002–07), das Liangzhu-Museum (Kulturstätte Liangzhu, China, 2003–07), das Neue Museum (Museumsinsel, Berlin, 1997–2009), die Ciutat de la Justícia (Barcelona, 2002–09) und das Anchorage Museum im Rasmuson Center (Anchorage, Alaska, 2003–09). Unlängst fertiggestellt wurden das Museum Folkwang (Essen, 2007–10), das Kaufhaus Tyrol (Innsbruck, 2007–10, hier vorgestellt), die Hepworth Gallery (Wakefield, GB, 2003–11), das Turner Contemporary (Margate, GB, 2006–11) sowie ein Flagship-Store für Peek & Cloppenburg (Wien, 2006–11, ebenfalls hier vorgestellt). In Arbeit sind derzeit u. a. die Stadt der Kulturen, Ansaldo-Komplex (Mailand, 2000–12), die Erweiterung des Saint Louis Art Museum (Saint Louis, Missouri, USA, 2005–13) und die Fertigstellung des Rockbund-Projekts (Schanghai, 2006–14).

Né à Londres en 1953, **DAVID CHIPPERFIELD** est diplômé en architecture de l'Architectural Association (Londres, 1977). Il a travaillé pour Norman Foster et Richard Rogers avant de créer David Chipperfield Architects (Londres, 1984). La société a désormais des bureaux à Londres, Berlin, Milan et Shanghai. Ses réalisations comprennent : le musée de l'Aviron (Henley-on-Thames, GB, 1989–97) ; la bibliothèque de Des Moines (Des Moines, Iowa, 2001–06) ; le Musée de la littérature moderne (Marbach am Neckar, Allemagne, 2002–06) ; le bâtiment de l'America's Cup « Veles et Vents » (Valence, Espagne, 2005–06) ; le musée de Liangzhu (village culturel de Liangzhu, Chine, 2003–07) ; Le Neues Museum (île des Musées, Berlin, 1997–2009) ; la Cité de la justice (Barcelone, 2002–09) et le musée d'Anchorage du Centre Rasmuson (Anchorage, Alaska, 2003–09). Plus récemment, l'agence a réalisé : le musée Folkwang (Essen, Allemagne, 2007–10) ; le grand magasin Kaufhaus Tyrol (Innsbruck, 2007–10, publié ici) ; la galerie Hepworth (Wakefield, GB, 2003–11) ; la Turner Contemporary (Margate, GB, 2006–11) et le magasin-phare de Peek & Cloppenburg (Vienne, 2006–11, publié ici). Les projets en cours de réalisation comptent : la Cité des cultures Ansaldo (Milan, 2000–12) ; l'extension du Musée d'art de Saint Louis (Missouri, 2005–13) et l'achèvement du projet Rockbund (Shanghai, 2006–14).

PEEK & CLOPPENBURG FLAGSHIP STORE

Vienna, Austria, 2006–11

Address: Kärntner Str. 29–33, 10100 Vienna, Austria, +43 1 890 48 88 / 0, www.peek-cloppenburg.at
Area: 11 838 m² (sales). Client: NAXOS Grundverwaltungs GmbH, Vienna
Cost: not disclosed

Having called on such prestigious architects as Renzo Piano (Cologne, 2005) and Richard Meier (Mannheim, 2007), it is not surprising that Peek & Cloppenburg commissioned David Chipperfield Architects for their Vienna flagship store situated on Kärntner Strasse, a shopping street in the historic center. Chipperfield emphasizes the contrast between his work and the older buildings in the vicinity while showing his ability to fit into this context, stating: "The design of the new building recalls the typology of 19th-century department stores and mediates between this tradition, the historic building fabric, and a contemporary architectural language. The solid façade is built using a light-colored, bush-hammered Danube limestone." The large windows of the new building are placed to harmonize them with neighboring structures, providing scale and a connection between inside and outside. White plaster walls and oak parquet mark the interiors of the textile sales areas, located on the basement, ground floor, and four levels above. The same Danube limestone employed for the façades is again found, in polished form, on the atrium floors.

Nachdem Peek & Cloppenburg bereits so renommierte Architekten wie Renzo Piano (Köln, 2005) und Richard Meier (Mannheim, 2007) verpflichtet hat, überrascht es nicht, dass David Chipperfield Architects mit der Gestaltung der Wiener Dependance auf der Kärntner Straße betraut wurde, einer Einkaufsstraße in der historischen Altstadt. Chipperfield betont den Kontrast zwischen seinem Entwurf und den Altbauten der Umgebung, stellt jedoch zugleich seine Fähigkeit unter Beweis, sich in den Kontext einzufügen: „Die Gestaltung des Neubaus erinnert an Kaufhaustypologien des 19. Jahrhunderts und wird zum Mittler zwischen Tradition, historischer Bausubstanz und zeitgenössischer Architektursprache. Die massive Fassade wurde aus hellem, scharriertem Donau-Kalkstein errichtet." Die Anordnung der großen Fenster des Neubaus ist harmonisch an den Nachbarbauten ausgerichtet, schafft ein Gefühl für die Raumgröße und eine Verknüpfung von innen und außen. Weiß verputzte Wände und Eichenparkett prägen die Verkaufsräume für Mode im Untergeschoss, im Parterre und den vier Obergeschossen. Für den Boden im Atrium wurde derselbe Donau-Kalkstein wie an der Fassade verwendet, hier jedoch poliert.

Après des architectes aussi prestigieux que Renzo Piano (Cologne, 2005) et Richard Meier (Mannheim, 2007), il n'y a rien d'étonnant à ce que Peek & Cloppenburg ait fait appel à David Chipperfield pour son magasin principal de Vienne, situé dans la Kärntner Strasse, une rue commerçante du centre historique. Chipperfield souligne le contraste entre son œuvre et les bâtiments plus anciens des alentours, tout en démontrant sa capacité d'adaptation : « Le design du nouvel édifice rappelle la typologie des grands magasins du XIXᵉ siècle et fait le lien entre cette tradition de construction historique et un langage architectural contemporain. La façade compacte est en calcaire bouchardé du Danube légèrement coloré. » Les grandes fenêtres sont disposées en harmonie avec les structures voisines, apportant de l'ampleur et créant un lien entre l'intérieur et l'extérieur. L'intérieur des espaces de vente textile au sous-sol, rez-de-chaussée et sur quatre niveaux est marqué par des murs de plâtre blanc et des parquets de chêne. On retrouve le calcaire du Danube de la façade, poli, sur le sol des halls.

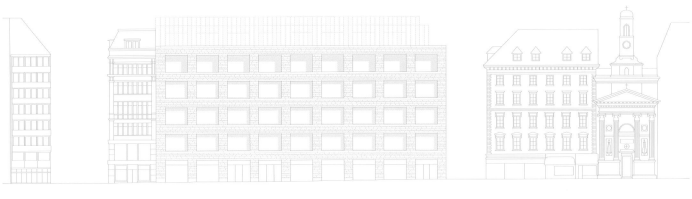

Interiors of the store, photographed here before occupation by the client, show the strict, minimalist architecture of David Chipperfield and the architect's mastery of light.

Ansichten des Gebäudeinneren, fotografiert, bevor die Räume bezogen wurden, zeigen die streng minimalistische Architektur David Chipperfields und seine meisterliche Lichtführung.

L'intérieur du magasin, photographié ici avant son occupation par le client, montre l'architecture strictement minimaliste de David Chipperfield et sa maîtrise de la lumière.

Generous overhead lighting irrigates
the space and makes customers feel
at ease inside. To the right, the store
photographed after its opening with
merchandise in place.

Großzügig von oben einfallendes Licht
durchflutet den Raum und trägt zum
Wohlbefinden der Kunden bei. Rechts
eine Ansicht des Kaufhauses nach
Bezug mit vollständiger Einrichtung.

Le généreux éclairage du plafond
inonde l'espace de lumière et donne
aux clients un sentiment de bien-être.
À droite, le magasin photographié
après son ouverture.

KAUFHAUS TYROL DEPARTMENT STORE

Innsbruck, Austria, 2007–10

Address: Maria-Theresien Str. 31, 6020 Innsbruck, Austria, +43 512 90 11–15, www. kaufhaus-tyrol.at
Area: 58 000 m². Client: Signa Holding GmbH, Innsbruck
Cost: not disclosed

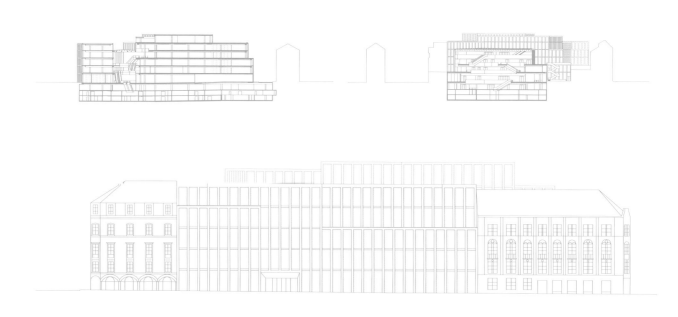

David Chipperfield took on the challenge of integrating this modern building into the historic center of Innsbruck on the Maria-Theresien Strasse. By angling the three precast concrete façade sections, the architect fits his structure into the rhythm of the old street. Rather than opting for smooth façades, Chipperfield articulates his design making use of light and shadow as well as the dimensions of neighboring building surfaces to further fit the mood of the city. The adjoining 16th-century Schindlerhaus also had its façade restored and a floor added, providing offices and meeting spaces and for the former Schindler Café. The interior of the **KAUFHAUS TYROL** contains a central, five-story, naturally lit atrium offering access to all the floors. Chipperfield's strength lies in not compromising modernity while still accepting the reality of the old city.

David Chipperfield stellte sich der Herausforderung, einen modernen Neubau in die Maria-Theresien-Straße im historischen Stadtzentrum von Innsbruck zu integrieren. Mit den schräg versetzten, vorgefertigten Fassadenelementen aus Beton bindet der Architekt seinen Bau in den Rhythmus des historischen Straßenzugs ein. Statt auf glatte Fassadenflächen zu setzen, gliedert der Architekt seinen Entwurf durch das Spiel von Licht und Schatten und greift die Proportionen der Bebauung in der Umgebung auf, um sich in das Stadtbild einzufügen. Auch das benachbarte Schindlerhaus aus dem 16. Jahrhundert erhielt eine sanierte Fassade sowie eine Etagenaufstockung, um Platz für Büros, Konferenzräume und das ehemalige Café Schindler zu schaffen. Innen erschließt ein helles zentrales, fünfstöckiges Atrium sämtliche Etagen des neuen **KAUFHAUSES TYROL**. Es ist Chipperfields Stärke, weder Kompromisse in der modernen Formensprache einzugehen noch die bauliche Realität der Altstadt zu ignorieren.

David Chipperfield a relevé le défi d'intégrer son bâtiment moderne au centre historique d'Innsbruck (Maria-Theresien Strasse). L'angle donné par l'architecte aux trois sections de la façade en béton précontraint leur permet de trouver leur place dans le rythme de la rue ancienne. Plutôt que des façades lisses et régulières, Chipperfield articule sa création autour de l'ombre et de la lumière et s'adapte aux dimensions des bâtiments voisins afin de mieux s'accorder à l'atmosphère de la ville. La façade de la Schindlerhaus contiguë du XVIe siècle a également été restaurée et un étage a été ajouté pour des bureaux, des espaces de réunion et l'ancien café Schindler. À l'intérieur du **KAUFHAUS TYROL**, le hall central éclairé naturellement donne accès aux cinq étages. La force de Chipperfield réside dans son talent à ne pas faire de compromis sur la modernité tout en tenant compte de la réalité d'une cité ancienne.

Despite its obvious modernity, the store fits into the patterned and irregular line of façades. Above, elevation and section drawings.

Trotz seiner offenkundigen Modernität fügt sich das Kaufhaus in die strukturierte, unregelmäßige Fassadenflucht ein. Oben ein Aufriss und Querschnitte.

En dépit de sa modernité évidente, le magasin s'intègre parfaitement à l'alignement irrégulier de façades ornementées. Ci-dessus, plans en élévation et en coupe.

Conserving his own style, the architect succeeds in making the design stand out while fitting into the urban patterns. Left, the active commercial spaces inside the building.

Der Architekt bleibt sich treu, indem er einen auffälligen Entwurf gestaltet, der sich dennoch in das urbane Raster fügt. Links die belebten Verkaufsflächen im Gebäude.

Tout en conservant son style propre, l'architecte a réussi à mettre le design en avant et à l'adapter à l'ensemble urbain. À gauche, les espaces commerciaux de l'intérieur en pleine activité.

CONCRETE

Concrete Architectural Associates BV
Oudezijds Achterburgwal 78a
1012 DR Amsterdam
The Netherlands

Tel: +31 20 520 02 00 / Fax: +31 20 520 02 01
E-mail: info@concreteamsterdam.nl
Web: www.concreteamsterdam.nl

Rob Wagemans was born in 1973. He created the interior design office **CONCRETE ARCHITECTURAL ASSOCIATES** in 1997 with Gilian Schrofer and Erik van Dillen. Wagemans studied at the Academies of Architecture in Amsterdam and Utrecht and completed his studies with an M.Arch degree focusing on interior design. The firm, with a staff of 30, includes interior designers, product, communication, and graphic designers, as well as architects. The firm is divided into three divisions— Concrete Architectural Associates, Concrete Reinforced, and Studio Models + Monsters. Concrete worked with the architects UNStudio on the Mercedes-Benz Museum shops and restaurants (Stuttgart, Germany, 2006), while recent and current work includes the citizenM Hotel, at Schiphol Airport (Amsterdam, the Netherlands, 2008); the Pearls and Caviar Restaurant (Abu Dhabi, UAE, 2008); VIP Lounge at Schiphol Airport (Amsterdam, the Netherlands, 2008); Supperclub (Singapore, 2008); De Bijenkorf Kitchen (Amsterdam, the Netherlands, 2008); Finca Pangola Eco Lodge (Costa Rica, 2009); Witteveen Brasserie, Ceintuurbaan (Amsterdam, the Netherlands, 2009, published here); Mazzo, Rozengracht (Amsterdam, the Netherlands, 2010, also published here); W Hotel (London, UK, 2010–11, also published here), citizenM Hotels in New York (USA, 2010–); Castell d'Emporda Hotel, Restaurant and Terrace (Girona, Spain, 2011–); and Hotel Bodrum (Bodrum, Turkey, 2011–).

Rob Wagemans wurde 1973 geboren. 1997 gründete er mit Gilian Schrofer und Erik van Dillen **CONCRETE ARCHITECTURAL ASSOCIATES**, ein Büro für Innen- architektur. Wagemans studierte Architektur in Amsterdam und Utrecht und schloss sein Studium mit einem M.Arch. (Schwerpunkt Innenarchitektur) ab. Das Büro be- schäftigt 30 Mitarbeiter, darunter Innenarchitekten, Produkt-, Kommunikations- und Grafikdesigner sowie Architekten. Die Firma gliedert sich in drei Bereiche: Concrete Architectural Associates, Concrete Reinforced sowie Studio Models + Monsters. Mit UNStudio arbeitete Concrete an den Museumsshops und -restaurants des Mercedes- Benz Museums (Stuttgart, Deutschland, 2006). Jüngere Projekte sind u. a. das Hotel citizenM am Flughafen Schiphol (Amsterdam, 2008), das Pearls & Caviar Restaurant (Abu Dhabi, VAE, 2008), die VIP Lounge am Flughafen Schiphol (Amsterdam, 2008), der Supperclub (Singapur, 2008), das Restaurant De Bijenkorf Kitchen (Amsterdam, 2008), die Finca Pangola Eco Lodge (Costa Rica, 2009), die Witteveen Brasserie, Ceintuurbaan (Amsterdam, 2009, hier vorgestellt), Mazzo, Rozengracht (Amsterdam, 2010, ebenfalls hier vorgestellt), das W Hotel am Leicester Square (London, 2010–11, ebenfalls hier vorgestellt), die Hotels citizenM in New York (USA, seit 2010), das Hotel Castell d'Emporda mit Restaurant und Terrasse (Girona, Spanien, seit 2011) sowie das Hotel Bodrum (Bodrum, Türkei, seit 2011).

Rob Wagemans est né en 1973. Il a créé le cabinet d'architecture intérieure **CONCRETE ARCHITECTURAL ASSOCIATES** en 1997 avec Gilian Schrofer et Erik van Dillen. Il a fait ses études aux académies d'architecture d'Amsterdam et d'Utrecht et a obtenu un M.Arch spécialisé en architecture d'intérieur. La société de 30 employés compte des architectes d'intérieur, des créateurs de produits, des designers communication, des graphistes et des architectes. Elle est divisée en trois sections : Concrete Architectural Associates, Concrete Reinforced et Studio Models + Monsters. Concrete a travaillé avec les architectes d'UNStudio aux boutiques et restaurants du musée Mercedes-Benz (Stuttgart, 2006), ses réalisations récentes et en cours comprennent : l'hôtel citizenM de l'aéroport de Schiphol (Amsterdam, 2008) ; le restaurant Pearls and Caviar (Abou Dhabi, EAU, 2008) ; l'espace VIP de l'aéroport de Schiphol (Amsterdam, 2008) ; le Supperclub (Singapour, 2008) ; le restau- rant De Bijenkorf Kitchen (Amsterdam, 2008) ; l'écolodge Finca Pangola (Costa Rica, 2009) ; la brasserie Witteveen de Ceintuurbaan (Amsterdam, 2009, publiée ici) ; le Mazzo, Rozengracht (Amsterdam, 2010, publié ici) ; l'hôtel W (Londres, 2010–11, publié ici) ; les hôtels citizenM de New York (2010–) ; l'hôtel-restaurant Castell d'Em- porda et sa terrasse (Gérone, Espagne, 2011–) et l'hôtel Bodrum (Bodrum, Turquie, 2011–).

WITTEVEEN BRASSERIE

Ceintuurbaan, Amsterdam, The Netherlands, 2009

Address: Ceintuurbaan 256–260, 1071 GH Amsterdam, The Netherlands,
+31 20 344 64 06, info@brasseriewitteveen.nl, www.brasseriewitteveen.nl
Area: 400 m². Client: IQ Creative. Cost: not disclosed

The décor is reductive but convivial, relying on repetitive elements such as the lighting fixtures and the colorful floor-tile patterns.

Das Dekor ist reduziert und einladend zugleich und verdankt seine Wirkung besonders einigen sich wiederholenden Motiven wie den Leuchten oder den bunten Bodenfliesen.

Le décor restreint mais convivial est basé sur la répétition d'éléments tels que les luminaires et les carreaux colorés du sol.

The bar holds a central place in the establishment, as seen in these photos, or in the section drawing below.

Die Bar ist der Dreh- und Angelpunkt der Brasserie, wie diese Aufnahmen und der Querschnitt unten belegen.

Le bar occupe une place centrale dans l'établissement, tel qu'on peut le voir sur ces photos ou sur le plan en coupe ci-dessous.

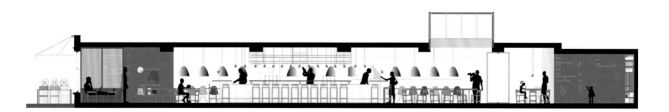

The IQ Creative group decided to revive this restaurant that was a well-known fixture of Amsterdam in the 1970s and 1980s. Referring to the Dutch tradition of putting Persian rugs on tables, Concrete designed a floor made of Portuguese cement tiles that recall the pattern of these rugs. In the style of a brasserie, **WITTEVEEN** is both a bar and a restaurant, open all day. The oak-top bar is clad with the same white metro tiles used in the restaurant area. A handmade 15-meter-long couch marks the café section of Witteveen. With its views into the kitchen, the restaurant is marked by three four-meter-long oak tables lined against the wall. Vintage Eames Dowel-Leg Side Chairs are provided for 14 guests at each table. A wine chamber with a bar and six stools, a fireplace room, and a family room round out the spaces of Witteveen, together with a year-round terrace covered by three gray canvas awnings. Concrete also developed the graphic design of Witteveen.

IQ Creative hatte die Idee, das Restaurant Witteveen – in den 1970er- und 1980er-Jahren ein fester Begriff in Amsterdam – neu aufleben zu lassen. In Anspielung auf die niederländische Eigenheit, kleine Perserteppiche auf Tische zu legen, entwarf Concrete einen Boden aus portugiesischen Zementfliesen, dessen Muster an diese Teppiche erinnert. **WITTEVEEN** ist eine Brasserie und damit zugleich Bar und Restaurant und den ganzen Tag geöffnet. Die Front der Eichenbar wurde mit denselben weißen Fliesen verblendet wie die Wände im Restaurantbereich. Markantes Merkmal der Cafézone ist ein 15 m langes, handgefertigtes Sofa. Im Restaurantbereich reihen sich drei 4 m lange Tische mit Blick auf die Küche an der Wand aneinander. An jedem Tisch finden bis zu 14 Gäste auf klassischen Eames-Dowel-Leg-Stühlen Platz. Eine Weinbar mit sechs Hockern, ein Kaminzimmer und ein Spielzimmer sowie eine ganzjährig nutzbare Terrasse mit grauen Segeltuchmarkisen vervollständigen das Angebot von Witteveen. Concrete gestaltete außerdem das grafische Erscheinungsbild des Restaurants.

Le groupe IQ Creative voulait faire revivre ce restaurant très connu à Amsterdam dans les années 1970 et 1980. En référence à la tradition néerlandaise de placer de petits tapis persans sur les tables, Concrete a imaginé un sol en carreaux de ciment portugais qui en rappellent les motifs. Dans le style d'une brasserie, **WITTEVEEN** est à la fois un bar et un restaurant, ouvert toute la journée. Le bar recouvert de chêne est revêtu des mêmes tuiles métro blanches que dans le restaurant. Le café est dominé par un canapé fait main de 15 m de long. Le restaurant, avec vue sur la cuisine, s'articule autour de trois tables de chêne de 4 m alignées contre le mur, chacune entourée de 14 chaises vintage Dowel-Leg d'Eames. Une cave de dégustation avec un bar et six tabourets, un coin du feu et une pièce familiale complètent les différents espaces de Witteveen avec une terrasse ouverte toute l'année et couverte de trois stores de toile grise. Concrete a également créé le graphisme de Witteveen.

With its visible ducts the Brasserie evoke an urban atmosphere whose conviviality is generated by careful attention to lighting and color schemes.

Durch die offenen Versorgungsleitungen gewinnt der Raum urbanes Flair. Einladend wird er durch sorgsam gewählte Details, etwa die Leuchten und die Farbpalette.

Avec ses canalisations apparentes, la brasserie évoque une ambiance urbaine dont la convivialité est assurée par la grande attention portée à l'éclairage et aux couleurs.

A children's play area, and a wine space are seen above. A large table with newspapers for clients is typical of Dutch bars and restaurants.

Oben der Spielbereich für Kinder und die Weinbar. Ein großer Tisch, auf dem Zeitungen für Gäste ausliegen, ist typisch für Bars und Restaurants in den Niederlanden.

Ci-dessus, l'espace de jeu pour les enfants et celui dédié au vin. La grande table garnie de journaux est typique des bars et restaurants néerlandais.

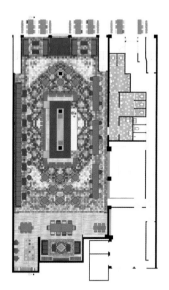

W HOTEL
London, UK, 2010–11

Address: 10 Wardour Street, Leicester Square, London W1D 6QF, UK, +44 20 77 58 10 00, www.wlondon.co.uk
Area: 8100 m². Client: McAleer & Rushe Group, Starwood Hotels and Resorts
Cost: not disclosed

A proliferation of faceted balls hanging from the ceiling and shiny desks greet guests in the check-in area of the hotel.

Ein Meer hängender Diskokugeln und hochglänzende Empfangstresen begrüßen die Gäste im Empfangsbereich des Hotels.

Une abondance de boules à facettes suspendues au plafond et des comptoirs scintillants accueillent les clients dans la réception de l'hôtel.

The check-in desks seen from another angle near the elevators. Right, a very large illuminated "W" signals the name of the hotel at the entrance.

Die Empfangstresen aus einem Blickwinkel bei den Aufzügen. Am Eingang signalisiert ein übergroßes „W" den Namen des Hotels.

Les comptoirs d'enregistrement vus sous un autre angle depuis les ascenseurs. À droite, un immense « W » illuminé indique le nom de l'hôtel dès l'entrée.

Areas worthy of particular attention in the **W HOTEL** designed by Concrete include the Sweat and AWAY Spa overlooking Leicester Square. The space has dark gray rubber flooring, multiple flat screens on the back wall, and two special wallpaper pieces, depicting dancers in sparkles of light by Marcel van der Vlugt. Saunas and steam baths share unisex cubicles with showers, toilets, and changing facilities. Spice Market London has a two-story, 24-meter-long spice cabinet. Gold mesh sliding screens, brass screen lanterns, *jatoba timbo* flooring, cozy booths, brass "birdcage" spiral stairs, and 600 wok-lights also mark the space. Monumental brass lanterns compliment the wok lamps for the lighting. Concrete also worked on room design ranging from the standard "Wonderful Room" to the Spectacular, Fabulous, Fantastic, Marvelous, and Wow Suites. The W Hotel entry has black granite floor tiles, black glass and frosted mirror walls, and a "cloud of 280 mirror balls mounted from the ceiling."

Zu den bemerkenswertesten Bereichen des **W HOTEL** zählt das von Concrete gestaltete Sweat and AWAY Spa mit Blick auf den Leicester Square: ein Raum mit dunkelgrauem Gummiboden, Flachbildschirmen an den Wänden und zwei großen Wandtapeten von Marcel van der Vlugt, die Tänzer in flirrendem Licht zeigen. Sauna und Dampfbad sind mit Unisex-Kabinen, Duschen, Toiletten und Umkleiden ausgestattet. Markenzeichen des Restaurants Spice Market London ist ein zweistöckiges, 24 m langes Gewürzregal; weitere Highlights sind die goldenen Metallparavents, Messinglaternen, ein Boden aus *jatoba timbo*, gemütliche Sitzkojen, eine von Messingstäben umschlossene Wendeltreppe sowie 600 Wokleuchten. Daneben sorgen monumentale Messinglaternen für Licht. Concrete gestaltete auch die Hotelzimmer, vom Standardzimmer „Wonderful Room" über die Kategorien Spectacular, Fabulous, Fantastic und Marvelous bis hin zu den sogenannten Wow-Suiten. Die Lobby des W Hotel wurde mit schwarzem Granitboden, schwarz mattiertem Spiegelglas und einer „Wolke aus 280 von der Decke hängenden Discokugeln" ausgestattet.

Le spa Sweat and AWAY qui donne sur Leicester Square est l'un des espaces les plus dignes d'attention de l'**HÔTEL W** conçu par Concrete. Le revêtement du sol est un caoutchouc gris sombre, le mur du fond comporte de multiples écrans plats et deux papiers peints représentant des danseurs dans des scintillements de lumière sont de Marcel van der Vlugt. Les saunas et bains de vapeur partagent des cabines unisexes avec douches et toilettes. Sur deux niveaux, le restaurant Spice Market London possède un cabinet d'épices long de 24 m. L'espace est marqué par les panneaux coulissants au maillage doré, les lanternes de bronze, le sol de jatoba timbo, les box confortables, la « volière » de bronze, l'escalier en colimaçon et les 600 lampes woks que complètent de monumentales lanternes de bronze. Concrete a aussi contribué au design intérieur, de la « chambre Merveilleuse » standard aux suites Spectaculaire, Fabuleuse, Fantastique, Merveilleuse et Wow. L'entrée de l'hôtel W est pavée de granit noir, les murs sont couverts de verre noir et de miroirs dépolis et un « nuage de 280 sphères miroir descend du plafond ».

A warm atmosphere and a central spiral staircase characterize the bar and dining area designed by Concrete for the W Hotel.

Bar und Restaurant des W Hotel, ebenfalls von Concrete entworfen, zeichnen sich durch ihre warme Atmosphäre und eine Wendeltreppe mitten im Raum aus.

L'espace bar et restaurant créé par Concrete pour l'hôtel W est caractérisé par une atmosphère chaleureuse et un escalier en colimaçon central.

A bar space shows the ability of the designers to vary the styles and effects they employ without undue heterogeneity. The project took 13 months to complete and was inaugurated on February 14, 2011.

Ein Barbereich belegt die Fähigkeit der Architekten, Stil- und Effektpalette zu variieren, ohne allzu heterogen zu werden. Das Projekt wurde in 13 Monaten realisiert und konnte am 14. Februar 2011 eröffnet werden.

Un espace bar montre le talent des designers à varier les styles et les effets sans obtenir un ensemble trop hétéroclite pour autant. Il a fallu 13 mois pour achever le projet, qui a été inauguré le 14 février 2011.

The design plays on contrasts between light and dark. Below, a gym
area. The overall design relies fre
quently on flowing curves.

*Das Design spielt mit dem Kontrast
von Licht und Dunkel. Unten ein Blick
in den Fitnessbereich. Insgesamt
setzt der Entwurf besonders auf flie-
ßende Formen.*

*Le design joue sur le contraste entre
l'obscurité et la lumière. Ci-dessous,
une salle de gymnastique. Les
courbes fluides dominent souvent le
design global.*

In the lobby, a hanging white architectonic element echoes the dark profile of the structured couch blocks.

Das hängende weiße architektonische Element in der Lobby greift die dunklen Konturen der strukturierten Sofalandschaft auf.

Dans le hall, un élément architectural blanc suspendu fait écho à la ligne sombre du bloc de canapés structurés.

An all-red bar seems to invite patrons to partake of somewhat sinful pleasures, in contrast with the white and black or willfully shiny atmosphere in lobby areas.

Die ganz in Rot gehaltene Bar verführt die Gäste zu kleinen Sünden: Ein auffälliger Gegensatz zum Schwarz-Weiß-Schema und den hochglänzenden Oberflächen im Lobbybereich.

Un bar tout en rouge semble inviter les clients à des plaisirs quelque peu coupables et contraste avec le noir et ·blanc ou l'atmosphère volontairement scintillante des différents espaces du hall.

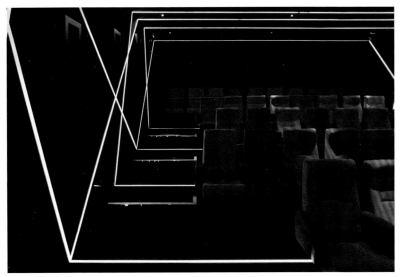

A small auditorium or theater space also makes use of a warm red palette to create an inviting ambiance. Concrete was responsible for 8000 square meters of space in the hotel.

Um ein einladendes Ambiente zu schaffen, wurde beim kleinen Kino- bzw. Theatersaal auf dieselbe warm-rote Palette gesetzt. Concrete zeichnete für die Gestaltung von insgesamt 8000 m² Gesamtfläche im Hotel verantwortlich.

Le petit auditorium ou théâtre a lui aussi recours à une palette de rouges chauds pour créer une atmosphère engageante. Concrete a été chargé d'agencer 8000 m² dans l'hôtel.

MAZZO

Rozengracht, Amsterdam, The Netherlands, 2010

*Address: Rozengracht 114, 1016 NH Amsterdam, The Netherlands, +31 20 344 64 02,
info@mazzoamsterdam.nl, www.mazzoamsterdam.nl. Area: 400 m²
Client: IQ Creative. Cost: not disclosed*

MAZZO, like the Witteveen Brasserie (page 132), is part of the IQ Creative group. Mazzo was a "famous and notorious disco" until six years ago. The bar is located in five-meter-high spaces on the Rozengracht. The darkest area in the old building was chosen for the kitchen, facing a restaurant seating area. Dear Ingo lights by Moooi are used in this seating area. Four portraits "provide an Italian family feeling." Another smaller space is the boardroom with its TV screen and fireplace, where family or business dinners can be organized. A narrower back room facing the Bloemstraat is used as a children's space during the day or a lounge with an 11-meter couch at night. A large-scale solid pine cupboard goes through all the spaces and unites the design. Concrete, chipped brickwork, stone, pine, and raw steel are the dominant materials. The designers added only the steel and wood elements to the original building. A "light object" made of raw steel in the form of the name Mazzo hangs above the bar.

MAZZO wird wie die Brasserie Witteveen (Seite 132) von IQ Creative betrieben. Bis vor sechs Jahren war Mazzo noch eine „berühmt-berüchtigte Disco". Die Bar liegt in 5 m hohen Räumen an der Rozengracht. Die Küche wurde im dunkelsten Bereich der Altbauräumlichkeiten mit Blick auf den Gastraum untergebracht. Im dort gelegenen Gastbereich hängen Dear-Ingo-Leuchten von Moooi. Vier großformatige Porträts „sorgen für italienisches Familiengefühl". Ein weiterer kleiner Bereich ist das „Sitzungszimmer" mit Monitor und Kamin, der für Familien- und Geschäftsessen genutzt werden kann. Ein schmales Hinterzimmer zur Bloemstraat dient tagsüber als Spielzimmer, abends als Lounge mit einer 11 m langen Couch. Ein großes Regal aus massiver Kiefer zieht sich als verbindendes Element durch den gesamten Raum. Vorherrschende Materialien sind Beton, freigelegtes Mauerwerk, Stein, Kiefernholz und Rohstahl. Einzig die Stahl- und Holzelemente wurden von den Architekten neu in den Altbau eingefügt. Über der Bar hängt der Schriftzug Mazzo als Lichtobjekt aus Rohstahl.

Comme la brasserie Witteveen (page 132), le **MAZZO** appartient au groupe IQ Creative. C'était une discothèque « famous and notorious » jusqu'il y a six ans. Le bar occupe des espaces de 5 m de haut dans la Rozengracht. La partie la plus sombre du bâtiment ancien a été dévolue à la cuisine, face à un espace de restauration aux lampes Dear Ingo par Moooi. Quatre portraits y « donnent une ambiance de famille italienne ». La salle de conférences occupe un autre espace plus petit avec un écran de télévision et une cheminée pour des repas d'affaires ou familiaux. À l'arrière, une pièce plus étroite qui donne sur la Bloemstraat est ouverte aux enfants la journée et tient lieu de salon avec un canapé long de 11 m le soir. Un immense placard massif en pin traverse les différents espaces dont il unifie le design. Les matériaux dominants sont le béton, les briques écornées, la pierre, le pin et l'acier brut, les designers n'ayant ajouté que ces deux derniers à la construction d'origine. Un « objet lumineux » d'acier brut formant le nom Mazzo est suspendu au-dessus du bar.

Fitting well into the line of façades along the Rozengracht, Mazzo can be understood as a subtle and successful combination of contemporary design with the feeling of an old restaurant.

Mazzo fügt sich ganz selbstverständlich in die Fassaden an der Rozengracht ein und kann als subtile und gelungene Verbindung aus zeitgenössischem Design und dem Flair eines alten Restaurants gelten.

Bien intégré à l'alignement de façades de la Rozengracht, le Mazzo peut être compris comme une combinaison subtile et réussie entre le design contemporain et l'atmosphère d'un restaurant ancien.

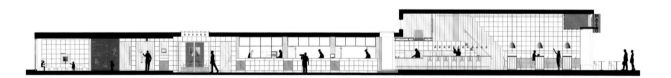

Different types of chairs and tables, combined with a repetition of items like the lighting fixtures, give a feeling of warm continuity not marked by the minimalism of past years.

Eine bunte Mischung verschiedener Tische und Stühle in Kombination mit wiederkehrenden Elementen wie den Leuchten sorgen für warme Beständigkeit jenseits des Minimalismus vergangener Jahre.

Différents modèles de tables et de chaises, associés à des objets répétés comme les luminaires, donnent un sentiment de continuité chaleureuse que ne marque plus le minimalisme des dernières années.

Large-scale photos of people eating with their hands mark the dining area. Below, a floor plan of Mazzo.

Großformatige Porträts von Menschen, die mit den Händen essen, dominieren den Gastraum. Unten ein Grundriss des Restaurants.

L'espace restauration est souligné par les photos grand format d'individus qui mangent avec les mains. Ci-dessous, un plan de niveau du Mazzo.

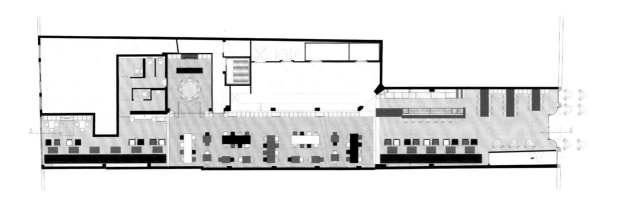

IVAN COTADO

Ivan Cotado
C/ Monte das Moas 15D, Office 6
15009 A Coruña
Spain

Tel: +34 981 92 26 96
E-mail: info@ivancotado.es
Web: www.ivancotado.es

IVAN COTADO was born in 1980 in O Barco de Valdeorras, Spain. He attended the Superior Technical School of Architecture in A Coruña (1998–2002), specializing in interior design. He created his own firm in A Coruña in 2005. Cotado says that it is important for him never to repeat an idea, a material, or a concept because he believes "in the realization of personal feelings and these are always unique." His work includes the A Coruña Apartment (A Coruña, 2005); El Sueño Húmedo Lounge Bar (O Barco de Valdeorras, Orense, 2006, published here); Glup Glup Jabonería (A Coruña, 2007); Tu Vision Óptica (Ponferrada, 2007); Gayco (Ponferrada, 2007); and a Madrid apartment (Madrid, 2010). Ongoing projects include the Vulcano Lounda (Medina de Rioseco, 2011–); Mundaka World (Milladoiro, Santiago de Compostela, 2011–); and the Aurum Hotel (O Barco de Valdeorras, Orense, 2011–), all in Spain.

IVAN COTADO wurde 1980 in O Barco de Valdeorras in Spanien geboren. Er besuchte die Technische Hochschule für Architektur in A Coruña (1998–2002), wo er sich auf Innenarchitektur spezialisierte. 2005 gründete er sein Büro in A Coruña. Cotado betont, ihm sei wichtig, keinerlei Ideen, Materialien oder Konzepte zu wiederholen, da er „an die Umsetzung persönlicher Empfindungen" glaubt, die „immer einzigartig" seien. Zu seinen Entwürfen zählen das Apartment A Coruña (A Coruña, 2005), die Lounge Bar El Sueño Húmedo (O Barco de Valdeorras, Orense, 2006, hier vorgestellt), Glup Glup Jabonería (A Coruña, 2007), Tu Vision Óptica (Ponferrada, 2007), Gayco (Ponferrada, 2007) sowie ein Apartment in Madrid (2010). Laufende Projekte sind u. a. Vulcano Lounda (Medina de Rioseco, seit 2011), Mundaka World (Milladoiro, Santiago de Compostela, seit 2011) und das Hotel Aurum (O Barco de Valdeorras, Orense, seit 2011), alle in Spanien.

IVAN COTADO est né en 1980 à O Barco de Valdeorras, Espagne. Il a suivi les cours de l'École supérieure technique de La Corogne (1998–2002) et s'est spécialisé en architecture d'intérieur. Il a créé son entreprise à La Corogne en 2005. Il importe toujours à Cotado de ne jamais répéter une idée, une matière ou un concept car il croit « en la réalisation de sentiments personnels et ces derniers sont toujours uniques ». Ses réalisations comprennent : l'appartement A Coruña (La Corogne, 2005) ; le lounge bar El Sueño Húmedo (O Barco de Valdeorras, Orense, Espagne, 2006, publié ici) ; la boutique de savon Glup Glup (La Corogne, 2007) ; l'opticien Tu Vision (Ponferrada, Espagne, 2007) ; le magasin Gayco (Ponferrada, 2007) et un appartement à Madrid (2010). Ses projets en cours comptent : Vulcano Lounda (Medina de Rioseco, 2011–) ; Mundaka World (Milladoiro, Saint-Jacques-de-Compostelle, 2011–) et l'hôtel Aurum (O Barco de Valdeorras, Orense, 2011–), tous en Espagne.

EL SUEÑO HÚMEDO LOUNGE BAR

O Barco de Valdeorras, Orense, Spain, 2006

Address: Pza. José Otero, s/n. O Barco de Valdeorras, Orense, Spain
Area: 90 m². Client: Nosgusloscu, SL. Cost: not disclosed

Variable colored lighting schemes, on the walls, ceilings, or even the floors, can modify the mood of the space.

Die Farben des Lichts an Wänden, Decken und sogar Böden können variiert werden und so die Stimmung des Raums verändern.

Des éclairages aux couleurs changeantes, sur les murs, les plafonds, ou même les sols, peuvent modifier l'ambiance de l'espace.

A façade view only suggests the
activity on the inside. Furnishings and
decorative elements are the same
throughout, giving a feeling of design
continuity, altered by changes in
color as required.

Ein Blick auf die Fassade lässt nur
ahnen, was sich hinter ihr verbirgt.
Einheitliches Mobiliar und Dekor im
gesamten Raum zeugen von gestalte-
rischer Konsequenz, können jedoch in
unterschiedliche Lichtstimmungen
getaucht werden.

La façade ne fait que suggérer l'activité de l'intérieur. Les meubles et
éléments de décor sont partout les
mêmes, donnant une impression de
continuité du design modifiée par les
changements de couleur à volonté.

A good part of the atmosphere of this lounge bar is based on a mixture of natural light and RGB LED lights that change according to the moment or the needs of the bar. Internally lit tables and backlit bands running along the bottom of the bar also contribute to the light effects. The use of computer-controlled LED lighting has had a considerable impact on interior design, in particular in such areas as fashion or bars and restaurants. Where each color formerly required its own lights, a LED can change color in a preordained or random sequence, changing mood and with it the perception of the interior design as a whole. Beyond the matter of lighting, Cotado says: "Bottle racks and bottles, never considered as design, are now elegantly intermingled with seating, bar, floor, and ceiling."

Einen Großteil ihrer Atmosphäre verdankt diese Lounge und Bar dem Zusammenspiel von Tageslicht und RGB-LEDs, die je nach Tageszeit oder Anforderungen der Bar in anderen Farben leuchten. Auch die von innen beleuchteten Tische und die Lichtstreifen auf dem Boden vor der Bar tragen zum Lichtspiel bei. Der Einsatz von computergesteuerten LEDs gewinnt in der Innenarchitektur immer größere Bedeutung, insbesondere in der Modebranche sowie in Bars und Restaurants. Erforderte früher noch jede Farbe ein eigenes Leuchtmittel, so lassen sich heutige LEDs in festgelegten oder zufälligen Sequenzen auf Farbwechsel programmieren, schaffen verschiedene Stimmungen und beeinflussen unsere Wahrnehmung eines Interieurs in seiner Gesamtheit. Abgesehen vom Licht merkt Cotado an: „Auch Flaschen und Flaschenregale, sonst nicht als Gestaltungselement gewürdigt, wurden hier elegant zwischen Sitzgelegenheiten, Bar, Boden und Decke integriert."

L'atmosphère de ce *lounge bar* est due en grande partie à un mélange de lumière naturelle et de lampes RGB à LED qui changent de couleur selon le moment ou les besoins. Des tables éclairées de l'intérieur et des bandes rétroéclairées qui longent le bar sur le sol contribuent aussi aux effets lumineux. L'utilisation d'un éclairage à LED contrôlé par ordinateur a un impact considérable sur le design intérieur, en particulier dans les endroits à la mode ou les bars et restaurants : si chaque couleur nécessitait autrefois sa propre lampe, une LED peut changer de teinte selon un ordre prédéfini ou aléatoire et modifier à chaque fois l'atmosphère et la perception du décor. Outre l'éclairage, Cotado a aménagé «les casiers à bouteilles et les bouteilles, qui n'étaient jamais considérés comme des éléments de design, et se mêlent désormais avec élégance aux sièges, au bar, au sol et au plafond».

Typical first names of men and women are marked on doors. To the right, an electric purple ambiance highlights the forms of the bar.

Typische männliche und weibliche Vornamen schmücken diese zwei Türen. Die Formen der Bar werden durch das faszinierende violette Lichtspiel betont.

Des prénoms masculins et féminins typiques sont inscrits sur les portes. À droite, une atmosphère violet électrique souligne les formes du bar.

ODILE DECQ BENOÎT CORNETTE

Odile Decq Benoît Cornette
Architectes Urbanistes
11 Rue des Arquebusiers
75003 Paris
France

Tel: +33 1 42 71 27 41 / Fax: +33 1 42 71 27 42
E-mail: odbc@odbc-paris.com
Web: www.odbc-paris.com

ODILE DECQ was born in 1955 in Laval, France, and obtained her degree in Architecture (DPLG) at UP6 in Paris in 1978. She studied Urbanism at the Institut d'Études Politiques in Paris (1979) and founded her office in 1980. Her former partner Benoît Cornette died in 1998. She has designed a number of apartment buildings in Paris; the French Pavilion at the 1996 Architecture Biennale in Venice (Italy); three buildings for Nantes University (1993–99); a refurbishment of the Conference Hall of Unesco in Paris (France, 2001); renovation of the Cureghem Veterinary School in Brussels (Belgium, 2001); and the Liaunig Museum (Neuhaus, Austria, 2004). Decq has been very much in the news with her recent MACRO Museum of Contemporary Art in Rome (Italy, 2004–10) and the Opéra Restaurant (Paris, France, 2008–11, published here). Winner of the Golden Lion at the Venice Architecture Biennale (1996) and the 1999 Benedictus Award for the Faculty of Economics and the Law Library at the University of Nantes, she is currently building the Flying Horse House (CIPEA, Nanjing, China) and continues work on the FRAC Contemporary Art Center in Rennes (France).

ODILE DECQ wurde 1955 in Laval, Frankreich, geboren und erlangte ihr Architekturdiplom (DPLG) 1978 an der UP6 in Paris. Sie studierte Städtebau am Institut d'Etudes Politiques in Paris (1979) und gründete 1980 ihr Büro. Ihr Partner Benoît Cornette verstarb 1998. Sie entwarf eine Reihe von Apartmenthäusern in Paris, den französischen Pavillon auf der Architekturbiennale 1996 in Venedig, drei Gebäude für die Universität Nantes (1993–99), verantwortete die Sanierung des Kongresszentrums der UNESCO in Paris (2001), die Sanierung der Fakultät für Veterinärmedizin Cureghem in Brüssel (2001) und das Museum Liaunig (Neuhaus, Österreich, 2004). Decq war mit ihrem jüngst realisierten MACRO Museum für zeitgenössische Kunst in Rom (2004–10) und dem Restaurant L'Opéra (Paris, 2008–11, hier vorgestellt) vielfach in den Medien. Odile Decq wurde mit dem Goldenen Löwen der Architekturbiennale Venedig (1996) sowie dem Benedictus-Preis der Fakultät für Wirtschaft und Recht der Universität Nantes (1999) ausgezeichnet. Derzeit im Bau sind das Flying Horse House (CIPEA, Nanjing, China) und das Zentrum für Zeitgenössische Kunst FRAC in Rennes (Frankreich).

ODILE DECQ, née en 1955 à Laval, est diplômée en architecture (DPLG) de l'UP6 (Paris, 1978). Elle a étudié l'urbanisme à l'Institut d'études politiques de Paris (1979) et créé son agence en 1980 avec son associé Benoît Cornette, décédé en 1998. Parmi ses réalisations figurent de nombreux immeubles de logements à Paris ; le Pavillon français à la Biennale d'architecture de Venise 1996 ; trois immeubles pour l'université de Nantes (1993–99) ; la rénovation de la salle de conférence de l'UNESCO à Paris (2001) ; la rénovation de l'École vétérinaire de Cureghem à Bruxelles (2001) et le musée Liaunig (Neuhaus, Autriche, 2004). Decq a beaucoup fait parler d'elle récemment avec le Musée d'art contemporain MACRO à Rome (2004–10) et le restaurant l'Opéra (Paris, 2008–11, publié ici). Lauréate du Lion d'or de la Biennale d'architecture de Venise 1996 et du prix Benedictus 1999 pour la faculté d'économie et la bibliothèque de droit de l'université de Nantes, elle construit actuellement la Maison du cheval volant (CIPEA, Nankin) et travaille au centre d'art contemporain FRAC de Rennes.

L'OPÉRA RESTAURANT

Paris, France, 2008–11

Address: Place Jacques Rouché, 75009 Paris, France, tel: 01 42 68 86 80, fax: 01 42 68 86 89,
www.opera-restaurant.fr. Area: 1100 m². Client: Gumery. Cost: €6 million

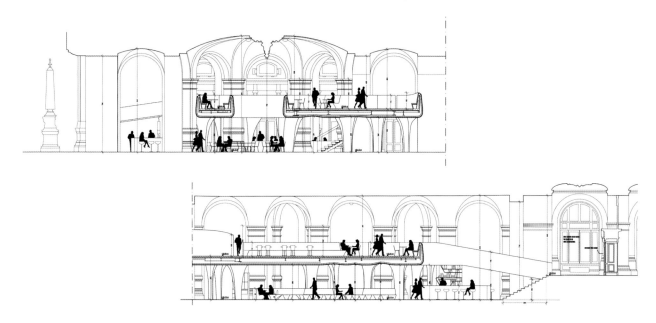

Located behind the east façade of the famous Opéra Garnier in Paris, this restaurant occupies spaces where horse-drawn carriages entered when the building was first erected. Given the historic monument status of the building, Odile Decq was obliged to create the restaurant without making use of any of the original walls, pillars, or ceiling. A "veil of undulating glass," held in place by a single strip of steel, was erected between the pillars. The program required that the restaurant be able to seat 90 and the architect accommodated this capacity with an added mezzanine situated in a "molded plaster hull." Odile Decq states: "Like a 'phantom,' silent and insidious, the soft protean curves of the mezzanine level float above the dinner guests, covering the space with a surface that bends and undulates." A lounge area, more intimate than the main dining space, is located at the back of the restaurant, with a long black bar and red booths. "The design for this project is based around creating a space that will highlight the restaurant inside the Opéra Garnier, without mimicking the existing monument, but respecting it while affirming its truly contemporary character," concludes Odile Decq.

Hinter der Ostfassade der berühmten Pariser Opéra Garnier liegt das Restaurant dort, wo früher die Pferdekutschen einfuhren. Die Denkmalschutzauflagen für das Gebäude stellten Odile Decq vor die Aufgabe, das Restaurant ohne jegliche Eingriffe in die historischen Mauern, Säulen oder Decken zu realisieren. So wurde zwischen den Säulen ein „geschwungener Glasvorhang" installiert, der lediglich mit einem Stahlband fixiert ist. Das Programm sah Kapazitäten für 90 Gäste vor, was die Architektin mit einem Mezzaningeschoss in „einem aus Gips geformten Körper" umsetzte. Odile Decq erklärt: „Still und heimlich, wie ein ‚Phantom', schweben die weichen, proteischen Kurven des Mezzanins über den Abendgästen und überfangen den Raum mit einer gewölbten, geschwungenen Decke." Im hinteren Bereich des Restaurants liegt eine Lounge, intimer als der Hauptsaal, mit einer langen schwarzen Bar und roten Nischen. „Der Entwurf entstand aus dem Gedanken, einen Raum zu schaffen, der das Restaurant in der Opéra Garnier ins rechte Licht rückt, ohne das alte Baudenkmal zu kopieren, sondern es respektiert und zugleich einen dezidiert zeitgenössischen Stil verfolgt", resümiert Odile Decq.

Situé derrière la façade est de l'opéra Garnier, à Paris, le restaurant occupe l'espace par lequel les attelages à chevaux entraient lorsque le bâtiment a été construit. Étant donné le caractère de « monument historique » de l'endroit, Odile Decq a été contrainte de laisser en l'état les murs, piliers et plafonds d'origine. Un « voile de verre ondulé » maintenu par une simple bande de métal a été érigé entre les piliers. Le cahier des charges prévoyait un restaurant de 90 places, une capacité que l'architecte a obtenue en ajoutant une mezzanine dans une « coque de plâtre moulée ». Selon les termes d'Odile Decq : « Comme un "fantôme", silencieux et insidieux, la mezzanine aux courbes douces et mouvantes flotte au-dessus des convives, nappant l'espace d'une surface sinueuse et ondulante. » Un espace salon, plus intime que la grande salle du restaurant, en occupe l'arrière avec un long bar noir et des alcôves rouges. « L'idée est de créer un espace qui mette en valeur le restaurant dans l'opéra Garnier sans pasticher le monument existant, mais en le respectant tout en affirmant son caractère résolument contemporain », conclut Odile Decq.

Section drawings show the volumes inserted by the architect into the venerable space of the Opéra Garnier. Right, curving surfaces, and bright red furnishings and carpets contrast with the old opera.

Querschnitte veranschaulichen die von der Architektin in die ehrwürdigen Räume der Opéra Garnier eingefügten Volumina. Rechts die mit dem alten Opernbau kontrastierenden, leuchtend roten Möbel und Teppiche.

Les plans en coupe montrent les volumes insérés par l'architecte au digne opéra Garnier. À droite, les surfaces courbes et le rouge vif des chaises et du tapis contrastent avec la construction ancienne.

A sensuous, curving seating area or cocktail space is located above the main part of the restaurant.

Sinnlich geschwungene Sitz- bzw. Cocktailnischen über dem zentralen Gastraum

Un espace cocktail assis aux courbes voluptueuses est situé au-dessus de la partie principale du restaurant.

Right, the Opéra Garnier seen from the outside at night. Interior views of Odile Decq's installation below show that it does not actually touch or interfere with the original architecture.

Rechts eine nächtliche Außenansicht der Opéra Garnier. Innenansichten der Installation von Odile Decq belegen, dass diese die alte bauliche Struktur tatsächlich nicht berührt oder in sie eingreift.

À droite, l'opéra Garnier la nuit vu de l'extérieur. Ci-dessous, les vues intérieures de l'installation d'Odile Decq montrent qu'elle n'altère ni n'affecte l'architecture originale.

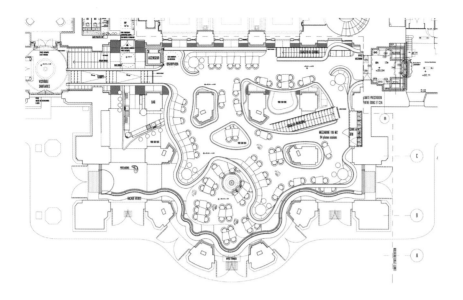

A plan showing the seating arrangements makes clear the emphasis on curving forms. The bright red and white curvilinear "object" that the architect inserted into the Napoleon III building can be seen in the two photos.

Ein Grundriss mit der Anordnung der Sitzgruppen macht deutlich, welch große Rolle geschwungene Formen hier spielen. Auf den Fotos das auffällig rot-weiße „Objekt", das die Architektin in den Bau aus Zeiten Napoleons III. setzte.

Un plan avec emplacements des sièges met en évidence l'accent qui est mis sur les formes courbes. L'« objet » curviligne rouge vif et blanc inséré par l'architecte au bâtiment Napoléon III peut être vu sur les deux photos.

TOM DIXON

Design Research Studio
The Wharf Building
344 Ladbroke Grove
London W10 5BU
UK

Tel: +44 20 74 00 05 26
Fax: +44 20 74 00 05 01
E-mail: contact@designresearchstudio.net
Web: www.designresearchstudio.net

TOM DIXON was born in 1959 in Sfax, Tunisia, and moved to the United Kingdom as a child. He began designing furniture in his 20s without formal training. Amongst his many well-known furniture designs, the S-bend Chair, Kitchen Chair, and Bird chaise longue have been fabricated by Capellini since the 1990s. Tom Dixon has taught at the Royal College of Art, Kingston Polytechnic, and Plymouth University, and was appointed head of design for Habitat in 1998. He is the Creative Director of British design brand Tom Dixon (established in 2002) and is also the Creative Director of the interior design arm of the brand Design Research Studio, which "is an interior design practice specializing in high-concept interiors, large-scale installations, and architectural design." Work of the Design Research Studio includes Tokyo Hipsters Club (Tokyo, Japan, 2006); Shoreditch House, a club created by Nick Jones (London, 2007); Paramount Club, located in the top three floors of Centre Point (London, 2008); the Joseph Store (London, 2009); Circus (London, 2010); the Tazmania Ballroom (Central district, Hong Kong, China, 2010, published here); and the Restaurant at the Royal Academy (London, 2011), all in the UK unless stated otherwise.

TOM DIXON wurde 1959 in Sfax, Tunesien, geboren und siedelte als Kind mit seiner Familie nach Großbritannien um. Mit Mitte 20 begann er, ohne formelle Ausbildung Möbel zu entwerfen. Seit den 1990er-Jahren wurden zahlreiche bekannt gewordene Entwürfe wie der Stuhl „S-bend", „Kitchen Chair" oder die Chaiselongue „Bird" von Capellini gefertigt. Tom Dixon lehrte am Royal College of Art, der Kingston Polytechnic und der Universität Plymouth und wurde 1998 Chefdesigner bei Habitat. Er ist Kreativdirektor des britischen Designunternehmens Tom Dixon (gegründet 2002) und Kreativdirektor der Innenarchitekturabteilung von Design Research Studio, „einem Büro für Innenarchitektur, das sich auf perfekt durchkonzeptionierte Interieurs, Großinstallationen und architektonische Gestaltung spezialisiert hat". Zu den Projekten von Design Research Studio zählen der Tokyo Hipsters Club (Tokio, 2006), Shoreditch House, ein von Nick Jones entworfener Club (London, 2007), der Paramount Club auf den obersten drei Etagen des Centre-Point-Hochhauses (London, 2008), der Joseph Store (London, 2009), das Circus (London, 2010), der Tazmania Ballroom (Central District, Hongkong, 2010, hier vorgestellt) und das Restaurant in der Royal Academy (London, 2011).

TOM DIXON est né en 1959 à Sfax, Tunisie, et a rejoint le Royaume-Uni dans son enfance. Il a commencé à imaginer des meubles dès ses vingt ans, sans aucune formation. Parmi ses nombreuses créations célèbres, la chaise *S-bend*, la chaise de cuisine et la chaise longue *Bird* sont fabriquées par Capellini depuis les années 1990. Tom Dixon a enseigné au Royal College of Art, à la Kingston Polytechnic et à l'université de Plymouth. Il a été nommé responsable du design d'Habitat en 1998. Il est le directeur artistique de la marque britannique Tom Dixon (créée en 2002) et du département Architecture d'intérieur de l'agence Design Research Studio, « un cabinet d'architecture intérieure spécialisé dans les intérieurs très conceptuels, les installations d'envergure et le design architectural ». Les réalisations de Design Research Studio comptent : le Tokyo Hipsters Club (Tokyo, 2006) ; le club Shoreditch House créé par Nick Jones (Londres, 2007) ; le Paramount Club, aux trois derniers étages du Centre Point (Londres, 2008) ; le magasin Joseph (Londres, 2009) ; le Circus (Londres, 2010) ; le club Tazmania Ballroom (Central district, Hong Kong, 2010, publié ici) et le restaurant de la Royal Academy (Londres, 2011), toutes au Royaume-Uni sauf mention contraire.

TAZMANIA BALLROOM

Central, Hong Kong, China, 2010

Address: 1/F LKF Tower, 33 Wyndham Street, Central, Hong Kong, China, +852 2801 5009,
info@tazmaniaballroom.com, www.tazmaniaballroom.com. Area: 300 m²
Client: Yield Trend Limited. Cost: not disclosed

The **TAZMANIA BALLROOM** is "an exclusive pool bar" in the Central district of Hong Kong. Tom Dixon's Design Research Studio was invited to create "a slick new interior," and inspiration, Dixon says, was "drawn from a traditional British games room and… reflected in elements such as the plaster book-lined feature wall and plush upholstery. These traditional items are contrasted with highly contemporary features, such as a blue chalk greeting station and an innovative cue storage case." The rough concrete of the building itself dictates the geometry of the interior wall finishes. A corridor with a faceted mirror cladding leads clients from the street into a "sharp rock cavern." Metal is used for the DJ booth, bar, and pool tables, in an unexpected departure from tradition.

Der **TAZMANIA BALLROOM** im Stadtteil Central in Hongkong ist „eine exklusive Billardbar". Tom Dixons Design Research Studio erhielt den Auftrag, „ein elegantes neues Interieur" zu gestalten. Inspiration fand Dixon im „traditionellen britischen Spielzimmer … was sich in Elementen wie der auffälligen Bücherwand aus Stuck und den luxuriösen Polstermöbeln widerspiegelt. Diese traditionellen Elemente kontrastieren mit ausgesprochen modernen Details wie dem im Blau von Billardkreide gehaltenen Empfangsbereich und einem ungewöhnlichen Queueschrank." Die geometrisch-skulpturale Ausgestaltung der Innenwände ergab sich geradezu zwingend aus der Sichtbetonoptik des Gebäudes. Durch einen mit facettierten Spiegeln verkleideten Korridor gelangen die Gäste von der Straße in eine „zerklüftete Felshöhle". Das DJ-Pult sowie die Bar und Pooltische in Metalloptik schaffen eine überraschende Distanz zur Tradition.

Le **TAZMANIA BALLROOM** est « un bar à billard sélect » situé dans le district central de Hong Kong. L'agence de Tom Dixon, Design Research Studio, a été invitée à créer « un nouvel intérieur lisse » et a puisé son inspiration « dans les salles de jeux traditionnelles britanniques… ce qui se reflète notamment dans le motif de livres alignés du mur de plâtre et les tissus luxueux. Ces éléments traditionnels contrastent avec d'autres extrêmement contemporains tels que la craie bleue de l'accueil et un espace de rangement allongé très innovant ». Le béton brut de la construction dicte la géométrie des finitions intérieures. Un couloir revêtu de miroirs à facettes mène les clients de la rue vers une « caverne taillée dans la roche ». Le métal se retrouve dans le box du DJ, le bar et les tables de la piscine et crée une distance inattendue avec la tradition.

A billiard table in front of the bar— the "plush" upholstery referred to by Tom Dixon, and the "plaster book-lined feature wall (below).

Ein Billardtisch im vorderen Bereich der Bar. Unten die „luxuriösen Polstermöbel" und die „auffällige Bücherwand aus Stuck".

Une table de billard devant le bar – le tissu « luxueux » évoqué par Tom Dixon et le motif de livres alignés du mur de plâtre (ci-dessous).

EVAN DOUGLIS

Evan Douglis Studio
63 Third Street, Suite 503
Troy, NY 12180
USA

Tel: +1 917 568 6337
E-mail: evan@evandouglis.com
Web: www.evandouglis.com

EVAN DOUGLIS participated in the Exchange Program of the Architectural Association in London (1980), before obtaining his B.A. degree from Cooper Union (1983) and his M.Arch from the Harvard GSD (1991). He worked in the offices of Tod Williams and Billie Tsien (1982–85), Emilio Ambasz (1985–87), and Agrest and Gandelsonas (1991–92), all in New York, before creating the Evan Douglis Studio in 1992. As he describes his work: "Evan Douglis Studio is an architecture and interdisciplinary design firm committed to the research and application of new self-generative systems, membrane technology, and contemporary fabrication techniques as applied to a range of projects." Douglis is currently the Dean of the School of Architecture at Rensselaer Polytechnic Institute (Troy, New York). His main projects include *Anamorphic Balloons* (Columbia University, New York, 2000); installation for a Jean Prouvé traveling exhibition (beginning in 2003); *Auto-Braids / Auto Breeding* (New York, Los Angeles, 2003–05); ECO Bars (Cape Verde Islands, Africa, 2003–04); and the REptile–Haku Japanese Restaurant (New York, 2005). More recent work includes *Helioscopes*, traveling mediascape (Orléans, France, 2004–05; Basel, Switzerland 2008); REptile, tile product line (2006–07); Moon Jelly, Choice: Kitchens and Bakery (Brooklyn, New York, 2009–10, published here); and "Blue Rain," a custom glass installation (Abu Dhabi, UAE, 2011), all in the USA unless stated otherwise.

EVAN DOUGLIS nahm am Austauschprogramm der Architectural Association in London (1980) teil, bevor er einen B.A. an der Cooper Union (1983) sowie einen M.Arch. an der Harvard GSD (1991) erwarb. Douglis arbeitete für so namhafte Büros wie Tod Williams und Billie Tsien (1982–85), Emilio Ambasz (1985–87) und Agrest & Gandelsonas (1991–92), alle in New York, ehe er 1992 sein eigenes Büro Evan Douglis Studio gründete. Er selbst nennt sein Studio „ein Architektur- und interdisziplinäres Büro, das sich der Erforschung und Anwendung neuartiger selbstgenerativer Systeme, der Membrantechnologie und aktuellen Fertigungsmethoden verschrieben hat, die auf ein breites Spektrum an Projekten angewendet werden". Douglis ist derzeit Dekan der Architekturfakultät am Rensselaer Polytechnic Institute (Troy, New York). Seine wichtigsten Projekte sind u. a. Anamorphic Balloons (Columbia University, New York, 2000), eine Installation für eine Jean-Prouvé-Wanderausstellung (seit 2003), Auto-Braids/Auto Breeding (New York, Los Angeles, 2003–05), die ECO Bars (Kap Verde, 2003–04) sowie das japanische Restaurant REptile–Haku (New York, 2005). Zu seinen jüngeren Arbeiten zählen Helioscopes, Wanderausstellung/Medienlandschaft (Orléans, 2004–05, Basel, 2008), die Fliesenkollektion REptile (2006–07), Moon Jelly, Choice: Kitchens and Bakery (Brooklyn, New York, 2009–10, hier vorgestellt) und *Blue Rain*, eine ortsspezifische Glasinstallation (Abu Dhabi, VAE, 2011).

EVAN DOUGLIS a participé au programme d'échange de l'Architectural Association de Londres (1980) avant d'obtenir un B.A. à Cooper Union (1983) et un M.Arch à Harvard GSD (1991). Il a travaillé dans les agences new-yorkaises de Tod Williams et Billie Tsien (1982–85), Emilio Ambasz (1985–87) et Agrest and Gandelsonas (1991–92) avant de fonder Evan Douglis Studio en 1992. Il décrit son travail comme suit : « Evan Douglis Studio est une agence d'architecture et de conception interdisciplinaire spécialisée dans la recherche et l'application de nouveaux systèmes autogénératifs, de la technologie des membranes et des techniques de production contemporaines telles qu'elles sont utilisées dans de nombreux projets. » Douglis est doyen de l'école d'architecture du Rensselaer Polytechnic Institute (Troy, New York). Ses projets principaux comprennent : *Anamorphic Balloons* (université Columbia, New York, 2000) ; une installation pour une exposition itinérante de Jean Prouvé (commencée en 2003) ; *Auto-Braids/Auto Breeding* (New York, Los Angeles, 2003–05) ; les bars ECO (Cap-Vert, 2003–04) et le restaurant japonais REptile–Haku (New York, 2005). Parmi ses réalisations plus récentes figurent : *Helioscopes*, un voyage médiatique (Orléans, 2004–05 ; Bâle, 2008) ; REptile, une ligne de produits en tuile (2006–07) ; Moon Jelly: Choice: Kitchens and Bakery (Brooklyn, New York, 2009–10, publié ici) et *Blue Rain*, une installation de verre sur commande (Abou Dhabi, EAU, 2011).

MOON JELLY
(CHOICE: KITCHENS AND BAKERY)

Brooklyn, New York, USA, 2009–10

Address: 108 Jay Street, Brooklyn, New York 11201, USA, +1 718 797 1695
Area: 186 m². Client: Cara Construction. Cost: $650 000

Evan Douglis created a custom modular ceiling system for this restaurant project that seeks to combine "a sense of old-world charm alongside a unique contemporary setting." According to the designer, the ceiling, which encloses the required mechanical, sprinkler and lighting systems, was "conceived as a beautiful theatrical cloud suspended above one's head." It is, he continues, "an extension of our continued interest in surface intricacy, animate form, and serial distraction as a totally immersive experience in architecture today." A custom glass chandelier was also part of the design. The ceiling is made with 3D-printed SLS master modular units, urethane molds, polyester resin slip cast modular units, and water-based metallic faux finish.

Evan Douglis entwickelte ein speziell gefertigtes modulares Deckensystem für das Restaurant, das „einerseits den Charme der Alten Welt vermittelt, andererseits in einen unverwechselbar zeitgenössischen Kontext passen sollte". Douglis zufolge wurde die Decke, in welche die erforderlichen Leitungen, Sprinkler- und Lichtsysteme integriert wurden, als „ästhetisch-dramatische, über den Köpfen der Gäste schwebende Wolke" gestaltet. Der Entwurf, so der Architekt weiter, „ist eine Vertiefung unseres Interesses an komplexen Oberflächen, dynamisch-bewegten Formen und serieller Streuung, um umfassende räumliche Gesamterlebnisse in der heutigen Architektur zu realisieren". Teil des Designs ist außerdem ein eigens entworfener Glaslüster. Gefertigt wurde die Decke mit ihrem metallischem, wasserbasiertem Acryllackfinish aus 3-D-gedruckten SLS-Mastermodulen, geformten Urethan-Elementen und gegossenen Polyesterharzmodulen.

Evan Douglis a créé pour ce restaurant un système de plafond modulaire qui vise à combiner « une impression de charme désuet et un décor contemporain unique ». Pour le designer, le plafond, qui renferme le mécanisme anti-incendie ou d'éclairage, a été « conçu comme un magnifique nuage théâtral suspendu au-dessus des têtes. C'est la poursuite de notre intérêt persistant pour la complexité des surfaces, la forme animée et la distraction séquentielle sous la forme d'une expérience d'immersion totale dans l'architecture ». L'ensemble comprend aussi un lustre de verre réalisé sur mesure. Le plafond est fait d'unités modulaires en SLS à impression 3D, de moulages d'uréthane, d'unités modulaires en résine polyester coulée en barbotine et de faux fini métallique à base d'eau.

Suspended above a rather simple interior décor, the ceiling of Moon Jelly is an extravagant adventure into the complexities of computer-generated forms.

Die über dem vergleichsweise schlichten Interieur schwebende Decke des Moon Jelly ist eine extravagante Abenteuerreise in die komplexe Welt computergenerierter Formen.

Suspendu au-dessus d'un décor intérieur plutôt simple, le plafond de Moon Jelly constitue une fantastique incursion dans le monde complexe des formes créées par ordinateur.

EM2N

EM2N | Mathias Müller Daniel Niggli
Josef Str. 92
8005 Zurich
Switzerland

Tel: +41 442 15 60 10 / Fax: +41 442 15 60 11
E-mail: em2n@em2n.ch
Web: www.em2n.ch

This Zurich office is run by **DANIEL NIGGLI**, born in 1970 in Olten, Switzerland, and **MATHIAS MÜLLER**, born in 1966 in Zurich. Both architects received their diplomas from the ETH (Zurich, 1990–96). Niggli worked in the offices of Tod Williams and Billie Tsien (New York, 1993) and VMX Architects (Amsterdam, 1997), before creating EM2N in 1997. Mathias Müller worked with Herzog & de Meuron (Basel, 1997) and Bürgin Nissen Wentzlaff Architekten (Basel, 1997), before teaming up with Niggli. Their work includes the Public Archives of Basel-Landschaft (Liestal, 2000); the 11 Theater (Zurich, 2006); Affoltern Apartments (Zurich, 2008); the City Garden Hotel (Zug, 2009); and the IM VIADUKT (Zurich, 2008–10, published here). They are currently working on the Toni-Areal project in Zurich with a school, apartments, and a cultural activity zone (2006–13); the International Center for Competitive and Popular Sports (Winterthur, 2010–13); the Swiss Cinémathèque (Penthaz, 2007–14); and a school in Inner Mongolia (Ordos, China, 2008–), all in Switzerland unless stated otherwise.

Das Züricher Büro arbeitet unter der Leitung von **DANIEL NIGGLI**, geboren 1970 in Olten, Schweiz, und **MATHIAS MÜLLER**, geboren 1966 in Zürich. Beide Architekten schlossen ihr Studium an der ETH Zürich (1990–96) mit einem Diplom ab. Niggli arbeitete vor der Gründung von EM2N 1997 für Tod Williams und Billie Tsien (New York, 1993) und VMX Architects (Amsterdam, 1997). Mathias Müller war für Herzog & de Meuron (Basel, 1997) und Bürgin Nissen Wentzlaff Architekten (Basel, 1997) tätig, bevor er sich Niggli anschloss. Zu ihren Projekten zählen das Staatsarchiv Basel-Landschaft (Liestal, 2000), das Theater 11 (Zürich, 2006), Wohnungen in Zürich-Affoltern (Zürich, 2008), das Hotel City Garden (Zug, 2009) und IM VIADUKT (Zürich, 2008–10, hier vorgestellt). Derzeit arbeitet das Büro am Toni-Areal in Zürich mit Hochschuleinrichtungen, Wohnungen und kulturellen Angeboten (2006–13), am Internationalen Zentrum für Leistungs- und Breitensport (Winterthur, 2010 bis 2013), der Cinémathèque Suisse (Penthaz, 2007–14) und einer Schule in der Inneren Mongolei (Ordos, China, seit 2008), alle in der Schweiz, sofern nicht anders angegeben.

Agence zurichoise dirigée par **DANIEL NIGGLI**, né en 1970 à Olten, Suisse, et **MATHIAS MÜLLER**, né en 1966 à Zurich, tous deux architectes diplômés de l'ETH (Zurich, 1990–96). Niggli a travaillé dans les agences de Tod Williams et Billie Tsien (New York, 1993) et chez VMX Architects (Amsterdam, 1997) avant de créer EM2N en 1997. Mathias Müller a travaillé avec Herzog & de Meuron (Bâle, 1997) et Bürgin Nissen Wentzlaff Architekten (Bâle, 1997) avant de rejoindre Niggli. Leurs réalisations comprennent : les archives publiques de Bâle-Campagne (Liestal, 2000) ; le théâtre 11 (Zurich, 2006) ; les appartements Affoltern (Zurich, 2008) ; l'hôtel City Garden (Zoug, 2009) et IM VIADUKT (Zurich, 2008–10, publié ici). Ils travaillent actuellement au projet de l'espace Toni-Areal à Zurich qui comprend une école, des appartements et une zone d'activité culturelle (2006–13) ; au Centre international de sports de compétition et populaires (Winterthur, 2010–13) ; à la Cinémathèque suisse (Penthaz, 2007–14) et à une école en Mongolie intérieure (Ordos, Chine, 2008–), tous en Suisse sauf mention contraire.

IM VIADUKT

Zurich, Switzerland, 2008–10

Address: Viaduk Str. / Limmat Str., 8005 Zurich, Switzerland, www.im-viadukt.ch
Area: 9008 m². Client: Stiftung PWG, Zurich. Cost: €32.9 million

This project concerns the refurbishment of existing railway viaduct arches and their reuse for shops or restaurants. The architects point out that their mission was to make this former urban barrier into a "linking structure" while upgrading the spaces bordering the viaduct. They explain: "The viaduct becomes a large-scale connecting machine and a linear building. We view this ambivalence as a fundamental quality and use it as the architectural leitmotiv to symbiotically connect the new uses with the viaduct structure. The characteristic Cyclopean masonry here forms the central atmospheric element. The new structures are deliberately restrained so as to emphasize the existing arches. In fitting-out the interiors, the future users can choose from a kit of elements or design the spaces themselves."

Hier ging es um die Sanierung eines Eisenbahnviadukts, dessen Bögen zur Umnutzung durch Läden und Restaurants vorgesehen waren. Die Architekten betonen, ihre Mission sei es gewesen, ein ehemals urbanes Hindernis zum „Bindeglied" zu machen und zugleich das bauliche Umfeld des Viadukts aufzuwerten. Sie führen aus: „Das Viadukt wird zur großräumigen Verbindungsmaschine, zum linearen Bauwerk. Für uns ist diese Ambivalenz eine grundlegende Qualität, ein architektonisches Leitmotiv, das wir einsetzen, um die neuen Nutzungen symbiotisch mit dem Viaduktbau zu verbinden. Das typische Mauerwerk wird zum zentralen atmosphärischen Element. Die Neubauelemente wurden bewusst zurückhaltend gestaltet, um die alten Bögen wirken zu lassen. Bei der Ausstattung der Innenräume können die künftigen Nutzer zwischen Baukastenelementen oder einer eigenen Gestaltung wählen."

Le projet consiste à réaménager les arches du viaduc de chemin de fer pour des magasins ou restaurants. Les architectes soulignent que leur mission a consisté à transformer cette ancienne barrière urbaine en une « structure de liaison » par la mise en valeur des espaces bordant le viaduc. Ils expliquent notamment que « le viaduc devient un mécanisme de connexion à grande échelle et un bâtiment linéaire. Nous avons vu cette ambivalence comme une qualité fondamentale et on avons fait le leitmotiv architectural qui relie de manière symbiotique les nouveaux usages du viaduc et sa structure. La maçonnerie cyclopéenne typique constitue ici l'élément central qui crée l'atmosphère. Les nouvelles structures sont volontairement restreintes afin de mettre en valeur les arches. Les utilisateurs peuvent aménager l'espace à partir d'un kit ou le dessiner eux-mêmes ».

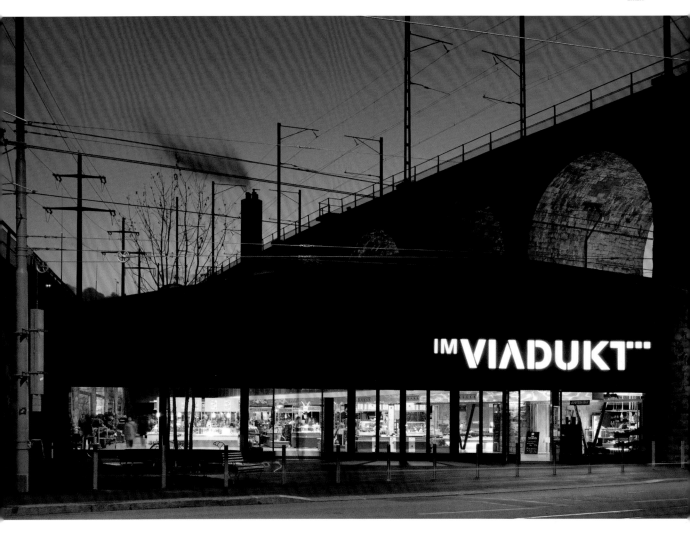

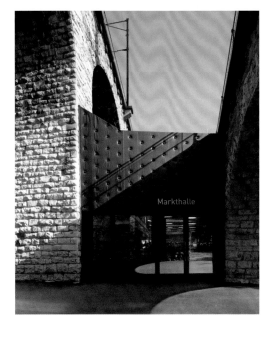

Markthalle

Located relatively close to Gigon & Guyer's new Prime Tower, the Viadukt complex improves on such earlier bids to use railway arches as the one in Paris on the Avenue Daumesnil.

Das Viadukt, nur unweit vom neuen Prime Tower von Gigon & Guyer, ist ein denkbarer Fortschritt zu früheren Umnutzungen von Bahnbögen, etwa an der Avenue Daumesnil in Paris.

Situé non loin de la Prime Tower de Gigon & Guyer, le complexe du Viadukt surpasse les projets antérieurs d'exploitation d'arches de viaducs de chemin de fer, tel celui de l'avenue Daumesnil à Paris.

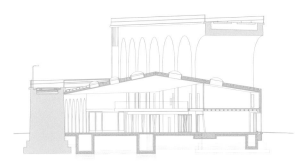

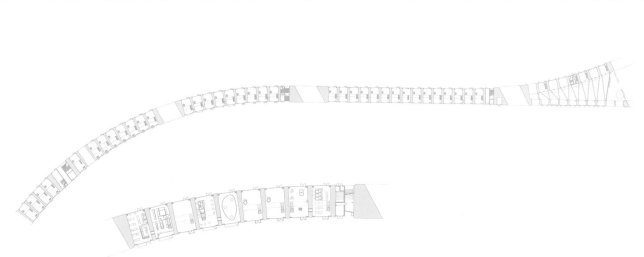

Generous spaces were installed inside of the stone arches, in these instances for the sale of clothing accessories or food. Above, a plan.

Unter den steinernen Bögen wurden großzügige Räume geschaffen, hier für den Verkauf von Modeaccessoires oder Lebensmitteln. Oben ein Grundriss.

Des espaces généreux ont été ménagés sous les arches de pierre pour la vente de vêtements, accessoires ou alimentation, comme ici. Plan ci-dessus.

With its broad arches and openings from one archway to the next, the existing structure provides ample space for a restaurant, or a wine bar (left).

Dank der ausgreifenden Gewölbe und Verbindungen zwischen den Bögen bietet das alte Bauwerk viel Platz für ein Restaurant und eine Weinbar (links).

La largeur des arches et les ouvertures de l'une à l'autre dans la structure existante offrent de larges espaces pour un restaurant ou un bar à vin (à gauche).

Unlike the Avenue Daumesnil arcade in Paris, the Viadukt sits beneath an operating train line as can be seen in the section drawings below. Right, design furniture and objects in a Viadukt store.

Anders als bei der Einkaufspassage an der Avenue Daumesnil in Paris liegt das Viadukt unter einer aktiven Bahnlinie, wie die Querschnitte unten belegen. Rechts Designmöbel und -objekte in einem der Viaduktläden.

Contrairement aux arcades de l'avenue Daumesnil à Paris, le Viadukt est situé sous une ligne de chemin de fer en activité, comme on le voit sur les plans en coupe ci-dessous. À droite, meubles et objets design dans une boutique.

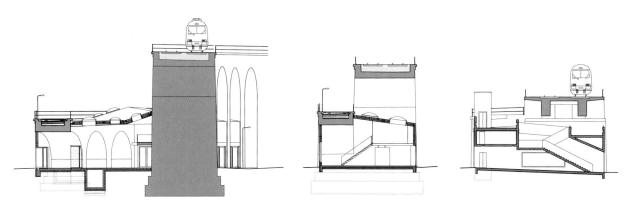

ESTUDIO NÓMADA

Estudio Nómada
Rua das Hedras 6, Nivel I, Loft E
15895 Santiago de Compostela
Spain

Tel: +34 981 59 59 59 / Fax: +34 981 59 59 69
E-mail: nomada@estudionomada.es
Web: www.estudionomada.es

JOSÉ ANTONIO VÁZQUEZ MARTÍN was born in 1972 in Orense, Spain. He received his architecture degree at the ETSA of A Coruña (1997). He worked after that for the apparel company STL for four years, before creating Estudio Nómada with **ENRIQUE DE SANTIAGO**, who was born in San Juan, Puerto Rico, in 1973. De Santiago obtained a BBA degree at Iowa State University in 1996 and an additional degree in Apparel Merchandising, Design, and Production. He then worked as a fashion buyer, before the creation of Nómada. Their work includes the Dominio do Bibei Winery cellar (Manzaneda, Orense, 2006); House in the Monteprincipe private compound (Boadilla del Monte, Madrid, 2007); Sterling Store (Orense, 2008); the Canteen at the City of Culture of Galicia (Santiago de Compostela, 2010, published here); House in Pazo Ramirás private compound (Orense, 2011); and the Fernández-Braso Art Gallery (Madrid, 2011), all in Spain.

JOSÉ ANTONIO VÁZQUEZ MARTÍN wurde 1972 in Orense, Spanien, geboren. Sein Architekturstudium schloss er an der ETSA in A Coruña ab (1997). Im Anschluss daran arbeitete er zunächst vier Jahre für die Bekleidungsfirma STL, ehe er mit **ENRIQUE DE SANTIAGO** das gemeinsame Büro Estudio Nómada gründete. De Santiago, geboren 1973 in San Juan, Puerto Rico, schloss sein Studium mit einem BBA an der Iowa State University (1996) sowie einem weiteren Abschluss in Textilmarketing, -gestaltung und -fertigung ab. Vor der Gründung von Nómada arbeitete er als Einkäufer in der Modebranche. Zu ihren Projekten zählen die Weinkellerei Dominio do Bibei (Manzaneda, Orense, 2006), ein Haus in der privaten Wohnanlage Monteprincipe (Boadilla del Monte, Madrid, 2007), der Sterling Store (Orense, 2008), die Kantine für die Cidade da Cultura de Galicia (Santiago de Compostela, 2010, hier vorgestellt), ein Haus in der privaten Wohnanlage Pazo Ramirás (Orense, 2011) sowie die Galerie Fernández-Braso (Madrid, 2011), alle in Spanien.

JOSÉ ANTONIO VÁZQUEZ MARTÍN est né en 1972 à Orense, Espagne. Il a obtenu son diplôme d'architecture à l'ETSA de La Corogne (1997) et a ensuite travaillé quatre ans dans la société d'habillement STL avant de créer Estudio Nómada avec **ENRIQUE DE SANTIAGO**. Né à San Juan, Porto Rico, en 1973 et titulaire d'un BBA de l'université de l'Iowa en 1996 et d'un diplôme complémentaire en commerce de l'habillement, design et production, il a travaillé auparavant comme acheteur de mode. Leurs réalisations comprennent : la cave du domaine Dominio do Bibei (Manzaneda, Orense, 2006) ; une maison dans le complexe privé de Monteprincipe (Boadilla del Monte, Madrid, 2007) ; le magasin Sterling (Orense, 2008) ; la cantine de la Cité de la culture de Galice (Saint-Jacques-de-Compostelle, 2010, publiée ici) ; une maison dans le complexe privé Pazo Ramirás (Orense, 2011) et la galerie d'art Fernández-Braso (Madrid, 2011), tous en Espagne.

CANTEEN AT THE CITY OF CULTURE OF GALICIA

Santiago de Compostela, Spain, 2010

Address: Rua de San Roque 2, 15704 Santiago de Compostela,
Galicia, Spain, +34 881 99 75 65, www.cidadedacultura.org. Area: 277 m²
Client: Fundacion Cidade da Cultura de Galicia. Cost: not disclosed

This project is situated in two structures next to the Archive of Galicia, part of Peter Eisenman's Galician City of Culture. The architects broke through preexisting walls to link the two spaces of café and shop with one long shared bar, recalling the typology of Galician village canteens. The architects explain: "To begin, we refer to the canteen as a model of traditional establishment in Galicia, a concept that permits reinterpretation through a modern filter. Abstracting this idea, the tables are arranged in parallel, elongated under schematic trees evoking popular festivities…" A "geometric and uninhibited" profusion of color is intended to bring to mind Galician folk art. Both this colorful décor and the trees referred to are abstract presences that fill and animate the space, while allowing the Canteen to remain light and airy.

Das Projekt liegt in zwei Bauten neben dem Galizischen Archiv, einem Teil der Cidade da Cultura de Galicia (Kulturstadt Galiziens) von Peter Eisenman. Mit Durchbrüchen im alten Mauerwerk und einem langen gemeinschaftlichen Tresen, der an die typischen Dorfkantinen Galiziens erinnert, verbanden die Architekten Café und Shop. Die Architekten erklären: „Ausgangspunkt ist die Bezugnahme auf die Kantine als traditionelle, typisch galizische Einrichtung, ein Konzept, das hier durch einen modernen Filter neu interpretiert wird. Abstrahiert wird diese Idee durch längs gestellte, parallele Tischreihen unter stilisierten ,Bäumen', eine Anspielung auf Dorffeste…" Eine Fülle von Farben, „geometrisch und überbordend", ist Hommage an die galizische Volkskunst. Das farbenfrohe Dekor und die „Bäume" bleiben abstrakt und prägen und beleben den Raum, sodass die Kantine hell und offen bleibt.

Le projet occupe deux bâtiments à proximité des Archives de Galice, dans la Cité de la culture construite par Peter Eisenman. Les architectes ont percé les murs existants pour relier les deux espaces café et boutique par un long bar commun rappelant les cantines des villages galiciens. Ils expliquent : « Pour commencer, nous pensons la cantine comme un modèle d'établissement traditionnel en Galice, ce qui permet sa réinterprétation à travers un filtre moderne. Pour résumer cette idée, les tables sont disposées en lignes parallèles sous des arbres schématisés qui évoquent les fêtes populaires… » Une profusion « géométrique et sans retenue » de couleurs évoque l'art folklorique galicien. Le décor coloré et les références aux arbres constituent des présences abstraites qui emplissent et animent l'espace tout en gardant sa luminosité aérienne à la cantine.

Treelike wooden frames rise above the tables. Left, in the second room, tall shelves rise up to the ceiling.

Ein zu Bäumen stilisiertes Holzgerüst ragt über den Tischen auf. Im zweiten Raum reichen Regale bis zur Decke (links).

Des arbres schématisés en bois se dressent au-dessus des tables. À gauche, dans la seconde pièce, des étagères montent jusqu'au plafond.

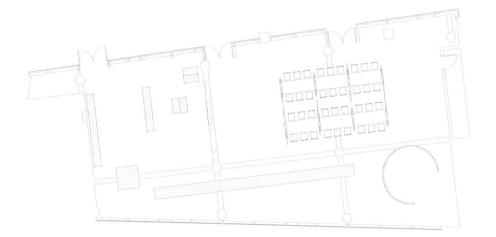

The "colorful décor" referred to by the architects is seen to the right in this otherwise white and tan environment.

Das von den Architekten zitierte farbenfrohe Dekor (rechts) in der ansonsten in Weiß und Naturtönen gehaltenen Umgebung

On aperçoit à droite le « décor coloré » évoqué par les architectes dans l'ensemble sinon blanc et brun clair.

FEARON HAY

Fearon Hay Architects Ltd.
PO Box 90311
Victoria Street West
Auckland 1142
New Zealand

Tel: +64 9309 0128 / Fax: +64 9309 0827
E-mail: contact@fearonhay.com
Web: www.fearonhay.com

JEFFREY FEARON was born in 1972 in Auckland, New Zealand, and received his B.Arch degree from the University of Queensland (1990–95). **TIM HAY** was born in 1973, also in Auckland, and received a B.Arch degree from Auckland University (1993–97). They established Fearon Hay Architects in 1998. As they describe their own practice and its largely residential work: "Fearon Hay projects include commissions in diverse environments—coastal, urban, rural, lakeside, and alpine. Works are located in both North and South Islands of New Zealand." Their projects include Coromandel Beach House (Coromandel Peninsula, 2000); Kellands Commercial Office Building (Auckland, 2001); Darling Point Apartment (Sydney, Australia, 2002); Parnell House (Auckland, 2002); Shark Alley Retreat (Great Barrier Island, 2002–03); Lake Wakatipu House (Queenstown, 2003); Sergeant to Dunn House (Auckland, 2005); Clooney Restaurant (Auckland, 2006); Northland Beach House (Rawhiti); Yates-Allison House (Tutukaka Coast, 2007); Sandhills Road House (Great Barrier Island, 2007); Sandy Bay Road House (Sandy Bay, Tutukaka Coast, 2007–08); Closeburg Station Guest House (Queenstown, 2008); Tribeca Loft (Manhattan, New York, USA, 2008); Wintergarden at The Northern Club (Auckland, 2008); and North Wharf (Auckland, 2010–11, published here), all in New Zealand unless stated otherwise.

JEFFREY FEARON wurde 1972 in Auckland geboren. Er schloss sein Studium an der Universität von Queensland (1990–95) mit einem B.Arch. ab. **TIM HAY** wurde 1973 ebenfalls in Auckland geboren und erwarb seinen B.Arch. an der Universität seiner Heimatstadt (1993–97). 1998 gründeten sie ihr Büro Fearon Hay Architects. Sie beschreiben ihre Firma und deren überwiegendes Engagement im Wohnungsbau wie folgt: „Zu den Projekten von Fearon Hay zählen Aufträge in den verschiedensten Kontexten – an der Küste, in der Stadt, auf dem Land, an Seen und in den Bergen. Die Projekte liegen auf der Nord- und Südinsel Neuseelands." Zu ihren Arbeiten zählen Coromandel Beach House (Coromandel-Halbinsel, 2000), Kellands Commercial Office Building (Auckland, 2001), Darling Point Apartment (Sydney, 2002), Parnell House (Auckland, 2002), Shark Alley Retreat (Great Barrier Island, 2002–03), Lake Wakatipu House (Queenstown, 2003), der Umbau des Sergeant House zum Dunn House (Auckland, 2005), Clooney Restaurant (Auckland, 2006), Northland Beach House (Rawhiti, 2007), Yates-Allison House (Tutukaka Coast, 2007), Sandhills Road House (Great Barrier Island, 2007), Sandy Bay Road House (Sandy Bay, Tutukaka Coast, 2007–08), Gästehaus Closeburg Station (Queenstown, 2008), ein Loft in Tribeca (New York, 2008), Wintergarden at The Northern Club (Auckland, 2008) sowie North Wharf (Auckland, 2010–11, hier vorgestellt), alle in Neuseeland, sofern nicht anders vermerkt.

JEFFREY FEARON est né en 1972 à Auckland, et a obtenu son B.Arch à l'université du Queensland (1990–95). **TIM HAY** est né en 1973, également à Auckland, et a obtenu son B.Arch à l'université d'Auckland (1993–97). Ils ont ouvert Fearon Hay Architects en 1998. Selon leurs propres termes : « Les projets commandés à Fearon Hay sont situés dans des milieux très divers – côtier, urbain, rural, lacustre et alpin, dans l'île du Nord comme dans celle du Sud de la Nouvelle-Zélande. » Ces projets comprennent : Coromandel Beach House (péninsule de Coromandel, 2000) ; l'immeuble de bureaux de Kellands Commercial (Auckland, 2001) ; un appartement à Darling Point (Sydney, 2002) ; Parnell House (Auckland, 2002) ; la résidence Shark Alley Retreat (île de la Grande Barrière, 2002–03) ; Lake Wakatipu House (Queenstown, 2003) ; Sergeant to Dunn House (Auckland, 2005) ; le restaurant Clooney (Auckland, 2006) ; Northland Beach House (Rawhiti) ; Yates-Allison House (côte de Tutukaka, 2007) ; Sandhills Road House (île de la Grande Barrière, 2007) ; Sandy Bay Road House (Sandy Bay, côte de Tutukaka, 2007–08) ; la pension Closeburg Station (Queenstown, 2008) ; le loft Tribeca (Manhattan, New York, 2008) ; Wintergarden at The Northern Club (Auckland, 2008) et North Wharf (Auckland, 2010–11, publié ici), tous en Nouvelle-Zélande sauf mention contraire.

NORTH WHARF

Auckland, New Zealand, 2010–11

Address: Wynyard Quarter, Auckland 1010, New Zealand, www.northwharf.co.nz
Area: 1659 m². Client: Waterfront Auckland. Cost: not disclosed
Collaboration: Stephen de Vrij, Robin Geiselhardt

The architects have played on and expanded the mood and typology of existing wharf architecture, creating a convivial public space where dock activities have waned.

An einem Ort, wo immer weniger Hafenarbeiten anfallen, schufen die Architekten einen belebten öffentlichen Raum. Atmosphäre und Typologie der alten Hafenanlagen wurden spielerisch aufgegriffen.

Les architectes ont prolongé et joué sur l'ambiance et la typologie de l'architecture du quai pour créer un espace public convivial où les activités liées au dock ont décliné.

Situated in the 2.5-hectare Wynyard Waterfront Development area, these three structures, one of which is a renovated historic cargo shed, are intended to allow for both retail and entertainment activities. **NORTH WHARF** in Auckland has been compared to Fisherman's Wharf in San Francisco. Fearon Hay placed their two new buildings somewhat behind the wharf edge to create a broader area for pedestrians. They also renovated the Old Red Shed on North Wharf, a 1930s building with distinctive red doors which was one of the three original cargo sheds located at the western end of the Auckland waterfront. Seeking to retain the "grittiness" of this building, Fearon Hay used the red doors as an inspiration for the new buildings that are located to either side. Old, pallet timber was used on the sides of the new buildings to reflect their intention to create a unity between the structures. "The interior of the shed reflects its former uses, with the original timber frame containing marks and paint from over the years still visible," according to Steven de Vrij from Fearon Hay. "It has basically been left in its original state, with only some of the ceiling partitions removed and an industrial strength vacuum cleaner used to clear dust and debris." In an interesting touch, "bio-retention" rain gardens that treat storm water and provide passive irrigation are located on the southern side of North Wharf. The architects have also recently won a competition to design a 5-star 300-room hotel nearby (in collaboration with Peddle Thorp Architects).

Die drei Gebäude im 2,5 ha großen Erschließungsgebiet Wynyard Waterfront, darunter ein sanierter historischer Frachtschuppen, sind für Läden und Freizeitangebote vorgesehen. **NORTH WHARF** in Auckland wurde u. a. mit Fisherman's Wharf in San Francisco verglichen. Fearon Hay setzten die zwei Neubauten zugunsten einer breiteren Fußgängerzone leicht von der Kaimauer zurück. Saniert wurde außerdem der Old Red Shed an der North Wharf, ein Altbau mit markant roten Toren aus den 1930er-Jahren und einer der drei ersten Schuppen am westlichen Ende des Aucklander Hafens. Bemüht, den „spröden" Charme des alten Gebäudes zu erhalten, ließen sich Fearon Hay für die flankierenden Neubauten von den roten Toren des alten Schuppens inspirieren. Die Verkleidung der Neubaustirnfronten mit Palettenholz betont die Zusammengehörigkeit des Komplexes. „Im Innern des Schuppens bleibt die frühere Nutzung erkennbar: Am alten Fachwerk sind die im Laufe der Jahr entstandenen Spuren und Farbreste sichtbar", so Steven de Vrij von Fearon Hay. „Im Grunde wurde der Originalzustand erhalten, nur ein Teil der Deckenabhängung wurde entfernt, Staub und Schutt mit Industriestaubsaugern beseitigt." Ein interessantes Element sind die Sickerbeete an der Südseite der North Wharf, die auch ein passives Bewässerungssystem versorgen. Unlängst gewannen die Architekten (mit Peddle Thorp Architects) in der Nähe einen Wettbewerb für ein Fünf-Sterne-Hotel mit 300 Betten.

Situées dans la zone de développement de 2,5 hectares Wynyard Waterfront, les trois structures, dont un abri à bateaux historique rénové, doivent accueillir des commerces de détail et activités de loisir. **NORTH WHARF** a été comparé au quartier Fisherman's Wharf de San Francisco. Fearon Hay ont placé leurs deux bâtiments neufs légèrement en retrait au bout du quai afin d'ouvrir un espace plus large aux pietons. Ils ont rénové l'abri à bateaux Old Red Shed sur le quai, une construction des années 1930 aux portes rouges caractéristiques et l'un des trois abris à bateaux d'origine à la pointe ouest du front de mer d'Auckland. Désireux de conserver la « crudité » du bâtiment, les architectes se sont inspirés des portes rouges pour les bâtiments neufs des autres côtés. De même, de vieilles palettes en bois sur les côtés des nouveaux bâtiments affichent leur intention de créer une unité entre les différentes structures. « L'intérieur de l'abri montre encore l'utilisation qui en a été faite, avec les ossatures de bois originales et la peinture qui reste visible », explique Steven de Vrij de Fearon Hay. « Il a été laissé pour l'essentiel dans son état d'origine, seules quelques cloisons du plafond ont été retirées et un aspirateur industriel a été utilisé pour éliminer la poussière et les débris. » Parmi les détails intéressants, des jardins à « bio rétention » côté sud traitent l'eau de pluie et assurent une irrigation passive. Les architectes ont récemment gagné un concours pour construire à côté un hôtel cinq étoiles de 300 chambres (en collaboration avec Peddle Thorp Architects).

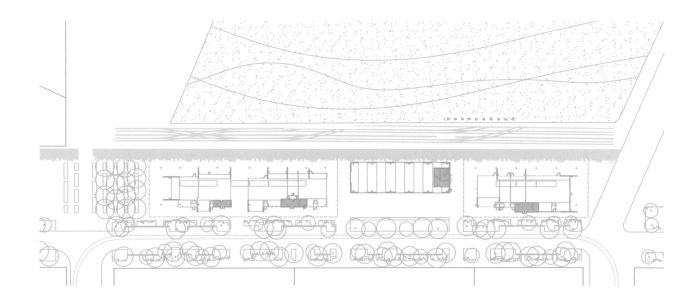

A site plan shows the two new buildings and the old restored structure.

Der Lageplan zeigt die beiden Neubauten und den sanierten alten Bau.

Un plan du site montre les deux bâtiments neufs et la structure ancienne rénovée.

Using glass and metal, Fearon Hay have imagined new buildings that do not conflict with the wharf atmosphere, while allowing for modern restaurant facilities, for example.

Mit Glas und Metall entwarfen Fearon Hay Neubauten, die die Atmosphäre der alten Hafenbebauung nicht zerstören und dennoch die Unterbringung moderner Einrichtungen wie Restaurants erlauben.

Avec du verre et du métal, Fearon Hay a créé de nouveaux bâtiments accueillant des restaurants modernes sans désavouer pour autant l'atmosphère générale du quai.

MASSIMILIANO AND DORIANA FUKSAS

Massimiliano and Doriana Fuksas
Piazza del Monte di Pietà 30
00186 Rome
Italy

Tel: +39 06 68 80 78 71 / Fax: +39 06 68 80 78 72
E-mail: press@fuksas.com
Web: www.fuksas.com

MASSIMILIANO FUKSAS was born in 1944 in Rome, Italy. He received his degree in Architecture at the "La Sapienza" University of Rome in 1969. He founded a studio in Rome in 1967, and opened an office in Paris in 1989. He won the 1999 Grand Prix d'Architecture in France. He was the Director of the 7th Architecture Biennale in Venice (1998–2000). He has worked with **DORIANA MANDRELLI FUKSAS** since 1985. She attended the Faculty of Architecture at the "La Sapienza" University of Rome and has been responsible for design in the firm since 1997. They have completed the Ferrari Operational Headquarters and Research Center (Maranello, Italy, 2001–04); the new Trade Fair (Rho-Pero, Milan, Italy, 2002–05); Zenith Strasbourg (Eckbolsheim, Strasbourg, France, 2003–07); the Armani Ginza Tower (Tokyo, Japan, 2005–07); Peres Peace House (Jaffa, Israel, 1999–2009); the Church of San Paolo in Foligno (Italy, 2001–09); MyZeil Shopping Mall (Frankfurt, Germany, 2002–09); Emporio Armani Fifth Avenue (New York, New York, USA, 2007–09); 18.Septemberplein (Eindhoven, the Netherlands, 2003–10); the Admirant Entrance Building (Eindhoven, the Netherlands, 2003–10); Lyon Confluence (Lyon, France, 2005–10); and the Palatino Center (Turin, Italy, 1998–2011, published here). Upcoming work includes the French National Archives (Paris, France, 2005–12); Terminal 3, International Shenzhen Bao'an Airport (Shenzhen, China, 2008–12); the House of Justice (Tblisi, Georgia, 2010–12); and the Eur New Congress Center (Rome, Italy, 1998–2013).

MASSIMILIANO FUKSAS wurde 1944 in Rom geboren und schloss sein Architekturstudium 1969 an der Universität La Sapienza in Rom ab. 1967 gründete er ein Büro in Rom, 1989 eines in Paris. 1999 erhielt er in Frankreich den Grand Prix d'Architecture. Fuksas war Direktor der VII. Architekturbiennale in Venedig (1998 bis 2000). Seit 1985 arbeitet er mit **DORIANA MANDRELLI FUKSAS** zusammen. Sie studierte an der Fakultät für Architektur an der La Sapienza in Rom und ist seit 1997 verantwortlich für die Entwürfe des Büros. Das Team realisierte den Hauptsitz von Ferrari mit Forschungszentrum (Maranello, Italien, 2001–04), die neue Messe Mailand (Rho-Pero, Mailand, 2002–05), das Zenith Strasbourg (Eckbolsheim, Frankreich, 2003–07), den Armani Ginza Tower (Tokio, 2005–07), das Peres-Friedenszentrum (Jaffa, Israel, 1999–2009), die Kirche San Paolo in Foligno (Italien, 2001–09), das Einkaufszentrum MyZeil (Frankfurt am Main, 2002–09), Emporio Armani Fifth Avenue (New York, 2007–09), 18. Septemberplein (Eindhoven, Niederlande, 2003–10), das Zugangsgebäude zum Komplex De Admirant (Eindhoven, Niederlande, 2003–10), Lyon Confluence (Lyon, 2005–10) und das Centro Palatino (Turin, 1998–2011, hier vorgestellt). In Planung bzw. im Bau sind u.a. das Französische Nationalarchiv (Paris, 2005–12), das Terminal 3 am Flughafen Shenzhen Bao'an (Shenzhen, China, 2008–12), der Gerichtshof in Tblisi (Georgien, 2010–12) und das neue Kongresszentrum im Stadtteil Eur (Rom, 1998–2013).

MASSIMILIANO FUKSAS, né en 1944 à Rome, est diplômé en architecture de l'université de Rome La Sapienza (1969). Il crée son agence à Rome en 1967 et ouvre un bureau à Paris en 1989. En 1999, il remporte le Grand Prix d'architecture français. Il a été directeur de la VIIᵉ Biennale d'architecture de Venise (1998–2000) et travaille avec **DORIANA MANDRELLI FUKSAS** depuis 1985. Celle-ci a également étudié à la faculté d'architecture de l'université de Rome La Sapienza. Elle est responsable du design à l'agence depuis 1997. Ils ont réalisé : le siège opérationnel et Centre de recherches Ferrari (Maranello, Italie, 2001–04), la nouvelle Foire de Milan (Rho-Pero, Milan, 2002–05) ; le Zénith de Strasbourg (Eckbolsheim, Strasbourg, 2003–07) ; la tour Armani à Ginza (Tokyo, 2005–07) ; Le Centre Peres pour la Paix (Jaffa, Israel, 1999–2009) ; l'église Saint-Paul de Foligno (Italie, 2001–09) ; le centre commercial MyZeil (Francfort, 2002–09) ; l'Emporio Armani Fifth Avenue (New York, 2007–09) ; la 18 Septemberplein (Eindhoven, Pays-Bas, 2003–10) ; l'immeuble d'entrée du centre commercial Admirant (Eindhoven, 2003–10) ; Lyon Confluence (Lyon, 2005–10) et le Palatino Center (Turin, 1998–2011, publié ici). Leurs futurs projets comprennent : les Archives nationales de France (Paris, 2005–12) ; le terminal 3 de l'aéroport international Bao'an (Shenzhen, Chine, 2008–12) ; le palais de justice (Tbilissi, Géorgie, 2010–12) et le nouveau Centre des congrès Eur (Rome, 1998–2013).

PALATINO CENTER

Turin, Italy, 1998–2011

*Address: corner Via Giulio Cesare / Corso Regina Margherita (Porta Palazzo area),
10152 Turin, Italy, www.centropalatino.it. Area: 13 000 m²
Client: City of Turin. Cost: €8.5 million. Collaboration: Imp. La Sorgente (Contractor),
AI Engineering (Engineering), iGuzzini (Lighting: lamp "Lavinia")*

The **PALATINO CENTER** is located in the Porta Palazzo market zone of Turin, one of the oldest areas of the city. Studio Fuksas won a 1998 competition to design a new indoor market hall for clothing housed in a new five-story building, with three levels above grade for commercial activities and restaurants. The central courtyard on the ground floor has "11 multistory prismatic pillars equipped with embedded metal shelves, to support the load of three metal bridges that connect the various floors." The first floor is organized like the ground floor with commercial areas along the perimeter: shops, coffee shops, and a service area in the southwest corner. The top floor is occupied by a restaurant with a panoramic terrace, offering views of the historic center. The external façade of the building consists of a system of layers of strips of glass with layers of steel that gradually replace the glass. The 2000-square-meter façade is clad with no less than 60 000 glass elements and 150 000 kilograms of steel. This external façade covers another in stone housing a fire escape and utility access, and allows spectacular night lighting of the edifice.

Das **PALATINO CENTER** liegt im Marktquartier Porta Palazzo von Turin, einem der ältesten Viertel der Stadt. 1998 hatte Studio Fuksas einen Wettbewerb für eine neue Markthalle für Bekleidung gewonnen, die in einem fünfgeschossigen Neubau untergebracht werden sollte – davon drei Obergeschosse für Verkaufsflächen und Restaurants. In der zentralen Halle des Erdgeschosses „leiten elf mehrgeschossige Prismenpfeilern mit integrierten Querverstrebungen aus Metall die Lasten der drei Metallbrücken ab, welche die verschiedenen Geschossebenen verbinden". Die Organisation des ersten Stocks entspricht dem Erdgeschoss mit rundum verlaufenden Gewerbeflächen, Läden und Cafés sowie mit Versorgungseinrichtungen in der südwestlichen Ecke. Im obersten Geschoss ist ein Restaurant mit Panoramaterrasse und Blick auf die Altstadt untergebracht. Der Außenbau wurde mit einer Doppelschichtfassade aus Glas und Metall realisiert; hier gehen Glas- und Metallsegmente fließend ineinander über. Die 2000 m² große Fassadenfläche wurde mit nicht weniger als 60 000 Glaselementen und 150 000 kg Stahl verblendet. Hinter der Außenhaut verbirgt sich eine zweite Fassade aus Stein, in die Fluchtwege und Versorgungszugänge integriert wurden und die nachts eine dramatische Beleuchtung des Baus erlaubt.

Le **PALATINO CENTER** est situé dans la zone commerciale de Porta Palazzo à Turin, l'un des plus anciens quartiers de la ville. L'agence Fuksas a gagné un concours en 1998 pour construire un marché couvert aux vêtements dans un nouvel immeuble de cinq étages, dont trois niveaux en surface destinés à des activités commerciales et des restaurants. La cour centrale, au rez-de-chaussée, a « 11 piliers prismatiques à étages aux rayonnages métalliques enchâssés qui supportent le poids de trois passerelles métalliques entre les différents niveaux ». Le premier étage est agencé comme le rez-de-chaussée avec des surfaces commerciales sur son périmètre : boutiques, cafés et une aire de services dans le coin sud-ouest. Le dernier étage est occupé par un restaurant à terrasse panoramique avec vue sur le centre historique. La façade extérieure est composée de couches de bandes vitrées remplacées progressivement par des couches d'acier, sa surface de 2000 m² est revêtue de 60 000 morceaux de verre et 150 000 kg d'acier. Elle recouvre une autre façade en pierre qui contient l'escalier de secours et l'accès au complexe, tout en permettant un éclairage nocturne spectaculaire.

With its dramatic cantilevered roof and generous interior spaces, the Palatino Center evokes the vocabulary of industrial architecture in the image above.

Mit seinem dramatisch auskragenden Dach und den weitläufigen Innenbereichen greift das Centro Palatino formal das Vokabular von Industriebauten auf (oben).

Avec son toit spectaculaire en porte-à-faux et ses généreux espaces intérieurs, le Palatino Center évoque l'architecture industrielle.

A sketch by Fuksas gives an idea of the structure that is almost as clear as the section drawings below.

Eine Skizze von Fuksas vermittelt eine fast ebenso präzise Vorstellung vom Bau wie die Querschnitte darunter.

Croquis de Fuksas donnant une idée de la structure presque aussi claire que le plan en coupe en dessous.

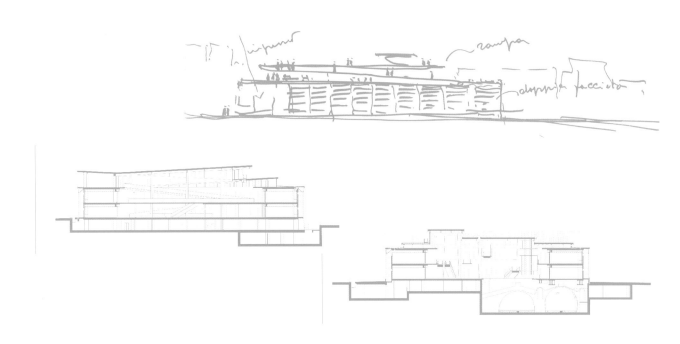

Long, gently sloping ramps cut through the very open space, with brightly colored pillars giving a vertical contrast to the largely horizontal space.

Lang gestreckte, sanft geneigte Rampen ziehen sich durch den sehr offenen Raum. Die leuchtend farbigen Pfeiler bilden einen vertikalen Kontrapunkt im ansonsten horizontal orientierten Bau.

De longues rampes en pente douce coupent la surface très ouverte où les piliers de couleurs vives forment un contraste vertical avec l'espace sinon largement horizontal.

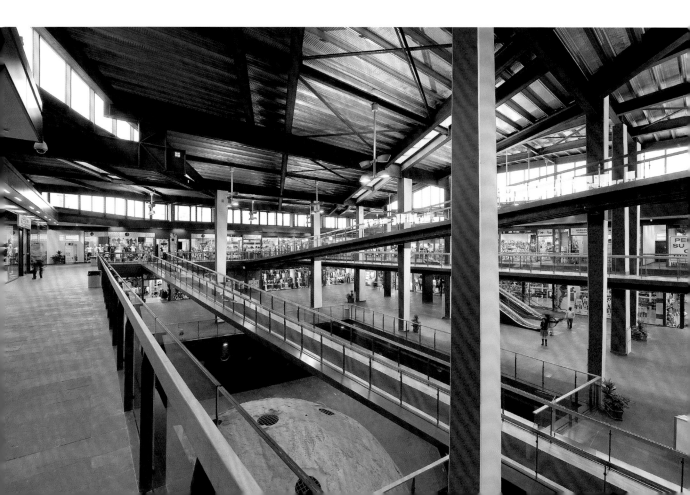

GRAFT

Graft Berlin
Heidestr. 50 / 10557 Berlin / Germany
Tel: +49 303 06 45 10 30 / Fax: +49 30 30 64 51 03 34
E-mail: berlin@graftlab.com / Web: www.graftlab.com

GRAFT was created in Los Angeles in 1998 "as a label for architecture, art, music, and the pursuit of happiness." Lars Krückeberg, Wolfram Putz, Thomas Willemeit, and Gregor Hoheisel are the Partners of Graft, which has about 100 employees worldwide. Graft maintains offices in Los Angeles, Berlin, and Beijing. Lars Krückeberg was educated at the Technical University, Braunschweig, Germany, as an engineer (1988–96) and at SCI-Arc in Los Angeles (1997–98). Wolfram Putz attended the Technical University, Braunschweig (1988–95); the University of Utah, Salt Lake City (1992–93); and SCI-Arc (1996–98). Thomas Willemeit was also educated in Braunschweig, and at the Bauhaus Dessau (1991–92), before working in the office of Daniel Libeskind (1998–2001). Gregor Hoheisel was also educated at the Technical University in Braunschweig (1988–95). They have built a studio and house for Brad Pitt in Los Angeles (2000–03) and, working with Brad Pitt and William McDonough + Partners, Graft are the lead architects for the Pink Project and Make It Right initiative in New Orleans (Louisiana, 2007–). They designed the Hotel Q! in Berlin (Germany, 2002–04), as well as restaurants in the Bellagio and Mirage casinos in Las Vegas (Nevada, USA, 2004 and 2006) and worked on several luxury resort hotels in the Caribbean. Their most recent work includes the Ginkgo Restaurant (Chengdu, China, 2008); Frankfurt Regionals Store at the International Airport (Frankfurt, Germany, 2009, published here); Wokalicious (Berlin, Germany, 2010–11, also published here); the Russian Jewish Museum of Tolerance (Moscow, Russia, 2007–12); and Ordos 20+10 Commercial Development (Ordos, Inner Mongolia, China, 2011–).

GRAFT entstand 1998 in Los Angeles als „ein Label für Architektur, Kunst, Musik und das Streben nach Glück". Lars Krückeberg, Wolfram Putz, Thomas Willemeit und Gregor Hoheisel sind Partner bei Graft, beschäftigen weltweit rund 100 Mitarbeiter und unterhalten Büros in Los Angeles, Berlin und Peking. Lars Krückeberg erhielt seine Ausbildung zum Ingenieur an der Technischen Universität Braunschweig (1988–96) und am SCI-Arc in Los Angeles (1997–98). Wolfram Putz besuchte die TU Braunschweig (1988–95), die University of Utah in Salt Lake City (1992–93) sowie das SCI-Arc (1996–98). Auch Thomas Willemeit studierte in Braunschweig sowie anschließend am Bauhaus Dessau (1991–92), ehe er im Büro von Daniel Libeskind arbeitete (1998–2001). Gregor Hoheisel studierte ebenfalls an der TU Braunschweig (1988–95). Sie bauten in Los Angeles ein Studio und Haus für Brad Pitt (2000–03). Gemeinsam mit Brad Pitt und William McDonough + Partners sind Graft leitende Architekten des Pink Project und der Make-It-Right-Initiative in New Orleans. Sie entwarfen das Hotel Q! in Berlin (2002–04) sowie Restaurants in den Kasinos Bellagio und Mirage in Las Vegas (Nevada, USA, 2004 und 2006) und arbeiteten an mehreren Luxusresorts in der Karibik. Zu ihren jüngsten Projekten zählen das Restaurant Ginkgo (Chengdu, China, 2008), der Frankfurt Regionals Store im Internationalen Flughafen (Frankfurt am Main, 2009, hier vorgestellt), Wokalicious (Berlin, 2010–11, ebenfalls hier vorgestellt), das Russisch-Jüdische Museum der Toleranz (Moskau, 2007–12) sowie das Bürogebäude Ordos 20+10 (Ordos, Innere Mongolei, China, seit 2011).

GRAFT a été créé à Los Angeles en 1998 « comme un label en architecture, art, musique et poursuite du bonheur ». Lars Krückeberg, Wolfram Putz, Thomas Willemeit et Gregor Hoheisel sont les partenaires de l'agence qui emploie près de 100 personnes dans le monde entier. Graft possède des bureaux à Los Angeles, Berlin et Pékin. Lars Krückeberg a fait des études d'ingénieur à l'Université technique de Brunswick, Allemagne (1988–96) et à l'école SCI-Arc de Los Angeles (1997–98). Wolfram Putz a fait ses études à l'Université technique de Brunswick (1988–95), l'université de l'Utah à Salt Lake City (1992–93) et l'école SCI-Arc (1996–98). Thomas Willemeit a également été formé à Brunswick et au Bauhaus de Dessau (1991–92) avant de travailler à l'agence de Daniel Libeskind (1998–2001). Gregor Hoheisel sort lui aussi de l'Université technique de Brunswick (1988–95). Ils ont construit un studio et une maison pour Brad Pitt à Los Angeles (2000–03) et sont les premiers architectes du projet Pink et de l'initiative Make It Right à La Nouvelle-Orléans (Louisiane, 2007–), en collaboration avec Brad Pitt et William McDonough + Partners. Ils ont créé l'hôtel Q! à Berlin (2002–04), ainsi que des restaurants des casinos Bellagio and Mirage de Las Vegas (Nevada, 2004 et 2006), et ont collaboré à plusieurs centres hôteliers de luxe dans les Caraïbes. Leurs réalisations les plus récentes comprennent : le restaurant Ginkgo (Chengdu, Chine, 2008) ; la boutique régionale à l'aéroport international de Francfort (2009, publiée ici) ; le restaurant Wokalicious (Berlin, 2010–11, publié ici) ; le Musée juif russe de la tolérance (Moscou, 2007–12) et la zone de développement commercial Ordos 20+10 (Ordos, Mongolie intérieure, Chine, 2011–).

WOKALICIOUS

Berlin, Germany, 2010–11

*Address: Litfass-Platz 1, Hackesches Quartier, 10178 Berlin, Germany, +49 30 27 58 10 10,
www.wokalicious.de. Area: 302 m²
Client: Jan Schäfer, Faris Nager, Rainer Wendt. Cost: not disclosed*

This "Thai fusion cuisine" restaurant is located in Berlin-Mitte. The design features large windows facing the street and a square, while the "restaurant's back wall is carried out as a horizontally structured wooden relief, which, in materiality, curvature and stacking, reminds the diner of the characteristic bamboo baskets in which the delicious dim sums are prepared and served." Reflective film is applied to the narrow sides of this wooden relief resulting in unexpected lighting effects. The three parts of the restaurant are a main dining area, a central bar and open kitchen, and a private dining area in the back. In contrast to the light, natural materials used in the dining area, the lavatories are black with gold glass-mosaic tiles and wallpaper.

Das Restaurant mit „Thai Fusion Cuisine" in Berlin-Mitte hat große Fenster mit Blick auf die Straße und einen Platz, während „die rückwärtige Wand des Restaurants als Holzrelief mit Querstruktur gestaltet wurde, das die Gäste durch Material, Wölbung und Schichtung an die typischen Bambuskörbe erinnert, in denen die köstlichen Dim Sums zubereitet und serviert werden". An den Schmalseiten des Holzreliefs wurde Spiegelfolie aufgebracht, wodurch überraschende Lichteffekte entstehen. Das Restaurant gliedert sich in Hauptspeisebereich, Bar und offene Küche, nach hinten schließt sich ein Raum für geschlossene Veranstaltungen an. Im Kontrast zu den hellen Naturmaterialien des Gastbereichs wurden die Toiletten schwarz mit goldenen Mosaikfliesen und Tapeten gestaltet.

Le restaurant de « cuisine thaï fusion » est situé dans le quartier de Berlin-Mitte. Les larges fenêtres ouvrent sur la rue et une place, tandis que « le mur du fond est réalisé sous la forme d'un relief horizontal de bois structuré qui, dans sa matérialité, sa courbure et son empilage, rappelle aux dîneurs les paniers de bambou typiques dans lesquels sont préparés et servis les délicieux dim sum. » Un film réfléchissant recouvre la tranche du bois et produit des effets d'éclairage inattendus. Le restaurant comporte trois parties, une salle principale, un bar central à cuisine ouverte et un espace privé à l'arrière. Les toilettes sont en noir, avec des carreaux en mosaïque de verre dorés et du papier peint qui contrastent avec les matériaux clairs et naturels de la partie restaurant.

The exterior of the restaurant is simple, but broadly glazed, with a bright white circle attracting attention to the name of the establishment.

Die Fassade des Restaurants ist schlicht und großflächig verglast. Ein leuchtender weißer Kreis lenkt die Aufmerksamkeit auf den Namen des Lokals.

L'extérieur du restaurant est simple mais largement vitré ; le cercle blanc lumineux attire l'attention sur son nom.

Interior spaces are simple, but warm,
with the amoeboid lighting fixtures
and patterned wood walls or dividers
giving the overall tone to the design.

Das Interieur ist schlicht und warm
gehalten. Amöbenhafte Lichtobjekte
sowie Wände und Raumteiler aus
strukturiertem Holz prägen die Atmosphäre.

Les espaces intérieurs sont sobres,
mais chaleureux, le luminaire ami-
boïde et les murs ou divisions en bois
à motifs donnent au design son ton
général.

The designers contrast matte, opaque surfaces with the freely formed hanging light fixtures.

Die Gestalter arbeiten mit Kontrasten zwischen den matten, lichtundurchlässigen Flächen und den frei geformten, hängenden Leuchten.

Les designers ont opposé les surfaces mates et opaques aux formes libres des lampes suspendues.

A floor plan shows the very efficient alignment to tables and other restaurant facilities. Below, the curving, wood-faced bar.

Ein Grundriss illustriert die höchst effiziente Anordnung der Tische und weiterer Einrichtungen des Restaurants. Unten die geschwungene holzverkleidete Bar.

Le plan met en évidence l'alignement très rationnel des tables et autres équipements du restaurant. Ci-dessous, le bar courbe à revêtement de bois.

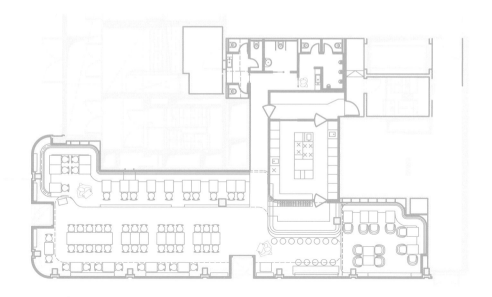

FRANKFURT REGIONALS STORE

Frankfurt International Airport, Frankfurt, Germany, 2009

*Address: Frankfurt International Airport, Frankfurt, Germany,
www.heinemann-dutyfree.com/frankfurt. Client: Gebr. Heinemann, Hamburg
Area: 40 m². Cost: not disclosed*

The curving, overlapping layers of the installation allow for the display of products, while rendering ordinary airport space inviting.

Die gerundeten, gestapelten Schichten der Installation dienen als Präsentationsfläche für Waren und verleihen den gewöhnlichen Flughafenräumen ein einladendes Flair.

Les courbes se chevauchant en couches multiples de l'installation servent de présentoirs et donnent un air engageant à un espace d'aéroport des plus ordinaires.

The structure designed by Graft fits into a broad, empty store, bringing its center to life and inviting clients to discover German products.

Die von Graft entwickelte Konstruktion integriert sich in den geräumigen Ladenbereich, belebt dessen Zentrum und regt Kunden an, deutsche Produkte zu entdecken.

La structure créée par Graft s'inscrit dans un vaste magasin vide, donnant vie au centre et invitant les clients à découvrir les spécialités allemandes.

Graft created a "dynamic tree installation" for this shop with stacked disks of oak, while an inlaid leaf design clads the floor, especially near the base of the tree structures. The space is meant to be essentially open, "like a forest glade." The "tree" structure serves an obvious display function and with its layered composition recalls contemporary architecture and design as much as any attempt to imitate a natural formation. The owner of the shop, Gebr. Heinemann, has called on other well-known architects, such as Hadi Teherani, for their airport stores. Heinemann operates 179 duty free shops in 49 airports. Graft saw this design as being a natural combination of a German element with their own international experience. Indeed, the point of this shop is to stock and sell typical German specialities for travelers. Graft's presence is marked, as is the German flavor of the shop, by the signage on the store.

Für diese Ladeneinrichtung realisierte Graft eine „dynamische Bauminstallation" aus geschichteten Eichenholzscheiben und einem Intarsienparkett mit Blattmuster am Sockel der Konstruktion. Der Bereich wurde „wie eine Waldlichtung" bewusst offen gestaltet. Die Bauminstallation wurde ganz auf die Präsentation der Waren zugeschnitten und erinnert dank der geschichteten Struktur an zeitgenössische Architektur und Design, ist jedoch ebenso natürlichen Formen nachempfunden. Der Shopbetreiber Gebr. Heinemann beauftragte auch andere bekannte Architekten mit der Gestaltung ihrer Flughafenfilialen, darunter Hadi Teherani. Heinemann betreibt 179 Duty-Free-Shops in 49 Flughäfen. Graft versteht den Entwurf als organisches Zusammenspiel zwischen einem gewissen deutschen Element und dem internationalen Profil des Büros. Tatsächlich präsentiert die Installation den Reisenden typisch deutsche Produkte und Spezialitäten. Der deutsche Schwerpunkt des Produktangebots und der Name des Büros wird mit entsprechenden Schriftzügen am Shop signalisiert.

Pour cette boutique, Graft a créé une « installation arborescente dynamique » en disques de chêne empilés, avec un motif de feuilles incrusté sur le sol, notamment autour de la base des structures arborescentes. L'espace se veut avant tout ouvert, « comme une clairière ». La structure « en arbre » a une fonction de présentation évidente et sa composition stratifiée rappelle autant l'architecture contemporaine et le design que d'autres tentatives d'imiter une formation naturelle. Le propriétaire, Gebr. Heinemann, a fait appel à d'autres architectes de renom, comme Hadi Teherani, pour ses boutiques d'aéroport – il gère 179 magasins duty free dans 49 aéroports. Pour Graft, cette réalisation a représenté l'association naturelle d'un élément allemand et de sa propre expérience internationale. De fait, la boutique vend des spécialités allemandes typiques aux voyageurs. La présence de Graft est affichée, comme l'atmosphère allemande de la boutique, par la signalisation.

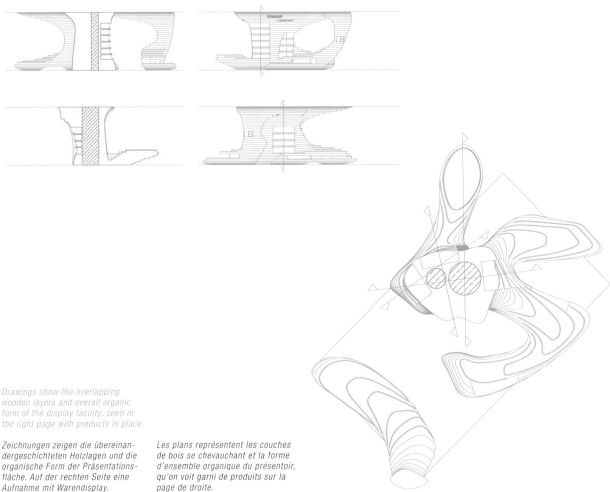

Drawings show the overlapping wooden layers and overall organic form of the display facility, seen in the right page with products in place.

Zeichnungen zeigen die übereinandergeschichteten Holzlagen und die organische Form der Präsentationsfläche. Auf der rechten Seite eine Aufnahme mit Warendisplay.

Les plans représentent les couches de bois se chevauchant et la forme d'ensemble organique du présentoir, qu'on voit garni de produits sur la page de droite.

HAKUHODO

Hakuhodo Inc.
5–3–1 Akasaka
Minato-ku
Tokyo 107–8766
Japan

Tel: +81 3 6441 8766 / Fax: +81 3 6441 8649
E-mail: atsushi.muroi@hakuhodo.co.jp
Web: www.hakuhodo.co.jp

ATSUSHI MUROI was born in Hiroshima, Japan, in 1975. He received a B.Arch degree from Tokyo University of Science. He worked on the AND Market (Kasumigaseki, Tokyo, 2011, published here) with **HATTORI KIMITARO**, who was born in Gifu, Japan (1977), and graduated from the Tokyo University of the Arts. They both work for Hakuhodo, a firm specialized in advertising, corporate communications, and marketing. Hakuhodo is the second largest advertising agency in Japan. Atsushi Muroi has also worked on the Nissan Omoiyari Balloon (Yokohama, 2009); Docomo Smartphone Lounge (Tokyo, 2010); and Zoff Park Harajuku (Tokyo, 2011), all in Japan.

ATSUSHI MUROI Atsushi Muroi wurde 1975 in Hiroshima geboren. Seinen B.Arch. machte er an der Naturwissenschaftlichen Universität Tokio. Am AND Market (Kasumigaseki, Tokio, 2011, hier vorgestellt) arbeitete er gemeinsam mit **HATTORI KIMITARO**, geboren 1977 in Gifu, Japan, der sein Studium an der Universität der Künste Tokio abschloss. Beide sind für Hakuhodo tätig, eine Agentur für Werbung, Kommunikation und Marketing. Hakuhodo ist Japans zweitgrößte Werbeagentur. Atsushi Muroi arbeitete außerdem an folgenden Projekten: Nissan Omoiyari Balloon (Yokohama, 2009), Docomo Smartphone Lounge (Tokio, 2010) und Zoff Park Harajuku (Tokio, 2011), alle in Japan.

ATSUSHI MUROI est né à Hiroshima en 1975. Il est titulaire d'un B.Arch de l'Université des sciences de Tokyo. Il a travaillé au projet AND Market (Kasumigaseki, Tokyo, 2011, publié ici) avec **HATTORI KIMITARO**, né à Gifu, Japon (1977) et diplômé de l'Université des arts de Tokyo. Ils sont tous les deux employés par Hakuhodo, une agence de publicité, communication d'entreprise et marketing – la deuxième agence de publicité du Japon. Atsushi Muroi a également collaboré au Nissan Omoiyari Balloon (Yokohama, 2009) ; au Smartphone Lounge Docomo (Tokyo, 2010) et au Zoff Park d'Harajuku (Tokyo, 2011).

AND MARKET

Kasumigaseki, Tokyo, Japan, 2011

Address: Kasumigaseki, Tokyo, Japan, www.and-market.com
Area: 31 m². Client: NEC Mobiling, Ltd. Cost: not disclosed

The **AND MARKET** concept was developed by Atsushi Muroi and Hattori Kimitaro for Japan's first smart phone retailer that is not part of a major mobile phone company. Customers can buy phones, accessories, and applications, and benefit from various membership services, not confined to any one certain carrier both in the retail shop and on their web site. Atsushi Muroi states: "Our project includes concept development, brand portfolio strategy, brand name and CI/VI development, and overall brand design, such as the retail shop, web site, promotional tools, and characters." The designer describes the concept as "neutral" meaning "achromatic in terms of design." For Muroi: "Without any heightened color, not even black or white, our design symbolizes the brand essence by depicting the balance of brightness between black and white. You cannot associate AND Market with traditional colors, since it is quite unique both in its services and brand designs."

Atsushi Muroi und Hattori Kimitaro entwickelten das Konzept des **AND MARKET** für Japans ersten netzwerkunabhängigen Smartphone-Anbieter. Die Kunden können in der Filiale wie auch im Webshop Telefone, Accessoires und Apps wählen und verschiedene Mitgliedervorteile nutzen, ohne an einen bestimmten Netzwerkbetreiber gebunden zu sein. Atsushi Muroi erklärt: „Unser Projekt war ein Gesamtpaket aus Konzeptentwicklung, Markenportfolio-Strategie, Entwicklung von Markennamen, Corporate Identity und Erscheinungsbild sowie dem gesamten Branding, einschließlich Filialgeschäft, Website, Werbemitteln und Typografie." Ihm zufolge ist das Konzept „neutral" im Sinne eines „achromatischen Designs". Muroi fügt hinzu: „Unser Design verzichtet auf prägnante Farben, einschließlich Schwarz und Weiß, und symbolisiert den Kern der Marke durch ein Gleichgewicht der Helligkeit zwischen Schwarz und Weiß. AND Market lässt sich nicht mit üblichen Farben assoziieren, schließlich sind Service und Markendesign einzigartig."

Le concept **AND MARKET** a été créé par Atsushi Muroi et Hattori Kimitaro pour le premier distributeur japonais de smart phones, qui n'appartient à aucune grande société de téléphonie mobile : les clients membres peuvent y acheter des téléphones, des accessoires, des applications et bénéficier de divers services sans être limités à un opérateur unique, que ce soit dans la boutique ou sur le site Web. Pour Atsushi Muroi : « notre projet associe le développement conceptuel, la stratégie de portefeuille de marque, le nom commercial et développement CI/VI et le design de marque global par le biais de la boutique, du site Web, des outils promotionnels et des personnages. » Le designer décrit le concept comme « neutre », soit « achromatique en termes de design. Sans rehausser aucune couleur, pas même le noir ou le blanc, notre design incarne l'essence même de la marque en représentant l'équilibre de clarté entre le noir et le blanc. AND Market ne peut être associé à aucune couleur traditionnelle car le concept est quasi unique, par ses services et ses designs de marques ».

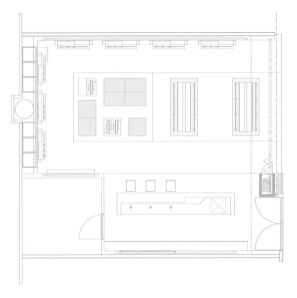

By pushing the logic of a black-and-white design, with repetitive elements such as the circular, disklike lighting fixtures, to its logical extreme, the designers create an unusual, intriguing space.

Indem sie die Logik ihres Schwarz-Weiß-Entwurfs mit wiederkehrenden Elementen wie den runden, scheibenförmigen Leuchten konzeptuell zuspitzen, gelingt es den Gestaltern, einen ungewöhnlich faszinierenden Raum zu realisieren.

En poussant à l'extrême la logique d'un design en noir et blanc aux éléments répétitifs comme les lampes circulaires en forme de disques, les designers ont créé un espace inédit et fascinant.

JOUIN MANKU

Agence Jouin Manku
8 Passage de la Bonne Graine
75011 Paris
France

Tel: +33 1 55 28 89 20 / Fax: +33 1 58 30 60 70
E-mail: agence@jouinmanku.com
Web: www.jouinmanku.com

Born in Nantes, France, in 1967, **PATRICK JOUIN** studied at the École Nationale Supérieure de Création Industrielle (ENSCI) in Paris and received his diploma in 1992. He worked in 1992 as a designer at the Compagnie des Wagons-Lits, and for the following two years at Tim Thom, Thomson Multimedia, under Philippe Starck, who was then Artistic Director of the brand. From 1995 to 1999, Patrick Jouin was a designer in Philippe Starck's Paris studio. He has designed numerous objects and pieces of furniture, while his architectural work includes the Alain Ducasse au Plaza Athénée Restaurant (Paris, 2000); 59 Poincaré Restaurant (Paris, 2000); Plaza Athénée Bar (Paris, 2001); Spoon Byblos Restaurant (Saint-Tropez, 2002); Terrasse Montaigne, Plaza Athénée (Paris, 2005), all in France; and the Gilt Restaurant and Bar (New York, USA, 2005). **SANJIT MANKU** was born in 1971 in Nairobi, Kenya. He received his B.Arch degree from Carleton University (Ottawa, Canada, 1995) and was a designer in the office of Yabu Pushelberg (Toronto, 1996–2001). Sanjit Manku joined Patrick Jouin in 2001 and became a Partner in 2006. Recently, Jouin Manku have completed Van Cleef & Arpels (Paris, France, 2006); Alain Ducasse at the Dorchester (London, UK, 2007); Le Jules Verne, Eiffel Tower (Paris, France, 2007); the Auberge de l'Ill (Illhaeusern, France, 2007); YTL Residence (Kuala Lumpur, Malaysia, 2004–08); Silvera Showroom (Paris, France, 2009); and the Mandarin Oriental, Paris (Paris, France, 2009–11, published here). They are currently working on a residence in Crimea (2010–13); and the Haras Brasserie and Hotel (Strasbourg, France, 2013).

PATRICK JOUIN, 1967 in Nantes, Frankreich, geboren, studierte an der École Nationale Supérieure de Création Industrielle (ENSCI) in Paris und machte sein Diplom 1992. Im selben Jahr arbeitete er als Designer für die Compagnie des Wagons-Lits und in den folgenden zwei Jahren für Tim Thom, Thomson Multimedia, bei Philippe Starck, der damals Art-Direktor war. 1995 bis 1999 war Jouin in Philippe Starcks Pariser Büro tätig. Er entwarf zahlreiche Objekte und Möbel. Zu seinen Architekturprojekten zählen: Restaurant Alain Ducasse au Plaza Athénée (Paris, 2000), Restaurant 59 Poincaré (Paris, 2000), Bar Plaza Athénée (Paris, 2001), Restaurant Spoon Byblos (Saint-Tropez, 2002), Terrasse Montaigne, Plaza Athénée (Paris, 2005), alle in Frankreich, sowie Restaurant und Bar Gilt (New York, 2005). **SANJIT MANKU** wurde 1971 in Nairobi, Kenia, geboren. Er machte seinen B.Arch. an der Carleton University (Ottawa, Kanada, 1995) und arbeitete an Entwürfen im Büro von Yabu Pushelberg (Toronto, 1996–2001). Manku schloss sich 2001 Jouin an und wurde 2006 Partner. In letzter Zeit realisierten Jouin Manku ein Ladenlokal für Van Cleef & Arpels (Paris, 2006), die Restaurants Alain Ducasse im Dorchester (London, 2007) und Le Jules Verne im Eiffelturm (Paris, 2007), die Auberge de l'Ill (Illhaeusern, Frankreich, 2007), die YTL Residence (Kuala Lumpur, Malaysia, 2004–08), einen Showroom für Silvera (Paris, 2009) und das Mandarin Oriental, Paris (Paris, 2009–11, hier vorgestellt). Derzeit arbeitet das Büro an einem Anwesen auf der Krim (2010–13) und dem Hotel Haras mit Brasserie (Straßburg, 2013).

Né à Nantes en 1967, **PATRICK JOUIN** a fait ses études à l'École nationale supérieure de création industrielle (ENSCI) de Paris dont il a obtenu le diplôme en 1992. Il a travaillé comme designer à la Compagnie des Wagons-Lits en 1992 et les deux années suivantes chez Tim Thom, Thomson Multimedia, sous la direction de Philippe Starck qui était alors le directeur artistique de la marque. De 1995 à 1999, Patrick Jouin a été l'un des designers du studio parisien de Philippe Starck. Il a créé de nombreux objets et meubles, ses réalisations architecturales comprennent : le restaurant Alain Ducasse au Plaza Athénée (Paris, 2000) ; le restaurant 59 Poincaré (Paris, 2000) ; lc bar Plaza Athénée (Paris, 2001) ; le restaurant Spoon Byblos (Saint-Tropez, 2002) ; la Terrasse Montaigne, Plaza Athénée (Paris, 2005), ainsi que le restaurant et bar Gilt (New York, 2005). **SANJIT MANKU** est né en 1971 à Nairobi, Kenya. Il a obtenu son B.Arch à l'université Carleton (Ottawa, Canada, 1995) et a été l'un des designers de l'agence de Yabu Pushelberg (Toronto, 1996–2001). Il a rejoint Patrick Jouin en 2001 et est devenu son partenaire en 2006. Récemment, Jouin Manku a réalisé le magasin Van Cleef & Arpels (Paris, 2006) ; le restaurant Alain Ducasse at the Dorchester (Londres, 2007) ; le restaurant de la tour Eiffel Le Jules Verne (Paris, 2007) ; l'Auberge de l'Ill (Illhaeusern, France, 2007) ; la résidence YTL (Kuala Lumpur, Malaisie, 2004–08) ; l'espace d'exposition Silvera (Paris, 2009) et le Mandarin Oriental (Paris, 2009–11, publié ici). Ils travaillent actuellement à une résidence en Crimée (2010–13) et à la brasserie et hôtel du Haras (Strasbourg, 2013).

MANDARIN ORIENTAL, PARIS

Paris, France, 2009–11

Address: 251 Rue Saint-Honoré, 75001 Paris, France, +33 1 70 98 78 88, www.mandarinoriental.com/paris
Area: Bar 8 130 m² + 210 m² garden; Le Sur Mesure 200 m²; Le Camélia 200 m² + 210 m² garden
Client: SFL. Cost: not disclosed

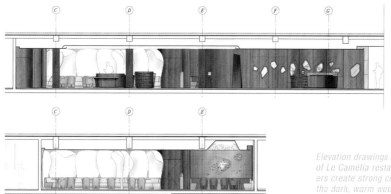

Aufrisse und ein Blick in das Restaurant Le Camélia. Die Gestalter schaffen auffällige Kontraste zwischen dem dunklen warmen Holz und den lichtdurchfluteten Räumen.

Elevation drawings and a view inside of Le Camélia restaurant. The designers create strong contrasts between the dark, warm wood and the light-filled space.

Plans en élévation et vue intérieure du restaurant Le Camélia. Les designers ont créé de forts contrastes entre le bois chaud et sombre et l'espace empli de lumière.

The architects designed two restaurants and one bar in the **MANDARIN ORIENTAL** Hotel on the Rue Saint-Honoré in Paris, recently refurbished by Jean-Michel Wilmotte. They call the Camélia a "bright, open space" that takes its inspiration from the garden onto which it opens. The restaurant is surrounded by white plaster petals. A wood and enamel cooking and dining counter, the "Asian Bar" occupies the center of the restaurant. A giant birdcage with seating for eight is located in one corner of the garden. Bar 8 is a "dark and mysterious space" that features a 12-ton stone bar. The architects explain: "The space is lined with plush, dark leather banquettes, custom-designed armchairs and stools, as well as smoked-glass tables. As in the Camélia, the bar continues into a courtyard with custom furniture…" The Sur Mesure is a gourmet restaurant where a series of alcoves are arrayed around a small glass-lined courtyard. Furniture, tablecloths, and even the tableware were custom-designed by Jouin Manku for the restaurant. White cloth that ranges from smooth surfaces to surprisingly varied and rippled or even torn sections characterizes the interior, while a large metal ring appears to hover in the courtyard space.

Die Architekten gestalteten zwei Restaurants und eine Bar im kürzlich von Jean-Michel Wilmotte renovierten Hotel **MANDARIN ORIENTAL** an der Pariser Rue Saint-Honoré. Das Camélia beschreiben die Planer als „hellen, offenen Raum", vom Garten inspiriert, zu dem es sich öffnet. Weiße, blütenblattähnliche Wandpaneele aus Gips rahmen das Restaurant. Herzstück des Restaurants ist die sog. Asien-Bar, ein Tresen aus Holz und Emaille, an dem auch gekocht wird. In einer Ecke des Innenhofs befindet sich ein „Vogelkäfig" mit Sitzgelegenheiten für acht Personen. Die Bar 8 ist ein „dunkler, geheimnisvoller Raum" mit einem 12 t schweren Bartresen aus Stein. Die Architekten erklären: „Der Raum wird von luxuriösen dunklen Lederbänken, eigens entworfenen Lehnsesseln, Hockern und Rauchglastischen gesäumt. Wie das Camélia, so setzt sich auch die Bar mit eigens entworfenen Möbeln in einem Innenhof fort…" Auch die Sitznischen des Gourmetrestaurants Sur Mesure säumen einen kleinen verglasten Innenhof. Möbel, Tischdecken und selbst das Besteck wurden von Jouin Manku eigens für das Restaurant gestaltet. Weiße Stoffe prägen das Interieur, von glatt über ungewöhnlich strukturiert und gerippt bis hin zu zerissenen Texturen. Über dem Innenhof schwebt ein großer Metallring.

Les architectes ont réalisé deux restaurants et un bar à l'hôtel **MANDARIN ORIENTAL** de la rue Saint-Honoré, récemment réaménagé par Jean-Michel Wilmotte. Ils ont conçu le Camélia comme un « espace clair et ouvert » qui puise son inspiration du jardin sur lequel il ouvre. Un comptoir gastronomique de bois et d'émail, l'« Asian Bar », occupe le centre du restaurant, entouré de pétales en plâtre blanc. Une cage à oiseaux géante pour huit convives est placée dans un coin du jardin. Le Bar 8 est un « lieu sombre et mystérieux » avec son bar en pierre de 12 tonnes. Les architectes le décrivent : « L'espace est bordé de luxueuses banquettes de cuir sombre, de fauteuils et tabourets spécialement créés et de tables de verre fumé. Comme le Camélia, le bar se prolonge par une cour aux meubles exclusifs… » Le Sur Mesure, enfin, est un restaurant gourmet dont les alcôves rayonnent autour d'une petite cour vitrée. Le mobilier, le linge de table, et même les couverts, ont été créés spécialement par Jouin Manku. L'intérieur est marqué par des drapés blancs dont les surfaces varient du lisse à des ondulations surprenantes, voire à des déchirures, tandis qu'un large anneau de métal semble planer dans l'espace de la cour.

An image taken inside Bar 8 within the Mandarin Oriental Hotel in Paris. The bar itself was made with 12 tons of stone.

Ein Blick in die Bar 8 im Hotel Mandarin Oriental in Paris. Der Bartresen wurde aus 12 t Stein gefertigt.

Vue de l'intérieur du Bar 8, à l'hôtel Mandarin Oriental de Paris. Le bar lui-même est fait de 12 tonnes de pierre.

The garden-like atmosphere and a "birdcage" seating area located in Bar 8. A plan and an elevation drawing explore the entire space.

L'atmosphère de jardin et une « cage à oiseaux » où s'asseoir dans le Bar 8. Le plan et l'élévation ci-dessous parcourent l'espace total.

Auch ein begrünter Innenhof samt „Vogelkäfig" mit Sitzgelegenheiten gehört zur Bar 8. Grundriss und Querschnitt zeigen die Bar im Überblick.

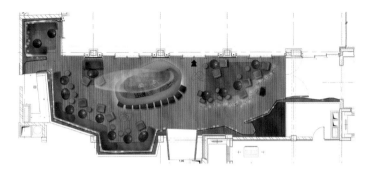

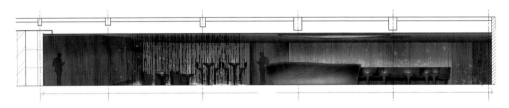

The architects explain that "heavily sculpted forms in tailored fabric wrap around the entire space." The arm chairs designed by Jouin are visible in the photo below.

Den Architekten zufolge wurde „der gesamte Raum mit maßgeschneiderten Stoffen ausgekleidet". Die von Jouin entworfenen Armlehnsessel unten im Bild.

Les architectes expliquent que « des formes puissamment sculptées dans des tissus sur mesure enveloppent complètement l'espace ». Sur la photo du bas, on voit les fauteuils créés par Jouin.

The restrooms of the Sur Mesure restaurant, also designed by Jouin Manku. Below, sketches by Patrick Jouin showing the armchair he designed for the Mandarin Oriental Hotel.

Die ebenfalls von Jouin Manku gestateten Toiletten des Restaurants Sur Mesure. Unten Skizzen von Patrick Jouin für den eigens für das Mandarin Oriental in Paris entworfenen Armlehnsessel.

Toilettes du Sur Mesure, également créées par Jouin Manku. Ci-dessous, croquis de Patrick Jouin du fauteuil qu'il a imaginé pour le Mandarin Oriental.

WOLFGANG KERGASSNER

Architekturbüro Wolfgang Kergaßner
Herzog-Carlstr. 2
Scharnhauser Park
73760 Ostfildern
Germany

Tel: +49 711 540 70 90 / Fax: +49 711 54 07 09 50
E-mail: buero@kergassner.com
Web: www.kergassner.com

WOLFGANG KERGASSNER was born in Dürnhof, Germany, in 1958. He studied architecture at the Technischen Hochschule Darmstadt (1983–88). He worked with Kauffmann Theilig (Stuttgart, 1988–94), and opened his own office in Stuttgart in 1996. In describing his method, Wolfgang Kergaßner emphasizes the issues of cost and scheduling that must be part of each project from the outset. He states: "The planning and execution process, which includes construction, cost, and project management, as well as the experience and evaluation of built projects, prove that very economical projects can be realized with innovative architecture." His work includes the Seele Headquarters (Gersthofen, 1998); Airbus Aircabin (Laupheim, 2001); Scharnhauser Park Office Building (Ostfildern, 2003); Linde Agora (Pullach-Höllriegelskreuth, 2006–08, published here); SAP "Haus im Park" (St. Ingbert, 2008); and Z-UP (Stuttgart, 2009), all in Germany.

WOLFGANG KERGASSNER wurde 1958 in Dürnhof, Deutschland, geboren. Er studierte Architektur an der Technischen Hochschule Darmstadt (1983–88). Nachdem er für Kauffmann Theilig (Stuttgart, 1988–94) tätig war, eröffnete er 1996 ein eigenes Büro in Stuttgart. Kergaßner ist es besonders wichtig, Kosten- und Terminfragen von Beginn an in den Planungsprozess miteinzubeziehen. Er erklärt: „Der kreative Zugriff auf den gesamten Planungs- und Ausführungsprozess, das heißt insbesondere Bauleitung, Kosten- und Projektmanagement, sowie die Erfahrung und Auswertung der gebauten Projekte belegen, dass mit innovativer Architektur sehr wirtschaftliche Projekte zu realisieren sind." Zu seinen Projekten zählen das Bürohaus Seele (Gersthofen, 1998), die Airbus Aircabin (Laupheim, 2001), das Bürohaus Scharnhauser Park (Ostfildern, 2003), die Linde Agora (Pullach-Höllriegelskreuth, 2006–08, hier vorgestellt), das „Haus im Park" für SAP (St. Ingbert, 2008) sowie das Z-UP (Stuttgart, 2009), alle in Deutschland.

WOLFGANG KERGASSNER est né à Dürnhof, Allemagne, en 1958. Il a étudié l'architecture à l'École supérieure technique de Darmstadt (1983–88), travaillé avec Kauffmann Theilig (Stuttgart, 1988–94) et ouvert son agence à Stuttgart en 1996. Lorsqu'il décrit sa méthode de travail, Wolfgang Kergaßner insiste sur la question du coût et le calendrier qui doit être intégré à chaque projet dès le début : « Le processus de planification et d'exécution, qui comprend la construction, l'étude des coûts et la gestion du projet, ainsi que l'expérience et l'évaluation des projets déjà construits, prouve que des projets très économiques peuvent être réalisés avec une architecture innovante. » Ses réalisations comprennent : le siège de Seele (Gersthofen, 1998) ; le bâtiment Airbus Aircabin (Laupheim, 2001) ; l'immeuble de bureaux Scharnhauser Park (Ostfildern, 2003) ; l'agora Linde (Pullach-Höllriegelskreuth, 2006–08, publiée ici) ; la « Haus im Park » de SAP (St. Ingbert, 2008) et l'immeuble Z-UP (Stuttgart, 2009), toutes en Allemagne.

LINDE AGORA

Pullach-Höllriegelskreuth, Germany, 2006–08

Address: Dr.-Carl-von-Lindestr. 6, 82049 Höllriegelskreuth, Germany,
www.linde.com. Area: 6700 m². Client: Linde Group. Cost: not disclosed
Collaboration: Armin Fies, Oliver Kettenhofen

The **LINDE AGORA** accommodates the staff restaurant with a capacity of 2000 meals a day, a staff cafeteria with 300 seats, and a hospitality area. The training and conference center on the first floor surrounds the Agora atrium. A "VIP-Forum" constitutes the upper part of the building, which offers a year-round panoramic view of the Alps. Linde is the world's largest supplier of industrial and medical gases. They are also one of the most important manufacturers of forklift trucks and warehouse equipment and are market leaders in refrigeration technology in Europe. The architects and the firm emphasize the "social perception of the project" as being a tribute to the employees, guests, and business partners of Linde. "These investments of the builder have nothing to do with any political calculation," according to the architect. "They are a visible sign of the respect for the most valuable asset of a business, its employees, and for the citizens of Pullach in the spirit of good, neighborly relations."

In der **LINDE AGORA** befinden sich ein Betriebsrestaurant mit einer Kapazität von täglich 2000 Mahlzeiten, ein Mitarbeitercafé mit 300 Plätzen sowie ein Bereich für Gäste. Das Schulungs- und Konferenzzentrum im ersten Stock säumt das Atrium. Im obersten Geschoss liegt das VIP-Forum, von dem aus sich ganzjährig das Panorama auf die Alpen öffnet. Linde ist weltweit größter Gaslieferant für Industrie und Medizin. Darüber hinaus zählt das Unternehmen zu den wichtigsten Herstellern von Gabelstaplern sowie Lagertechnik und ist europaweiter Marktführer in der Kältetechnik. Architekt wie Auftraggeber betonen die „soziale Wahrnehmung des Projekts" als eine Hommage an die eigenen Angestellten, Gäste und Geschäftspartner der Firma Linde. „Diese Investition des Bauherren erfolgt völlig losgelöst von jeglichem politischem Kalkül", so der Architekt. „Sie ist sichtbares Zeichen der entgegengebrachten Achtung vor dem wertvollsten Gut eines Unternehmens, vor seinen Mitarbeiterinnen und Mitarbeitern und den Bürgerinnen und Bürgern von Pullach im Sinne einer guten Nachbarschaft."

L'**AGORA LINDE** accueille le restaurant d'entreprise, d'une capacité de 2000 repas par jour, une cafétéria de 300 couverts et un espace salon. Le centre de formation et de conférences au premier étage entoure l'atrium. Un « forum VIP » occupe le haut du bâtiment et offre toute l'année une vue panoramique sur les Alpes. Linde est le premier fournisseur mondial de gaz industriels et médicaux, c'est aussi l'un des premiers fabricants de chariots élévateurs et systèmes d'entreposage et le leader du marché européen des technologies de réfrigération. Les architectes et l'entreprise soulignent l'« image sociale du projet », tribut aux employés, aux invités et aux partenaires commerciaux de Linde. « Ces investissements du constructeur n'ont rien d'un calcul politique, selon l'architecte, ils sont le signe visible du respect pour le bien le plus précieux d'une entreprise, ses employés, et pour les habitants de Pullach, dans un esprit de relations de bon voisinage. »

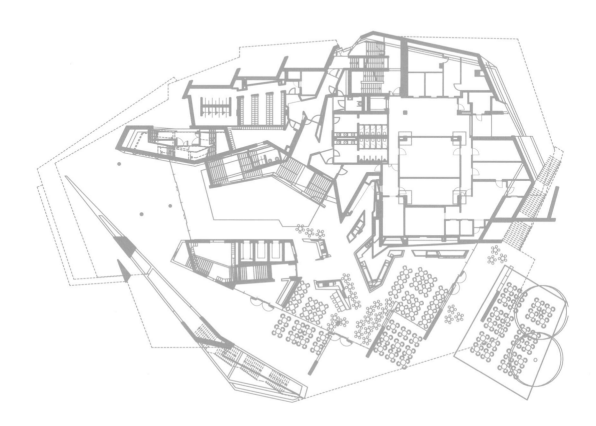

The complex, angled composition of the structure is visible in the drawing to the left, and equally, in the photo above.

Die komplexe schiefwinklige Komposition des Baus ist auf der Zeichnung links zu sehen, ebenso wie auf der Ansicht oben.

La composition complexe et anguleuse de la structure ressort du plan à gauche et de la photo ci-dessus.

The cafeteria area features furnishings that are very much in the spirit of the building itself, with their muted colors and strong angles.

Die Einbauten der Cafeteria mit ihren gedämpften Farben und spitzen Winkeln entsprechen ganz der Formensprache des Gebäudes.

Le mobilier de l'espace cafétéria est conforme à l'esprit de la construction avec ses couleurs douces et ses angles marqués.

WARO KISHI

Waro Kishi + K. Associates/Architects
4F Yutaka Building, 366 Karigane-cho
Nakagyo-ku
Kyoto 604–8115
Japan

Tel: +81 75 213 0258 / Fax: +81 75 213 0259
E-mail: mail@k-associates.com
Web: www.k-associates.com

Born in Yokohama, Japan, in 1950, **WARO KISHI** graduated from the Department of Electronics of Kyoto University in 1973, and from the Department of Architecture of the same institution two years later. He completed his postgraduate studies in Kyoto in 1978, and worked in the office of Masayuki Kurokawa in Tokyo from 1978 to 1981. He created Waro Kishi + K. Associates/Architects in Kyoto in 1993. His work includes the Memorial Hall (Ube, Yamaguchi, 1997); a House in Higashi-nada (Kobe, 1997); a House in Suzaku (Nara, 1997–98); a House in Fukaya (Fukaya, Saitama, 2000); House II in Kurakuen (Nishinomiya, Hyogo, 2001); the Zen Lounge ONO/ Kyoto (Kyoto, 2003, published here); and the Luna di Miele Omotesando Building (Tokyo, 2004). More recently he has completed the Kit House, Student Union Building for the Kyoto Institute of Technology (Kyoto, 2010); Tokyo International Air Terminal Commercial Zone (Toky, 2010); and the Nitto Pharma Centennial Hall (Kyoto, 2011), all in Japan.

Der 1950 im japanischen Yokohama geborene **WARO KISHI** schloss sein Studium 1973 an der Fakultät für Elektrotechnik der Universität Kioto ab, zwei Jahre später folgte ein Abschluss in Architektur an derselben Hochschule. 1978 beendete er dort ein Aufbaustudium. Kishi war von 1978 bis 1981 für Masayuki Kurokawa in Tokio tätig, 1993 gründete er sein Büro Waro Kishi + K. Associates/Architects in Kioto. Zu seinen Projekten zählen die Memorial Hall (Ube, Yamaguchi, 1997), ein Haus in Higashi-nada (Kobe, 1997), ein Haus in Suzaku (Nara, 1997–98), ein Haus in Fukaya (Fukaya, Saitama, 2000), das Haus II in Kurakuen (Nishinomiya, Hyogo, 2001), die Zen Lounge ONO/Kyoto (Kioto, 2003, hier vorgestellt) sowie das Luna di Miele Omotesando Building (Tokio, 2004). In jüngster Zeit konnte er das Kit House für das Studentenwerk der Technischen Universität Kioto (2010) fertigstellen sowie Verkaufsflächen im Terminalgebäude des Internationalen Flughafens Tokio (2010) und die Jahrhunderthalle für Nitto Pharma (Kioto, 2011), alle in Japan.

Né à Yokohama en 1950, **WARO KISHI** est diplômé en électronique de l'université de Kyoto (1973) et en architecture deux ans plus tard. Il a achevé ses études de troisième cycle à Kyoto en 1978 et a travaillé dans l'agence de Masayuki Kurokawa à Tokyo de 1978 à 1981. Il a fondé Waro Kishi + K. Associates/Architects à Kyoto en 1993. Ses réalisations comprennent : le hall du mémorial (Ube, Yamaguchi, 1997) ; une maison à Higashi-nada (Kobe, 1997) ; une maison à Suzaku (Nara, 1997–98) ; une maison à Fukaya (Fukaya, Saitama, 2000) ; la Maison II à Kurakuen (Nishinomiya, Hyogo, 2001) ; le Zen Lounge ONO/Kyoto (Kyoto, 2003, publié ici) et le bâtiment Luna di Miele Omotesando (Tokyo, 2004), toutes au Japon. Plus récemment, il a terminé la Kit House, bâtiment du syndicat étudiant pour l'Institut de technologie de Kyoto (Kyoto, 2010) ; la zone commerciale du terminal aérien international de Tokyo (2010) et la salle séculaire de Nitto Pharma (Kyoto, 2011).

ZEN LOUNGE ONO/KYOTO

Kyoto, Japan, 2003

Address: Nakagyo-ku, Kyoto, Japan. Area: 79 m²
Client: not disclosed. Cost: not disclosed

ONO/Kyoto is a "store" dealing in religious vestments and Buddhist altar articles for the Soto sect of Zen Buddhism. Business is not conducted here as it is in most stores. The customers are mainly priests of the Soto sect, and they come as much to talk as to buy. The architect states: "The client wanted a space that was as unobtrusive as possible—a store that was not recognized as such by passersby—even though the place faces a major street in the middle of the city." Japanese chestnut and zelkova with an adze finish were used for the interior. A floating screen of steel plate inside a partly frosted pane of glass shuts off the view from the street while allowing light in. A brick wall in the middle of the shop and an L-shaped fabric surface define the space. "My intention was to limit the elements to horizontal and vertical surfaces and to display in the space composed of those minimal elements a wealth of different material qualities," says Waro Kishi.

ONO/Kyoto ist ein Geschäft für religiöse Gewänder und Altarbedarf für Praktizierende des Soto-Zen-Buddhismus. Doch Geschäfte werden hier nicht wie in den meisten Läden abgewickelt. Die Kunden sind überwiegend Priester des Soto-Zen, die ebensosehr hierherkommen um etwas zu kaufen, wie um das Gespräch zu suchen. Der Architekt erklärt: „Der Bauherr wünschte einen Raum, der so unaufdringlich wie möglich ist – ein Ladenlokal, das von Passanten nicht als solches zu erkennen ist – obwohl das Geschäft an einer innerstädtischen Hauptstraße liegt." Für den Innenraum wurde mit der Dechsel bearbeitete japanische Kastanie und Zelkove verarbeitet. Zur Straße hin schützt ein Schirm aus schwebenden Stahlblechen hinter einem teilweise satinierten Fenster vor Blicken, lässt aber dennoch Licht einfallen. Gegliedert wird das Geschäft durch eine mittig im Raum platzierte Backsteinwand und eine L-förmige Textilbespannung. „Mein Ziel war die Reduktion der einzelnen Elemente auf horizontale und vertikale Flächen; zugleich wollte ich in diesem aus minimalistischen Elementen komponierten Raum eine Vielzahl von Materialqualitäten zeigen", so Waro Kishi.

ONO/Kyoto est un « magasin » qui distribue des vêtements religieux et articles d'autels pour la secte bouddhiste zen Soto. Les affaires ne sont pas ici réalisées comme dans les autres magasins. Les clients sont pour la plupart des prêtres Soto qui viennent autant pour parler que pour acheter. L'architecte explique que « le client souhaitait un espace le plus discret possible – un magasin que les passants ne verraient pas comme tel – même s'il donne sur une grande artère du centre ». L'intérieur est en bois de châtaignier du Japon et de zelkova avec des finitions en liège herminette. Une plaque d'acier flottante dans un panneau de verre partiellement dépoli ferme l'accès aux regards de la rue tout en laissant pénétrer la lumière. L'espace est défini par un mur de briques en son milieu et une surface de tissu en forme de L. « J'ai voulu limiter les éléments aux surfaces horizontales et verticales et afficher dans l'espace composé par ces éléments minimalistes une richesse de différentes qualités de matériaux », explique Waro Kishi.

Though minimal décors are rather typical of Japanese architecture and design, the Zen Lounge goes a step further in the direction of complete minimalism.

Obwohl sparsames Dekor typisch für japanische Architektur und japanisches Design ist, geht die Zen Lounge doch einen Schritt weiter in Richtung eines konsequenten Minimalismus.

Si les décors minimaux sont assez typiques de l'architecture et du design japonais, le Zen Lounge fait un pas de plus vers le minimalisme total.

An axonometric drawing of the space
and two photos that emphasize the
broad flat areas and spotlights near
walls and the limited object display
space.

*Eine Axonometrie des Raums und
zwei Aufnahmen zeigen die großen,
schmucklosen Oberflächen sowie die
wandnahe Spotbeleuchtung und die
reduzierten Präsentationsflächen.*

Le plan axonométrique de l'espace et
les deux photos soulignent les vastes
surfaces planes, les spots proches
des murs et l'espace d'étalage réduit.

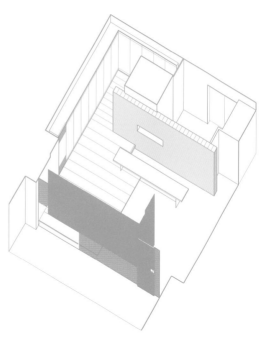

MARCIO KOGAN

Marcio Kogan
Studio MK27
Alameida Tiete 505
04616–001 São Paulo, SP
Brazil

Tel: +55 11 3081 3522 / Fax: +55 11 3063 3424
E-mail: info@marciokogan.com.br / Web: www.marciokogan.com.br

Born in 1952, **MARCIO KOGAN** graduated in 1976 from the School of Architecture at Mackenzie University in São Paulo. He received an IAB (Brazilian Architects Institute) Award for UMA Stores (1999 and 2002); Coser Studio (2002); Gama Issa House (2002); and Quinta House (2004). He also received the Record House Award for Du Plessis House (2004) and BR House (2005). In 2002 he completed a Museum of Microbiology in São Paulo and in 2003 he made a submission for the World Trade Center Site Memorial. He worked with Isay Weinfeld on the Fasano Hotel in São Paulo (2001–03). He also participated with Weinfeld in the 25th São Paulo Biennale (2002) with the project for a hypothetical city named Happyland. Kogan is known for his use of boxlike forms, together with wooden shutters, trellises, and exposed stone. Amongst Kogan's recent residential projects are the Cury House (São Paulo, 2004–06); the Primetime Nursery (São Paulo, 2005–07); the E-Home, a "super-technological" house (Santander, Spain, 2007); an "extreme house" on an island in Paraty (Rio de Janeiro, 2007); Warbler House (Los Angeles, California, USA, 2008); a villa in Milan (Italy, 2008); House 53 (São Paulo, 2008); and two other houses in Brasilia, all in Brazil unless stated otherwise. He has recently completed Bahia House (Salvador, Bahia, Brazil, 2010); L'AND Vineyards, near Évora (Alentejo, Portugal, 2011, published here); and is currently working on a "green building" in New Jersey (USA, 2008–).

MARCIO KOGAN, geboren 1952, schloss sein Studium 1976 an der Architekturfakultät der Universität Mackenzie in São Paulo ab. Für seine UMA Stores (1999 und 2002), sein Coser Studio (2002), das Haus Gama Issa (2002) sowie das Haus Quinta (2004) wurde er mit dem Preis des IAB (Brasilianisches Institut für Architektur) ausgezeichnet. Darüber hinaus erhielt er den Record-House-Preis für sein Haus Du Plessis (2004) und das Haus BR (2005). 2002 konnte er das Museum für Mikrobiologie in São Paulo fertigstellen, 2003 gestaltete er einen Entwurf für die Gedenkstätte am ehemaligen World Trade Center. Mit Isay Weinfeld arbeitete er am Fasano Hotel in São Paulo (2001–03). Ebenfalls mit Weinfeld entwarf er die fiktive Stadt „Happyland" für die 25. Biennale von São Paulo (2002). Kogan ist bekannt für seine kastenartigen Formen, die er mit Holzläden, -gittern und freigelegtem Mauerwerk kombiniert. Zu Kogans jüngeren Wohnbauten zählen das Haus Cury (São Paulo, 2004–06), die Primetime Nursery (São Paulo, 2005–07), das E-Home, ein „hochtechnisiertes" Haus (Santander, Spanien, 2007), ein „extremes Haus" auf einer Insel in Paraty (Rio de Janeiro, 2007), das Warbler House (Los Angeles, Kalifornien, 2008), eine Villa in Mailand (2008), das Haus 53 (São Paulo, 2008) sowie zwei weitere Häuser in Brasília. Kürzlich fertiggestellt wurden das Haus Bahia (Salvador, Bahia, Brasilien, 2010) und das Weingut L'AND bei Évora (Alentejo, Portugal, 2011, hier vorgestellt). Aktuell arbeitet das Büro an einem „Grünen Haus" in New Jersey (USA, 2008).

Né en 1952, **MARCIO KOGAN** a obtenu son diplôme de l'École d'architecture de l'université Mackenzie de São Paulo en 1976. Il a reçu un prix de l'IAB (Institut des architectes brésiliens) pour les magasins UMA (1999 et 2002) ; le studio Coser (2002) ; la maison Gama Issa (2002) et la maison Quinta (2004). Il a également remporté le Record House Award pour la maison Du Plessis (2004) et la maison BR (2005). En 2002, il a réalisé un musée de microbiologie à São Paulo et a fait une proposition pour le mémorial sur le site du World Trade Center en 2003. Il a travaillé avec Isay Weinfeld à l'hôtel Fasano de São Paulo (2001–03) et a participé avec lui au projet d'une cité hypothétique baptisée Happyland pour la XXVe Biennale de São Paulo (2002). Kogan est connu pour son emploi des formes rappelant des boîtes, des volets en bois, des treillages et de la pierre nue. Parmi ses projets résidentiels récents figurent la maison Cury (São Paulo, 2004–06) ; la nursery Primetime (São Paulo, 2005–07) ; l'E-Home, une maison « super technologique » (Santander, Espagne, 2007) ; une « maison extrême » sur une île à Paraty (Rio de Janeiro, 2007) ; la maison Warbler (Los Angeles, 2008) ; une villa à Milan (2008) ; la maison 53 (São Paulo, 2008) et deux maisons à Brasilia, tous au Brésil sauf si précisé. Il vient d'achever la maison Bahia (Salvador, Bahia, 2010) ; le domaine viticole L'AND près d'Évora (Alentejo, Portugal, 2011, publié ici) et travaille à un « bâtiment vert » dans le New Jersey (2008–).

L'AND VINEYARDS

Évora, Alentejo, Portugal, 2011

Address: Estrada Nacional 4, Herdade das Valadas, 7050–031 Montemor-o-Novo, Évora, Alentejo, Portugal,
tel: +351 266 24 24 00, fax: +351 266 24 24 01, info@landvineyards.com, www.l-andvineyards.com/pt
Area: 4000 m². Client: L'AND Vineyards. Cost: not disclosed

Marcio Kogan designed this interior space, which is very much in the spirit of his own architecture.

Ein von Marcio Kogan gestalteter Innenraum, stilistisch eng mit seiner Architektur verwandt.

Marcio Kogan a conçu un espace intérieur très proche de l'esprit qui domine dans son architecture.

Located in the Alentejo area of Portugal, the **L'AND VINEYARDS** include a 22-suite exclusive country club hotel and a residential development. Marcio Kogan, Diana Radomysler, and Suzana Glogosky, from Studio MK27, designed the interiors of the central building and the hotel suites. The central reception building contains "a contemporary reinterpretation of Roman and Arabic atrium architecture," creating a generous living room, library, and gift shop offering vineyard products. The central building also houses a winery, a "wine club," an 800-square-meter luxury spa, a courtyard restaurant, and lobby lounge area. Marcio Kogan used natural stone, slate, and wood as his main materials for the interiors he designed. The overall development is made up of six residential clusters, designed by five architects.

Das **WEINGUT L'AND** in der portugiesischen Region Alentejo umfasst ein exklusives Country-Club-Hotel mit 22 Suiten und eine Wohnanlage. Marcio Kogan, Diana Radomysler und Suzana Glogosky von Studio MK27 zeichnen verantwortlich für die Innenarchitektur des Hauptgebäudes und die Hotelsuiten. Das zentrale Empfangsgebäude ist „eine zeitgenössische Interpretation römischer und arabischer Hofbauweise" und umfasst einen großzügigen Wohnraum, eine Bibliothek und einen Souvenirshop, in dem Produkte rund um das Weingut angeboten werden. Im Hauptgebäude befinden sich zudem eine Weinkellerei, ein „Weinclub", ein 800 m² großes Luxus-Spa, ein Hofrestaurant sowie ein Loungebereich in der Lobby. Als Hauptmaterialien für die Gestaltung der Interieurs wählte Marcio Kogan Naturstein, Schiefer und Holz. Die gesamte Anlage umfasst sechs Wohnbereiche, die von fünf verschiedenen Architekten entworfen wurden.

Situé dans la région portugaise de l'Alentejo, **LE DOMAINE VITICOLE L'AND** comprend un hôtel country club sélect de 22 suites et un ensemble résidentiel. Marcio Kogan, Diana Radomysler et Suzana Glogosky de Studio MK27 ont conçu l'intérieur du bâtiment central et les suites de l'hôtel. Le bâtiment de réception central affiche « une réinterprétation contemporaine de l'architecture romaine et arabe des atriums » avec un salon généreux, une bibliothèque et une boutique de cadeaux offrant les produits du vignoble, ainsi qu'une cave, un « wine club », un spa luxueux de 800 m², un restaurant dans la cour et un espace lounge. Marcio Kogan a principalement utilisé la pierre naturelle, l'ardoise et le bois. L'ensemble est composé de six unités résidentielles conçues par cinq architectes.

An unusually shaped outdoor pool and area with its irregular stone path and lounge chairs.

Die formal ungewöhnliche Außenpoolanlage mit unregelmäßigen Steinpfaden und Sonnenliegen.

Une piscine et un espace extérieurs à la forme inhabituelle avec leurs sentiers de pierres irréguliers et chaises longues.

A rough stone wall, wood, and broad glazing mark a small indoor pool in the vineyard complex.

Der kleine Innenpool des Weinguts, geprägt von rauem Mauerwerk, Holz und großen Fensterflächen.

La petite piscine intérieure est marquée par un mur de pierres brutes, du bois et un large vitrage.

An outdoor walled courtyard with an unusual central fire feature.

Ein von Mauern gesäumter Innenhof unter freiem Himmel, in seiner Mitte eine ungewöhnliche Feuerstelle.

Cour extérieure entourée de murs avec une cheminée centrale très originale.

LOT-EK

LOT-EK
55 Little West 12th Street
New York, NY 10014
USA

Tel: +1 212 255 9326 / Fax: +1 212 255 2988
E-mail: info@lot-ek.com
Web: www.lot-ek.com

ADA TOLLA was born in 1964 in Potenza, Italy. She received her M.Arch from the Architecture Faculty of the "Federico II" University (Naples, 1982–89) and did postgraduate studies at Columbia University (New York, 1990–91). She is one of the two founding Partners of LOT-EK, created in Naples, Italy, in 1993 and in New York in 1995. She is currently an Associate Professor at Columbia University in the Graduate School of Architecture, Planning, and Preservation. **GIUSEPPE LIGNANO** was born in Naples, Italy, in 1963. He also received his M.Arch degree from the "Federico II" University (1982–89) and did postgraduate studies at Columbia at the same time as Ada Tolla. He is the other founding Partner of LOT-EK and is currently an Associate Professor at Columbia University in the Graduate School of Architecture, Planning, and Preservation. Their temporary work includes "X-Static Process" (Deitch Projects, New York, 2003); Uniqlo Container Stores (New York, 2006); the Theater for One (Princeton University, Princeton, New Jersey, 2007); PUMACity (Alicante, Spain, and Boston, Massachusetts, 2008); PUMA DDSU (South Street Seaport, New York, 2010); APAP OpenSchool (Anyang, South Korea, 2010); and Van Alen Books (New York, New York, 2011, published here). Current projects include Pier 57 (New York, 2011–); Carroll Townhouse (Brooklyn, New York, 2011–in development); and The City (Eindhoven, the Netherlands, 2011–in development), all in the USA unless stated otherwise.

ADA TOLLA wurde 1964 in Potenza, Italien, geboren. Sie machte ihren M.Arch. an der Fakultät für Architektur der Universität Federico II (Neapel, 1982–89) sowie ein Aufbaustudium an der Columbia University (New York, 1990–91). Sie ist eine der beiden Gründungspartner von LOT-EK, gegründet 1993 in Neapel (1995 in New York). Derzeit lehrt Ada Tolla als außerordentliche Professorin am Graduiertenprogramm für Architektur, Stadtplanung und Denkmalschutz der Columbia University. **GIUSEPPE LIGNANO** wurde 1963 in Neapel geboren. Auch er machte seinen M.Arch. an der Universität Federico II (1982–89) sowie ein Aufbaustudium an der Columbia University, zeitgleich mit Ada Tolla. Er ist der andere Gründungspartner von LOT-EK und derzeit ebenfalls außerordentlicher Professor am Graduiertenprogramm für Architektur, Stadtplanung und Denkmalschutz der Columbia University. Zu den temporären Projekten des Teams zählen *X-Static Process* (Deitch Projects, New York, 2003), Uniqlo Container Stores (New York, 2006), das Theater for One (Princeton University, Princeton, New Jersey, 2007), PUMACity (Alicante, Spanien, und Boston, Massachusetts, 2008), PUMA DDSM (South Street Seaport, New York, 2010), die APAP OpenSchool (Anyang, Südkorea, 2010) und Van Alen Books (New York, 2011, hier vorgestellt). Aktuelle Projekte sind Pier 57 (New York, seit 2011), das Carroll Townhouse (Brooklyn, New York, seit 2011) und The City (Eindhoven, Niederlande, seit 2011).

ADA TOLLA, née en 1964 à Potenza (Italie), a obtenu son M.Arch à la faculté d'architecture de l'université Federico II de Naples (1982–89) et a effectué des études supérieures à l'université Columbia (New York, 1990–91). Elle est l'une des deux associés fondateurs de l'agence LOT-EK, créée à Naples en 1993 et à New York en 1995. Elle est actuellement professeur associé à l'université Columbia (Graduate School of Architecture, Planning, and Preservation). **GIUSEPPE LIGNANO**, né à Naples en 1963, a également obtenu son M.Arch à l'université Federico II (1982–89) et étudié à l'université Columbia en même temps qu'Ada Tolla avec laquelle il a fondé LOT-EK. Il y est lui aussi professeur associé (Graduate School of Architecture, Planning, and Preservation). Parmi leurs projets d'architecture temporaire : l'installation *X-Static Process* (Deitch Projects, New York, 2003) ; les magasins Uniqlo Container (New York, 2006) ; le Theater for One (université de Princeton, New Jersey, 2007) ; PUMACity (Alicante, Espagne et Boston, Massachusetts, 2008) ; PUMA DDSU (South Street Seaport, New York, 2010) ; l'OpenSchool APAP (Anyang, Corée-du-Sud, 2010) et Van Alen Books (New York, 2011, publiée ici). Les projets actuels comprennent : Pier 57 (New York, 2011–) ; Carroll Townhouse (Brooklyn, New York, 2011–) et The City (Eindhoven, Pays-Bas, 2011–).

VAN ALEN BOOKS

New York, New York, USA, 2011

Address: 30 West 22nd Street, New York, NY 10010, USA, +1 212 924 7000,
vanalenbooks@vanalen.org, www.vanalen.org/books
Area: 47 m². Client: Van Alen Institute. Cost: not disclosed

Located at the Van Alen Institute at 30 West 22nd Street in Manhattan, this is a new architecture and design bookstore and public reading room and is the only facility of its kind in New York. Named after the American architect William Van Alen (1883–1954) who designed Manhattan's Chrysler Building, the Institute is a non-profit organization that seeks to improve design in the public domain through publications, exhibitions, and competitions. The installation includes a 4.3-meter seating platform forming large steps, or an amphitheater, that was made with 70 recycled doors. The architects explain: "The solid wood doors form a triangular installation evoking the steps of Times Square's TKTS booth, an iconic project originated through Van Alen Institute's 1999 design competition." As is often the case in the work of LOT-EK, a bright yellow color and strong graphics characterize the space.

Die in Manhattan, neben dem Van Alen Institute an der 30 West 22nd Street gelegene neue Buchhandlung ist auf Architektur und Design spezialisiert und die einzige ihrer Art in New York. Das nach dem amerikanischen Architekten William Van Alen (1883–1954) – dem Baumeister des Chrysler Building in Manhattan – benannte Institut ist eine gemeinnützige Einrichtung zur Förderung von gutem Design im öffentlichen Raum. Dies geschieht durch Publikationen, Ausstellungen und Wettbewerbe. Die Rauminstallation umfasst eine 4,30 m hohe Sitzplattform bzw. ein Amphitheater mit breiten Stufen, das aus 70 recycelten Türen gebaut wurde. Die Architekten führen aus: „Die massiven Holztüren bilden eine Dreiecksform, die an die Treppenkonstruktion der TKTS-Theaterkasse am Times Square erinnert – ein echtes Wahrzeichen, das 1999 aus einem Entwurfswettbewerb hervorging, den das Van Alen Institute initiiert hatte." Wie oft bei Entwürfen von LOT-EK, wird der Raum von leuchtendem Gelb und auffälligen Schriftzügen dominiert.

Située dans l'Institut Van Alen, 30 Ouest 22e Rue à Manhattan, cette nouvelle librairie d'architecture et de design avec salle de lecture publique est la seule de ce type à New York. L'institut, qui porte le nom de l'architecte américain auteur du Chrysler Building de Manhattan William Van Alen (1883–1954), est une organisation à but non lucratif qui vise à faire progresser le design dans le domaine public par des publications, des expositions et des concours. L'ensemble comporte une plate-forme de 4,3 m formant de larges marches, ou un amphithéâtre, et est faite de 70 portes recyclées. Les architectes expliquent que « les solides portes de bois forment une installation triangulaire qui rappelle les marches du kiosque TKTS de Times Square, un projet emblématique qui doit son origine au concours de design de l'Institut Van Alen en 1999 ». Comme souvent dans les projets de LOT-EK, l'espace est marqué par le jaune vif et un graphisme très dynamique.

LOT-EK has realized a number of temporary installations with elements such as shipping containers—here their typical bright colors and an unexpected suspended stair give the small space a dynamic feeling.

LOT-EK realisierte eine Reihe temporärer Installationen mit Modulen wie Schiffscontainern – hier gewinnt der kleine Raum durch die für LOT-EK typischen leuchtenden Farben und eine ungewöhnliche abgehängte Treppenkonstruktion an Dynamik.

LOT-EK a réalisé beaucoup d'installations temporaires avec des conteneurs maritimes – leurs couleurs vives caractéristiques et un étonnant escalier suspendu donnent ici un grand dynamisme au petit espace.

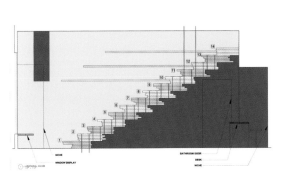

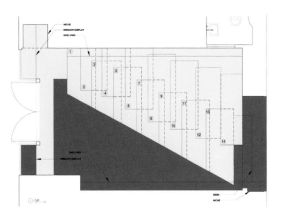

DAVID LYNCH

Silencio
142 Rue Montmartre
75002 Paris
France

Tel: +33 1 40 13 12 32
E-mail: contact@silencio-club.com
Web: www.silencio-club.com

DAVID LYNCH was born in Missoula, Montana, in 1946. He studied painting at the Pennsylvania Academy of Fine Arts and went on to create noted movies such as *Eraserhead* (1977); *The Elephant Man* (1980); *Dune* (1984); *Blue Velvet* (1986); *Wild at Heart* (1990); *Twin Peaks: Fire Walk with Me* (1992); *Lost Highway* (1997); *The Straight Story* (1999); *Mulholland Drive* (2001); and *Inland Empire* (2006), as well as a number of television series such as Twin Peaks (1990–91). He won three Academy Awards as Best Director (1980, 1987, and 2002), a Palme d'Or at the Cannes Film Festival (1990), and a Golden Lion at the Venice Film Festival for his entire career (2006). He has also worked extensively in the area of music. In collaboration with the Paris-based multidisciplinary designer Raphaël Navot, Silencio (Paris, France, 2010–11, published here) was Lynch's first design project, although he has been designing and building furniture for many years. Navot has designed projects for Cappellini, Alessi, Arthus Bertrand, and the Luxembourg Museum of Modern Art among others. He worked with David Lynch throughout every step of the creation and conception of Silencio. The architectural agency ENIA, directed by Brice Piechaczyk, Mathieu Chazelle, and Simon Pallubicki, was responsible for the architecture and project management.

DAVID LYNCH wurde 1946 in Missoula, Montana, geboren. Er studierte Malerei an der Pennsylvania Academy of Fine Arts und schuf später bekannte Filme wie *Eraserhead* (1977), *Der Elefantenmensch* (1980), *Dune – Der Wüstenplanet* (1984), *Blue Velvet* (1986), *Wild at Heart* (1990), *Twin Peaks – Der Film* (1992), *Lost Highway* (1997), *Eine wahre Geschichte* (1999), *Mulholland Drive* (2001) und *Inland Empire* (2006) sowie eine Reihe von Fernsehserien, darunter *Twin Peaks* (1990–91). Ausgezeichnet wurde er dreimal mit dem Oscar als bester Regisseur (1980, 1987 und 2002), einer Goldenen Palme in Cannes (1990) und einem Goldenen Löwen für sein Lebenswerk in Venedig (2006). Darüber hinaus arbeitet Lynch auch zunehmend im Musikbereich. Silencio (Paris, 2010–11, hier vorgestellt), realisiert in Zusammenarbeit mit dem multidisziplinär arbeitenden Pariser Designer Raphaël Navot, war Lynchs erstes Designprojekt, obwohl er seit Jahren Möbel entwirft und baut. Navot hat u. a. Designs für Cappellini, Alessi, Arthus Bertrand und das Museum für moderne Kunst in Luxemburg entwickelt. Für Silencio arbeitete er während des gesamten Konzeptions- und Realisierungsprozesses eng mit David Lynch zusammen. Die Architekturagentur ENIA unter Leitung von Brice Piechaczyk, Mathieu Chazelle und Simon Pallubicki zeichnete für Architektur und Projektmanagement verantwortlich.

DAVID LYNCH est né à Missoula, Montana, en 1946. Il a étudié la peinture à l'Académie des beaux-arts de Pennsylvanie et a ensuite créé des films remarqués tels qu'*Eraserhead* (1977) ; *Elephant Man* (1980) ; *Dune* (1984) ; *Blue Velvet* (1986) ; *Sailor et Lula* (1990) ; *Twin Peaks, les sept derniers jours de Laura Palmer* (1992) ; *Lost Highway* (1997) ; *Une histoire vraie* (1999) ; *Mulholland Drive* (2001) et *Inland Empire* (2006), ainsi que plusieurs séries télé comme *Twin Peaks* (1990–91). Il a remporté trois oscars du meilleur réalisateur (1980, 1987 et 2002), une Palme d'or au festival de Cannes (1990) et un Lion d'or au festival de Venise pour l'ensemble de sa carrière (2006). Il a aussi beaucoup travaillé dans le domaine musical. Réalisé en collaboration avec le designer parisien multidisciplinaire Raphaël Navot, Silencio (Paris, 2010–11, publié ici) est le premier projet d'architecture d'intérieur de Lynch, même s'il crée et fabrique des meubles depuis des années. Navot a conçu des projets pour Cappellini, Alessi, Arthus Bertrand et le Musée d'art moderne du Luxembourg. Il a travaillé avec Lynch à toutes les étapes de la création et de la conception. L'agence d'architecture ENIA, dirigée par Brice Piechaczyk, Mathieu Chazelle et Simon Pallubicki, est responsable de l'architecture et de la gestion du projet.

SILENCIO

Paris, France, 2010–11

Address: 142 Rue Montmartre, Paris 75002, France, +33 1 40 13 12 32,
www.silencio-club.com. Area: 650 m². Client: Savoir Faire
Cost: €3 million. Collaboration: Raphaël Navot, Thierry Dreyfus, Domeau & Pérès, Les Ateliers Gohard

SILENCIO is located at 142 Rue Montmartre in Paris, in an 1883 building on the site of the headquarters of the newspaper *La France*. The structure subsequently served as the Paul Dupont printing house. David Lynch conceived the interior design and furniture, and even the carpets of Silencio. The basic color scheme is a gold monochrome, including a good deal of actual gold leaf. Randomly scattered raw wood cladding is one of the most unusual features of the interior design. Silencio includes a stage for live performances, a cinema, art library, and smoking room. Black Bird seats, Wire seats, sofas, and tables (manufactured by Domeau & Pérès), and cinema seats (manufactured by Quinette) are amongst the objects created especially for the space by David Lynch and developed by Raphaël Navot. Open from 6:00 p.m. to 6:00 a.m., Silencio features a varied series of events, such as a quarterly "Carte Blanche" invitation to discover the universe of a given artist, or a "Cabinet des curiosités" created around an artistic theme.

SILENCIO liegt in der Pariser Rue Montmartre 142 in einem Gebäude von 1883, gegenüber der Hauptredaktion von *La France*. Später wurde der historische Bau von der Druckerei Paul Dupont genutzt. David Lynch gestaltete die Innenarchitektur für den Club, einschließlich der Möbel, bis hin zu den Teppichen. Die Farbpalette basiert auf Goldtönen, darunter ein erheblicher Teil echtes Blattgold. Einer der ungewöhnlichsten Aspekte des Interieurs ist die Wandverkleidung mit unbehandeltem Holz in einzelnen Bereichen. Zum Club gehören eine Bühne für Liveauftritte, ein Kinoraum, eine Kunstbibliothek und ein Raucherzimmer. Eigens von Lynch entworfen und von Raphaël Navot umgesetzt wurden u. a. die Black-Bird-Sessel, die Wire-Sessel, Sofas und Tische (gefertigt von Domeau & Pérès) sowie Kinosessel (produziert von Quinette). Silencio, von sechs Uhr abends bis sechs Uhr morgens geöffnet, bietet ein ambitioniertes Programm, darunter vierteljährliche „Carte Blanche"-Events, die Gelegenheit bieten, das Werk eines bestimmten Künstlers zu entdecken, oder das „Cabinet des curiosités" zu einem künstlerischen Thema.

Le **SILENCIO** est situé au 142 rue Montmartre à Paris dans un immeuble de 1883, siège du journal *La France*, qui a ensuite abrité l'imprimerie Paul Dupont. David Lynch en a imaginé l'architecture intérieure et les meubles, jusqu'aux moquettes. La teinte de base est un doré monochrome, obtenu notamment par de la feuille d'or en abondance. Le revêtement en bois brut disposé au hasard est l'un des aspects les plus insolites. Le Silencio comprend une scène pour performances live, un cinéma, une bibliothèque d'art et un fumoir. Parmi les objets créés par David Lynch et développés par Raphaël Navot figurent des sièges Black Bird, des chaises métalliques, des canapés et des tables (fabrication par Domeau & Pérès) ou des sièges de cinéma (fabrication par Quinette). Ouvert de 18 h à 6 h, le Silencio propose des manifestations variées telles qu'une « Carte Blanche » trimestrielle, invitation à découvrir l'univers d'un artiste, ou un « Cabinet des curiosités » autour d'un thème artistique.

A contrast between light and dark or translucent and opaque surfaces lends an air of mystery to these interior views.

Der Kontrast zwischen hellen und dunklen bzw. lichtdurchlässigen und opaken Oberflächen verleiht diesen Ansichten ein geheimnisvolles Flair.

Le contraste entre obscurité et lumière, ou surfaces transparentes et opaques, donne un air mystérieux à l'intérieur.

An arching ceiling with a random pattern of small wood panels. The Wire chair design seen here is by David Lynch (Domeau & Pérès).

Ein Gewölbe, verkleidet mit einem Zufallsmuster aus kleinteiligen Holztafeln. Auch der hier abgebildete Wire-Sessel ist ein Entwurf von David Lynch (Domeau & Pérès).

Un plafond voûté revêtu de petits panneaux de bois formant un motif aléatoire. Les chaises métalliques ont été créées par David Lynch (Domeau & Pérès).

MARCH STUDIO

March Studio
134 Langford Street
North Melbourne
3051 Victoria
Australia

Tel: +61 3 9348 9199 / Fax: +61 3 9348 9499
E-mail: info@marchstudio.com.au
Web: www.marchstudio.com.au

RODNEY EGGLESTON, born in 1981, is an Australian architect and a founding Director of March Studio. Eggleston was trained at RMIT (1999–2005). Toward the end of his study, Eggleston completed a two-year internship with OMA / Rem Koolhaas in Rotterdam. He returned to Australia and in 2007 set up March Studio with Parisian graphic artist **ANNE-LAURE CAVIGNEAUX** (born in 1980). March Studio has completed Aesop Saint-Honoré (Paris, France, 2010, published here); Aesop Westfield City (Sydney, NSW, 2011); and the bakery Baker D. Chirico (Carlton, Victoria, 2011). Current projects include the O'Keefe Residence (Ivanhoe East, Victoria, 2012); Rose Street Market, restaurant and bar alterations and addition (Fitzroy, Victoria, 2012); and Aesop (New York, USA, 2012), all in Australia unless stated otherwise.

Der australische Architekt **RODNEY EGGLESTON**, geboren 1981, ist einer der Gründer von March Studio. Eggleston studierte am RMIT (1999–2005). Nach Ende seines Studiums absolvierte er ein zweijähriges Praktikum bei OMA/Rem Koolhaas in Rotterdam. 2007 kehrte er nach Australien zurück und gründete mit der Pariser Grafikdesignerin **ANNE-LAURE CAVIGNEAUX** (geboren 1980) March Studio. Das Team realisierte Aesop Saint-Honoré (Paris, 2010, hier vorgestellt), Aesop Westfield City (Sydney, NSW, 2011) und die Bäckerei Baker D. Chirico (Carlton, Victoria, 2011). Laufende Projekte sind u. a. die O'Keefe Residence (Ivanhoe East, Victoria, 2012), Um- und Anbauten eines Restaurants und einer Bar am Rose Street Market (Fitzroy, Victoria, 2012) und Aesop (New York, 2012), alle in Australien, sofern nicht anders vermerkt.

L'architecte australien **RODNEY EGGLESTON**, né en 1981, est directeur fondateur de March Studio. Formé à la RMIT (1999–2005), il a fait un stage de deux ans à la fin de ses études chez OMA/Rem Koolhaas à Rotterdam. De retour en Australie, il a créé March Studio en 2007 avec la graphiste parisienne **ANNE-LAURE CAVIGNEAUX** (née en 1980). March Studio a réalisé les boutiques Aesop Saint-Honoré (Paris, 2010, publiée ici) ; Aesop Westfield City (Sydney, 2011) et la boulangerie Baker D. Chirico (Carlton, Victoria, 2011). Leurs projets en cours comprennent la résidence O'Keefe (Ivanhoe East, Victoria, 2012) ; Rose Street Market, variations et extension de restaurant et bar (Fitzroy, Victoria, 2012) et Aesop (New York, 2012), tous en Australie sauf mention contraire.

AESOP SAINT-HONORÉ

Paris, France, 2010

Address: 256, Rue Saint-Honoré, 75001 Paris, +33 1 40 20 96 14, sainthonore@aesop.com, www.aesop.com
Area: 100 m². Client: Aesop. Cost: not disclosed
Collaboration: Julian Canterbury, Sam Rice, CBD Contracting

The description given by March Studio of this project conveys its spirit and execution as clearly as any other text. "We began by looking at the possibilities of plaster, but soon became intrigued by the parquetry floors one sees throughout Paris. We wanted to explore inhabiting the space with one material, used in one encompassing way. We envisaged using cut wood in such a fashion that it covered the floor, walls, and ceiling, lending a cohesive texture and warmth to the room. The wood of choice for this store is Victorian ash, a timber grown in renewable forests across Australia. The wood was cut in a factory in Melbourne's inner-city suburb of Richmond, then each of the approximately 3500 pieces was hand-cut, hand-sanded, sealed, and numbered according to meticulously drafted plans, before being strategically packed in shipping crates." Created in 1987 in Melbourne, Aesop markets products for skin, hair, and body, presented here on an accumulation of ash planks.

Die Beschreibung von March Studio erklärt die Philosophie und Entstehungsgeschichte des Projekts besser als jeder andere Text: „Anfangs überlegten wir, welche Möglichkeiten Putz bieten könnte, begeisterten uns dann aber bald für Parkettböden, die es überall in Paris gibt. Wir wollten sehen, wie man den Raum mit einem einzigen Material gestalten könnte und suchten nach einer Gesamtlösung. Wir dachten daran, Holz zuschneiden zu lassen und Böden, Wände und Decken damit zu verkleiden, sodass der Raum eine geschlossene Textur und Wärme gewinnen würde. Wir entschieden uns hier für Riesen-Eukalyptus, ein Holz, das überall in Australien in nachhaltiger Forstwirtschaft angebaut wird. Das Holz wurde in einer Fabrik in Richmond, einem innerstädtischen Bezirk von Melbourne, zugesägt. Anschließend wurde jeder der fast 3500 Abschnitte von Hand zugeschnitten, geschliffen und versiegelt, dann nach genauesten Plänen nummeriert und schließlich strategisch in Transportkisten verpackt." Aesop, 1987 in Melbourne gegründet, vertreibt Kosmetikprodukte zur Haut-, Haar- und Körperpflege, die hier auf einer Vielzahl von Eukalyptusholzbrettchen präsentiert werden.

La description que fait March Studio de ce projet en donne mieux que toute autre l'esprit et l'exécution : « Nous avons commencé par chercher des possibilités en plâtre, mais avons vite été intrigués par les sols en parqueterie qu'on voit partout à Paris. Nous voulions essayer une occupation de l'espace avec un seul matériau. Nous avons pensé couper le bois de manière à ce qu'il couvre le sol, les murs et le plafond, ce qui donne une texture cohérente et de la chaleur à la pièce. Le bois choisi est du sorbier des oiseleurs, cultivé dans des forêts renouvelables en Australie. Il a été découpé dans une usine de Richmond, une banlieue défavorisée de Melbourne, puis chacun des 3500 morceaux a été taillé et poncé à la main, collé et numéroté selon un plan méticuleux avant d'être emballé stratégiquement dans des caisses à claire-voie pour expédition. » Fondé en 1987 à Melbourne, Aesop distribue des produits pour la peau, les cheveux et les soins du corps présentés ici sur d'innombrables étagères de sorbier.

The interior of the store is reminiscent of stacks of wood—projecting from the walls just enough to allow for the display of a wide range of Aesop products.

Der Innenausbau des Ladens erinnert an gestapeltes Holz – das gerade weit genug aus der Wand herausragt, um darauf die ganze Bandbreite des Aesop-Sortiments zu präsentieren.

L'intérieur de la boutique fait penser à des piles de bois – qui dépassent juste assez des murs pour permettre d'y présenter une large gamme de produits Aesop.

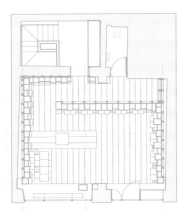

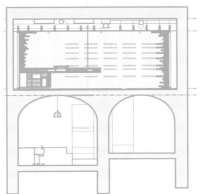

PETER MARINO

Peter Marino Architect, PLLC
150 East 58th Street
New York, NY 10022
USA

Tel: +1 212 752 5444 / Fax: +1 212 759 3727
E-mail: press@petermarinoarchitect.com
Web: www.petermarinoarchitect.com

PETER MARINO received an architecture degree from Cornell University and began his career at Skidmore, Owings & Merrill. He created his present firm in 1978 in New York and currently has seven associates and more than 140 employees, with satellite offices in Philadelphia and Southampton. He has designed shops for Fendi, Armani, Valentino, Louis Vuitton, Dior, Ermenegildo Zegna, Chanel, Loewe, Barneys New York, and Donna Karan. Notable and recently completed retail projects include boutiques for Chanel in New York (2010, published here), Paris (2010), and Singapore (2010); a Hublot flagship on Place Vendôme (Paris, 2010), and a boutique on Madison Avenue in New York (2010); boutiques for Christian Dior in New York (2010), Shanghai (2010), Paris (2010), and Hong Kong (2011); for Ermenegildo Zegna in Shanghai (2010), and Paris (2011); and for Louis Vuitton in Singapore (2011) and Shanghai (2011), as well as the Louis Vuitton Maison on London's New Bond Street (2010, also published here). Marino's cultural design projects include the Zwinger Porcelain Collection and Meissen Animal Gallery at the Dresden Museum (Dresden, Germany, 2006/2010); and a 2010 retrospective of the work of Claude and François-Xavier Lalanne at the Musée des Arts Décoratifs in Paris (France). Current work includes a flagship store for Céline (New York, 2012); and a Hotel, Spa, and Retail Complex in Beirut (Lebanon, 2014).

PETER MARINO schloss sein Architekturstudium an der Cornell University ab und begann seine Laufbahn bei Skidmore, Owings & Merrill. Sein heutiges Büro gründete Marino 1978 in New York. Er beschäftigt derzeit sieben Partner und über 140 Mitarbeiter, weitere Dependancen gibt es in Philadelphia und Southampton. Marino gestaltete Ladenlokale für Fendi, Armani, Valentino, Louis Vuitton, Dior, Ermenegildo Zegna, Chanel, Loewe, Barneys New York und Donna Karan. Wichtige, in jüngster Zeit fertiggestellte Projekte sind u. a. Boutiquen für Chanel in New York (2010, hier vorgestellt), Paris (2010) und Singapur (2010), einen Hublot-Flagshipstore an der Place Vendôme (Paris, 2010) und eine Boutique auf der Madison Avenue in New York (2010), Boutiquen für Christian Dior in New York (2010), Schanghai (2010), Paris (2010) und Hongkong (2011), für Ermenegildo Zegna in Schanghai (2010) und Paris (2011) sowie für Louis Vuitton in Singapur (2011) und Schanghai (2011) und die Louis Vuitton Maison auf der Londoner New Bond Street (2010, ebenfalls hier vorgestellt). Marinos Projekte im kulturellen Bereich sind u. a. die Präsentation der Porzellansammlung im Dresdner Zwinger einschließlich der Meißner Tiere (Dresden, 2006/2010) sowie die Retrospektive von Claude und François-Xavier Lalanne am Musée des Arts Décoratifs in Paris (2010). Zu den laufenden Projekten zählen ein Flagshipstore für Céline (New York, 2012) und ein Hotel-, Spa- und Einkaufszentrum in Beirut (2014).

PETER MARINO est diplômé en architecture de l'université Cornell et a commencé sa carrière chez Skidmore, Owings & Merrill. Il a ouvert son agence en 1978 à New York : elle compte actuellement sept associés et plus de 140 employés avec des filiales à Philadelphie et Southampton. Il a créé des boutiques pour Fendi, Armani, Valentino, Louis Vuitton, Dior, Ermenegildo Zegna, Chanel, Loewe, Barneys New York et Donna Karan. Ses projets récents et notables de commerces comprennent des magasins pour Chanel à New York (2010, publié ici), Paris (2010) et Singapour ; le magasin-phare place Vendôme (Paris, 2010) et une boutique Madison Avenue à New York (2010) pour Hublot ; des boutiques pour Christian Dior à New York (2010), Shanghai (2010), Paris (2010) et Hong Kong (2011) ; pour Ermenegildo Zegna à Shanghai (2010) et Paris (2011) et pour Louis Vuitton à Singapour (2011) et Shanghai (2011), ainsi que le grand magasin londonien Louis Vuitton de New Bond Street (2010, publié ici). Les projets culturels design de Marino comprennent la collection de porcelaine du Zwinger et la Galerie des animaux de Meißen au musée de Dresde (Allemagne, 2006/2010) et une rétrospective de l'œuvre de Claude et François-Xavier Lalanne au Musée des arts décoratifs de Paris (2010). Il travaille actuellement à un magasin pour Céline (New York, 2012) et à un complexe hôtelier, spa et commercial à Beyrouth (2014).

LOUIS VUITTON NEW BOND STREET

London, UK, 2010

*Address: 17–20 New Bond Street, London WIS 2 RB, UK, +44 20 32 14 92 00,
www.louisvuitton.co.uk. Area: 1500 m². Client: Louis Vuitton
Cost: not disclosed*

The architects play on patterns, reflections, and the unexpected alternation of opaque surfaces with cut-out transparencies.

Die Architekten spielen mit Mustern, Spiegelungen und dem überraschenden Wechsel von opaken Flächen und scherenschnitthaften Durchblicken.

Les architectes ont joué avec les motifs, les reflets et l'alternance inattendue de surfaces opaques et de transparences découpées.

Substantial height is amplified with the use of a ceiling mirror. A living-room atmosphere with couches, a table, and books creates a sense of relaxation where fine objects can be viewed.

Die erhebliche Raumhöhe wird durch eine verspiegelte Decke optisch noch gesteigert. Sofas, ein Tisch und Bücher schaffen eine entspannte Atmosphäre, in der sich erlesene Objekte betrachten lassen.

La hauteur déjà substantielle est encore amplifiée par le miroir du plafond. Une ambiance de salon avec des canapés, une table et des livres crée un lieu de détente où admirer de beaux objets.

"The New Bond Street Maison," explain the architects, "was conceived of as the home of a collector who loves the best and rarest and, as such, was planned as a series of unique, exotic environments ranging from vast and luxuriously light-filled to restrained and intimate." The store occupies four floors in two buildings that occupy half the block at the corner of Clifford Street. Since the buildings are listed, outside changes were limited. These constraints did not apply to the interior, thus a three-story void was cut from the structures and lined with a metal mesh curtain. A bridge crossing the void allows clients to view the entire space. A three-story glass staircase was placed in the void. Louis Vuitton accessories, including luggage and objects designed specifically for the New Bond Street store, are displayed on the ground floor, as are original works of art by Richard Prince and Takashi Murakami. Menswear, with its "masculine, clubby, and intimate mood," is displayed on the lower ground floor, as is a 2005 work by Gilbert & George entitled *Paws*. Womenswear is located on the first floor, together with a "librairie" art bookshop with works by Anish Kapoor, Chris Ofili, and Gary Hume. Private client suites accessible by invitation only are on the second floor.

„Die Maison an der New Bond Street", so der Architekt, „wurde wie das Haus eines Kunstsammlers gestaltet, der nur die besten und erlesensten Dinge liebt. Entsprechend wurden einzigartige, exotische Räume geplant – von weitläufig und opulent-lichtdurchflutet bis hin zu zurückhaltend und intim." Das Geschäft erstreckt sich über vier Ebenen in zwei Gebäuden, die einen halben Häuserblock an der Kreuzung zur Clifford Street einnehmen. Denkmalschutzauflagen ließen nur begrenzte Eingriffe am Außenbau zu. Die Einschränkungen betrafen jedoch nicht den Innenraum, sodass ein dreigeschossiger Schacht durch den Bau gezogen wurde, gerahmt von einem Paravent aus Metallgeflecht. Von einer Brücke, die beide Bauten verbindet, haben die Kunden den gesamten Raum im Blick. In den Schacht wurde eine dreistöckige Glastreppe gesetzt. Das Erdgeschoss ist den Accessoires von Louis Vuitton, Taschen und Gepäck sowie einer eigens für die Maison an der New Bond Street entworfenen Produktlinie vorbehalten. Hier sind auch Werke von Richard Prince und Takashi Murakami zu sehen. Herrenmode wird in „maskuliner, intimer Clubatmosphäre" im Untergeschoss präsentiert, neben der 2005 entstandenen Arbeit *Paws* von Gilbert & George. Damenmode befindet sich im ersten Stock, ebenso wie eine „Librairie", eine Kunstbuchhandlung, mit Werken von Anish Kapoor, Chris Ofili und Gary Hume. Suiten für die private Kundenberatung (exklusiv auf Einladung) liegen im zweiten Stock.

« La maison de New Bond Street, expliquent les architectes, a été conçue comme celle d'un collectionneur qui aime ce qu'il y a de mieux et de plus rare et en tant que telle, se compose de plusieurs environnements uniques et exotiques, du vaste espace luxueux baigné de lumière au plus sobre et intime. » Le magasin occupe quatre étages de deux immeubles au coin de Clifford Street. Comme il s'agit de bâtiments classés, les modifications extérieures étaient limitées. Ces contraintes ne s'appliquaient cependant pas à l'intérieur où un vide a été découpé sur trois niveaux et tapissé d'un rideau de mailles métallique. Une passerelle l'enjambe et permet aux clients de visualiser la totalité de l'espace. Un escalier de verre à trois étages y a été placé. Les accessoires Louis Vuitton, notamment les bagages et objets spécialement conçus pour le magasin, sont exposés au rez-de-chaussée avec des œuvres originales de Richard Prince et Takashi Murakami. Le rayon hommes et son « ambiance masculine et intime de club » occupe le sous-sol, ainsi qu'une œuvre de 2005 de Gilbert & George intitulée *Paws*. Le rayon femmes se trouve au premier étage, flanqué de la « Librairie » d'art et d'œuvres d'Anish Kapoor, Chris Ofili et Gary Hume. Des suites privées uniquement accessibles sur invitation sont situées au deuxième étage.

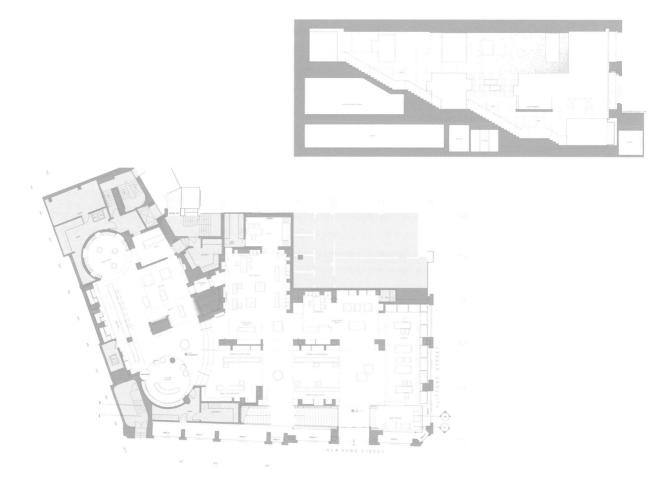

Left, a plan of the store with New Bond Street at the bottom. Right, the stairway with its three-story void and display alcoves.

Links ein Grundriss der Boutique, mit der New Bond Street unten im Bild. Rechts die Treppe in ihrem dreigeschossigen Schacht mit Schaufensteralkoven.

À gauche, un plan du magasin avec New Bond Street en bas. À droite, l'escalier avec son vide de trois étages et ses étalages dans des niches.

To the left, a display area is complemented by an original work by the English artists Gilbert & George.

Links ein Verkaufsbereich, der durch ein Original der englischen Künstler Gilbert & George zusätzlich an Wirkung gewinnt.

À gauche, un espace de présentation est complété par une œuvre originale des artistes anglais Gilbert & George.

Left, a circular eyewear display space with a reflecting ceiling and cylindrical exhibition stands. Below, another rounded room with a work by the noted Japanese artist Takashi Murakami.

Links ein runder Verkaufsraum für Brillenmode mit einer verspiegelten Decke und Säulendisplays. Unten ein weiterer runder Raum mit einem Werk des namhaften japanischen Künstlers Takashi Murakami.

À gauche, un espace circulaire de présentation de lunettes, au plafond réfléchissant et à présentoirs cylindriques. Ci-dessous, une autre pièce ronde avec une œuvre du célèbre artiste japonais Takashi Murakami.

CHANEL SOHO
New York, New York, USA, 2010

*Address: 139 Spring Street, Manhattan, New York 10012, USA, +1 212 334 0055,
www.chanel.com. Area: 387 m². Client: Chanel. Cost: not disclosed*

Reflective surfaces and high ceilings create a distinctive atmosphere where black and white dominate, immediately bringing out Chanel's clothing and objects.

Spiegelnde Oberflächen und hohe Decken schaffen eine ganz eigene Atmosphäre. Hier dominieren Schwarz und Weiß, was Chanels Mode und Objekte besonders zur Geltung bringt.

Les surfaces réfléchissantes et les hauts plafonds créent une atmosphère singulière dominée par le noir et le blanc qui fait ressortir d'emblée les vêtements et accessoires Chanel.

The plan of the store is rectangular (right), but columns and furniture break up and enliven the space according to the types of product on display.

Der Grundriss der Boutique ist ein schlichtes Rechteck (rechts), das jedoch durch Pfeiler und auf die jeweiligen Produktreihen abgestimmte Einbauten aufgelockert wird.

Le plan du magasin est strictement rectangulaire (à droite), mais les colonnes et meubles brisent l'espace et lui donnent vie selon les types de produits présentés.

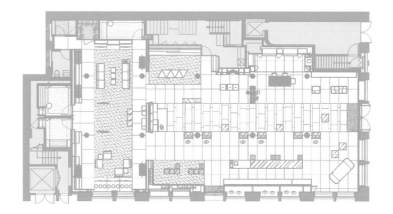

Visitors to this new SoHo space are greeted by a three-meter-high acrylic bottle of the iconic Chanel No. 5 perfume with a surface that shows video images. The architect explains: "Works by artists Peter Belyi, Robert Greene, Gregor Hildebrandt, Alan Rath, and Richard Woods were specially commissioned to highlight the space and meld with the streamlined black-and-white graphicism of the boutique's interior to provide an appropriate edge for the customer that lives, works, and shops in SoHo." The artworks, like the black-and-white woodblock pattern by Richard Woods enclosing columns in the accessories area or the *Flying Eyeballs* work by Alan Rath in the area where sunglasses are sold, are directly related to the retailing strategy of the store. Vintage molded records in a metal structure (Record Wall) by Gregor Hildebrandt mark the ready-to-wear section of the boutique. The mixture of artworks and high-end retail architecture may not be a first, but, in this instance, Peter Marino carries the idea a step further than others, an appropriate gesture given the active art scene in the SoHo area.

Besucher der neuen Chanel-Boutique in SoHo werden von einer 3 m hohen Nachbildung des legendären Chanel-No.-5-Flakons aus Acrylglas begrüßt; ein darin integrierter Monitor zeigt Videos. Der Architekt führt aus: „Als Highlight der Räume wurden Werke von Künstlern wie Peter Belyi, Robert Greene, Gregor Hildebrandt, Alan Rath und Richard Woods in Auftrag gegeben. Integriert in das grafische Schwarz-Weiß-Thema des Interieurs sorgen sie für das gewisse Etwas, das Kunden, die in SoHo arbeiten, leben und einkaufen, erwarten." Kunstwerke wie das schwarz-weiße Holzschnittmotiv von Richard Woods, das die Säulen im Verkaufsbereich für Accessoires schmückt, oder die Arbeit *Flying Eyeballs* von Alan Rath im Verkaufsbereich für Sonnenbrillen, sind unmittelbar mit der Verkaufsstrategie des Geschäfts verschränkt. Der Ready-to-Wear-Bereich der Boutique wird von der *Record Wall* von Gregor Hildebrandt geprägt, einer Installation aus geschmolzenen Schallplatten in einem Metallgestell. Die Verbindung von Kunst und Architektur in gehobenen Ladeneinrichtungen ist sicherlich nichts Neues, doch in diesem Fall geht Peter Marino einen Schritt weiter als die meisten – eine naheliegende Geste in einer so aktiven Kunstszene wie in SoHo.

Les visiteurs du nouvel espace de SoHo sont accueillis par un flacon en acrylique haut de 3 m de l'emblématique Chanel N° 5, sur la surface duquel des images vidéo sont projetées. Selon les architectes, « les œuvres des artistes Peter Belyi, Robert Greene, Gregor Hildebrandt, Alan Rath et Richard Woods ont été spécialement chargées de mettre en valeur l'espace et se mêlent à l'austère graphisme noir et blanc de la boutique pour une approche adaptée aux clients qui vivent, travaillent et achètent à SoHo. » Les œuvres, comme le motif de blocs de bois noir et blanc par Richard Woods qui entoure les colonnes au rayon accessoires ou *Flying Eyeballs* par Alan Rath aux lunettes de soleil, sont en lien direct avec la stratégie commerciale du magasin. D'anciens disques moulés dans une structure métallique (*Record Wall*) par Gregor Hildebrandt marquent la partie prêt-à-porter du magasin. Le mélange d'art et d'architecture haut de gamme n'est peut-être pas nouveau, mais Peter Marino franchit ici un pas de plus que les autres, et le geste prend toute sa pertinence au vu du dynamisme de la scène artistique de SoHo.

The black-and-white décor is interrupted by image screens, but the overall impression is one of strict, usually linear continuity.

Das in Schwarz-weiß gehaltene Dekor wird von Bildtafeln aufgelockert, doch der Gesamteindruck bleibt streng und von überwiegend linearer Stringenz.

Le décor noir et blanc est entrecoupé d'images sur écrans mais l'impression globale reste celle d'une continuité stricte majoritairement linéaire.

Columns are integrated into the design, as are patterned screens, dividing the space, but also giving a hint of what lies beyond.

Integriert in den Entwurf sind sowohl Pfeiler als auch gemusterte Paravents, die den Raum gliedern und zugleich ahnen lassen, was hinter ihnen liegt.

Les colonnes sont intégrées au design comme les écrans à motifs qui divisent l'espace tout en laissant transparaître ce qu'ils cachent.

Camper Store

MIRALLES TAGLIABUE EMBT

Miralles Tagliabue Arquitectes Associats EMBT
Passatge de la Pau, 10 Bis. Pral.
08002 Barcelona
Spain

Tel: +34 93 412 53 42 / Fax: +34 93 412 37 18
E-mail: info@mirallestagliabue.com
Web: www.mirallestagliabue.com

Born in Barcelona, Spain, in 1955 (d. 2000), Enric Miralles received his degree from the ETSA in that city in 1978, and went on to form a partnership with Carme Pinós in 1983. **BENEDETTA TAGLIABUE** was born in Milan, Italy, and graduated from the IUAV in Venice in 1989. She studied and worked in New York (with Agrest and Gandelsonas) from 1987 to 1989. She worked for Enric Miralles, beginning in 1992, first becoming a Partner, then leading the studio after his death. The work of Miralles includes the Olympic Archery Ranges (Barcelona, 1989–91); Igualada Cemetery Park (Barcelona, 1985–92); La Mina Civic Center (Barcelona, 1987–92); Morella Boarding School (Castelló, 1986–94); and the Huesca Sports Hall (1988–94). The most visible recent project of the firm was the Scottish Parliament (Edinburgh, UK, 1998–2004); while other recent work includes the Rehabilitation of the Santa Caterina Market (Barcelona, 1997–2005); the Principal Building for the University Campus (Vigo, 2006); the Public Library (Palafolls, 1997–2007); headquarters for Gas Natural (Barcelona, 2007); the Camper Store (Barcelona, 2010, published here); and the Spanish Pavilion for the Shanghai 2010 Expo (China), all in Spain unless stated otherwise.

Enric Miralles, geboren 1955 in Barcelona (gestorben 2000), beendete sein Studium 1978 an der ETSA Barcelona und schloss sich 1983 mit Carme Pinós als Partnerin zusammen. **BENEDETTA TAGLIABUE**, geboren in Mailand, schloss ihr Studium 1989 an der IUAV Venedig ab. Von 1987 bis 1989 studierte und arbeitete sie in New York (bei Agrest & Gandelsonas). Ab 1992 war sie für Enric Miralles tätig, wurde Partnerin und übernahm nach seinem Tod die Leitung des Studios. Zu Miralles' Projekten zählen die Olympische Bogenschießanlage (Barcelona, 1989–91), die Gartenanlagen des Friedhofs Igualada (Barcelona, 1985–92), das Stadtteilzentrum in La Mina (Barcelona, 1987–92), ein Internat in Morella (Castelló, 1986–94) sowie das Sportzentrum in Huesca (1988–94). Bekanntestes Projekt des Büros in jüngerer Zeit ist das Schottische Parlament (Edinburgh, 1998–2004). Weitere neuere Projekte sind der Umbau der Markthalle Santa Caterina (Barcelona, 1997–2005), das Hauptgebäude auf dem Universitätscampus von Vigo (2006), die Bibliothek von Palafolls (1997–2007), die Zentrale für Gas Natural (Barcelona, 2007), der Camper Store (Barcelona, 2010, hier vorgestellt) und der Spanische Pavillon für die Expo 2010 in Shanghai (China), alle in Spanien, soweit nicht anders angegeben.

Né à Barcelone en 1955 (mort en 2000), Enric Miralles y a obtenu son diplôme de l'ETSA en 1978 et s'est associé à Carme Pinós en 1983. **BENEDETTA TAGLIABUE** est née à Milan et a obtenu son diplôme de l'IUAV à Venise en 1989. Elle a fait des études et a travaillé à New York (avec Agrest and Gandelsonas) de 1987 à 1989. Elle a travaillé pour Enric Miralles dès 1992, d'abord en tant que partenaire, et dirige l'agence depuis sa mort. Leurs réalisations comprennent : le terrain de tir à l'arc olympique (Barcelone, 1989–91) ; le cimetière d'Igualada (Barcelone, 1985–92) ; le centre administratif de La Mina (Barcelone, 1987–92) ; le pensionnat de Morella (Castelló, Espagne, 1986–94) et la salle de sports de Huesca (Espagne, 1988–94). Le projet récent le plus représentatif est le parlement écossais (Édimbourg, 1998–2004) ; parmi les autres réalisations récentes figurent la rénovation du marché Santa Caterina (Barcelone, 1997–2005) ; le bâtiment directeur du campus universitaire (Vigo, 2006) ; la bibliothèque publique (Palafolls, 1997–2007) ; le siège de Gas Natural (Barcelone, 2007) ; la boutique Camper (Barcelone, 2010, publiée ici) et le pavillon de l'Espagne à l'Exposition universelle de Shanghai en 2010 (Chine), toutes en Espagne sauf mention contraire.

CAMPER STORE

Barcelona, Spain, 2010

Address: Passeig de Gracia 2–4, Barcelona 08002, Spain, +34 93 467 4148,
www.camper.com. Area: 52 m². Client: Camper. Cost: not disclosed
Collaboration: Karl Unglaub (Project Director)

This interior design project was created with the idea of seeing fashion through children's eyes, or "shoes in front of the twisted mirrors of an amusement park." The architects also visited a Camper shoe factory where "flat leather sheets are cut and, like magic, with a couple of stitches and a mold, they become beautiful three-dimensional wrappings!" The result of this observation was that EMBT used MDF sheets "cut like shoes," creating benches, tables, and other surfaces, together with the mirrors that they also refer to. Finally, Benedetta Tagliabue states: "Camper has much to do with *el campo*, that is the countryside, the fields… to walk in the fields… and so we imagined shoes stepping on irregular surfaces, like when we walk on earth."

Hinter dieser Innenarchitektur steckt der Gedanke, Mode durch die Augen eines Kindes zu sehen, wie „Schuhe in einem Zerrspiegel auf dem Jahrmarkt". Die Architekten besuchten ein Camper-Werk, wo „Lederstücke zugeschnitten und wie durch Zauberhand mit ein paar Stichen und einem Leisten zu wunderschönen dreidimensionalen Hüllen werden!" Diese Beobachtungen veranlassten EMBT, mit MDF-Platten zu arbeiten, die „wie Schuhe zugeschnitten" wurden, um Bänke, Tische und weitere Präsentationsflächen zu schaffen, die mit den eingangs erwähnten Spiegelelementen kombiniert wurden. Benedetta Tagliabue resümiert: „Camper hat viel mit *el campo* zu tun, dem Land, den Feldern … Spaziergängen in den Feldern … weshalb wir ein bestimmtes Bild vor Augen hatten: Schuhe, die auf unebenen Grund treten, so als würden wir über erdigen Grund laufen."

Ce projet d'architecture intérieure a été créé avec l'idée de voir la mode à travers des yeux d'enfant ou « des chaussures dans les miroirs déformants d'un parc de loisirs ». Les architectes ont visité une usine de chaussures Camper et vu « les feuilles de cuir découpées à plat devenir, comme par magie, avec un ou deux points de couture et une forme, de superbes emballages en trois dimensions ! » À la suite de cette observation, EMBT a choisi d'utiliser des feuilles MDF « coupées à la manière de chaussures », créant bancs, tables et autres surfaces avec les miroirs qu'ils évoquent. Benedetta Tagliabue conclut : « Camper est très proche d'*el campo*, la campagne, les champs… marcher à travers champs… nous avons donc imaginé des chaussures qui arpentent des surfaces irrégulières, comme lorsque nous marchons sur la terre. »

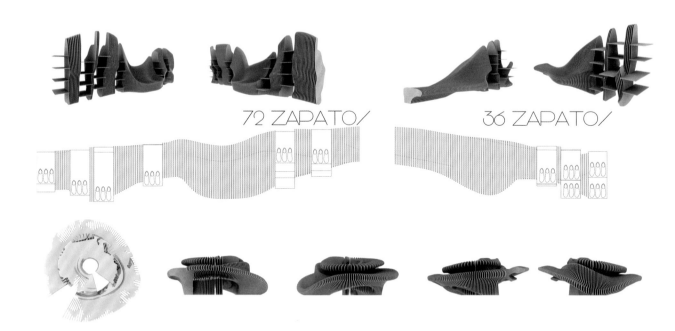

72 ZAPATO/   36 ZAPATO/

Above, three-dimensional drawings show the design of the display stands, visible in situ in the images to the right. An ordinary shop interior is transformed by the addition of this irregular, seemingly mobile installation.

Dreidimensionale Zeichnungen (oben) veranschaulichen das Design der Präsentationsinseln, rechts auf einer Aufnahme vor Ort. Die asymmetrische, scheinbar mobile Installation verwandelt den gewöhnlichen Verkaufsraum.

Ci-dessus, plans 3D du design du présentoir visible in situ sur les photos de droite. L'installation aux formes irrégulières et en apparence mobiles transforme l'intérieur d'une boutique ordinaire.

MOATTI-RIVIÈRE

Agence Moatti et Rivière
11 Cité de l'Ameublement
75011 Paris
France

Tel: +33 1 45 65 44 04 / Fax: +33 1 45 65 10 01
E-mail: communication@moatti-riviere.com
Web: www.moatti-riviere.com

ALAIN MOATTI received his DPLG degree in 1986 and worked on theater and exhibition décors (1985–90), décors for the Lyon Opera, Centre de Congrès (Tours), and Centre de conferences internationals de Paris (Agence Babel, 1990–93). From 1993 to 1995 he worked with the architect Jacques Moussafir (Paris), before creating his own office for architecture and décors (1994–2001). Henri Rivière received a degree in Construction and Cabinetmaking (Paris, 1985) and his diploma from the École Camondo (Paris, 1990). He worked in the office of Francis Soler (Paris, 1990–95), and Christian Hauvette, Jakob + MacFarlane, Dusapin & Leclercq, Patrick Bouchain and François Confino for Expo 2000 in Hanover (1995–2000). He passed away in 2010. Moatti and Rivière started working together in 1990. Their work includes the Champollion Museum (Figeac, 2005–07); Historial Charles de Gaulle (Paris, 2008); Cité de la dentelle et de la mode (Calais, 2006–09); a number of luxury retail spaces such as the 65 Croisette complex (Cannes, 2007–08); and S.T.A.Y. and Sweet Tea (Beirut, Lebanon, 2011, published here). The firm is currently refurbishing the first floor of the Eiffel Tower (Paris, 2011–13); building a 5-star hotel in Courchevel (2011–13); and the Museum of Decorative Arts and Fashion (Marseille, 2013), all in France unless stated otherwise.

ALAIN MOATTI erwarb seinen Architekturabschluss (DPLG) 1986 und gestaltete Bühnenbilder und Ausstellungsarchitekturen (1985–90), Bühnenbilder für die Oper in Lyon, Projekte für das Centre de Congrès (Tours) sowie das Centre de conferences internationals de Paris (Agence Babel, 1990–93). Von 1993 bis 1995 kooperierte er mit dem Architekten Jacques Moussafir (Paris) und gründete schließlich ein eigenes Büro für Architektur und Bühnenbild (1994–2001). Henri Rivière absolvierte eine Ausbildung als Bau- und Kunsttischler (Paris, 1985) sowie ein Architekturdiplom an der École Camondo (Paris, 1990). Er arbeitete in den Büros von Francis Soler (Paris, 1990–95) und Christian Hauvette, Jakob + MacFarlane, Dusapin & Leclercq, Patrick Bouchain und François Confino für die Expo 2000 in Hannover (1995 bis 2000). Er starb 2010. 1990 begannen Moatti und Rivière ihre Zusammenarbeit. Zu ihren Projekten zählen das Champollion Museum (Figeac, 2005–07), das Historial Charles de Gaulle (Paris, 2008) und die Cité de la dentelle et de la mode (Museum für Spitze und Mode, Calais, 2006–09) sowie mehrere Luxusboutiquen, darunter der Einkaufskomplex 65 Croisette (Cannes, 2007–08), und S.T.A.Y. and Sweet Tea (Beirut, 2011, hier vorgestellt). Derzeit arbeitet das Büro an der Sanierung des ersten Stockwerks des Eiffelturms (Paris, 2011–13), einem Fünfsternehotel in Courchevel (2011–13) sowie dem Museum für Mode und Kunstgewerbe in Marseille (2013).

ALAIN MOATTI a obtenu son DPLG en 1986 et a surtout travaillé à des décors de théâtre et d'expositions (1985–90) pour l'Opéra de Lyon, le Centre des Congrès (Tours) et le Centre international de conférences de Paris (Agence Babel, 1990–93). Il a travaillé de 1993 à 1995 avec l'architecte Jacques Moussafir (Paris) avant de créer sa propre agence d'architecture et de décors (1994–2001). Henri Rivière est diplômé de construction et d'ébénisterie (Paris, 1985), ainsi que de l'École Camondo (Paris, 1990). Il a travaillé dans les agences de Francis Soler (Paris, 1990–95), Christian Hauvette, Jakob + MacFarlane, Dusapin & Leclercq, Patrick Bouchain et François Confino pour l'Exposition universelle 2000 de Hanovre (1995–2000). Il est mort en 2010. Moatti et Rivière ont commencé à travailler ensemble en 1990. Leurs réalisations comprennent le musée Champollion (Figeac, 2005–07) ; l'Historial Charles de Gaulle (Paris, 2008) ; la Cité de la dentelle et de la mode (Calais, 2006–09) ; de nombreux commerces de luxe parmi lesquels le complexe 65 Croisette (Cannes, 2007–08) et S.T.A.Y. and Sweet Tea (Beyrouth, Liban, 2011, publié ici). L'agence travaille actuellement à la rénovation du premier étage de la tour Eiffel (2011–13) ; la construction d'un hôtel cinq étoiles à Courchevel (2011–13) et au Musée des arts décoratifs et de la mode (Marseille, 2013).

S.T.A.Y. AND SWEET TEA

Beirut, Lebanon, 2011

Address: Fakhry Bey Street and Jewelry Souk, Beirut Souks, Beirut Central District, Beirut, Lebanon,
+ 961 0 1 99 97 57, reservations@staybeirut.com.lb, www.yannick-alleno.fr. Area: 2055 m²
Client: Solidere, Groupe Yannick Alléno. Cost: not disclosed
Collaboration: Mathilde Felix-Faure (Project Manager), Albane Macé de Lepinay (Designer)

This project, involving a restaurant and a tea salon for the chef Yannick Alléno, is located in the central Souk area of Beirut, that has been thoroughly restored by Solidere since the war years. S.T.A.Y. (Simple Table Alléno Yannick) is the 1440-square-meter restaurant with 157 square meters of terraces, which can accommodate 96 people inside, 60 on the terrace, and a further 64 people at the bar. By taking out a ceiling in the building on Fakhry Bey Street that had been intended for offices, the architects allowed for very high ceilings. Moatti-Rivière imagined the inside of the space like a blue boat shell made in molded GRP, recalling the seafaring traditions of Lebanon. The firm designed everything inside the restaurant, including wall coverings, tables, and seating. Sweet Tea measures 390 square meters with a 68-meter terrace area and is accessed directly from the Souk (designed by Rafael Moneo). It seats 24 inside and 79 on the terrace. The architects explain: "It is a refined space that is as precious as a jewel box on the ground floor and as intimate as a secret garden on the first floor. It is enlivened by a very cheerful chromatic universe composed of blue, yellow, pink, and green. These are the same colors used for the pastries and the packaging for the desserts."

Das Restaurant mit Teesalon für den Koch Yannick Alléno liegt im Soukviertel im Zentrum von Beirut, das seit den Kriegsjahren umfassend von Solidere saniert wurde. Das Restaurant S.T.A.Y. (Simple Table Alléno Yannick) bietet 1440 m² Nutzfläche und zusätzliche 157 m² an Terassenfläche. Neben 96 Sitzplätzen innen kommen weitere 60 auf der Terrasse und 64 an der Bar hinzu. Durch das Entfernen der Decken aus dem ursprünglich als Büro geplanten Bau an der Fakhry Bey Street entstanden besonders hohe Räume. Im Innenbereich arbeiteten Moatti-Rivière mit dem Motiv eines blauen Bootsrumpfes aus Fiberglas, eine Anspielung auf die libanesische Seefahrertradition. Das Büro entwarf das gesamte Interieur, einschließlich der Wandverkleidungen, Tische und Sitzmöbel. Der Teesalon Sweet Tea hat neben 390 m² Grundfläche eine 68 m² große Terrasse und ist unmittelbar vom Souk (einem Entwurf von Rafael Moneo) zugänglich. Der Teesalon hat 24 Plätze innen sowie 79 auf der Terrasse. Die Architekten erklären: „Die hochwertigen Räume sind im Erdgeschoss wie ein Schmuckkästchen gehalten, im ersten Stock so privat wie ein geheimer Garten. Belebt werden sie durch heitere chromatische Farben: Blau, Gelb, Pink und Grün. Dieselben Farben finden sich auch beim Gebäck und den Verpackungen der Süßigkeiten."

Le projet, qui comprend un restaurant et un salon de thé pour le chef Yannick Alléno, est situé dans le souk central de Beyrouth, complètement restauré par Solidere depuis la guerre. S.T.A.Y. (Simple Table Alléno Yannick) est un restaurant de 1440 m² et 157 m² de terrasses qui peut accueillir 96 personnes à l'intérieur, 60 sur la terrasse et 64 au bar. Les architectes ont retiré un plafond du bâtiment de la rue Fakhry Bey qui aurait dû abriter des bureaux, ce qui leur a permis d'obtenir une très grande hauteur. Moatti-Rivière ont imaginé un espace intérieur comme une coque de bateau bleue faite de stratifié-verre moulé qui rappelle les traditions maritimes du Liban. L'agence a entièrement conçu l'intérieur du restaurant, y compris les revêtements des murs, les tables et les sièges. Sweet Tea a une surface de 390 m² et une terrasse de 68 m², il est directement accessible depuis le souk (créé par Rafael Moneo). Il dispose de 24 places à l'intérieur et 79 sur la terrasse. Les architectes le décrivent comme un « espace raffiné aussi précieux qu'une boîte à bijoux au rez-de-chaussée et aussi intime qu'un jardin secret au premier étage. Il est animé par un univers chromatique très gai composé de bleu, jaune, rose et vert. Les mêmes couleurs se retrouvent dans les pâtisseries et les emballages des desserts ».

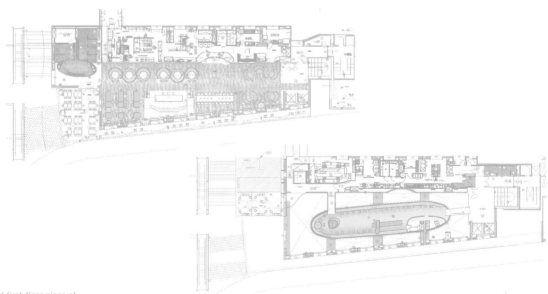

Above, ground and first-floor plans of the S.T.A.Y. restaurant.

Grundrisse von Parterre und erstem Stock des Restaurants S.T.A.Y. (oben).

Ci-dessus, plans du rez-de-chaussée et du premier étage du restaurant S.T.A.Y.

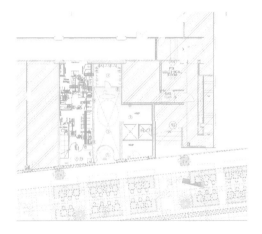

Above, he Fakhry Bey ground floor and mezzanine plans. Below, interior images of the Sweet Tea space.

Oben die Grundrisse von Parterre und Mezzaningeschoss des Gebäudes an der Fakhry Bey Street. Unten Ansichten des Teesalons Sweet Tea.

Ci-dessus, plan du rez-de-chaussée et de la mezzanine rue Fakhry Bey. Ci-dessous, vues intérieures du Sweet Tea.

To the right, two interior views of the restaurant with its curving seating arrangement, all purpose-designed by Moatti-Rivière.

Rechts zwei Innenansichten des Restaurants mit den geschwungenen Sitznischen. Sämtliche Details wurden speziell von Moatti-Rivière entworfen.

À droite, deux vues intérieures du restaurant et de ses tables disposées selon des lignes courbes, le tout spécialement créé par Moatti-Rivière.

Below, a section drawing of the restaurant with its unusual ceiling feature and an outdoor terrace (left).

Unten ein Querschnitt des Restaurants mit der ungewöhnlichen Deckenkonstruktion und einer Außenterrasse (links).

Ci-dessous, un plan en coupe du restaurant avec son étonnant plafond et une terrasse (à gauche).

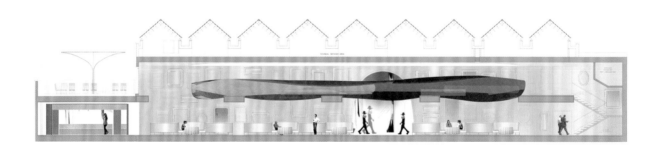

Below, the blue bar contrasts in its colors with the overall gray and white color scheme of the restaurant. The suspended ceiling fixture is meant to symbolize a boat, since the Souks are near the former Phoenician port of the city.

Die blaue Bar (unten) kontrastiert farblich mit der ansonsten grau-weißen Palette des Restaurants. Die hängende Deckeninstallation soll ein Boot symbolisieren, denn das Soukviertel liegt unweit des alten phönizischen Hafens der Stadt.

Ci-dessous, le bar en bleu contraste avec la gamme générale grise et blanche du restaurant. Le plafonnier suspendu symbolise un bateau car les souks sont proches de l'ancien port phénicien de la ville.

A covered outdoor courtyard with a vertical garden and chairs created by the designers.

Ein geschützter Innenhof mit einem vertikalen Garten und ebenfalls von den Architekten entworfenen Stühlen.

Une cour couverte avec son jardin vertical et des chaises créées par les designers.

YUKO NAGAYAMA

Yuko Nagayama & Associates
2–19–18–5F, Kamiogi
Suginamiku
Tokyo 167–0043
Japan

Tel: +81 3 3392 5428 / Fax: +81 3 3392 5429
E-mail: contact@yukonagayama.co.jp
Web: www.yukonagayama.co.jp

YUKO NAGAYAMA was born in Tokyo, Japan, in 1975. She graduated from Showa Women's University in 1998 and worked from that year until 2002 in the office of Jun Aoki in Tokyo. She established Yuko Nagayama & Associates in 2002. In Japan, she received the Best New Female Architect Award (2007), and she lectures at Tokyo University of Science and Showa Women's University. Since establishing her firm, she has worked on a large number of residential and retail projects, such as interior and façade design for afloat-f, a hair salon (Tokyo, 2002); design for the showroom at Fields (Tokyo, 2003); façade design for the Louis Vuitton flagship store in Kyoto (Kyoto Daimariu, 2004); façade design for Wontana, a restaurant (Kyoto, 2007); design for tea ceremony room at Azumaya (Ciba, 2007); architecture of the Louis Vuitton Urbanprem Minami-Aoyama (Tokyo, 2008); interior design of Anteprima (Roppongi Hills, Tokyo, 2008); the renovation of Kayaba Coffee Shop in Tokyo (2009, published here); and design for Sisii, a showroom and office (Kobe, 2010), all in Japan.

YUKO NAGAYAMA wurde 1975 in Tokio geboren. Sie schloss ihr Studium 1998 an der Frauenuniversität Showa ab und arbeitete anschließend bis 2002 im Büro von Jun Aoki in Tokio. 2002 gründete sie Yuko Nagayama & Associates. Sie wurde in Japan 2007 als beste junge Architektin ausgezeichnet und lehrt an der Naturwissenschaftlichen Universität Tokio und der Frauenuniversität Showa. Seit Gründung ihres Büros arbeitete sie an einer Vielzahl von Wohnbauten und Ladeneinrichtungen, hierzu zählen: Interieur und Fassadengestaltung für den Friseursalon afloat-f (Tokio, 2002), Gestaltung des Showrooms Fields (Tokio, 2003), Gestaltung und Fassadendesign für den Louis Vuitton Flagshipstore in Kioto (Kyoto Daimariu, 2004), Fassade für das Restaurant Wontana (Kioto, 2007), Gestaltung des Teezeremonie-Salons in Azumaya (Ciba, 2007), architektonische Planung für Louis Vuitton Urbanprem Minami-Aoyama (Tokio, 2008), Innenarchitektur für Anteprima (Roppongi Hills, Tokio, 2008), Renovierung des Kaffeegeschäfts Kayaba in Tokio (2009, hier vorgestellt) sowie die Gestaltung eines Büros und Showrooms für Sisii (Kobe, 2010), alle in Japan.

YUKO NAGAYAMA est née à Tokyo en 1975. Elle a obtenu son diplôme à l'Université féminine de Showa en 1998 et a ensuite travaillé jusque 2002 à l'agence de Jun Aoki à Tokyo. Elle a ouvert Yuko Nagayama & Associates en 2002. Au Japon, elle a remporté le prix de la meilleure nouvelle architecte (2007) et elle enseigne à l'Université des sciences de Tokyo et l'Université féminine de Showa. Depuis la création de son agence, elle a réalisé de nombreux projets résidentiels et commerciaux, tels que le salon de coiffure afloat-f (Tokyo, 2002) ; le design de la salle d'expositions Fields (Tokyo, 2003) ; la façade du magasin-phare de Louis Vuitton à Kyoto (Daimariu, 2004) ; la façade du restaurant Wontana (Kyoto, 2007) ; la conception d'une pièce pour la cérémonie du thé à Azumaya (Ciba, 2007) ; l'architecture du bâtiment Louis Vuitton Urbanprem de Minami-Aoyama (Tokyo, 2008) ; l'architecture intérieure d'Anteprima (Roppongi Hills, Tokyo, 2008) ; la rénovation du café Kayaba à Tokyo (2009, publié ici) et le design de la salle d'expositions et de bureaux Sisii (Kobe, 2010), tous au Japon.

KAYABA COFFEE

Tokyo, Japan, 2009

*Address: 6–1–29 Yanaka, Taito-ku, Tokyo, Japan, +81 3 3823 3545,
mail@kayaba-coffee.com, www.kayaba-coffee.com
Area: 45 m². Client: Scai The Bathhouse / Contemporary Art, Inc. Cost: not disclosed*

Yuko Nagayama undertook the rather delicate task of restoring and modernizing a coffee house in Tokyo that is more than a century old. Buildings of this type, remnants of the Tokyo of another era, are relatively rare given the history of the city, rendering her assignment all the more complex. While retaining the exterior forms of the building, she converted the ground floor into a warm yet quite minimalistic seating area for clients. Most importantly, the coffee shop retains the Japanese atmosphere that it had originally while affirming a modern identity. Although **KAYABA COFFEE** has a usable floor area of just 45 square meters, Yuko Nagayama managed to use the upper floor for a comfortable seating zone with a selection of contemporary art books.

Yuko Nagayama stellte sich der sensiblen Aufgabe, ein über 100-jähriges Kaffeehaus in Tokio zu renovieren. Bauten dieser Art sind Zeugen einer vergangenen Zeit und angesichts der Geschichte Tokios recht selten, was die Aufgabe umso anspruchsvoller machte. Die Architektin wahrte die äußere Erscheinung des Gebäudes und baute das Erdgeschoss zu einem warmen und dennoch minimalistischen Gastbereich um. Das Wichtigste war, dass das Kaffeehaus seinen ursprünglichen japanischen Charakter bewahren konnte, dabei jedoch eine deutlich moderne, neue Identität erhielt. Obwohl **KAYABA COFFEE** eine Nutzfläche von nur 45 m² hat, gelang es Yuko Nagayama, das Obergeschoss als bequemen Sitzbereich mit einer Auswahl an Büchern über zeitgenössische Kunst zu gestalten.

Yuko Nagayama a entrepris ici la tâche délicate de restaurer et moderniser un café de Tokyo vieux de plus d'un siècle. Les constructions de ce type, vestiges du Tokyo d'une autre époque, sont plutôt rares étant donné l'histoire de la ville, ce qui rend cette mission d'autant plus complexe. L'architecte a conservé l'aspect extérieur du bâtiment, mais a converti le rez-de-chaussée en un espace assis chaleureux bien que plutôt minimaliste. Le plus important est que le café conserve son atmosphère d'origine, typiquement japonaise, tout en affirmant sa nouvelle identité modernisée. Malgré une surface utile au sol de seulement 45 m², Yuko Nagayama est parvenue à transformer l'étage du **CAFÉ KAYABA** en une salle confortable présentant une sélection d'ouvrages d'art contemporain.

The interior of the coffee shop (seen from the street, below) has been entirely redone, but retains the typically Japanese atmosphere of the original.

Das Interieur des Cafés (rechts eine Außenansicht von der Straße) wurde vollständig erneuert, bewahrt jedoch die typisch japanische Atmosphäre des Originals.

L'intérieur du café (vu de la rue ci-dessous) a été entièrement refait mais conserve l'atmosphère typiquement japonaise d'origine.

NINOM

Ninom
400 North Suzhou Rd, Apt 706
200085 Shanghai
China

Tel: +86 158 0217 4855
E-mail: info@ninom.com
Web: www.ninom.com

The founding Directors of Ninom, **ELENA PÉREZ GARRIGUES** and **DANIEL BLANCO COHEN**, were both born in 1975 in Madrid and they both obtained their M.Arch degrees from the ETSA in Madrid (1993–2002). They created their own firm in in 2006 "with the idea of integrating architecture with disciplines such as dance, photography, and scenery," with offices in Madrid and Shanghai. Their work includes the Viñedos del Contino Winery (Laguardia, Álava, 2006–07); the Abejera wine shop (Laguardia, Álava 2008); the CVNE Winery tasting hall and reception area (Haro, La Rioja, 2008–09, published here); and the Fosca luxury hotel restaurant (La Fosca, Gerona, 2010). As scenographers, they have developed their work together with the contemporary dance choreographer Michelle Man (*Tussore*, Teatro Real Madrid, 2006; and *Tent*, Casar, Cáceres, 2009).

ELENA PÉREZ GARRIGUES und **DANIEL BLANCO COHEN**, Gründungsdirektoren von Ninom, wurden beide 1975 in Madrid geboren und schlossen ihr Studium jeweils mit einem M.Arch. an der ETSA in Madrid ab (1993–2002). 2006 gründeten sie ihr Büro mit Niederlassungen in Madrid und Schanghai mit der Absicht, „Architektur mit Disziplinen wie Tanz, Fotografie und Bühnenbild zu verbinden". Zu ihren Projekten zählen das Weingut Viñedos del Contino (Laguardia, Álava, 2006–07), die Weinhandlung Abejera (Laguardia, Álava 2008), die Empfangs- und Weinverkostungshalle für CVNE (Haro, La Rioja, 2008–09, hier vorgestellt) und das Restaurant im Luxushotel Fosca (La Fosca, Gerona, 2010). Als Bühnenbilder realisierten sie Entwürfe in Zusammenarbeit mit der Choreografin für zeitgenössischen Tanz, Michelle Man (*Tussore*, Teatro Real Madrid, 2006, und *Tent*, Casar, Cáceres, 2009).

Les directeurs fondateurs de Ninom, **ELENA PÉREZ GARRIGUES** et **DANIEL BLANCO COHEN**, sont nés tous les deux en 1975 à Madrid et ont obtenu leur M. Arch à l'ETSA de Madrid (1993–2002). Ils ont créé leur entreprise en 2006 « avec l'idée d'intégrer l'architecture à des disciplines telles que la danse, la photographie et la création de décors » et des agences à Madrid et Shanghai. Leurs réalisations comprennent : la cave Viñedos del Contino (Laguardia, Álava, 2006–07) ; le caviste Abejera (Laguardia, Álava 2008) ; la salle de dégustation et l'espace de réception de la cave CVNE (Haro, La Rioja, 2008–09, publiés ici) et l'hôtel-restaurant de luxe Fosca (La Fosca, Gérone, 2010), tous en Espagne. En tant que scénographes, ils ont travaillé avec la chorégraphe contemporaine Michelle Man (*Tussore*, Teatro Real Madrid, 2006 et *Tent*, Casar, Cáceres, 2009).

CVNE WINE HALL
AND RECEPTION AREA

Barrio de la Estación, Haro, La Rioja, Spain, 2009

*Address: Barrio de la Estación S/N, 26200 Haro, La Rioja, Spain, +34 941 30 48 09,
www.cvne.com. Area: 1920 m². Client: CVNE. Cost: €550 000*

Making intelligent use of an existing building, the architects inserted a metallic box structure allowing for the vineyard to receive clients and taste wine.

Die Architekten nutzten einen Altbau auf intelligente Weise, indem sie eine Box aus Metall in die bestehende Hülle setzten. Das Weingut gewann so einen Empfangs- und Verkostungsraum für Besucher.

Exploitant astucieusement une construction existante, les architectes y ont introduit un caisson métallique où recevoir les clients et déguster le vin du domaine.

CVNE is an old and prestigious winery located in the Rioja Alta region of Spain. The new tasting and reception area is part of a larger project aimed at developing the oldest part of the facilities for "new dynamic activities centered around wine." This project was carried out in an 1879 building and the surrounding area. In a stone and oak structure used for storing barrels, the architects inserted an "iron box" within the original walls. They explain: "The box is understood as a system. Its dry construction is based on a basic mechanism of a tubular structure upon which multiple layers overlap, including sound insulation and different finishes according to needs. This structure is split in two, to lodge the mechanical and electrical components and a storage space that is fully accessible from both sides." Ninom gave importance to lighting in the spaces, using both spot projectors and fiber optics.

CVNE ist ein alteingesessenes, renommiertes Weingut in der spanischen Region Rioja Alta. Der neue Empfangs- und Verkostungsbereich entstand im Zuge größerer Sanierungsarbeiten am ältesten Teil des Guts, um „neue, dynamische Aktivitäten rund um das Thema Wein" anbieten zu können. Realisiert wurde der Entwurf in einem Altbau von 1879 und umliegenden Bereichen. Die Architekten setzten eine „eiserne Box" in das alte Gebäude aus Mauerwerk und Eiche, in dem früher Fässer gelagert wurden. Sie erklären: „Die Box ist als System zu verstehen. Ihre Trockenkonstruktion basiert auf einem Grundgerüst, über das mehrere Schichten gelegt wurden, darunter eine Schalldämmung und je nach Erfordernis verschiedene Oberflächenbehandlungen. Diese Konstruktion ist zweigeteilt, zur Unterbringung technischer und elektrischer Anlagen sowie als Lagerraum, und ist von beiden Seiten frei zugänglich." Ninom legte besonderen Wert auf die Beleuchtung der Räume und arbeitet sowohl mit Spots als auch mit Faseroptik.

CVNE est un domaine viticole de prestige dans la région espagnole de Rioja Alta. Le nouvel espace de dégustation et de réception fait partie d'un projet plus vaste visant à mettre en valeur la partie la plus ancienne de l'ensemble – un bâtiment de 1879 et ses environs – pour développer « de nouvelles activités et une nouvelle dynamique autour du vin ». Les architectes ont inséré une « boîte en fer » dans les murs d'origine d'une structure de pierre et chêne où étaient stockés les fûts. Ils expliquent que « la boîte est à comprendre comme un système. Sa construction sèche repose sur le mécanisme de base d'une structure tubulaire recouverte de plusieurs couches se chevauchant qui comprennent l'isolation acoustique et différentes finitions selon les besoins. La structure est coupée en deux pour loger les éléments mécaniques et électriques et former un espace de stockage accessible des deux côtés ». Ninom a veillé tout particulièrement à l'éclairage des différents espaces, à l'aide de projecteurs spots et de fibre optique.

Using a geometric cutout in the metallic skin of their installation, the architects allow for bottles of wine to be seen.

Durch einen geometrischen Einschnitt in die Metallhaut der Installation geben die Architekten den Blick frei auf gelagerte Weinflaschen.

Un découpage géométrique dans l'enveloppe métallique de l'installation permet de voir les bouteilles de vin.

As seen from this angle, the installation appears to be only a thin skin of metal subdividing the existing space and rendering it contemporary.

Aus diesem Blickwinkel scheint die Installation kaum mehr als eine dünne Metallhaut zu sein, die den vorhandenen Raum gliedert und ihm ein zeitgenössisches Gesicht gibt.

Vue sous cet angle, l'installation semble une simple enveloppe métallique fine qui divise l'espace existant et lui donne un caractère contemporain.

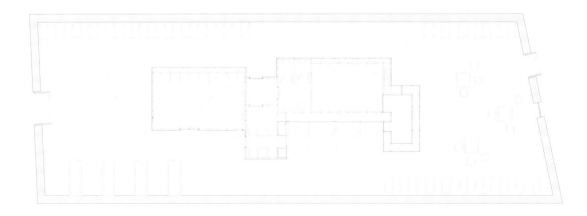

An old stone wall, wooden beams, a cement floor, and the new dark metal walls seem to go together in a nearly seamless way. Right, an exploded axonometric drawing of the installation.

L'ancien mur de pierre, les poutres en bois, le sol de ciment et les nouvelles parois de métal sombre semblent s'associer de manière homogène. À droite, un plan axonométrique explosé de l'installation.

Eine alte Steinmauer, Holzstreben, ein Zementboden und die neuen dunklen Metallwände fügen sich fast nahtlos zu einem Ganzen. Rechts eine Explosions-Axonometrie der Installation.

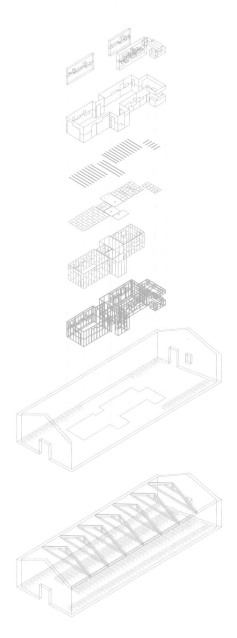

JEAN NOUVEL

Ateliers Jean Nouvel
10 Cité d'Angoulème
75011 Paris
France

Tel: +33 1 49 23 83 83 / Fax: +33 1 43 14 81 10
E-mail: info@jeannouvel.fr / Web: www.jeannouvel.com

JEAN NOUVEL was born in 1945 in Fumel, France. He studied in Bordeaux and then at the École des Beaux-Arts (Paris, 1964–72). From 1967 to 1970, he was an assistant of the noted architects Claude Parent and Paul Virilio. He created his first office with François Seigneur in Paris in 1970. Jean Nouvel received the RIBA Gold Medal in 2001 and the Pritzker Prize in 2008. His first widely noted project was the Institut du Monde Arabe (Paris, France, 1981–87, with Architecture Studio) and the Fondation Cartier (Paris, France, 1991–94), made him one of the most renowned French architects. Major projects since 2000 are the Music and Conference Center (Lucerne, Switzerland, 1998–2000); the Agbar Tower (Barcelona, Spain, 2001–03); an extension of the Reina Sofia Museum (Madrid, Spain, 1999–2005); the Quai Branly Museum (Paris, France, 2001–06); an apartment building in SoHo (New York, New York, USA, 2006); the Guthrie Theater (Minneapolis, Minnesota, USA, 2006); the Danish Radio Concert House (Copenhagen, Denmark, 2003–09); Le Loft Restaurant, Hotel Stephansdom Vienna (Vienna, Austria, 2006–10, published here); an office tower in Doha (Qatar, 2010); two apartment buildings in Ibiza (Spain, 2006–11); the City Hall in Montpellier (France, 2008–11); the Excelsior-Milano (Milan, Italy, 2010–11, also published here); and a hotel in Barcelona (Spain, 2011). Current work includes the new Philharmonic Hall in Paris (France, 2012); the Louvre Abu Dhabi (UAE, 2009–13); the Tour de Verre in New York (New York, USA); and the National Museum of Qatar (Doha, Qatar, 2015). Jean Nouvel is the architect-manager of all the projects for the Ile Seguin in Boulogne-Billancourt (Paris, France, 2012–23).

JEAN NOUVEL, geboren 1945 in Fumel, Frankreich, studierte zunächst in Bordeaux und schließlich an der Pariser École des Beaux-Arts (1964–72). Von 1967 bis 1970 war er Assistent bei den renommierten Architekten Claude Parent und Paul Virilio. 1970 gründete er mit François Seigneur sein erstes Büro in Paris. 2001 wurde Jean Nouvel mit der RIBA-Goldmedaille, 2008 mit dem Pritzker-Preis ausgezeichnet. Sein erstes weithin bekannt gewordenes Projekt, das Institut du Monde Arabe (mit Architecture Studio, Paris, 1981–87), und die Fondation Cartier (Paris, 1991–94) machten ihn zu einem der bekanntesten Architekten Frankreichs. Seine bedeutendsten Projekte seit 2000 sind das Kultur- und Kongresszentrum Luzern (Schweiz, 1998–2000), der Agbar-Turm (Barcelona, 2001–03), die Erweiterung des Museums Reina Sofia (Madrid, 1999–2005), das Museum am Quai Branly (Paris, 2001–06), ein Apartmenthaus in SoHo (New York, 2006), das Guthrie-Theater (Minneapolis, 2006), das Konzerthaus für den dänischen Rundfunk (Kopenhagen, 2003–09), das Restaurant Le Loft im Hotel Stephansdom Vienna (Wien, Österreich, 2006–10, hier vorgestellt), ein Bürohochhaus in Doha (Katar, 2010), zwei Apartmenthäuser auf Ibiza (Spanien, 2006–11), das Rathaus in Montpellier (Frankreich, 2008–11), das Excelsior-Milano (Mailand, 2010–11, ebenfalls hier vorgestellt) und ein Hotel in Barcelona (2011). Laufende Projekte sind u. a. die Philharmonie in Paris (Frankreich, 2012), der Louvre Abu Dhabi (VAE, 2009–13), der Tour de Verre in New York und das Nationalmuseum von Katar (Doha, 2014). Jean Nouvel ist zudem leitender Projektmanager sämtlicher Bauvorhaben auf der Ile Seguin in Boulogne-Billancourt (Paris, 2012–23).

Né en 1945 à Fumel, **JEAN NOUVEL** étudie à Bordeaux, puis à l'École des beaux-arts de Paris (1964–72). De 1967 à 1970, il est l'assistant des célèbres architectes Claude Parent et Paul Virilio. En 1970, il crée une première agence à Paris avec François Seigneur. Il reçoit la médaille d'or du RIBA en 2001 et le prix Pritzker en 2008. Son premier projet largement salué est l'Institut du monde arabe (Paris, 1981–87, en collaboration avec Architecture Studio), tandis que la Fondation Cartier (Paris, 1991–94) en a fait l'un des architectes français les plus connus. Ses principaux projets depuis 2000 sont le Centre de congrès et de musique (Lucerne, Suisse, 1998–2000) ; la tour Agbar (Barcelone, 2001–03) ; une extension du musée Reina Sofia (Madrid, 1999–2005) ; le musée du quai Branly (Paris, 2001–06) ; un immeuble d'appartements à SoHo (New York, 2006) ; le Guthrie Theater (Minneapolis, Minnesota, 2006) ; la salle de concert de la radio danoise (Copenhague, 2003–09) ; le restaurant Le Loft du Sofitel Stephansdom à Vienne (Autriche, 2006–10, publié ici) ; une tour de bureaux à Doha (Qatar, 2010) ; deux immeubles d'appartements à Ibiza (Espagne, 2006–11) ; l'hôtel de ville de Montpellier (2008–11) ; le centre commercial Excelsior-Milano (Milan, 2010–11, publié ici) et un hôtel à Barcelone (2011). Il travaille actuellement à : la nouvelle salle philharmonique à Paris (2012) ; le Louvre Abou Dhabi (EAU, 2009–13) ; la Tour de verre à New York et le Musée national du Qatar (Doha, 2015). Jean Nouvel est aussi l'architecte chargé de coordonner les projets pour l'île Seguin à Boulogne-Billancourt (Paris, 2012–23).

LE LOFT RESTAURANT

Hotel Stephansdom Vienna, Vienna, Austria, 2006–10

*Address: Prater Str. 1, Hotel Sofitel Vienna Stephansdom, 1020 Vienna,
Austria, +43 1 90 61 60, www.sofitel.com. Area: 800 m²
Client: UNIQA Praterstrasse Projekterrichtungs GmbH. Cost: not disclosed*

This restaurant is located in the heart of the Austrian capital, in the Sofitel Vienna Stephansdom, also by Jean Nouvel. The restaurant, situated at the top of the hotel on the 18th floor, and other spaces in the building were designed by Nouvel in collaboration with the noted Swiss artist Pipilotti Rist. Rist's intervention, which represents a willful contrast with the powerful, strict lines of Nouvel's architecture, is expressed in glossy, colorful video ceilings. The full-height glazing of the restaurant allows patrons to view the city, but also means that the work by Rist can be seen at night from the exterior. Born in Grab (near St. Gallen in Switzerland), in 1962, Rist studied commercial art, illustration, and photography at the Institute of Applied Arts in Vienna (1982–86). The combination of her talents with those of Jean Nouvel makes this restaurant one of the most spectacular and artistically interesting realizations of recent years.

Das Restaurant liegt im Herzen der österreichischen Hauptstadt Wien im Sofitel Vienna Stephansdom, ebenfalls ein Entwurf von Jean Nouvel. Das ganz oben im 18. Stock gelegene Restaurant wurde, ebenso wie andere Bereiche des Hotels, in Zusammenarbeit mit der Schweizer Künstlerin Pipilotti Rist gestaltet. Rists Interventionen, ein bewusst gewählter Kontrast zu den strengen Linien der Architektur Nouvels, sind hochglänzende, farbintensive Video-Deckeninstallationen. Die raumhohe Verglasung des Restaurants bietet den Gästen einen Ausblick über die Stadt und bedeutet zugleich, dass die Installation von Rist nachts auch von außen sichtbar ist. Die 1962 in Grab (bei St. Gallen) geborene Rist studierte Gebrauchs- und Illustrationsgrafik sowie Fotografie an der Hochschule für angewandte Kunst in Wien (1982–86). Das Zusammenspiel ihres Könnens mit dem Talent Nouvels macht das Restaurant zu einem der spektakulärsten und künstlerisch interessantesten Projekte der letzten Jahre.

Le restaurant se trouve au cœur de la capitale autrichienne, dans le Sofitel Vienna Stephansdom également réalisé par Jean Nouvel. Il occupe le haut de l'hôtel, au 18e étage, et a été conçu, avec d'autres espaces de l'ensemble, par Nouvel en collaboration avec l'artiste suisse de renom Pipilotti Rist dont le travail, qui contraste volontairement avec les lignes puissantes et strictes de l'architecture de Nouvel, prend la forme de plafonds vidéo brillants et colorés. Le vitrage du restaurant sur toute sa hauteur donne aux clients vue sur la ville mais permet également à l'œuvre de Rist d'être admirée de l'extérieur la nuit. Née à Grab (près de Saint-Gall, en Suisse) en 1962, Rist a étudié l'art publicitaire, l'illustration et la photographie à l'Institut des arts appliqués de Vienne (1982–86). L'association de son talent et de celui de Jean Nouvel font du restaurant l'une des réalisations les plus spectaculaires et artistiquement intéressantes de ces dernières années.

Above, exterior views showing the hotel in its urban setting. Right, a spectacular night-time view with the work by Pipilotti Rist reflected in the ceiling of the restaurant.

Außenansichten (oben) zeigen das Hotel in seinem urbanen Umfeld. Rechts eine spektakuläre Nachtansicht mit einer Spiegelung der Deckeninstallation Pipilotti Rists im Restaurant.

Ci-dessus, vues extérieures de l'hôtel dans son cadre urbain. À droite, la vue nocturne spectaculaire et l'œuvre de Pipilotti Rist se reflétant au plafond du restaurant.

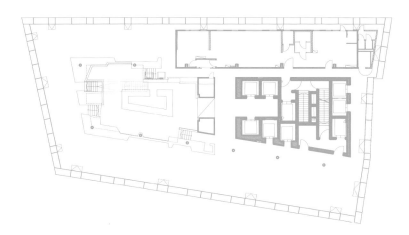

The restaurant is visible at the top of the hotel in this night view. Left, a plan of the restaurant and above, an overall view of the top-floor dining area.

Das Restaurant ist auf dieser Nachtansicht des Hotels ganz oben zu erkennen. Links ein Grundriss des Restaurants sowie oben ein Blick über den Speisebereich unter dem Dach.

On voit le restaurant en haut de l'hôtel sur cette photo de nuit. À gauche, plan du restaurant et ci-dessus, vue d'ensemble de la salle du dernier étage.

EXCELSIOR-MILANO

Milan, Italy, 2010–11

Address: Galleria del Corso 4, 20100 Milano, Italy, +39 02 76 01 51 76, www.excelsiormilano.com
Area: 5000 m². Client: Gruppo Coin SPA. Cost: not disclosed

Jean Nouvel has often expressed an interest in film, as he did in The Hotel (Lucerne, Switzerland, 2001). This interest in cinema finds a natural outlet in this Milan retail space that mixes fashion, food, and design around the existing Excelsior movie theater. Closed for a number of years, the Excelsior, located in the Galleria del Corso, saw its volumes preserved. Nouvel states that the "relation between the preexisting structure and the new one occurs by reflection: the inner walls of the old movie theater are coated with reflecting paints, while the exterior parapets of the new floors, isolated at the center of the building, support LED screens all along the outer edge. The light from the screens on the reflecting surface generates a kaleidoscopic and ever-changing periphery." The main façade of the complex, on the Via Passarella, has horizontal louvers in matte glazed aluminum, and mirror-polished aluminum that reflects the LED screens inside. A large entrance hall and "detached" floors mark the interior with its four levels above grade. Matte, dark-colored floors and ceilings contrast with the screens and the products sold in the store.

Sein Interesse am Film hat Jean Nouvel schon häufig zum Ausdruck gebracht, etwa bei seinem Projekt The Hotel (Luzern, Schweiz, 2001). Dieses Fasziniertsein vom Kino findet ein ideales Forum im Mailänder Einkaufszentrum mit Modegeschäften und Gastronomie rund um das alte Excelsior-Filmtheater. Das seit Jahren geschlossene Kino in der Galleria del Corso konnte erhalten werden. Nouvel erklärt: „Die Beziehung zwischen alten und neuen baulichen Komponenten beruht auf Spiegelungen: Die Innenwände des alten Filmtheaters wurden mit reflektierender Farbe gestrichen, während an den Geländern der neuen Ebenen im Kern des Gebäudes flächendeckende LED-Monitore angebracht wurden. Das Licht der Monitore erzeugt ein permanentes, kaleidoskopartiges Wechselspiel auf den reflektierenden Wandflächen." Die Hauptfassade des Komplexes an der Via Passarella wurde mit Querjalousien aus matt lackiertem Aluminium ausgestattet, in denen sich die LED-Monitore spiegeln. Eine großzügige Eingangshalle und „schwebende" Ebenen dominieren den Innenraum mit seinen vier Obergeschossen. Kontraste ergeben sich auch zwischen den matt dunklen Bodenbelägen und Decken, den Monitoren und dem Warenangebot der Läden.

Jean Nouvel a souvent exprimé son intérêt pour le cinéma, comme dans The Hotel (Lucerne, Suisse, 2001). Cette passion trouve un débouché naturel dans le centre commercial milanais qui associe mode, restauration et design autour de l'ancien cinéma Excelsior fermé depuis des années. Les volumes de l'établissement situé Galleria del Corso ont été conservés et Nouvel explique que « le lien entre la structure préexistante et la nouvelle structure est créé par réflexion : les murs intérieurs de l'ancien cinéma sont couverts de peintures réfléchissantes, tandis que les parapets des nouveaux étages, isolés au centre du bâtiment, sont surmontés d'écrans LED sur toute leur longueur extérieure. La lumière des écrans sur la surface réfléchissante crée une enceinte kaléidoscopique en mouvement permanent ». La façade principale du complexe, Via Passarella, est fermée par des persiennes horizontales en aluminium mat vitré et poli miroir qui reflètent les écrans de l'intérieur. L'intérieur et ses quatre niveaux au-dessus du sol est marqué par un vaste hall d'entrée et des étages « isolés ». Les sols et plafonds de couleurs sombres mates contrastent avec les écrans et les produits vendus.

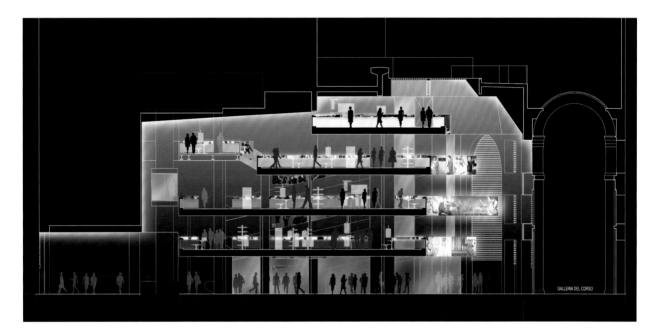

Above, a section drawing of the store showing the different levels and the relation of the structure to neighboring buildings.

Oben ein Querschnitt des Einkaufszentrums. Erkennbar sind die verschiedenen Ebenen und der Bezug zur angrenzenden Bebauung.

Ci-dessus, plan en coupe du centre commercial avec les différents niveaux et le rapport du bâtiment aux bâtiments voisins.

In these street views of the building, Jean Nouvel's innovative use of moving imagery is clearly visible.

Auf den Fassaden des Gebäudes wird Jean Nouvels innovativer Umgang mit bewegten Bildern deutlich.

L'emploi innovant des images en mouvement par Jean Nouvel est très visible sur ces vues de la rue.

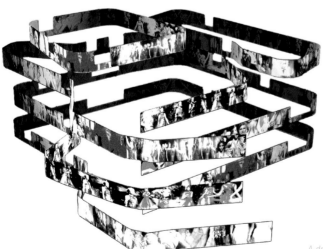

A drawing and images show how the movie band winds through the store space. Nouvel has long been interested in motion pictures and their use in one form or another in his architecture.

Eine Zeichnung und Ansichten zeigen das Filmband, das sich durch das Kaufhaus zieht. Schon lange interessiert sich Nouvel für bewegte Bilder und ihren Einsatz – auf die eine oder andere Weise – in seiner Architektur.

Le plan et les photos montrent comment la bande cinématographique s'enroule à travers l'espace du magasin. Nouvel s'intéresse depuis longtemps aux images en mouvement et leur utilisation sous différentes formes dans son architecture.

MUTI RANDOLPH

Muti Randolph
Praia de Botafogo 68/601
22250–040 Rio de Janeiro, RJ
Brazil

Tel: +55 21 9179 6290
E-mail: info@mutirandolph.com
Web: www.mutirandolph.com

MUTI RANDOLPH is an illustrator, graphic art designer, set maker, and creator of a number of noted interiors. His clubs like D-Edge or U-Turn (both in São Paulo) are inspired by "computers and electronic equipment," since, as he says: "My main concern is to design space that changes over time, reacting to music through the use of digital technology." Born in 1967 in Rio de Janeiro, Muti Randolph studied Visual Communications and Industrial Design at the Pontificia Universidade Católica do Rio de Janeiro. He started his career as a graphic designer and illustrator in the late 1980s. One of the pioneers in computer art, 3D illustration, and animation in Brazil, he began shifting from virtual 3D to real 3D spaces. His interest in music and technology is very apparent in his projects, where he explores the relation between music and space. He has been developing software to synch live music and video used in some current permanent and temporary works. Some of his noted projects are U-Turn Nightclub (São Paulo, 1997); D-Edge Nightclub (Campo Grande, 2001); D-Edge Nightclub (São Paulo, 2003); Galeria Melissa (São Paulo, 2005); São Paulo Fashion Week (2005); the opera *I Capuleti e i Montecchi* at the Theatro Municipal do Rio de Janeiro (2006); D-Edge 2.0 (São Paulo, 2009–10, published here); "Tube," The Creators Project, Galeria Baró (São Paulo, 2010); and "Deep Screen," The Creators Project (Beijing, China, 2010), all in Brazil unless stated otherwise.

MUTI RANDOLPH ist Illustrator, Grafikdesigner sowie Bühnenbildner und wurde durch seine Gestaltung zahlreicher Interieurs bekannt. Seine Clubs wie D-Edge oder U-Turn (beide in São Paulo) sind inspiriert von „Computern und elektronischen Geräten". „Mein Ziel ist in erster Linie, einen Raum zu gestalten, der sich mit der Zeit verändert, der durch digitale Technik auf Musik reagiert", erklärt Randolph. Der 1967 in Rio de Janeiro geborene Designer studierte Visuelle Kommunikation und Industriedesign an der Pontificia Universidade Católica do Rio de Janeiro. Seine Laufbahn begann er in den späten 1980er-Jahren als Grafikdesigner und Illustrator. Randolph, einer der Pioniere der digitalen Kunst, 3-D-Illustration und Animation in Brasilien, verlegte sich zunehmend von der Gestaltung virtueller auf reale 3-D-Räume. Sein Interesse an Musik und Technik spiegelt sich deutlich in seinen Projekten, in denen er sich mit der Beziehung von Musik und Raum befasst. Er entwickelte eine Software zur Synchronisierung von Livemusik und Videos, die bei verschiedenen temporären und permanenten Installationen zum Einsatz kommt. Zu seinen bekannten Projekten zählen die Clubs U-Turn (São Paulo, 1997), D-Edge (Campo Grande, 2001) und D-Edge (São Paulo, 2003), die Galeria Melissa (São Paulo, 2005), die São Paulo Fashion Week (2005), die Oper *I Capuleti e i Montecchi* am Theatro Municipal do Rio de Janeiro (2006), D-Edge 2.0 (São Paulo, 2009–10, hier vorgestellt), *Tube,* The Creators Project, Galeria Baró (São Paulo, 2010) und *Deep Screen,* The Creators Project (Peking, 2010), alle in Brasilien, sofern nicht anders vermerkt.

MUTI RANDOLPH est illustrateur, graphiste, typographe et auteur de nombreux projets d'aménagement intérieur remarqués. Les clubs qu'il a réalisés, dont le D-Edge ou le U-Turn (tous les deux à São Paulo), lui ont été inspirés par « des équipements informatiques et électroniques » puisque, ainsi qu'il l'explique : « Mon principal objectif est de concevoir des espaces qui se modifient dans le temps, réagissant à la musique grâce aux technologies numériques. » Né en 1967 à Rio de Janeiro, il a étudié la communication visuelle et le design industriel à l'Université catholique pontificale de Rio de Janeiro et débuté sa carrière de graphiste et illustrateur à la fin des années 1980. Pionnier de l'art numérique, de l'illustration en 3D et de l'animation au Brésil, il a commencé à évoluer de la 3D virtuelle vers de vrais espaces tridimensionnels. Son intérêt pour la musique et la technologie ressort particulièrement dans des projets où il explore les relations entre la musique et l'espace. Il a développé un logiciel de synchronisation en temps réel de musiques et de vidéos qu'il utilise dans certains projets permanents ou temporaires. Parmi ses réalisations remarquées : le night-club U-Turn (São Paulo, 1997) ; le night-club D-Edge (Campo Grande, 2001) ; le night-club D-Edge (São Paulo, 2003) ; la Galeria Melissa (São Paulo, 2005) ; la Semaine de la mode de São Paulo (2005) ; l'opéra *I Capuleti e i Montecchi* au Théâtre municipal de Rio de Janeiro (2006) ; D-Edge 2.0 (São Paulo, 2009–10, publié ici) ; l'installation *Tube*, The Creators Project, Galeria Baró (São Paulo, 2010) et l'installation *Deep Screen*, The Creators Project (Pékin, 2010), tous au Brésil sauf si spécifié.

D-EDGE 2.0

São Paulo, São Paulo, Brazil, 2009–10

*Address: Av. Auro Soares de Moura Andrade 141 (in front of the Latin America Memorial),
Barra Funda, São Paulo, São Paulo, Brazil, +55 11 3665 9500, www.d-edge.com.br
Area: 400 m². Client: Renato Ratier Cost: not disclosed
Collaboration: Marcelo Pontes, Eduardo Chalabi, Paula Zemel*

D-EDGE is a fashionable São Paulo nightclub accommodating up to 800 clients that opened in 2003. Muti Randolph states: "The computer is to me what the mirror was to Alice." By bringing his Alice in Wonderland vision of the computer together with light and sound Randolph forms D-Edge. The architect writes that "the space is determined by the light, and the light is determined by the music. The main idea is to show the relation of music and space through lighting, using software that analyzes the sound and makes the light change accordingly." When the owner bought the house next door and commissioned an expansion of the club, the brief was simple: more comfort, an open smoking area, and most importantly to create the same impact as the original D-Edge. A new terrace offers a view of Oscar Niemeyer's Latin America Memorial across the street. One of the walls of the new space is a large mirror that reflects lights covering a 20-meter window with embedded LED light boxes that partially obstruct the view. The new façade is a corrugated aluminum box with a window that shows some of the light action inside.

D-EDGE ist ein angesagter Club für bis zu 800 Gäste, der 2003 in São Paulo eröffnet wurde. Muti Randolph schreibt: „Für mich ist der Computer, was der Spiegel für Alice war." Aus seiner digitalen Alice-im-Wunderland-Vision entstand mithilfe von Licht und Sound das D-Edge. Der Architekt schreibt: „Der Raum wird vom Licht definiert, das Licht wiederum durch die Musik. Entscheidend ist vor allem, das Verhältnis von Musik und Raum in Licht zu übersetzen; eine Software analysiert die Musik und steuert die Lichtwechsel entsprechend." Als der Eigentümer das Nachbargebäude kaufte und eine Erweiterung des Clubs plante, war die Aufgabenstellung klar: mehr Komfort, ein offener Raucherbereich und insbesondere dieselbe Wirkung wie das ursprüngliche D-Edge. Eine neue Terrasse bietet Ausblick auf Oscar Niemeyers Memorial da América Latina auf der gegenüberliegenden Straßenseite. Eine Wand des neuen Clubs wurde verspiegelt und reflektiert ein 20 m breites Fenster mit integrierten LED-Boxen, die den Blick hinaus teilweise brechen. Die neue Fassade wurde als Box aus Aluminiumwellblech gestaltet, durch ein Fenster sind die Lichteffekte im Club teilweise von außen sichtbar.

D-EDGE est un night-club de São Paulo à la mode, ouvert en 2003, qui peut accueillir jusqu'à 800 clients. Muti Randolph déclare : « L'ordinateur est pour moi ce que le miroir était à Alice. » Il a créé D-Edge en associant sa vision de l'ordinateur tirée d'Alice au Pays des merveilles à la lumière et au son, écrivant notamment que « l'espace est déterminé par la lumière et la lumière par la musique. L'idée est de montrer la relation entre la musique et l'espace par l'éclairage, au moyen de logiciels qui analysent le son et modifient les effets lumineux en conséquence ». Lorsque le propriétaire a acheté la maison voisine et commandé l'extension du club, la consigne était simple : plus de confort, un espace fumeurs ouvert et, surtout, le même impact que le D-Edge d'origine. Une nouvelle terrasse donne sur le mémorial de l'Amérique latine d'Oscar Niemeyer, de l'autre côté de la rue. L'un des murs est un immense miroir qui reflète les lumières sur une fenêtre de 20 m où sont enchâssés des caissons lumineux à LED qui bouchent partiellement la vue. La nouvelle façade est un cube d'aluminium ondulé avec une fenêtre qui laisse voir les lumières à l'intérieur.

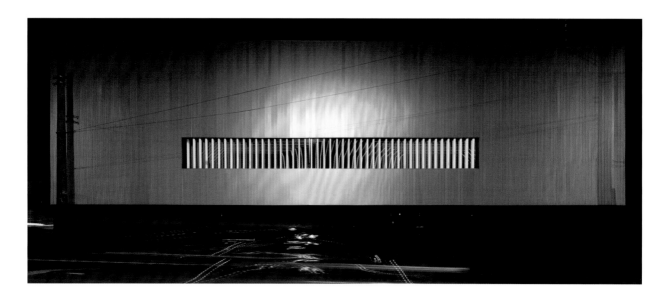

The plan on the right shows the simple rectangle form of the club—made unusual and easily modifiable by its sophisticated lighting systems.

Der Grundriss rechts lässt die schlichte Rechteckform des Clubs erkennen – die erst durch das aufwendige Lichtsystem ungewöhnlich und leicht veränderbar wird.

Le plan de droite montre la forme rectangulaire simple du club – auquel le système d'éclairage raffiné confère un caractère insolite et facilement modifiable.

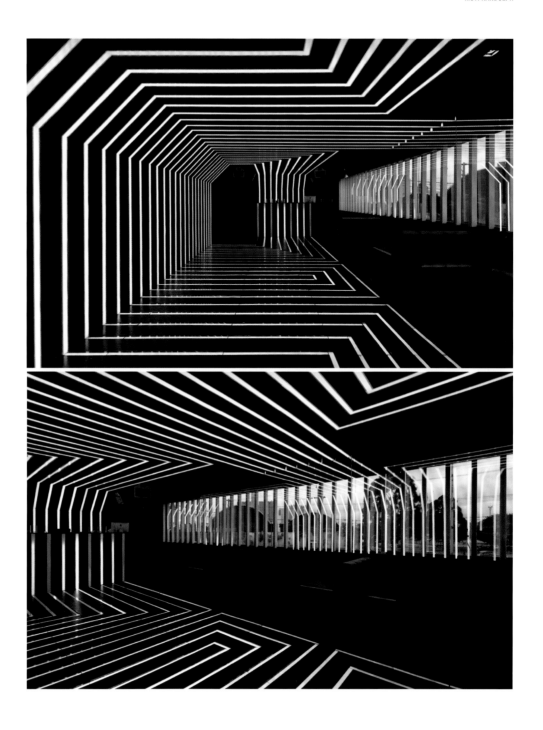

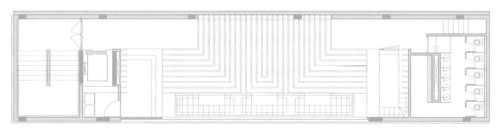

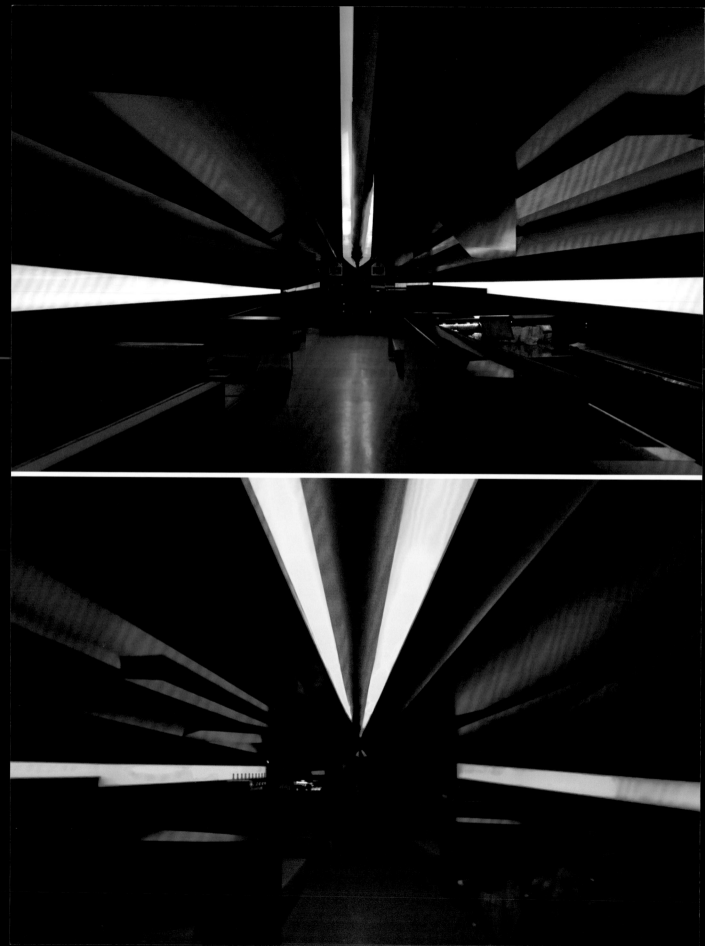

Spectacular lighting effects generated with a computer-controlled system can be modified in accordance with the music. Below, section drawings showing the club in its architectural context.

Spektakuläre computergesteuerte Lichteffekte können je nach Musik abgestimmt werden. Unten ein Querschnitt des Clubs in seinem architektonischen Kontext.

Les effets lumineux spectaculaires générés par un système contrôlé par ordinateur peuvent être modifiés selon la musique. Ci-dessous, les plans en coupe montrent le club dans son contexte architectural.

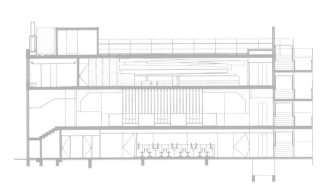

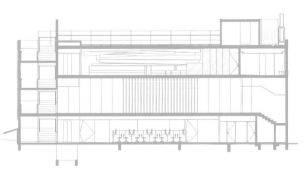

STEFANO RIVA

Stefano Riva
Rua de Santa Justa n° 60 - es
1100–485 Lisbon
Portugal

Tel: +351 93 432 14 00 / Fax: +351 21 152 42 72
E-mail: riva@stefanoriva.net
Web: www.stefanoriva.net

STEFANO RIVA was born in 1969, in Besana Brianza, Italy. He completed his studies at the State Art Institute in Monza and graduated in Architecture from Milan Polytechnic in 1997. Since 1995, he has lived and worked in Lisbon. He began his architectural career collaborating as a designer with ARX Portugal Architects (1997–2003). Since then he developed several commercial and residential projects for private and public clients. In 2004 he founded his own studio that currently works in Portugal and Italy. His work includes Intermezzo Bar (Lisbon, 2008); Portas do Sol Bar (Lisbon, 2009, published here); Two Houses in the Woods (with Marco and Massimo Bigozzi, Venegono, Italy, 2006–11); the Juso House (with ARX Portugal, Aldeia do Juso, 2008–11); South Portugal House (with ARX Portugal, Aldeia do Juso, 2009–11); a House in Monsaraz (Reguengos de Monsaraz, 2009–11); the Babel São Sebastião Library (Lisbon, 2010); and Ten Houses in Monsaraz (Reguengos de Monsaraz, 2008–20), all in Portugal unless stated otherwise.

STEFANO RIVA wurde 1969 in Besana Brianza, Italien, geboren. Er studierte am Staatlichen Kunstinstitut in Monza und machte seinen Architekturabschluss 1997 an der Polytechnischen Hochschule Mailand. Seit 1995 lebt und arbeitet er in Lissabon. Er begann seine architektonische Laufbahn mit Entwürfen für ARX Portugal Architects (1997–2003). Seither realisierte er verschiedene Gewerbe- und Wohnprojekte für private und öffentliche Auftraggeber. 2004 gründete er sein eigenes Studio, das derzeit in Portugal und Italien tätig ist. Zu seinen Projekten zählen: Intermezzo Bar (Lissabon, 2008), Portas do Sol Bar (Lissabon, 2009, hier vorgestellt), zwei Häuser im Wald (mit Marco und Massimo Bigozzi, Venegono, Italien, 2006–11), das Haus Juso (mit ARX Portugal, Aldeia do Juso, 2008–11), das Haus Südportugal (mit ARX Portugal, Aldeia do Juso, 2009–11), ein Haus in Monsaraz (Reguengos de Monsaraz, 2009–11), die Bibliothek Babel São Sebastião (Lissabon, 2010) und zehn Häuser in Monsaraz (Reguengos de Monsaraz, 2008–20), alle in Portugal, sofern nicht anders vermerkt.

STEFANO RIVA est né en 1969 à Besana Brianza, en Italie. Il a fait ses études à l'Institut d'art de Monza et a obtenu son diplôme d'architecture à l'École polytechnique de Milan en 1997. Il vit et travaille à Lisbonne depuis 1995. Il a débuté sa carrière d'architecte en tant que designer pour ARX Portugal Architects (1997–2003). Depuis, il a réalisé plusieurs projets commerciaux et résidentiels pour des clients publics et privés. En 2004, il a créé son agence, qui travaille actuellement au Portugal et en Italie. Ses réalisations comprennent : le bar Intermezzo (Lisbonne, 2008) ; le bar Portas do Sol (Lisbonne, 2009, publié ici) ; deux Maisons dans les bois (en collaboration avec Marco et Massimo Bigozzi, Venegono, Italie, 2006–11) ; la maison Juso (avec ARX Portugal, Aldeia do Juso, 2008–11) ; la maison du Sud du Portugal (avec ARX Portugal, Aldeia do Juso, 2009–11) ; une maison à Monsaraz (Reguengos de Monsaraz, 2009–11) ; la bibliothèque Babel São Sebastião (Lisbonne, 2010) et dix maisons à Monsaraz (Reguengos de Monsaraz, 2008–20), toutes au Portugal sauf mention contraire.

PORTAS DO SOL BAR

Lisbon, Portugal, 2009

Address: Largo das Portas do Sol, Castelo, Lisbon, Portugal, +351 21 88 512 99
Area: 220 m². Client: Miguel Cristo. Cost: not disclosed
Collaboration: Pietro Druido, Jimmy Ballando

The architect explains that this project aims to emphasize the contrast between the "brightness and vastness" of the outside world, and in particular the view on the Tagus, with the atmosphere of a dark cave. The interior walls and ceiling are finished in bare concrete, a rough atmosphere confirmed by the exposed ceiling ducts. Wood marks the curving counter like a "skin in a circular motion in front of the beautiful view outside." Interior tables and chairs are quite simple in the spirit of the entire design. An RGB lighting system, made up of "points of light" in the form of large halos, changes tone and color "in a continuous dialogue with the outside light." Clients more inclined to the exterior can take in the view from the broad terrace with its simple white furnishings.

Dem Architekten geht es bei diesem Projekt in erster Linie darum, den Kontrast zwischen der „Helligkeit und Weite" der Außenwelt, besonders dem Blick auf den Tejo, und der dunklen, höhlenartigen Atmosphäre der Bar zu unterstreichen. Durch Sichtbetonwände und -decken entsteht eine spröde Optik, die durch die offen an der Decke verlaufenden Versorgungsleitungen noch unterstrichen wird. Die geschwungene Bartheke ist mit Holz verblendet, ein Material, das den Tresen „vis à vis der wunderbaren Aussicht in großem Bogen wie eine zweite Haut überzieht". Tische und Stühle in der Bar entsprechen der schlichten Philosophie des Designs. RGB-Leuchten aus „Lichtpunkten" schweben wie große Heiligenscheine im Raum und wechseln Intensität und Farbe „im permanenten Dialog mit den draußen herrschenden Lichtverhältnissen". Wer lieber im Freien ist, kann die Aussicht von der großen Terrasse mit ihrem schlichten weißen Mobiliar genießen.

Pour l'architecte, ce projet vise à souligner le contraste entre la « luminosité et l'immensité » du monde extérieur, notamment la vue sur le Tage, et l'atmosphère d'une cave obscure. Les murs et le plafond sont en béton nu pour une atmosphère brute marquée par les canalisations apparentes au plafond. Le comptoir aux lignes courbes présente un revêtement de bois qui le met en relief, telle « une peau en mouvement circulaire face à la vue extérieure splendide ». Les tables et chaises sont très simples, dans la ligne du design global. Un système d'éclairage RVB fait de « points lumineux » sous forme de larges halos change de ton et de couleur « en un dialogue continu avec la lumière extérieure ». Les clients qui préfèrent rester dehors peuvent apprécier la vue depuis la terrasse simplement meublée de blanc.

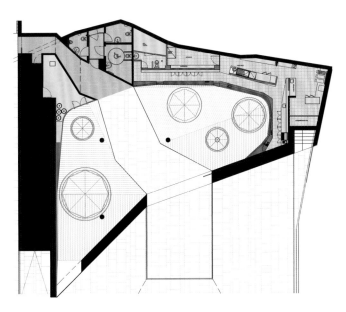

Within the irregular contours of the bar, the rounded lighting fixtures are capable of generating a large variety of colorful lighting effects.

Mit den runden Lichtobjekten, platziert im asymmetrischen Kontext der Bar, lässt sich eine große Bandbreite farbiger Lichteffekte erzeugen.

Dans le cadre aux contours irréguliers du bar, les luminaires ronds peuvent générer une grande variété d'effets lumineux colorés.

RIZOMA ARQUITETURA

Rizoma Arquitetura
Rua Juvenal Melo Senra, 395/1107
30320660 Belo Horizonte, MG
Brazil

Tel/Fax: +55 31 2555 9048
E-mail: rizoma.arquitetura@gmail.com
Web: www.rizoma.arq.br

MARIA PAZ was born in 1985, in Belo Horizonte, Brazil. She received her B.A. in Architecture and Urbanism in 2009, from FUMEC University (Belo Horizonte), and her M.A. in Architecture and Discourse in 2011, from Cornell University (Ithaca, New York). She worked as an intern at Jo Coenen & Co in Luxembourg (2007) and has been Partner and Principal of Rizoma since 2008. **THOMAZ REGATOS** was born in 1981, in Belo Horizonte. He received his B.A. in Architecture and Urbanism in 2004, from the Centro Metodista Izabela Hendrix (Belo Horizonte), and his M.A. in Theory and Practice of Architectural Projects in 2008, from the Universitat Politècnica de Catalunya (Barcelona, Spain, 2008). He also received an M.B.A. degree in Strategic Management in 2010, from the Centro Universitário UNA (Belo Horizonte). Thomaz Regatos worked with the Spanish architect Emilio Donato in 2006 and has been Partner and Principal of Rizoma since 2008. Their current work includes the Inhotim reception area (Brumadinho, 2010); Oiticica Restaurant (Inhotim, Brumadinho, 2010, published here); a Music School (Inhotim, Brumadinho, 2011); Tunga Gallery (Inhotim, Brumadinho, 2011); Lygia Pape Gallery (Inhotim, Brumadinho, 2011); a Botanical Shop (Inhotim, Brumadinho, 2011, also published here); and Filadelfia Advertising Company (Belo Horizonte, 2011–under construction), all in Brazil.

MARIA PAZ wurde 1985 in Belo Horizonte, Brasilien, geboren. Sie machte ihren B.A. in Architektur und Stadtplanung 2009 an der Universität FUMEC (Belo Horizonte) und einen M.A. in Architektur und Diskurs 2011 an der Cornell University (Ithaca, New York). Nach einem Praktikum bei Jo Coenen & Co in Luxemburg (2007) ist sie seit 2008 leitende Partnerin bei Rizoma. **THOMAZ REGATOS** wurde 1981 in Belo Horizonte geboren. Er schloss sein Studium 2004 mit einem B.A. in Architektur und Stadtplanung am Centro Metodista Izabela Hendrix (Belo Horizonte) ab und absolvierte 2008 einen M.A. in Theorie und Praxis architektonischer Projektplanung an der Universitat Politècnica de Catalunya (Barcelona, 2008). Darüber hinaus absolvierte er einen M.B.A. in Strategischem Management (2010) am Centro Universitário UNA (Belo Horizonte). Thomaz Regatos arbeitete 2006 für den spanischen Architekten Emilio Donato und ist seit 2008 leitender Partner bei Rizoma. Jüngere Projekte des Teams sind der Empfangsbereich des Inhotim (Brumadinho, 2010), das Oiticica Restaurant (Inhotim, Brumadinho, 2010, hier vorgestellt), eine Musikschule (Inhotim, Brumadinho, 2011), die Tunga-Galerie (Inhotim, Brumadinho, 2011), die Lygia-Pape-Galerie (Inhotim, Brumadinho, 2011), ein Geschäft für Pflanzen und Gartenbedarf (Inhotim, Brumadinho, 2011, ebenfalls hier vorgestellt) und die Werbeagentur Filadelfia (Belo Horizonte, seit 2011 im Bau), alle in Brasilien.

MARIA PAZ est née en 1985 à Belo Horizonte, au Brésil. Elle a obtenu son B.A. en architecture et urbanisme en 2009 à l'université FUMEC (Belo Horizonte) et son M.A. en architecture et discours architectural en 2011 à l'université Cornell (Ithaca, New York). Elle a effectué un stage chez Jo Coenen & Co à Luxembourg (2007) et est partenaire et directrice de Rizoma depuis 2008. **THOMAZ REGATOS** est né en 1981 à Belo Horizonte. Il a obtenu son B.A. en architecture et urbanisme en 2004 au Centre universitaire méthodiste Izabela Hendrix (Belo Horizonte) et son M.A. en théorie et pratique de projets architecturaux en 2008 à l'Université polytechnique de Catalogne (Barcelone, 2008). Il est également titulaire d'un M.B.A. en gestion stratégique obtenu en 2010 au centre universitaire UNA (Belo Horizonte). Thomaz Regatos a travaillé avec l'architecte espagnol Emilio Donato en 2006 et est partenaire et directeur de Rizoma depuis 2008. Leurs réalisations actuelles comprennent l'espace de réception d'Inhotim (Brumadinho, 2010) ; le restaurant Oiticica (Inhotim, Brumadinho, 2010, publié ici) ; une école de musique (Inhotim, Brumadinho, 2011) ; la galerie Tunga (Inhotim, Brumadinho, 2011) ; la galerie Lygia Pape (Inhotim, Brumadinho, 2011) ; un magasin botanique (Inhotim, Brumadinho, 2011, publié ici) et la société de publicité Filadelfia (Belo Horizonte, 2011–), toutes au Brésil.

OITICICA RESTAURANT

Brumadinho, Minas Gerais, Brazil, 2010

Address: Rua B, 20, Inhotim, Brumadinho, MG 35460–000, Brazil, +55 31 32271 0001, info@inhotim.org.br,
www.inhotim.org.br. Area: 704 m². Client: Inhotim. Cost: $435 000. Collaboration: Virginia Paz

Inhotim is a contemporary art center created by the entrepreneur Inhotim Bernardo Paz in the mid 1980s. A botanical garden was created in 2005, and the center committed itself to the social welfare of the population of Brumadinho and its region. Located in the state of Minas Gerais, Brumadinho is part of the metropolitan region of Belo Horizonte, and is about 60 kilometers from the city. The 320-seat restaurant was conceived as a low-cost building, making maximum use of brise-soleils and natural ventilation. Existing vegetation on the site was protected, making the structure blend smoothly into its setting. The architects state: "The openings of the restaurant to the park, with its colors, textures, and shapes, contaminates the interior, transforming the visitor's stay into an even more pleasant one." The structure was built in just three months.

Inhotim ist ein Zentrum für zeitgenössische Kunst und wurde Mitte der 1980er-Jahre von dem Unternehmer Inhotim Bernardo Paz gegründet. 2005 wurde ein botanischer Garten angelegt, das Zentrum selbst hat sich dem gesellschaftlichen Wohl der Bevölkerung von Brumadinho und seiner Region verschrieben. Das im Staat Minas Gerais gelegene Brumadinho ist Teil der Großstadtregion von Belo Horizonte und liegt rund 60 km von der Großstadt entfernt. Das Restaurant mit 320 Plätzen, ein kostengünstiger Bau, profitiert maßgeblich von den Sonnenschutzblenden und der natürlichen Belüftung. Die bestehende Vegetation des Grundstücks wurde erhalten und lässt den Bau mit seiner Umgebung verschmelzen. Die Architekten erklären: „Die Öffnung des Restaurants zum Park und dessen Farben, Texturen und Formen durchdringt und prägt die Innenarchitektur und macht den Aufenthalt für die Besucher umso angenehmer." Der Bau wurde in nur drei Monaten realisiert.

Inhotim est un centre d'art contemporain créé par l'entrepreneur Inhotim Bernardo Paz au milieu des années 1980. Un jardin botanique y a été ouvert en 2005 et le centre est voué à la sécurité sociale de la population de Brumadinho et de sa région. Située dans l'État du Minas Gerais, Brumadinho appartient à la zone métropolitaine de Belo Horizonte dont elle est éloignée de 60 km environ. Le restaurant de 320 places a été conçu comme un bâtiment peu onéreux faisant un usage optimal des brise-soleil et de la ventilation naturelle. La végétation sur le site a été protégée pour intégrer l'ensemble au décor tout en douceur. Les architectes constatent que « les ouvertures du restaurant sur le parc, ses couleurs, textures et formes, se répercutent sur l'intérieur pour rendre le séjour des visiteurs encore plus agréable ». La structure a été construite en seulement trois mois.

The very simple lines of the restaurant can be seen in these images and in the section drawings below. Concrete and glass are the essential materials.

Auf diesen Ansichten und den Querschnitten unten sind die äußerst schlichten Linien des Restaurants deutlich zu erkennen. Zentrale Materialien sind Beton und Glas.

Les lignes très simples du restaurant sont visibles sur les photos et les plans en coupe ci-dessous. Le béton et le verre sont les principaux matériaux utilisés.

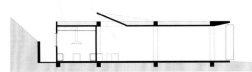

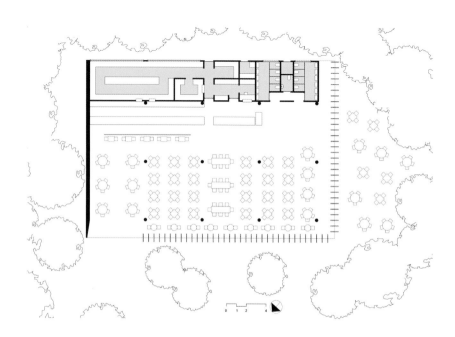

A floor plan shows the simple outlines of the building. The teardrop lighting fixtures add curved forms to the otherwise rectilinear design.

Ein Grundriss zeigt die schlichten Konturen des Baus. Die tränenförmigen Leuchten bringen geschwungene Formen in das ansonsten geradlinige Design.

Le plan au sol montre le tracé très simple du bâtiment. Les lampes en gouttes d'eau ajoutent des courbes au design sinon rectiligne.

Section drawings show the movement of air and rainwater through and around the structure.

Querschnitte illustrieren die Zirkulation von Luftströmen und Regenwasser rund um das Gebäude.

Les coupes illustrent la circulation de l'air et de l'eau de pluie dans et autour de l'ensemble.

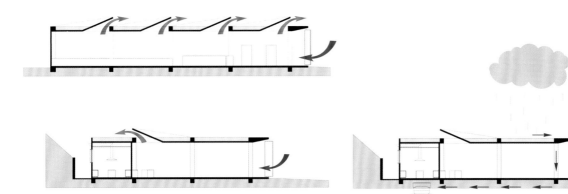

BOTANICAL SHOP

Brumadinho, Minas Gerais, Brazil, 2011

*Address: Rua B, 20, Inhotim, Brumadinho, MG 35460–000, Brazil, +55 31 32271 0001,
info@inhotim.org.br, www.inhotim.org.br. Area: 198 m². Client: Inhotim
Cost: $125 000. Collaboration: Virginia Paz*

Also located in the grounds of the Inhotim Contemporary Art Center, this shop is intended for the sale of plants and garden utensils. The architects explain: "The shop is simply an open shelter to keep the products protected from the weather. It consists only of four elements: two service boxes and two walls. The walls articulate the interior selling spaces and, at the same time, they connect the exterior and the interior. The openness of the building invites the visitors in and emphasizes the products on display." Like the Oiticica Restaurant, the Botanical Shop, made with concrete, wood, and stone, was erected in a very brief three-month period.

Das ebenfalls im Zentrum für zeitgenössische Kunst Inhotim gelegene Ladenlokal bietet Pflanzen und Gartenbedarf an. Die Architekten führen aus: „Der Laden ist ganz einfach ein offener Überbau, der das Produktangebot vor der Witterung schützt. Er besteht aus vier Elementen: zwei Serviceboxen und zwei Wänden. Die Wände definieren den Verkaufsraum und sind zugleich Bindeglied zwischen Außen- und Innenraum. Der offene Charakter des Baus lädt die Besucher ein und lässt die ausgestellten Produkte zur Geltung kommen." Wie das Restaurant Oiticica wurde auch der Laden für Pflanzen- und Gartenbedarf in sehr kurzer, dreimonatiger Bauzeit errichtet.

Également situé sur le terrain du centre d'art contemporain Inhotim, ce magasin vend des plantes et ustensiles de jardin. Les architectes expliquent que « le magasin est un simple abri ouvert pour protéger les produits des intempéries. Il se compose de quatre éléments : deux box de services et deux murs. Les murs articulent les espaces de vente de l'intérieur tout en reliant l'intérieur et l'extérieur. La nature ouverte de l'ensemble invite à entrer et met en valeur les produits présentés. » Comme le restaurant Oiticica, le magasin de béton, bois et pierre a été construit très rapidement, en trois mois.

With its simple concrete slab and column design, the Botanical Shop is a minimalist architectural gesture.

Der Laden für Pflanzen- und Gartenbedarf ist mit seiner schlichten Betonplatten- und Stützenkonstruktion eine minimalistische architektonische Geste.

Avec son design très simple en forme d'abri à colonnes, le magasin botanique est une démonstration d'architecture minimaliste.

The open nature of the structure
means that plants can practically
grow inside, or at any rate, at close
proximity.

Dank der Offenheit der Konstruktion
können die Pflanzen gewissermaßen
im Innern des Baus wachsen oder
zumindest ganz in der Nähe.

La nature ouverte de la structure permet aux plantes de pousser à l'intérieur, ou au moins tout près.

Pictures taken just after the Botanical Shop went into use show how the apparently cold concrete structure is brought to life by the plants and other objects sold there.

Kurz nach Eröffnung des Ladens entstandene Aufnahmen belegen, wie der vermeintlich kalte Betonbau durch die Pflanzen und weiteres angebotenes Zubehör zum Leben erwacht.

Ces photos prises peu après l'ouverture du magasin botanique montrent comment les plantes et autres objets donnent vie à la structure en béton d'apparence plutôt froide.

The brown stone floor and the metallic arch structure seen above contrast with the bare concrete walls and ceiling.

Der braune Steinboden und die metallische Dachkonstruktion (oben) kontrastieren mit den schmucklosen Betonwänden und -decken.

Le sol de pierre brune et les arches métalliques ci-dessus contrastent avec les murs et le plafond de béton nu.

ROJKIND ARQUITECTOS

Rojkind Arquitectos
Tamaulipas 30, Piso12
Col. Hipódromo Condesa,
México D.F. 06140
Mexico

Tel: +52 55 280 8521
E-mail: info@rojkindarquitectos.com
Web: www.rojkindarquitectos.com

MICHEL ROJKIND was born in 1969 in Mexico City, where he studied architecture and urban planning at the Universidad Iberoamericana. In 2002, he established his own firm, Rojkind Arquitectos, in Mexico City. **GERARDO SALINAS** joined the firm as a Partner in 2010. He received his B.Arch from the Universidad Nacional Autonoma de Mexico (Mexico City, 1993) and his M.Arch from the University of Maryland (Baltimore, 1995). Their work includes the Nestlé Chocolate Museum (Toluca, 2007); Nestlé Application Group (Querétaro, 2009); R432 Skyscraper (Mexico City, 2009, under construction); High Park (Monterrey, 2010, under construction); Cineteca Nacional del Siglo XXI (Mexico City, 2011, under construction); the Tori Tori Restaurant (Polanco, Mexico City, 2011, published here); and the Liverpool Department Store (Mexico City 2011), all in Mexico.

MICHEL ROJKIND wurde 1969 in Mexiko-Stadt geboren, wo er Architektur und Städtebau an der Universidad Iberoamericana studierte. 2002 gründete er in Mexiko-Stadt sein eigenes Büro. **GERARDO SALINAS** schloss sich ihm 2010 als Partner an. Salinas machte einen B.Arch. an der Universidad Nacional Autonoma de Mexico (Mexiko-Stadt, 1993) sowie einen M.Arch. an der University of Maryland (Baltimore, 1995). Realisiert wurde das Nestlé-Schokoladenmuseum (Toluca, 2007), die Nestlé Application Group (Querétaro, 2009), der R432-Wolkenkratzer (Mexiko-Stadt, seit 2009), High Park (Monterrey, seit 2010), die Cineteca Nacional del Siglo XXI (Mexiko-Stadt, seit 2011), das Tori Tori Restaurant (Polanco, Mexiko-Stadt, 2011, hier vorgestellt) und das Warenhaus Liverpool (Mexiko-Stadt, 2011).

MICHEL ROJKIND est né en 1969 à Mexico où il a étudié l'architecture et l'urbanisme à l'Université ibéro-américaine. En 2002, il ouvre sa propre agence, Rojkind Arquitectos, à Mexico. Son partenaire **GERARDO SALINAS** l'a rejoint en 2010. Il a obtenu son B.Arch à l'Université nationale autonome de Mexico (1993) et son M.Arch à l'université du Maryland (Baltimore, 1995). Parmi ses projets figurent le musée Nestlé du chocolat (Toluca, 2007) ; le Nestlé Application Group (Querétaro, 2009) ; le gratte-ciel R432 (Mexico, 2009, en construction) ; High Park (Monterrey, 2010, en construction) ; la Cineteca Nacional del Siglo XXI (Mexico, 2011, en construction) ; le restaurant Tori Tori (Polanco, Mexico, 2011, publié ici)) et le grand magasin Liverpool (Mexico 2011), tous au Mexique.

TORI TORI RESTAURANT

Polanco, Mexico City, Mexico, 2011

Address: Temistocles 61, Col. Polanco, 11560 Mexico City, Mexico, www.toritori.com.mx
Area: 629 m². Client: Dr. Kumoto. Cost: not disclosed
Collaboration: Esrawe Studio

This project was carried out in a former house, whose residential interior was stripped out. The client sought a "Japanese interpretation" that would be "contemporary and cosmopolitan." An "organic façade and landscape" were designed to create a strong connection between the interior and exterior of the restaurant. A collection of chairs and tables for interior and exterior use were developed for the restaurant with Esrawe Studio, which shares credit for the overall project with Rojkind. The unusual façade was made of two self-supporting layers of steel plates cut with a CNC machine and then handcrafted. Michel Rojkind points out that the complex geometry of the façade was translated "into very simple and understandable drawings that benefit from local manufacturing… in Mexico City."

Das Projekt wurde in einem ehemaligen Wohnhaus realisiert, das zunächst vollständig entkernt wurde. Der Bauherr wünschte sich eine „japanische Interpretation", die zugleich „zeitgenössisch und kosmopolitisch" sein sollte. Um eine hohe Durchlässigkeit von Innen- und Außenraum des Restaurants zu gewährleisten, entwarf der Architekt eine „organische Fassade und Landschaft". In Zusammenarbeit mit Esrawe Studio (das mit Rojkind für das gesamte Projekt verantwortlich zeichnet) entstand eine Kollektion von Stühlen und Tischen für das Restaurant, die innen wie außen genutzt werden können. Die außergewöhnliche Fassade besteht aus zwei tragenden Stahlblechschichten, die mit einer CNC-Maschine zugeschnitten und von Hand nachbearbeitet wurden. Michel Rojkind weist darauf hin, dass die komplexe Geometrie der Fassade „in sehr einfache, lesbare Zeichnungen" übersetzt wurde, „die in lokaler Fertigung … in Mexiko-Stadt" hergestellt werden konnten.

Le projet a été réalisé dans une ancienne maison dont le plan d'habitation intérieur a été entièrement démantelé. Le client voulait une « interprétation japonaise » à la fois « contemporaine et cosmopolite ». Une « façade biologique et paysagère » a été conçue pour créer un lien fort entre l'intérieur et l'extérieur. Un ensemble de chaises et de tables d'intérieur et d'extérieur a été spécialement développé en collaboration avec Esrawe Studio qui partage la paternité du projet global avec Rojkind. La façade originale est faite de deux couches autoporteuses de plaques d'acier découpées CNC et ouvragées. Michel Rojkind souligne que sa géométrie complexe a été traduite « en un dessin très simple et compréhensible grâce à la production locale… à Mexico ».

The unusual steel web that surrounds the restaurant is seen in these images taken at nightfall—and also in the elevation drawing below.

Das ungewöhnliche Stahlnetz, das das Restaurant umfängt, ist auf diesen abendlichen Aufnahmen gut zu sehen – ebenso wie auf dem Querschnitt unten.

On voit ici l'étrange « toile » d'acier qui entoure le restaurant photographiée à la tombée de la nuit, ainsi que sur le plan en élévation ci-dessous.

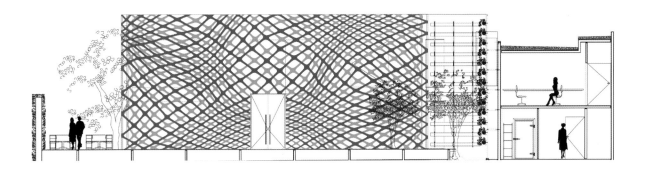

*Right, a plan of the facility. A black
stairway and wooden floors create an
ambiance that is warm but decidedly
modern.*

*Rechts ein Grundriss der Anlage. Eine
schwarze Treppe und Holzböden
schaffen ein warmes, aber auch dezidiert modernes Ambiente.*

*À droite, un plan de l'ensemble.
L'escalier noir et le bois des sols
créent une atmosphère chaleureuse
mais résolument moderne.*

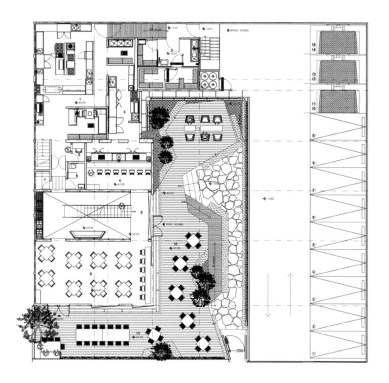

The bar and dining areas of the restaurant give a somewhat more traditional appearance than might be assumed from the exterior.

Bar und Speisebereich wirken etwas traditioneller, als der Blick auf die Außenfassade vermuten ließe.

Le bar et les espaces de restauration présentent une apparence un peu plus traditionnelle qu'on peut deviner de l'extérieur.

In an area where sushi is served, the space is marked by wood cladding, but also by the purpose-designed furniture conceived by Esrawe Studio. A vertical garden completes the space.

Der Bereich, in dem Sushi serviert wird, wird besonders durch seine Holzvertäfelung geprägt, jedoch auch durch die eigens entworfenen Möbel von Esrawe Studio. Ein vertikaler Garten rundet das Ensemble ab.

Dans une pièce où sont servis des sushis, l'espace est marqué par le revêtement en bois et le mobilier spécialement conçu par Esrawe Studio, complété par un jardin vertical.

SAQ

SAQ Architects
Arenbergstraat 44
1000 Brussels
Belgium

Tel: +32 2 300 59 10
Fax: +32 2 300 59 19
E-mail: info@saq.eu
Web: www.saq.eu

SAQ is an interdisciplinary design and architecture agency specialized in developing spatial scenography and concepts. Roel Dehoorne and Frederik Vaes are two Principals of the firm. Initially intended as a side activity of design manufacturer Quinze & Milan and the artist Arne Quinze, SAQ has further developed into an independent architecture studio, focusing on projects as diverse in scale as in program. Recent examples of these are the single-family Diamond House (Roeselare, 2011); and light installations such as BBASS (Ghent, 2011); and Botox Cloud (Berlin, Germany, 2011). Some of the latest high-end realizations of their interior architecture department, aside from retail projects such as the JAGA Experience Truck (2006) and Ferrer (Nieuwpoort-Bad, 2008), are the high-end concept store L'Eclaireur (Paris, France, 2009); the KWINT Restaurant (Brussels, 2009, published here); and SQUARE event-space (Brussels, 2009), all in Belgium unless stated otherwise. SAQ is currently also involved in the conceptualization of mixed-use developments in both Berlin and Brussels, where its offices are located.

SAQ ist eine interdisziplinäre Design- und Architekturagentur, die sich auf Raumszenografien und Konzepte spezialisiert hat. Roel Dehoorne und Frederik Vaes leiten die Firma. Ursprünglich als Projekt neben dem Designlabel Quinze & Milan und der Arbeit von Arne Quinze als Künstler geplant, hat sich SAQ zum eigenständigen Architekturstudio entwickelt, das Aufträge unterschiedlichster Größenordnung und Programme realisiert. Jüngste Beispiele sind etwa das Einfamilienhaus Diamond (Roeselare, 2011) und Lichtinstallationen wie BBASS (Gent, 2011) und Botox Cloud (Berlin, 2011). Zu den aktuellen anspruchsvollen Innenarchitekturprojekten von SAQ zählen neben Ladeneinrichtungen wie dem JAGA Experience Truck (2006) und Ferrer (Nieuwpoort-Bad, 2008) auch der Luxus-Konzeptstore L'Eclaireur (Paris, 2009), das Restaurant KWINT (Brüssel, 2009, hier vorgestellt) und die Event-Location SQUARE (Brüssel, 2009). Derzeit arbeitet SAQ u. a. an Konzepten für Projekte mit gemischter Nutzung in Berlin und Brüssel, wo die Agentur Büros unterhält.

SAQ est une agence de design et d'architecture interdisciplinaire spécialisée dans la scénographie et la conception spatiales. Roel Dehoorne et Frederik Vaes sont deux directeurs de l'agence. Ouverte au départ comme une activité annexe du producteur d'objets design Quinze & Milan et de l'artiste Arne Quinze, SAQ s'est développée et est devenue une agence d'architecture indépendante aux projets à l'envergure et la programmation très diverses. Parmi les exemples récents figurent la maison individuelle Diamond House (Roulers, Belgique, 2011) et des installations lumineuses comme *BBASS* (Gand, 2011) et *Botox Cloud* (Berlin, 2011). Les dernières réalisations haut de gamme du département Architecture d'intérieur, outre des projets commerciaux comme JAGA Experience Truck (2006) et Ferrer (Nieuwpoort-Bad, 2008), comprennent le concept store L'Eclaireur (Paris, 2009) ; le restaurant KWINT (Bruxelles, 2009, publié ici) et l'espace événementiel SQUARE (Bruxelles, 2009), toutes en Belgique sauf mention contraire. SAQ travaille actuellement à des concepts de structures à usage mixte à Berlin et Bruxelles où sont situés ses bureaux.

KWINT

Brussels, Belgium, 2009

Address: Mont des Arts 1 (Rue des Sols, parking Albertine, -3), 1000 Brussels,
+32 2 505 95 95, info@kwintbrussels.com, www.kwintbrussels.com
Area: 250 m². Client: Square & GL-Events. Cost: €900 000

Located in the center of Brussels, leading up to the Mont des Arts, the restaurant **KWINT** is near the new Brussels SQUARE Conference Center. SAQ renovated an arcaded space for KWINT. A 30-meter-long sculpture created by Arne Quinze emerges from the bar at the end of the room, "almost like a living and articulated organism" hanging above the seating space. An upholstered wall reduces noise and houses the service conduits. The glossed copper of the sculpture gives the tone for the basic color of the restaurant. The furniture in the restaurant is by Quinze & Milan. Large windows can be opened on warmer days allowing for a broad view over the old part of Brussels.

Das Restaurant **KWINT** liegt im Zentrum von Brüssel, auf dem Weg zum Mont des Arts, unweit des neuen Konferenzzentrums SQUARE. Für KWINT renovierte SAQ Räumlichkeiten in einem Arkadengang. Eine 30 m lange Skulptur von Arne Quinze „wächst" aus der Bartheke am Ende des Restaurants hervor und schwebt „geradezu wie ein lebendiges, vielgliedriges Wesen" über dem Sitzbereich. Eine gepolsterte Wandverkleidung sorgt für Schalldämmung und kaschiert die Versorgungsleitungen. Der glänzende Kupferton der Skulptur gibt die Grundfarbe des Restaurants vor; das Mobiliar im Restaurant stammt von Quinze & Milan. Die großen Fenster lassen sich bei warmem Wetter öffnen und bieten einen großzügigen Ausblick über die Brüsseler Altstadt.

Au centre de Bruxelles en allant vers le mont des Arts, le restaurant **KWINT** est situé à proximité du nouveau centre de conférences SQUARE. SAQ y a rénové l'espace sous arcades. À l'extrémité de la pièce, une sculpture de 30 m de long par Arne Quinze surgit du bar, « presque comme un organisme vivant et articulé » suspendu au-dessus des sièges. Le mur matelassé réduit le niveau sonore et abrite les canalisations de service. Le cuivre lustré de la sculpture donne le ton de la gamme de couleurs du restaurant. Le mobilier est de Quinze & Milan. De larges fenêtres peuvent être ouvertes par temps chaud pour une vue dégagée sur la vieille ville de Bruxelles.

The 30-meter-long sculpture that rises above the dining tables transforms the otherwise rectangular space into a surprising art installation.

Die 30 m lange Skulptur, die über den Tischen schwebt, lässt den ansonsten rechteckigen Raum zur erstaunlichen Kunstinstallation werden.

La sculpture de 30 m de long suspendue au-dessus des tables du restaurant en transforme l'espace rectangulaire en une étonnante installation artistique.

The brick and stone arches of the restaurant and its generous glazing are perturbed by the presence of the sculpture, which nonetheless leaves the dining space perfectly unimpeded.

Die Präsenz der Skulptur sorgt für einen Bruch in der großzügig verglasten Gewölbearchitektur aus Backstein und Mauerwerk. Dennoch behindert sie den Restaurantbereich in keiner Weise.

La présence de la sculpture parmi les arches de brique et de pierre du restaurant et son vitrage généreux s'avère troublante, même si elle laisse l'espace parfaitement libre.

A floor plan (below) shows the sculpture (seen above and left) in the lower part of the drawing.

Ein Grundriss (unten) zeigt die Skulptur (oben und links im Bild) im unteren Bereich der Zeichnung.

Un plan au sol (ci-dessous) montre la sculpture (ci-dessus et à gauche) dans sa partie inférieure.

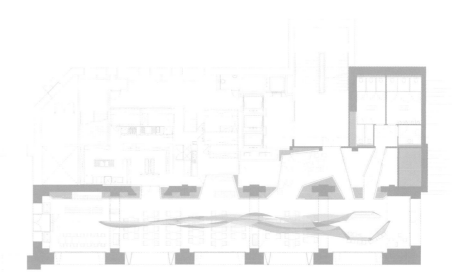

SINATO

Sinato
3–12–5–101 Tsurumaki
Setagaya-ku
Tokyo 154–0016
Japan

Tel: +81 3 6413 9081 / Fax: +81 3 6413 9082
E-mail: central@sinato.jp
Web: www.sinato.jp

CHIKARA OHNO was born in Osaka, Japan, in 1976. He graduated from the Department of Civil Engineering at Kanazawa University in 1999, and established his firm Sinato in Tokyo in 2004. He has designed numerous objects, such as the Punyupunyu light (2003) and the Sakazuk bowl (2004), and his work includes VIGORE (Tokyo, 2006); REI (Tokyo, 2006); Kinari (Tokyo, 2007); YURAS (Tokyo, 2007); Clover Clover (Kanagawa, 2007); House of Table (Shiga, 2007); Duras Ambient Funabashi (Funabashi, Chiba, 2008); Salire Hiroshima (Hiroshima, 2008); TTE (Tokyo, 2008); TOYOTA TSUSHO (Aichi, 2008); House O (Mie, 2009); the Patrick Cox store (Tokyo, 2009); Salon des Saluts Wine Bistro (Tokyo, 2009); and Duras Daiba Store (Tokyo, 2009). Recent work includes "Rolls" (Minato-ku, Tokyo, 2010, published here); Schichirigahama House (Kamakura, 2010); the +Green restaurant (Tokyo, 2010); and Lara Kofu Store (Kofu-shi, Yamanashi, 2011), all in Japan.

CHIKARA OHNO wurde 1976 in Osaka geboren. Er schloss sein Studium 1999 an der Fakultät für Bauingenieurwesen der Universität Kanazawa ab und gründete sein Büro Sinato 2004 in Tokio. Er gestaltete verschiedene Objekte, darunter die Leuchte Punyupunyu (2003) und die Schale Sakazuk (2004). Zu seinen Projekten zählen VIGORE (Tokio, 2006), REI (Tokio, 2006), Kinari (Tokio, 2007), YURAS (Tokio, 2007), Clover Clover (Kanagawa, 2007), House of Table (Shiga, 2007), Duras Ambient Funabashi (Funabashi, Chiba, 2008), Salire Hiroshima (Hiroshima, 2008), TTE (Tokio, 2008), TOYOTA TSUSHO (Aichi, 2008), House O (Mie, 2009), der Patrick Cox Store in Tokio (2009), das Weinbistro Salon des Saluts (Tokio, 2009) und der Duras Daiba Store (Tokio, 2009). Neuere Entwürfe sind u. a. *Rolls* (Minato-ku, Tokio, 2010, hier vorgestellt), Schichirigahama House (Kamakura, 2010), das Restaurant +Green (Tokio, 2010) und der Lara Kofu Store (Kofu-shi, Yamanashi, 2011), alle in Japan.

CHIKARA OHNO est né à Osaka en 1976. Il a obtenu son diplôme au département de génie civil de l'université de Kanazawa en 1999 et a créé son entreprise, Sinato, à Tokyo en 2004. Il a créé de nombreux objets comme la lampe Punyupunyu (2003) ou le bol Sakazuki (2004) et ses réalisations comprennent sinon : VIGORE (Tokyo, 2006) ; REI (Tokyo, 2006) ; Kinari (Tokyo, 2007) YURAS (Tokyo, 2007) ; Clover Clover (Kanagawa, 2007) ; House of Table (Shiga, 2007) ; Duras Ambient Funabashi (Funabashi, Chiba, 2008) ; Salire Hiroshima (Hiroshima, 2008) ; TTE (Tokyo, 2008) ; TOYOTA TSUSHO (Aichi, 2008) ; House O (Mie, 2009) ; le magasin Patrick Cox (Tokyo, 2009) ; le bistrot à vin Salon des Saluts (Tokyo, 2009) et le magasin Duras Daiba (Tokyo, 2009). Ses projets récents comprennent *Rolls* (Minato-ku, Tokyo, 2010, publié ici) ; Schichirigahama House (Kamakura, 2010) ; le restaurant +Green (Tokyo, 2010) et la boutique Lara Kofu (Kofu-shi, Yamanashi, 2011), tous au Japon.

"ROLLS"

Minato-ku, Tokyo, Japan, 2010

Address: n/a. Area: 93 m²
Client: Diesel Japan Co. Ltd. Cost: ¥1.75 million

ROLLS was an installation in the Diesel Denim Gallery Aoyama in Tokyo, which is well known for calling on contemporary artists and architects. In this instance, Chikara Ohno inserted a single long strip of aluminum from the entrance to the back of the shop. The wavy form of the aluminum band was intended to change its function as it advanced through the space. Chikara Ohno states: "The flexible quality of the material (aluminum) represents a gentle connection between the softness of clothes and the hardness of architecture." Using rolls of sheet aluminum, the architect created a veritable sculpture in the space, emphasizing the almost weightless appearance of the metal.

ROLLS war eine Installation in der Diesel Denim Gallery Aoyama in Tokio. Die Galerie ist bekannt dafür, zeitgenössische Künstler und Architekten zu beauftragen. Für sein Projekt installierte Chikara Ohno einen durchgängigen, langen Streifen aus Aluminiumblech vom Eingang bis zum hinteren Ende der Galerie. Die geschwungene Form des Aluminiumbands sollte verschiedenste Funktionen im Raum erfüllen. Chikara Ohno erklärt: „Die Flexibilität des Materials (Aluminium) steht für eine subtile Verbindung zwischen weicher Kleidung und harter Architektur." Mithilfe von Aluminiumblechrollen schuf der Architekt eine echte Skulptur im Raum und ließ die fast schwerelose Leichtigkeit des Metalls in den Vordergrund treten.

ROLLS était une installation à la galerie Diesel Denim Aoyama de Tokyo, connue pour exposer des artistes contemporains et des architectes. Chikara Ohno a ici déroulé un long ruban d'aluminium de l'entrée au fond du magasin, sa forme onduleuse devant changer de fonction en avançant à travers l'espace. Chikara Ohno déclare : « Le caractère souple du matériau (aluminium) représente une transition douce entre la souplesse des vêtements et la dureté de l'architecture. » L'architecte a créé une véritable sculpture à l'aide de rouleaux de feuilles d'aluminium, soulignant l'apparence d'extrême légèreté presque aérienne du métal.

A plan and photos show the simple rectangular layout of the space, with the aluminum rolls that rise up to the ceiling and reconfigure the volume.

Grundriss und Ansichten zeigen die schlichte Rechteckform des Raums und die Aluminiumrollen, die zur Decke aufsteigen und den Raum neu konfigurieren.

Le plan et les photos illustrent la forme rectangulaire simple de l'espace, dont les rouleaux d'alumi- nium qui montent au plafond remodèlent le volume.

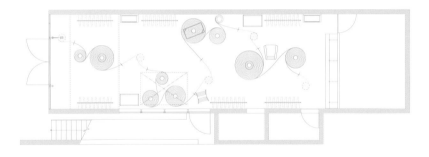

Like bolts of cloth that unravel into the sky, the aluminum rolls used by Sinato make an unexpected, almost magical space.

Wie in den Himmel steigende Stoffballen verwandeln die von Sinato installierten Aluminiumrollen den Raum in einen überraschenden, geradezu magischen Ort.

Tels des rouleaux de tissu qui se déroulent vers le ciel, les rubans d'aluminium utilisés par Sinato créent un espace inédit, presque magique.

SOTERO ARQUITETOS

Sotero Arquitetos
Avenida Contorno 1010
40015–160 Bahia Marina Salvador, BA
Brazil

Tel/Fax: +55 71 3321 0987
E-mail: contato@soteroarquitetos.com.br
Web: www.soteroarquitetos.com.br

ADRIANO MASCARENHAS was born in 1974. He graduated from the Universidade Federal da Bahia (UFBA) in 1999. After graduation, he worked in Brazil for the French firm Citélum as a lighting designer for two years. In 2003 he joined DB Arquitetos (David Bastos) as a Partner and over a period of six years developed private projects in Brazil and other countries, such as the United Arab Emirates (Dubai) and Portugal. He founded Sotero Arquitetos in 2007 in Salvador, Bahia. Sotero's recent projects include the Soho Paseo Restaurant (Salvador, 2008); Gurilândia School (Salvador, 2010); AABB Concert Hall (Salvador, 2011); the Soho Restaurant at Lago Sul (Brasilia, 2011); Ferraz Gourmet (Salvador, 2011, published here); Monorail Stations for public transport (Salvador, 2011); Tecnocentro, a building for the seat of government of the State of Bahia in the technology park TecnoBahia (Salvador, 2008–); and Bahia Marina Design Hotel (Salvador, 2011–), all in Brazil.

ADRIANO MASCARENHAS, geboren 1974, schloss sein Studium 1999 an der Universidade Federal da Bahia (UFBA) ab. Nach seinem Abschluss arbeitete er zunächst zwei Jahre in Brasilien als Leuchtendesigner für die französische Firma Citélum. 2003 schloss er sich DB Arquitetos (David Bastos) als Partner an und entwickelte in den folgenden sechs Jahren private Projekte in Brasilien und weiteren Ländern, darunter den Vereinigten Arabischen Emiraten (Dubai) und Portugal. 2007 gründete er Sotero Arquitetos in Salvador, Bahia. Zu Soteros jüngeren Projekten zählen das Restaurant Soho Paseo (Salvador, 2008), die Gurilândia-Schule (Salvador, 2010), das Konzerthaus AABB (Salvador, 2011), das Restaurant Soho in Lago Sul (Brasilia, 2011), Ferraz Gourmet (Salvador, 2011, hier vorgestellt), Monorail-Stationen für den Nahverkehr (Salvador, 2011), Tecnocentro, ein Gebäude für den Regierungssitz des Staates Bahia im Technologiepark TecnoBahia (Salvador, seit 2008) sowie das Designhotel Bahia Marina (Salvador, seit 2011), alle in Brasilien.

ADRIANO MASCARENHAS est né en 1974. Il est diplômé (1999) de l'Université fédérale de Bahia (UFBA). Il a ensuite travaillé au Brésil pour l'entreprise française Citélum comme créateur de luminaires pendant deux ans. En 2003, il a rejoint DB Arquitetos (David Bastos) dont il est devenu partenaire et a réalisé des projets privés pendant six ans au Brésil et dans d'autres pays comme les Émirats arabes unis (Dubaï) et le Portugal. Il a fondé Sotero Arquitetos en 2007 à Salvador, Bahia. Ses projets récents comprennent : le restaurant Soho Paseo (Salvador, 2008) ; l'école Gurilândia (Salvador, 2010) ; la salle de concerts AABB (Salvador, 2011) ; le restaurant Soho de Lago Sul (Brasilia, 2011) ; Ferraz Gourmet (Salvador, 2011, publié ici) ; des stations de monorail pour les transports publics (Salvador, 2011) ; Tecnocentro, un bâtiment pour le siège du gouvernement de l'État de Bahia dans le parc technologique TecnoBahia (Salvador, 2008–) et l'hôtel design Bahia Marina (Salvador, 2011–), tous au Brésil.

FERRAZ GOURMET

Salvador, Bahia, Brazil, 2011

Address: Rua Ceará 339, Pituba, Salvador, Bahia, Brazil, +55 71 3355 0027
Area: 320 m². Client: Sergio and Ricardo Ferraz. Cost: not disclosed

FERRAZ GOURMET was created on the occasion of the return of chef Ricardo Ferraz to Brazil after seven years working in acclaimed Italian restaurants (La Bastiglia, Il Rigoletto). The architects sought out the "cozy tone of tropical Sucupira wood" to define the atmosphere of the space. The restaurant remains open to the busy urban environment thanks to broad glazed surfaces but, within, the use of wood for the walls, linings, and furniture, together with gray limestone for the floor, counter, and lower walls, defines a space that is set apart from the city. As a counterpoint to the largely monochromatic décor, a specially commissioned work by the Bahian artist Bel Borba evokes themes related to gastronomy. The wood and leather furniture used in this project were entirely designed by Sotero. The restaurant occupies four levels, with toilets and employees' area in the basement, the main dining area, bar, and balcony on the ground floor, and the upper levels reserved for the kitchen and storage spaces.

FERRAZ GOURMET wurde von Ricardo Ferraz gegründet, nachdem er sieben Jahre in berühmten italienischen Restaurants gearbeitet hatte (La Bastiglia, Il Rigoletto) und schließlich nach Brasilien zurückgekehrt war. Die Architekten entschieden sich bewusst für den „warmen Farbton des tropischen Sucupira-Holzes", um Atmosphäre zu schaffen. Dank großzügiger Verglasung bleibt das Restaurant seinem belebten urbanen Umfeld verbunden, doch innen sorgt der Einsatz von Holz für die Wände, Verkleidungen und das Mobiliar im Zusammenspiel mit grauem Kalkstein für Böden, Tresen und Sockelzone für eine Stimmung, die sich von der Stadt abzusetzen versteht. Als Kontrapunkt zum überwiegend monochromatischen Dekor greift ein Auftragswerk von Bel Borba, einem Künstler aus Bahia, Motive aus der Welt der Gastronomie auf. Das gesamte Mobiliar aus Holz und Leder wurde von Sotero entworfen. Das Restaurant verteilt sich über vier Ebenen: Mitarbeiterräume und Toiletten liegen im Untergeschoss, Hauptgastraum, Bar und Balkon im Parterre sowie Küche und Lagerräume in zwei Obergeschossen.

FERRAZ GOURMET a été créé pour le retour au Brésil du chef Ricardo Ferraz après sept ans passés à travailler dans des restaurants italiens remarqués (*La Bastiglia*, *Il Rigoletto*). Les architectes ont eu recours au « ton chaleureux du bois tropical de sucupira » pour créer l'atmosphère de l'espace. Le restaurant est ouvert sur l'environnement urbain animé par de larges surfaces vitrées, mais à l'intérieur le choix du bois pour les murs, les revêtements et le mobilier, associé au calcaire gris du sol, du comptoir et du bas des murs, permet de définir un espace qui se distingue de la ville. En contrepoint du décor majoritairement monochrome, une œuvre spécialement commandée à l'artiste de Bahia Bel Borba évoque des thèmes liés à la gastronomie. Le mobilier de bois et de cuir a été entièrement créé par Sotero. Le restaurant occupe quatre niveaux : les toilettes et l'espace réservé aux employés au sous-sol, la salle principale, le bar et le balcon au rez-de-chaussée, les étages supérieurs étant réservés à la cuisine et à des espaces de rangement.

The warm, wood-clad atmosphere of the restaurant is complemented by purpose-designed furniture, a bar that displays bottles individually, and the green and red artwork seen at the back of the images.

Das warme, holzvertäfelte Ambiente des Restaurants wird ergänzt durch speziell entworfenes Mobiliar, eine Bar, die Flaschen als Solitäre präsentiert, und das grüne und rote Kunstwerk im Hintergrund.

L'atmosphère chaleureuse du restaurant lambrissé de bois est parachevée par le mobilier spécialement créé, le bar aux présentoirs de bouteilles individuels et l'œuvre d'art rouge et verte vue à l'arrière-plan des photos.

The enveloping texture of the wood creates a convivial space that is interrupted only by artworks or pottery.

Holz prägt den einladenden Raum als großes Thema. Kontrapunkte sind allein die Kunstwerke und einzelne Keramikobjekte.

La texture enveloppante du bois crée un espace convivial uniquement entrecoupé par des œuvres d'art ou des poteries.

Spotlights highlight the artworks but also the tables and other furnishings, making them stand out from the wood background.

Punktbeleuchtung hebt die Kunstwerke hervor, ebenso die Tische und andere Einbauten, die sich so vor dem Hintergrund aus Holz behaupten.

Des spots éclairent les œuvres d'art, mais aussi les tables et d'autres meubles, les faisant ressortir sur le fond de bois.

SUPPOSE DESIGN OFFICE

Suppose Design Office
13–2–3F Kako-machi
Naka-ku
Hiroshima 730–0812
Japan

Tel: +81 82 247 1152 / Fax: +81 82 298 5551
E-mail: info@suppose.jp
Web: www.suppose.jp

MAKOTO TANIJIRI was born in Hiroshima, Japan, in 1974. He worked in Motokane Architects Office (Hiroshima, 1994–99), and HAL Architects Office (Hiroshima, 1999–2000), before creating his own firm, Suppose Design Office, in 2000. It currently employs 15 people in Hiroshima and Tokyo, and the work of the office includes the design and supervision of architecture, interiors, landscapes, and exhibitions. It also designs and supervises renovations and design products and furniture. Tanijiri has been a lecturer at the Anabuki Design College, Department of Architecture Design, since 2003. His work in 2008 included a house in Sakuragawa, a house in Takasu 02, a house in Matsuyama, and a house in Minamimachi 02. In 2009, as well as the installation "Nature Factory" (Tokyo), he worked on houses in Obama, Hiro, Koamichyo, Kamiosuga, Moriyama, Jigozen, Kitakamakura, and Danbara. In 2010 and 2011, he designed houses in Seya, Tokushima, Hidaka, Fukawa, Fukuyama, and Kodaira, together with Café Day (Shizuoka, 2010, published here); and 52 (Shizuoka, 2011, also published here), all in Japan. In all, Tanijiri has designed over 60 houses.

MAKOTO TANIJIRI wurde 1974 in Hiroshima geboren. Er arbeitete für Motokane Architects (Hiroshima, 1994–99) und HAL Architects (Hiroshima, 1999–2000), bevor er 2000 sein eigenes Büro Suppose Design Office gründete. Derzeit beschäftigt das Büro 15 Mitarbeiter in Hiroshima und Tokio, das Spektrum reicht vom Entwurf bis zur Realisierung von Architektur, Innenarchitektur, Landschaften und Ausstellungsarchitekturen. Außerdem realisiert Suppose Sanierungen, Designprodukte und Möbel. Seit 2003 ist Tanijiri Dozent an der Architekturfakultät des Anabuki Design College. 2008 baute er u. a. ein Haus in Sakuragawa, ein Haus in Takasu 02, ein Haus in Matsuyama und ein Haus in Minamimachi 02. 2009 realisierte er neben der Installation *Nature Factory* (Tokio) auch Häuser in Obama, Hiro, Koamichyo, Kamiosuga, Moriyama, Jigozen, Kitakamakura und Danbara. 2010 und 2011 entwarf er Häuser in Seya, Tokushima, Hidaka, Fukawa, Fukuyama und Kodaira sowie das Café Day (Shizuoka, 2010, hier vorgestellt) und 52 (Shizuoka, 2011, ebenfalls hier vorgestellt), alle in Japan. Insgesamt hat Tanijiri über 60 Häuser gestaltet.

MAKOTO TANIJIRI est né à Hiroshima en 1974. Il a travaillé dans les cabinets d'architectes Motokane (Hiroshima, 1994–99) et HAL (Hiroshima, 1999–2000) avant de créer sa propre entreprise, Suppose Design Office, en 2000. Elle a actuellement 15 employés à Hiroshima et Tokyo et travaille à la conception et la supervision de projets architecturaux, d'intérieurs, de paysages et d'expositions, ainsi qu'à la conception et supervision de projets de rénovations et de design de produits et de mobilier. Tanijiri enseigne à l'école supérieure de design Anabuki, département de design architectural, depuis 2003. Ses projets en 2008 comprenaient une maison à Sakuragawa, une maison à Takasu 02, une maison à Matsuyama et une maison à Minamimachi 02. En 2009, outre l'installation *Nature Factory* (Tokyo), il a travaillé à des maisons à Obama, Hiro, Koamichyo, Kamiosuga, Moriyama, Jigozen, Kitakamakura et Danbara. En 2010 et 2011, il a créé des maisons à Seya, Tokushima, Hidaka, Fukawa, Fukuyama et Kodaira, ainsi que le Café Day (Shizuoka, 2010, publié ici) et 52 (Shizuoka, 2011, publié ici), tous au Japon. En tout, Tanijiri est l'auteur de plus de 60 maisons.

CAFÉ DAY
Shizuoka, Japan, 2010

Address:1–6–2–6 Numakitacho, Numazu, Shizuoka Prefecture, Japan
Area: 74 m². Client: Kenichiro Kano, Hiromi Kano. Cost: not disclosed
Collaboration: Hajime Nagano (Project Director)

CAFÉ DAY is located in an existing building where two traditional Japanese bars had been located in a residential area five minutes away form the Namazu-shi Shizuoka train station. The architect was inspired by the yellow cars of a local driving school and chose that tone for the new café, almost as though it had become part of the school. The two bars were converted into a single space by demolishing parts of the wall that divided them. The asphalt of the nearby street was continued into the store, with white lines marking the distinction between interior and exterior, highlighting the idea of an open café, with sliding glass walls that can be opened in warm weather. A bench inside mimics bus stop seating and modified car seats were used as a sofa, while outdoor seating seems to be part of the parking area.

CAFÉ DAY liegt in einem Wohnviertel rund fünf Minuten vom Bahnhof Namazu-shi Shizuoka entfernt: Im Gebäude befanden sich früher zwei traditionelle Bars. Inspirieren ließ sich der Architekt von den gelben Fahrzeugen einer ansässigen Fahrschule, seine Farbwahl für das neue Café lässt fast den Eindruck entstehen, es gehöre zur Schule. Aus den ehemals zwei Bars wurde durch einen Teildurchbruch der trennenden Wand ein großer Raum. Der Asphaltbelag der nahe gelegenen Straße setzt sich im Ladenlokal fort. Weiße Linien markieren den Übergang von Innen- und Außenraum und unterstreichen das Konzept eines offenen Cafés, dessen Glasschiebetüren bei warmem Wetter geöffnet werden können. Eine Bank im Café erinnert an eine Bushaltestelle, umgebaute Autositze dienen als Sofa, und das Mobiliar draußen wirkt, als gehöre es zum Parkplatz.

Le **CAFÉ DAY** occupe un bâtiment qui abritait auparavant deux bars traditionnels japonais, dans une zone résidentielle à cinq minutes de la gare Namazu-shi de Shizuoka. Inspiré par les voitures jaunes d'une auto-école voisine, l'architecte a choisi cette couleur pour le nouveau café, presque comme s'il faisait lui aussi partie de l'auto-école. Les deux bars ont été transformés en un espace unique en démolissant partiellement le mur qui les séparait. L'asphalte de la rue voisine avance jusque dans le café, des lignes blanches marquant la limite entre intérieur et extérieur de manière à souligner l'idée d'un café ouvert, aux baies vitrées coulissantes qui peuvent être ouvertes par temps chaud. À l'intérieur, un banc imite les sièges des arrêts de bus et des sièges de voiture modifiés tiennent lieu de canapé, tandis que les sièges extérieurs semblent faire partie du parking.

The café relies on a simple but clever design that makes outdoor asphalt space appear to be part of the interior.

Das Café setzt auf ein einfaches, aber gewitztes Design, das den asphaltierten Außenraum ganz einfach in die Innenraumgestaltung mit einbezieht.

Le café affiche un design simple, mais astucieux, dans lequel l'asphalte extérieur semble faire partie de l'intérieur.

The markings on the floor are in direct continuity with the outside street lines. Windows open broadly obviating any remaining distinction between interior and exterior.

Die Markierungen auf dem Boden knüpfen unmittelbar an die Straßenmarkierungen im Außenbereich an. Die sich weit öffnenden Fenster verwischen endgültig jede Grenze zwischen Innen- und Außenraum.

Le marquage au sol forme une continuité avec le marquage urbain extérieur. Les fenêtres s'ouvrent largement afin d'effacer la dernière distinction entre intérieur et extérieur.

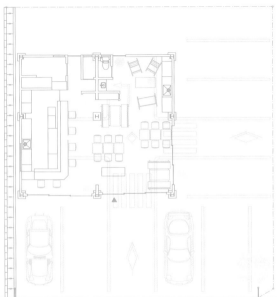

The furnishings and, indeed, the overall finishing of the café are relatively modest, in keeping with the roadway imagery used for the overall scheme.

Das Mobiliar und die gesamte Ausstattung des Cafés sind recht schlicht gehalten, eine stimmige Entscheidung angesichts des zentralen Motivs: der Straßenmarkierungen.

Le mobilier et les finitions du café dans son ensemble sont assez modestes, assortis à l'imaginaire routier utilisé pour le projet global.

52

Shizuoka, Japan, 2011

Address: 4–12–50–2 Shizuoka, Shizuoka Prefecture, Japan
Area: 113 m². Client: not disclosed. Cost: not disclosed
Collaboration: Masashi Shiino (Project Director)

For this clothing store, the architect considered the way natural light is often used in art galleries to highlight the real colors of the works on display. His concept was to "create a room that is like the outside… and to create a room that is like the inside." A nine-millimeter metal sheet wall was erected in a zigzag arrangement to create the two spaces with generous openings between them. The area with natural lighting was conceived for outdoor wear and shoes. The section with artificial light was reserved for clothing to be worn inside, and for stationary or other goods. Makoto Tanijiri states: "By creating an internal space and external space in a building using only natural light effects, we were able to find a new relationship between outdoor and indoor space."

Für dieses Bekleidungsgeschäft machte sich der Architekt den typischen Einsatz von Tageslicht in Kunstgalerien zu eigen, um die Farben der angebotenen Waren unverfälscht zur Wirkung zu bringen. Sein Konzept war es „einen Raum zu gestalten, der das Gefühl vermittelt, draußen zu sein… und einen Raum, der wie ein Innenraum wirkt". Um die beiden Raumzonen zu realisieren, wurde eine im Zickzack verlaufende Trennwand aus 9 mm starkem Stahlblech mit großzügigen Öffnungen eingezogen. Die Tageslichtzone ist Kleidung und Schuhen vorbehalten, die draußen getragen werden. Der künstlich belichtete Bereich präsentiert Kleidung, die drinnen getragen wird, sowie Schreibwaren und weitere Produkte. Makoto Tanijiri erklärt: „Durch die Simulation von Innen- und Außenraum in einem Gebäude, und dies ausschließlich durch die Nutzung von Tageslichteffekten, ist es uns gelungen, ein ganz neues Verhältnis von Außen- und Innenräumen zu definieren."

Pour cette boutique de vêtements, l'architecte a pensé à la manière dont la lumière naturelle est souvent exploitée dans les galeries d'art pour mettre en valeur les couleurs réelles des œuvres exposées. Son concept était de « créer une pièce qui soit comme extérieure… et une pièce qui soit comme intérieure ». Un mur fait d'une feuille métallique de 9 mm a été érigé en zigzag pour délimiter les deux espaces en ménageant de vastes ouvertures entre eux. La partie à la lumière naturelle était destinée aux vêtements d'extérieur et aux chaussures, celle à la lumière artificielle réservée aux vêtements d'intérieur et petits articles ou autres produits. Makoto Tanijiri déclare qu'« en créant un espace intérieur et un espace extérieur dans un bâtiment avec seulement de la lumière naturelle, nous avons pu découvrir une nouvelle relation entre intérieur et extérieur ».

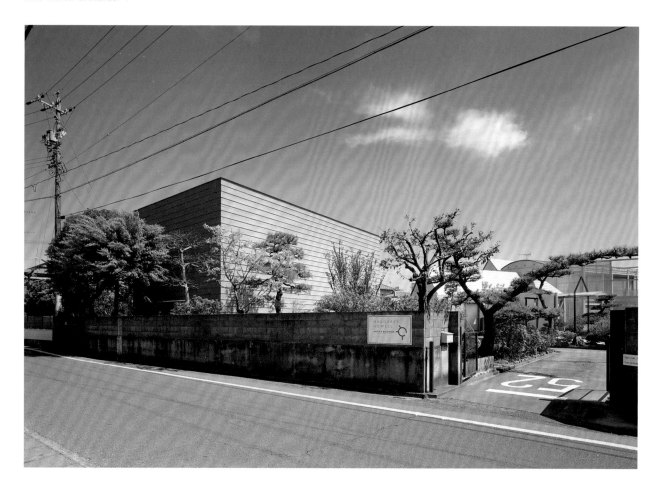

The interior of 52 gives an impression of radical simplicity, with one planted tree and hanging lightbulbs being the only added elements, aside from a changing "tent" and minimal hangers for the clothing.

Die Innenausstattung von 52 ist von radikaler Schlichtheit: Ein gepflanzter Baum und hängende Glühbirnen sind die einzigen ergänzenden Elemente, abgesehen von der „Zelt"-Umkleide und den minimalistischen Kleiderständern.

L'intérieur du 52 donne une impression d'absolue simplicité, l'arbre et les ampoules suspendues en constituent les seuls éléments ajoutés avec une « tente » d'essayage et des cintres minimalistes.

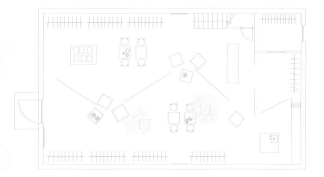

The interior space varies between generous daylight and the relatively shadowed stairway space seen above. Items on display are kept to a strict minimum.

Der Innenraum changiert zwischen großzügig einfallendem Tageslicht und der vergleichsweise schattigen Zone nahe der Treppe (oben). Die präsentierten Waren sind auf ein absolutes Minimum beschränkt.

L'espace intérieur se partage entre la lumière naturelle abondante et l'escalier plutôt sombre vu ci-dessus. Le nombre d'articles présentés est maintenu à un strict minimum.

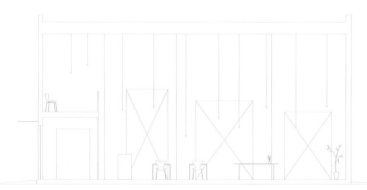

CATERINA TIAZZOLDI / NUOVA ORDENTRA

Caterina Tiazzoldi / Nuova Ordentra
Corso Vinzaglio 21
10121 Turin
Italy

Tel: +39 34 77 79 08 57
E-mail: info@tiazzoldi.org
Web: www.tiazzoldi.org

Born in Turin, Italy, in 1972, **CATERINA TIAZZOLDI** is the Principal of Nuova Ordentra, an interdisciplinary practice based in Turin and New York. She teaches at Columbia University, where she directs the Research Lab NSU. She is also a Postdoctoral Fellow at DIPRADI Politecnico di Torino. She was finalist for the Renzo Piano Foundation Prize for Young Talents (2011) and was nominated for the 2012 Cooper Hewitt National Design Award. As she explains, her research "is based on digital and physical manipulation of spatial attributes and material properties permitting to alter the way in which spaces are used or perceived." The installation "Social Cave" she developed with NSU, was commissioned by the Salone Satellite on the occasion of the 50th anniversary of Milan Furniture Fair (2011). Her projects include Onion Pinch (Lisbon, Portugal, 2009); Toolbox, Torino Office Lab (Turin, Italy, 2010); and the temporary illyshop (Milan, Italy, 2011, published here).

CATERINA TIAZZOLDI, geboren 1972 in Turin, ist Geschäftsführerin von Nuova Ordentra, einem interdisziplinären Büro mit Sitz in Turin und New York. Sie lehrt an der Columbia University, wo sie das Foschungslabor NSU leitet. Darüber hinaus ist sie Post Doctoral Fellow der DIPRADI Politecnico di Torino. Sie war Finalistin beim Preis für junge Talente der Renzo Piano Foundation (2011) und 2012 nominiert für den Cooper Hewitt National Design Award. Wie sie erklärt, basiert ihre Forschung „auf der digitalen und physikalischen Manipulation räumlicher Attribute und materieller Eigenschaften, durch die sich unsere Nutzung und Wahrnehmung von Räumen verändern lässt". Die Installation *Social Cave,* die sie mit NSU entwickelte, war ein Auftrag von Salone Satellite anlässlich des 50. Geburtstags der Möbelmesse in Mailand (2011). Zu ihren Projekten gehören Onion Pinch (Lissabon, 2009), Toolbox, Torino Office Lab (Turin, 2010), und der temporäre illyshop (Mailand, 2011, hier vorgestellt).

Née à Turin en 1972, **CATERINA TIAZZOLDI** est la directrice de Nuova Ordentra, un cabinet interdisciplinaire basé à Turin et New York. Elle enseigne à l'université Columbia où elle dirige le laboratoire de recherches NSU. Elle est également boursière postdoctorale du département DIPRADI de Politecnico di Torino. Elle a été finaliste du prix de la Fondation Renzo Piano pour les jeunes talents (2011) et nominée en 2012 pour le prix Cooper Hewitt National Design Award. Elle explique que sa recherche « est basée sur la manipulation numérique et physique d'attributs spatiaux et de propriétés physiques pour modifier la façon dont les espaces sont exploités ou perçus ». Son installation *Social Cave*» développée avec NSU a été commandée par Salone Satellite à l'occasion du 50ᵉ anniversaire du Salon du meuble de Milan (2011). Ses projets comprennent Onion Pinch (Lisbonne, Portugal, 2009) ; Toolbox, Torino Office Lab (Turin, 2010) et la boutique temporaire illy (Milan, 2011, publiée ici).

ILLYSHOP

Milan, Italy, 2011

Address: n/a. Area: 35 m²
Client: illycaffè. Cost: €60 000

The **ILLYSHOP** is a concept store that was installed in the Galleria San Carlo in Milan. Caterina Tiazzoldi describes it as a "reconfigurable store, characterized by different modulations of a single element, a 'cube' based on a 45 x 45-centimeter square." By varying depth, thickness, or opacity, she creates the possibility of generating over 3000 configurations using the same basic module. The 200 cubes used for the shop were specifically designed to adapt to illycaffè products. The module, covering the space from floor to ceiling, was used for the table, desk counter, storage space, lighting system, video frames, communication, and recycling bins. Since a number of the modules can be moved, the user can reconfigure part of the space himself. The designer states: "This idea reflects the illy concept as a unique product having the capacity to reconfigure in different formats."

Der **ILLYSHOP** ist ein Konzeptstore, der in der Galleria San Carlo in Mailand realisiert wurde. Caterina Tiazzoldi beschreibt ihn als „rekonfigurierbares Geschäft, das auf Modulationen eines einzigen Elements beruht, eines ‚Würfels', ausgehend von einem 45 x 45 cm großen Quadrat". Durch Variationen der Tiefe, Materialstärke oder Opazität der Elemente entwickelte sie über 3000 verschiedene Konfigurationen mit ein und demselben Modul. Die 200 im Ladengeschäft verbauten Kuben wurden speziell auf die Produktpalette von illycaffè zugeschnitten. Das Modul zieht sich vom Boden bis zur Decke durch den gesamten Raum und dient als Tisch, Tresen, Lagerfläche, Lichtsystem, Rahmen für Videomonitore, Kommunikation sowie als Recyclingbehälter. Einzelne Module lassen sich bewegen und erlauben dem Nutzer so, den Raum teilweise selbst zu verändern. Die Gestalterin erklärt: „Die Idee ist ein Spiegel des illy-Konzepts: ein unverwechselbares Produkt, das sich zu verschiedensten Formaten rekonfigurieren lässt."

La **BOUTIQUE ILLY** est un concept store qui a été installé Galleria San Carlo à Milan. Caterina Tiazzoldi la décrit comme « un magasin reconfigurable, caractérisé par différentes modulations d'un seul élément, un cube de 45 x 45 cm² de base ». En variant la profondeur, l'épaisseur ou l'opacité, on peut générer plus de 3000 configurations à partir du même module de base. Les 200 cubes utilisés pour le magasin ont été spécialement conçus pour s'adapter aux produits illycaffè. Ils recouvrent l'espace du sol au plafond et servent de table, caisse, comptoir, espace de rangement, éclairage, images vidéo, communication et poubelles. Un certain nombre de modules peut être déplacé pour permettre à l'utilisateur de reconfigurer lui-même une partie de l'espace. Pour la designer, « l'idée reflète le concept illy en tant que produit unique pouvant être reconfiguré en différents formats ».

Like open drawers or a display for works of art, the grid of white boxes employed by the architect enlivens the space while meeting its commercial requirements.

Wie offene Schubladen oder Sockel für Kunstobjekte belebt das von der Architektin entwickelte Raster aus weißen Boxen den Raum und erfüllt zugleich seinen kommerziellen Zweck.

Tels autant de tiroirs ouverts ou de présentoirs pour œuvres d'art, le maillage de cubes blancs donne vie à l'espace tout en répondant à ses exigences commerciales.

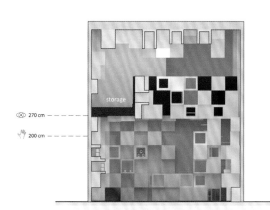

270 cm
200 cm

storage

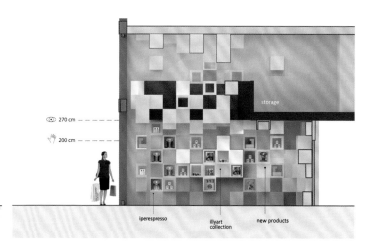

270 cm
200 cm

storage

iperespresso   illyart collection   new products

ALFONS TOST

Alfons Tost Interiorisme
Passatge Marimón
708021 Barcelona
Spain

Tel: +34 93 200 22 65
E-mail: info@alfonstost.com
Web: www.alfonstost.com

ALFONS TOST I SOLÀ was born in Tortosa, Spain, in 1966. He studied interior design at Eina University (Barcelona) and product design with Ramón Benedito. In 1994 he created Tost, a firm dedicated to the design, manufacture, and commercialization of furniture. In 1999 he created Accions interiorisme i flors, intended "as a multidisciplinary space where different teams make interior design, flower compositions, and ephemeral spaces." His firm for interior design execution, Alfons Tost interiorisme, was launched in 2008. As well as Fastvínic (Barcelona, 2010, published here), current projects include Monvínic Restaurant (Barcelona); Coure Restaurant (Barcelona); Espai Sucre Restaurant and School (Barcelona); Equestrian Center Restaurant (Barcelona); and Arrels Florist Shop (Martorello), all in Spain.

ALFONS TOST I SOLÀ wurde 1966 in Tortosa, Spanien, geboren. Er studierte Innenarchitektur an der Universität Eina in Barcelona sowie Produktdesign bei Ramón Benedito. 1994 gründete er Tost, ein auf Möbeldesign, -fertigung und -vertrieb spezialisiertes Büro. 1999 folgte die Gründung von Accions interiorisme i flors „als multidisziplinärer Raum, in dem verschiedene Teams innenarchitektonische Projekte, Floristik und flüchtige Räume realisieren können". Sein Büro für Innenarchitektur, Alfons Tost interiorisme, wurde 2008 gegründet. Neben Fastvínic (Barcelona, 2010, hier vorgestellt) sind seine aktuellen Projekte u. a. die Restaurants Monvínic (Barcelona), Coure (Barcelona), Espai Sucre (mit Schule, Barcelona) und das Restaurant im Reitsportzentrum (Barcelona) sowie das Blumengeschäft Arrels (Martorello), alle in Spanien.

ALFONS TOST I SOLÀ est né à Tortosa en Espagne en 1966. il a étudié l'architecture intérieure à l'université Eina (Barcelone) et le design produits avec Ramón Benedito. En 1994, il crée Tost, une société qui se consacre à la création, la fabrication et la commercialisation de meubles. En 1999, il crée Accions interiorisme i flors, conçu « comme un espace multidisciplinaire où différentes équipes font de l'architecture d'intérieur, des compositions florales et des espaces éphémères ». Sa société d'architecture intérieure, Alfons Tost interiorisme, a été lancée en 2008. Avec le Fastvínic (Barcelone, 2010, publié ici), ses projets en cours comprennent le restaurant Monvínic (Barcelone) ; le restaurant Coure (Barcelone) ; le restaurant et école Espai Sucre (Barcelone) ; le restaurant du centre équestre (Barcelone) et la boutique de fleuriste Arrels (Martorello), tous en Espagne.

FASTVÍNIC

Barcelona, Spain, 2010

Address: C/ Diputacío 251, 08007 Barcelona, Spain, +34 93 487 32 41, www.fastvinic.com
Area: 144 m² (first floor), 146 m² (basement). Client: not disclosed
Cost: not disclosed. Collaboration: Montse Hernando

Intended as an "environmental and sustainable project," this restaurant is arrayed on two levels, with a ground-floor kitchen and dining room, and the offices and toilets located in the basement. Tost uses what he calls "Meccano shelves" to form much of the furnishing, with green plants on the uppermost level to highlight "the compromise with nature and to help regenerate the oxygen." Indeed, all elements of the restaurant are designed to be recyclable and dismountable. The kitchen, located in the entrance, is imagined as a "domestic space" where clients can watch the work and select their menus. Gray water is recovered, all lighting is assured with LEED certified appliances, the wood employed is from renewable forests, and any packaging is 100% compostable.

Das Restaurant, konzipiert als „umweltfreundliches und nachhaltiges Projekt", verteilt sich über zwei Ebenen: Küche und Gastraum im Erdgeschoss sowie Büros und Toiletten im Untergeschoss. Tost arbeitete mit einem, wie er sagt, „Meccano-Regalsystem", mit dem er einen Großteil der Einrichtung realisierte. Auf der obersten Regalebene platzierte er Grünpflanzen als Zeichen für einen „Kompromiss mit der Natur und als Beitrag zur Sauerstoffproduktion". Tatsächlich sind sämtliche Elemente der Restauranteinrichtung recycelbar und demontierbar. Die am Eingang gelegene Küche wurde als „Wohnbereich" konzipiert; hier können die Gäste bei der Zubereitung zuschauen und ihr Menü wählen. Grauwasser wird aufbereitet, sämtliche Leuchten sind LEED-zertifiziert, das Holz stammt aus nachhaltiger Forstwirtschaft, und alle Verpackungsmaterialien sind zu 100 % kompostierbar.

Conçu comme un « projet environnemental et durable », ce restaurant se déploie sur deux niveaux, la cuisine et la salle au rez-de-chaussée, les bureaux et les toilettes au sous-sol. Tost utilise ce qu'il appelle des « étagères meccano » pour la plupart des meubles, les plantes vertes tout en haut devant éclairer « le compromis avec la nature et contribuer à régénérer l'oxygène ». Tous les éléments du restaurant sont recyclables et démontables. La cuisine, placée à l'entrée, est conçue comme un « espace domestique » où les clients peuvent voir le travail et choisir leurs menus. L'eau usée est récupérée, l'éclairage est assuré par des lampes certifiées LEED, le bois utilisé provient de forêts renouvelables et l'emballage est 100 % biodégradable.

The colorful décor immediately transmits a feeling of simplicity and proximity to a more natural environment than the Barcelona address might imply.

Die farbenfrohe Innenausstattung vermittelt sofort einen Eindruck von großer Einfachheit und einem naturnäheren Umfeld, als es die Adresse in Barcelona vermuten lassen würde.

Le décor coloré donne immédiatement une impression de simplicité et de proximité avec un environnement plus naturel que l'adresse à Barcelone ne le laisserait supposer.

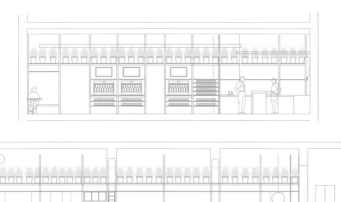

Section drawings and photos show
the highly simple design with seating
areas placed in part below shelf
space with boxes and plants arrayed
above the clients.

Querschnitte und Ansichten zeigen
das ausgesprochen schlichte Design.
Die Sitzplätze befinden sich teilweise
unterhalb der Regalkonstruktion, über
den Gästen schweben Kisten und
Pflanzen.

Les plans en coupe et les photos
illustrent l'extrême simplicité du
design, avec des tables disposées en
partie dans l'espace sous des étagères qui alignent caisses et plantes
au-dessus des clients.

The architects employ what they call a "Meccano" system, which is clearly a simple shelving design that lends informality to the space.

Die Architekten arbeiten mit einem „Meccano-System", einem einfachen Regalsystem, das dem Raum eine entspannte Atmosphäre verleiht.

Les architectes ont eu recours à ce qu'ils appellent un système « meccano », en fait un simple ensemble d'étagères qui donne un caractère décontracté au lieu.

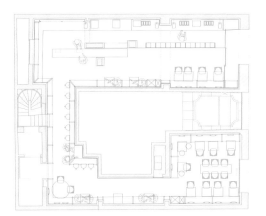

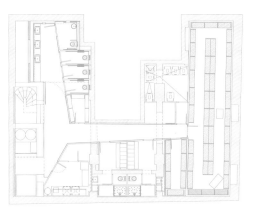

TRIPTYQUE

Triptyque
Al. Gabriel Monteiro da Silva 484
01442–000 São Paulo, SP, Brazil

Tel: +55 11 3081 3565
E-mail: com@triptyque.com / Web: www.triptyque.com

Triptyque
38 Rue de Rochechouart
75009 Paris, France

Tel: +33 1 75 43 42 16

Gregory Bousquet was born in 1973 in Evry, France. He received his degree as an architect from the École d'Architecture Paris la Seine (1991–97), and further DEA degrees from the École d'Architecture Paris Villemin and Paris IV (Sorbonne, in philosophy, 1998). He worked with the firm Jumeau & Paillard (Paris, 1999), before creating **TRIPTYQUE** in Paris in 2000. Triptyque moved to Rio in Brazil in 2001, and to São Paulo in 2002. Carolina Bueno was born in São Paulo, Brazil, in 1974. She received a DEFA degree from the École d'Architecture Paris la Seine (1993–95) and her DPLG from the same institution (1998–2000), as well as a Landscape Certificate from the Brazilian Institute (BRAP) in 2005. She was also a founding Partner of Triptyque. Olivier Raffaelli, born in 1973 in Neuilly-sur Seine, France, also received his DPGL at the École d'Architecture Paris la Seine (1991–97), as did Guillaume Sibaud, born in 1973 in Saint-Julien-les-Villas, France. Both Raffaelli and Sibaud were also founding Partners of the firm. Their work includes Sonique (São Paulo, Brazil, 2009, published here); the Jabuticaba Concert Hall (São Paulo, Brazil, 2011); a Médiathèque (Osny, France, 2010–12); an office building for INPI in Courbevoie (France, 2012); and two apartment buildings in São Paulo (Brazil, 2013).

Gregory Bousquet wurde 1973 in Evry, Frankreich, geboren. Er studierte Architektur an der École d'Architecture Paris la Seine (1991–97) und machte weitere DEA-Abschlüsse an der École d'Architecture Paris Villemin sowie der Universität Paris IV (Sorbonne, Philosophie, 1998). Er arbeitete für Jumeau & Paillard (Paris, 1999), ehe er 2000 in Paris das Büro **TRIPTYQUE** gründete. 2001 zog Triptyque nach Brasilien, zunächst nach Rio, 2002 nach São Paulo. Carolina Bueno wurde 1974 in São Paulo geboren. Sie machte ihren DEFA an der École d'Architecture Paris la Seine (1993–95), ihren DPLG an derselben Institution (1998–2000) und erhielt 2005 ein Landschaftsdiplom des Brazilian Institute (BRAP). Auch sie ist Gründungspartnerin von Triptyque. Olivier Raffaelli, geboren 1973 in Neuilly-sur-Seine, erwarb ebenfalls sein DPGL an der École d'Architecture Paris la Seine (1991–97), ebenso wie Guillaume Sibaud, geboren 1973 in Saint-Julien-les-Villas. Auch Raffaelli und Sibaud sind Gründungspartner des Büros. Zu ihren Projekten zählen Sonique (São Paulo, 2009, hier vorgestellt), die Konzerthalle Jabuticaba (São Paulo, 2011), eine Mediathek (Osny, Frankreich, 2010–12), ein Bürogebäude für INPI in Courbevoie (Frankreich, 2012) sowie zwei Apartmenthäuser in São Paulo (2013).

Gregory Bousquet est né en 1973 à Evry. Il a obtenu son diplôme d'architecte à l'École d'architecture Paris Seine (1991–97), puis des DEA de l'École d'architecture Paris Villemin and Paris IV (Sorbonne, en philosophie, 1998). Il a travaillé avec Jumeau & Paillard (Paris, 1999) avant de créer **TRIPTYQUE** à Paris en 2000. Triptyque a déménagé à Rio, au Brésil, en 2001 et à São Paulo en 2002. Carolina Bueno est née à São Paulo en 1974. Elle a obtenu un DEFA (1993–95) et un DPLG (1998–2000) de l'École d'architecture Paris la Seine, ainsi qu'un certificat de paysagiste de l'Institut brésilien (BRAP) en 2005. Elle est aussi un partenaire fondateur de Triptyque. Olivier Raffaelli, né en 1973 à Neuilly-sur-Seine, a également obtenu son DPGL à l'École d'Architecture Paris la Seine (1991–97), ainsi que Guillaume Sibaud, né en 1973 à Saint-Julien-les-Villas, France. Raffaelli et Sibaud sont aussi des partenaires fondateurs de la société. Leurs projets comprennent : le bar Sonique (São Paulo, 2009, publié ici) ; la salle de concerts Jabuticaba (São Paulo, 2011) ; une médiathèque (Osny, France, 2010–12) ; un immeuble de bureaux pour l'INPI à Courbevoie (2012) et deux immeubles d'habitation à São Paulo (2013).

SONIQUE

São Paulo, São Paulo, Brazil, 2009

*Address: Rua Bela Cintra 461, Consolação, São Paulo 01415–000, Brazil, +33 11 2628 8707,
www.soniquebar.com.br. Area: 420 m². Client: Alexandre Nadaechi, Beto Lago, Lelo Ramos, Rubens Cohen
Cost: €520 000. Collaboration: Isabela Gebard (Project Director),
Alexandre D'Agostini (Lighting), Sassumo Yagina Carlos (Engineer)*

The architects call **SONIQUE** "an informal, democratic, and gregarious space with no barriers. The bar's idea is that the customer can come alone or accompanied, on foot, by car or subway, listen to music, have a drink, meet interesting people, and learn more about the city's cultural programs." Sonique, located in the Baixo Augusta, a "bohemian" area of São Paulo, features materials such as concrete used in their "raw state." There is a large central hall with a bar, and two mezzanine spaces, with bathrooms and the kitchen in the rear. The central bar is conceived as an organizing point around which furniture can be arranged according to the use of the space. Monochrome (white) neon lights follow the design of the plaster décor of the ceiling.

Die Architekten beschreiben **SONIQUE** als „entspannten, demokratischen und aufgeschlossenen Ort ohne Grenzen. Das Prinzip der Bar ist, dass Gäste allein oder in Begleitung kommen können, zu Fuß, mit dem Auto oder mit der U-Bahn, Musik hören, etwas trinken, interessante Leute treffen und mehr über das kulturelle Leben der Stadt erfahren können". Sonique liegt im Baixo Augusta, einem kreativen Viertel von São Paulo; Highlight sind u. a. Materialien wie Beton „im Rohzustand". Neben einem zentralen Hauptraum mit Bar gibt es zwei Mezzaningeschosse mit Toiletten sowie einer Küche im hinteren Bereich. Die Bartheke funktioniert zugleich als zentraler Dreh- und Angelpunkt, um den herum sich das Mobiliar je nach Nutzung des Raums organisieren lässt. Monochrome (weiße) Neonröhren zeichnen die Konturen einer stuckierten Kassettendecke nach.

Les architectes qualifient **SONIQUE** d'« espace informel, démocratique et grégaire sans barrières. L'idée est que les clients puissent venir seuls ou accompagnés, à pied, en voiture ou en métro, écouter de la musique, boire un verre, rencontrer des gens intéressants et en apprendre plus sur le programme culturel de la ville ». Situé dans le Baixo Augusta, une zone « bohème » de São Paulo, le bar affiche des matériaux comme le béton « à l'état cru ». L'ensemble comporte un vaste hall central avec un bar et deux mezzanines avec des toilettes et la cuisine à l'arrière. Le bar central est conçu comme un point autour duquel l'espace est organisé et le mobilier disposé selon l'emploi qui en est fait. Des éclairages au néon monochromes (blancs) suivent le dessin du décor en plâtre du plafond.

The bunker-like atmosphere of the exterior cedes to a dark, high interior space where lighting effects can change the mood as required.

Die bunkerartige Anmutung des Außenbaus führt in dunkle, hohe Innenräume. Hier lässt sich die Stimmung nach Bedarf durch Lichteffekte beeinflussen.

L'apparence extérieure de bunker ouvre sur un espace intérieur sombre et haut dont les jeux de lumière peuvent changer l'ambiance à volonté.

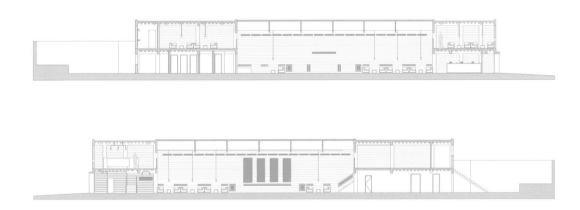

UNSTUDIO

UNStudio
Stadhouderskade 113
1073 AX Amsterdam
The Netherlands

Tel: +31 20 570 20 40 / Fax: +31 20 570 20 41
E-mail: info@unstudio.com
Web: www.unstudio.com

BEN VAN BERKEL was born in Utrecht, the Netherlands, in 1957 and studied at the Rietveld Academy in Amsterdam and at the Architectural Association (AA) in London, receiving the AA Diploma with honors in 1987. After working briefly in the office of Santiago Calatrava in 1988, he set up his practice in Amsterdam with Caroline Bos, under the name United Network Studio (UNStudio). Their work includes the Erasmus Bridge in Rotterdam (1996), the Karbouw and ACOM (1989–93) office buildings, and the REMU Electricity Station (1989–93), all in Amersfoort; and the Aedes East Gallery for Kristin Feireiss in Berlin, Germany. Other projects include the Möbius House (Naarden, 1993–98); Het Valkhof Museum (Nijmegen, 1998); and NMR Laboratory (Utrecht, 2000), all in the Netherlands; a Switching Station (Innsbruck, Austria, 1998–2001); VilLA NM (Upstate New York, USA, 2000–06); and the Mercedes-Benz Museum (Stuttgart, Germany, 2003–06). Recent work includes the Music Theater (Graz, Austria, 1998–2008); Research Laboratory, Groningen University (Groningen, the Netherlands, 2003–08); Star Place (Kaohsiung, Taiwan, 2006–08); Burnham Pavilion (Chicago, Illinois, USA, 2009); and Galleria Centercity (Cheonan, South Korea, 2008–10, published here). They are also working on I'Park City (Suwon, South Korea, 2008–12); Arnhem Station (the Netherlands, 1996–2014); Raffles City (Hangzhou, China, 2008–14); Ponte Parodi (Genoa, Italy, 2001–14); SUTD, the Singapore University of Technology and Design (Singapore, 2010–); and Scotts Tower (Singapore, 2010–).

BEN VAN BERKEL wurde 1957 in Utrecht geboren und studierte an der Rietveld-Akademie in Amsterdam sowie der Architectural Association (AA) in London, wo er 1987 das Diplom mit Auszeichnung erhielt. Nach einer kurzen Beschäftigung 1988 bei Santiago Calatrava gründete er mit Caroline Bos sein eigenes Büro in Amsterdam, das den Namen United Network Studio (UNStudio) trägt. Zu ihren Projekten zählen die Erasmusbrücke in Rotterdam (1996), die Büros für Karbouw und ACOM (1989–93) und das Kraftwerk REMU (1989–93), alle in Amersfoort, sowie die Galerie Aedes East für Kristin Feireiss in Berlin. Weitere Projekte sind das Haus Möbius (Naarden, 1993–98), das Museum Het Valkhof (Nijmegen, 1998) und das Labor NMR (Utrecht, 2000), alle in den Niederlanden, ein Umspannwerk (Innsbruck, 1998 bis 2001), die VilLA NM (bei New York, 2000–06) und das Mercedes-Benz-Museum (Stuttgart, 2003–06). Jüngere Arbeiten sind u. a. ein Musiktheater in Graz (1998–2008), ein Forschungslabor der Universität Groningen (2003–08), Star Place (Kaohsiung, Taiwan, 2006–08), der Burnham-Pavillon (Chicago, 2009) und die Galleria Centercity (Cheonan, Südkorea, 2008–10, hier vorgestellt). Außerdem arbeitet das Büro an I'Park City (Suwon, Südkorea, 2008–12), dem Bahnhof Arnhem (Niederlande, 1996 bis 2014), Raffles City (Hangzhou, China, 2008–14), der Ponte Parodi (Genua, 2001–14), der Universität für Technik und Design in Singapur (seit 2010), sowie am Scotts Tower (Singapur, seit 2010).

BEN VAN BERKEL, né à Utrecht, Pays-Bas, en 1957, a étudié à l'Académie Rietveld à Amsterdam et à l'Architectural Association (AA) de Londres, dont il est sorti diplômé avec mention en 1987. Après avoir brièvement travaillé pour Santiago Calatrava en 1988, il a créé, en association avec Caroline Bos, son agence United Network Studio (UNStudio) à Amsterdam. Leurs projets comprennent : le pont Erasmus à Rotterdam (1996), les immeubles de bureaux Karbouw et ACOM (1989–93) et la centrale électrique REMU (1989–93) à Amersfoort, ainsi que la galerie Aedes East pour Kristin Feireiss à Berlin. Plus récemment, l'agence a signé la maison Möbius (Naarden, 1993–98) ; le musée Het Valkhof (Nimègue, 1998) et le laboratoire NMR (Utrecht, 2000), tous aux Pays-Bas ; une station de transformation (Innsbruck, Autriche, 1998–2001) ; la VilLA NM (Upstate New York, 2000–06) et le musée Mercedes-Benz (Stuttgart, 2003–06). Les projets récents comprennent une maison de la musique et théâtre musical (Graz, Autriche, 1998–2008) ; un laboratoire de recherches pour l'université de Groningue (Pays-Bas, 2003–08) ; le centre commercial Star Place (Kaohsiung, Taïwan, 2006–08) ; le pavillon Burnham (Chicago, Illinois, 2009) et le centre commercial Galleria Centercity (Cheonan, Corée-du-Sud, 2008–10, publiée ici). Ils travaillent aussi à I'Park City (Suwon, Corée-du-Sud, 2008–12) ; la gare d'Arnhem (Pays-Bas, 1996–2014) ; Raffles City (Hangzhou, Chine, 2008–14) ; Ponte Parodi (Gênes, 2001–14) ; SUTD, l'Université de technologie et design de Singapour (2010–) et la tour Scotts (Singapour, 2010–).

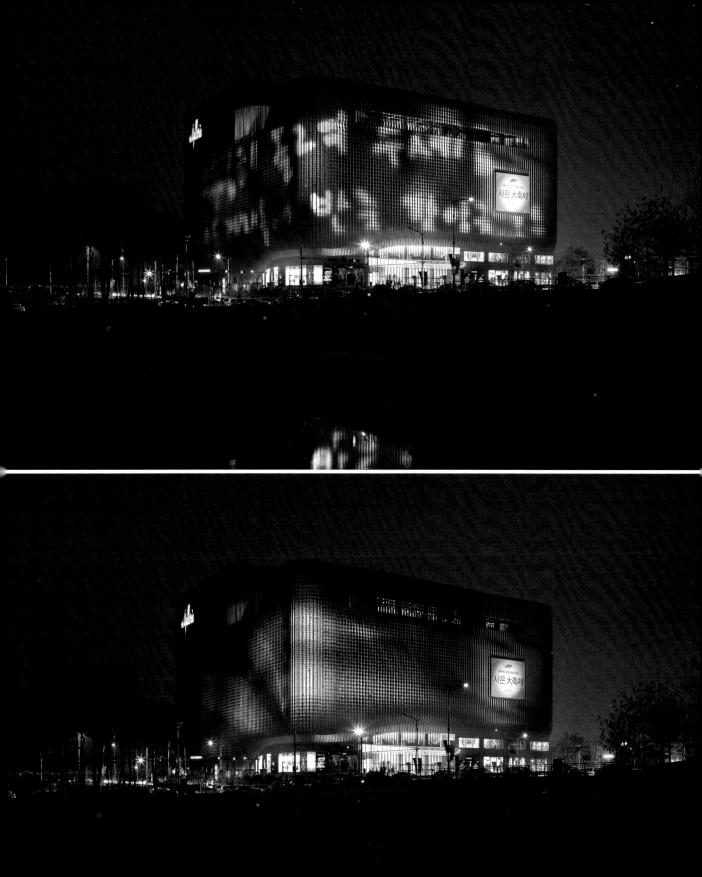

GALLERIA CENTERCITY

Cheonan, South Korea, 2008–10

Address: 521–3 Buldangedong, Seobukgu, Cheonan, Choongchung Province, South Korea
Area: 66 700 m² (retail). Client: Hanwha Galleria Co. Ltd. Cost: not disclosed
Collaboration: Astrid Piber, Ger Gijzen, Marc Herschel

Cheonan, located 80 kilometers south of Seoul, has a population of about 540 000 people. This Galleria department store is located near a new high-speed train station. UNStudio had previously renovated a Galleria store in Seoul (2003). The architects state: "The main architectural theme is that of dynamic flow. This is found both inside and outside." The exterior appearance of the building creates an "optical illusion" with "two layers of customized aluminum extrusion profiles on top of a back layer of composite aluminum cladding," which yields a moiré effect. Waves of color cross the façade at night. Computer-controlled animations designed by UNStudio refer to the themes related to the department store: fashion, events, art, and public life. The interior is organized around "rounded plateaus on long columns." A central atrium is defined as "a kind of spatial waterfall." Each floor is divided into a public area near the central void and a peripheral zone. The architects have also created a VIP Room, art center, and customer-service zones. A food court and speciality supermarket are situated in the basement, while upper level terraces provide extra public space.

Cheonan, 80 km südlich von Seoul gelegen, hat rund 540 000 Einwohner. Das Kaufhaus Galleria liegt unweit eines Bahnhofs für Hochgeschwindigkeitszüge. Schon 2003 hatte UNStudio ein Kaufhaus der Galleria-Kette in Seoul saniert (2003). Die Architekten erklären: „Das zentrale architektonische Thema ist ein dynamischer Fluss. Dieser zeigt sich innen wie außen am Bau." Der Außenbau erzeugt durch „eine Doppelschicht maßgefertigter extrudierter Aluminiumprofile über einer Verkleidung aus schwarzen Aluminiumverbundplatten" einen Moirée-Effekt, eine „optische Täuschung". Nachts ziehen farbige Wellen über die Fassade. Von UNStudio entwickelte, computergesteuerte Animationen nehmen Bezug auf Themen rund um das Kaufhaus: Mode, Veranstaltungen, Kunst und öffentliches Leben. Innen organisiert sich der Bau um „rundkonturige Plateaus auf hohen Säulen". Ein zentrales Atrium wurde als „eine Art räumlicher Wasserfall" gestaltet. Jedes Geschoss gliedert sich in eine zum Atrium orientierte öffentliche Zone und eine Peripherie. Die Architekten gestalteten außerdem einen VIP-Bereich, ein Kunstzentrum und Kundendienstbereiche. Im Untergeschoss sind ein Gastronomiebereich und ein Spezialitätensupermarkt untergebracht, auf den Terrassen der Obergeschosse wurde weitere öffentliche Bereiche realisiert.

Cheonan, à 80 km au sud de Séoul, a une population d'environ 540 000 habitants. Le grand magasin Galleria est situé à proximité d'une nouvelle gare de trains à grande vitesse. UNStudio a déjà rénové un magasin Galleria à Séoul (2003). Les architectes expliquent : « Le thème architectural principal est celui des flux dynamiques. On le retrouve à l'intérieur comme à l'extérieur. » L'aspect extérieur du bâtiment crée une « illusion d'optique » avec « deux couches de profilés par extrusion en aluminium sur mesure au-dessus d'une couche arrière de revêtement aluminium composite », qui créent un effet moiré. Des ondulations colorées traversent la façade la nuit. Les animations commandées par ordinateur évoquent les thèmes liés au grand magasin : mode, événements, art et vie publique. L'intérieur est organisé autour de « plateaux ronds sur de longues colonnes ». Un atrium central est défini comme « un genre de cascade spatiale ». Chaque étage comprend un espace public près du vide central et une zone périphérique. Les architectes ont aussi créé un espace VIP, un centre d'art et des zones de service après-vente. L'aire de restauration et un supermarché de spécialités sont situés au sous-sol, tandis que les terrasses des niveaux supérieurs fournissent un espace supplémentaire.

The aluminum extrusion profiles that form the façades of the Galleria (seen above and in the drawings to the right) can be used to project bright, changing color effects at night.

Die extrudierten Aluminiumprofile an der Fassade des Kaufhauses (oben und Zeichnungen rechts) lassen sich nachts zur Projektion leuchtender, wechselnder Farbeffekte nutzen.

Les profilés par extrusion en aluminium des façades du Galleria (ci-dessus et dans les plans à droite) peuvent servir d'écran de projection de divers effets lumineux et colorés la nuit.

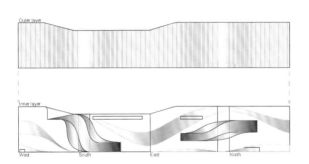

North-West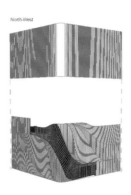

South-East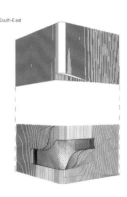

The complex interior of the Galleria is conceived like an unfolding ribbon as seen in the small drawing at the bottom of this page.

Der komplexe Innenraum der Galleria entspricht einer sich entfaltenden Schleife, wie auf der kleinen Zeichnung unten zu sehen ist.

L'intérieur complexe du Galleria est conçu à l'image d'un ruban qui se déroule, comme le montre le petit plan ci-dessous.

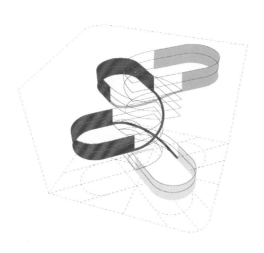

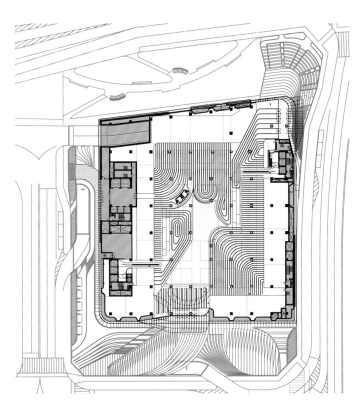

A plan shows that the apparent complexity of the architecture is resolved into well aligned spaces that are used below, for example, as a cafeteria area.

Der Grundriss veranschaulicht, wie sich die vermeintlich komplexe Architektur in klar organisierte Bereiche gliedert, die hier etwa als Cafeteria genutzt werden (unten).

On voit sur le plan que l'apparente complexité architecturale est ramenée à des espaces bien alignés qui abritent, par exemple, la cafétéria ci-dessous.

Continuous bands of lighting give a sense of continuity to this grocery store space, where a white ceiling cedes to a black one in the background.

Durch umlaufende Lichtbänder gewinnt dieser Lebensmittelmarkt Kontinuität. Im Hintergrund geht die weiße Decke in eine schwarze über.

Des bandes lumineuses ininterrompues donnent une impression de continuité à cet espace épicerie où un plafond blanc cède la place à un noir à l'arrière-plan.

ISAY WEINFELD

Isay Weinfeld
Rua Wisard 305, 7° andar
05434–080 São Paulo, SP
Brazil

Tel: +55 11 3079 7581 / Fax: +55 11 3079 5656
E-mail: contato@isayweinfeld.com
Web: www.isayweinfeld.com

ISAY WEINFELD was born in 1952 in São Paulo, Brazil. He graduated from the School of Architecture at Mackenzie University in São Paulo in 1975. In an unusual mixture of careers, Weinfeld has also worked in cinema since 1974, making 14 short films that have received numerous international awards. In 1988, he wrote and directed his first full-length movie, *Fogo e Paixão*, considered one of the 10 best comedies produced that year worldwide. In 1989, the São Paulo Art Critics' Association awarded him the Prize for Best New Director. Weinfeld has completed dozens of private homes, commercial projects, banks, advertising agencies, discotheques, a bar, a restaurant, an art gallery, and the Hotel Fasano (São Paulo, 2001–03, with Marcio Kogan). He has worked with Kogan on numerous projects, including the 2001 exhibit "Umore and Architektur" at the Casa Brasileira Museum. Recent work includes Livraria da Vila (São Paulo, 2006–07); the Sumaré House (São Paulo, 2007); Kesley Caliguere Antique Shop (São Paulo, 2007); Havaianas (São Paulo, 2008–09); Grecia House (São Paulo, 2008–09); Numero Bar (São Paulo, 2010, published here); Las Piedras Fasano, Hotel Bar (Punta del Este, Uruguay, 2008–11); Fasano Restaurant (Punta del Este, Uruguay, 2010–11, also published here); Square Nine Hotel (Belgrade, Serbia, 2011); and the 360° Building (São Paulo, under construction), all in Brazil unless stated otherwise.

ISAY WEINFELD wurde 1952 in São Paulo geboren. 1975 schloss er sein Architekturstudium an der Mackenzie Universität in São Paulo ab. Weinfeld verbindet zwei Laufbahnen auf ungewöhnliche Weise: Seit 1974 ist er auch Filmemacher – seine 14 Kurzfilme wurden mit zahlreichen internationalen Preisen ausgezeichnet. 1988 schrieb er das Drehbuch für seinen ersten Spielfilm, *Fogo e Paixão,* bei dem er auch Regie führte und der als eine der zehn besten Komödien gilt, die in diesem Jahr weltweit produziert wurden. 1989 zeichnete ihn der Kunstkritikerverband São Paulo als besten neuen Regisseur aus. Weinfeld realisierte Dutzende von privaten Wohnbauten, gewerbliche Projekte, Banken, Werbeagenturen, Diskotheken, eine Bar, ein Restaurant, eine Galerie sowie das Hotel Fasano (São Paulo, 2001–03, mit Marcio Kogan). Bei zahlreichen Projekten kooperierte er mit Marcio Kogan, etwa für die Ausstellung „Umore and Architektur" am Casa Brasileira Museum (2001). Jüngere Arbeiten sind u. a. die Livraria da Vila (São Paulo, 2006–07), das Haus Sumaré (São Paulo, 2007), die Antiquitätenhandlung Kesley Caliguere (São Paulo, 2007), Havaianas (São Paulo, 2008–09), das Haus Grecia (São Paulo, 2008–09), die Numero Bar (São Paulo, 2010, hier vorgestellt), Hotel und Bar Las Piedras Fasano (Punta del Este, Uruguay, 2008–11), das Fasano Restaurant (Punta del Este, Uruguay, 2010–11, ebenfalls hier vorgestellt), das Square Nine Hotel (Belgrad, Serbien, 2011) und das 360° Building (São Paulo, im Bau), alle in Brasilien soweit nicht anders angegeben.

ISAY WEINFELD, né en 1952 à São Paulo, est diplômé de l'école d'architecture de l'université Mackenzie à São Paulo (1975). Sa carrière étonnamment variée l'a conduit à s'intéresser au cinéma et depuis 1974, il a réalisé 14 courts métrages qui ont reçu de nombreux prix internationaux. En 1988, il écrit et réalise son premier long métrage, *Fogo e Paixão*, considéré comme l'une des dix meilleures comédies produites dans le monde cette année-là. En 1989, l'Association des critiques d'art de São Paulo lui remet le prix du meilleur nouveau metteur en scène. Weinfeld a réalisé des dizaines de résidences privées, de projets commerciaux, de banques, d'agences de publicité, de discothèques, un bar, un restaurant, une galerie d'art et l'hôtel Fasano (São Paulo, 2001–03, en collaboration avec Marcio Kogan). Il a collaboré avec Kogan à de nombreux projets dont l'exposition de 2001 « Humour et architecture » au Musée de la maison brésilienne. Parmi ses réalisations récentes : la librairie da Vila (São Paulo, 2006–07) ; la maison Sumaré (São Paulo, 2007) ; le magasin d'antiquités Kesley Caliguere (São Paulo, 2007) ; le magasin Havaianas (São Paulo, 2008–09) ; la maison Grecia (São Paulo, 2008–09) ; le bar Numero (São Paulo, 2010, publié ici) ; l'hôtel bar Fasano Las Piedras (Punta del Este, Uruguay, 2008–11) ; le restaurant Fasano (Punta del Este, Uruguay, 2010–11, publié ici) ; l'hôtel Square Nine (Belgrade, Serbie, 2011) et le 360 ° Building (São Paulo, en construction).

NUMERO BAR

São Paulo, São Paulo, Brazil, 2010

Address: Rua da Consolação 3585, Jardim Paulista, São Paulo 01416–001, Brazil,
+55 11 3061 3995. Area: 551 m²
Client: not disclosed. Cost: not disclosed

The rectangular **NUMERO BAR** occupies a narrow and long strip of land in the prestigious Jardins area of São Paulo. A hallway lined with mirrors leads from the street to the main space. The ceiling height of the space increases to the rear of the space. A private-function room, with a low ceiling, is set on the lower floor. The walls are covered with old posters and poster fragments, and windows offer a view of tropical vegetation. The architect states: "The low and indirect lighting throughout lends the ambience a pleasant and cozy atmosphere, perfect for a relaxing drink at the end of the day, accompanied by friends and to the sound of good music."

Die als Rechteck angelegte **NUMERO BAR** liegt auf einem langen schmalen Grundstück in dem angesehenen Viertel Jardins von São Paulo. Ein spiegelgesäumter Korridor führt von der Straße in den Hauptraum. Die Deckenhöhe nimmt mit zunehmender Tiefe des Raums zu. Im Untergeschoss befindet sich ein Raum für private Veranstaltungen. Die Wände sind mit alten Plakaten und Ausrissen aus Plakaten tapeziert, Fenster bieten Ausblick auf eine tropische Vegetation. Der Architekt erklärt: „Das gedämpfte, indirekte Licht schafft eine angenehme, harmonische Stimmung, ideal für einen entspannten Drink am Ende des Tages, in Begleitung von Freunden und bei guter Musik".

Le bar rectangulaire **NUMERO** occupe une bande étroite et longue dans le prestigieux quartier des Jardins de São Paulo. Un hall couvert de miroirs mène de la rue à l'espace principal. La hauteur sous plafond augmente à l'arrière. Une pièce privée basse de plafond occupe l'étage du bas. Les murs sont couverts de vieux posters et fragments de posters, tandis que les fenêtres donnent à voir la végétation tropicale. Les architectes déclarent : « L'éclairage faible et indirect rend l'atmosphère plaisante et agréable, parfaite pour boire un verre et se détendre à la fin de la journée, en compagnie d'amis et au son de la bonne musique. »

The dark interiors open into a lush garden, which contrasts with the comfortable leather couches.

Die dunklen Räume öffnen sich zu einem üppig grünen Garten: ein Kontrast zu den bequemen Ledersofas.

L'intérieur sombre ouvre sur un luxuriant jardin qui contraste avec les confortables canapés de cuir.

Another image inside the bar with the garden in the background. Below, a section drawing shows the floor levels and the garden to the right.

Eine weitere Ansicht der Bar mit dem Garten im Hintergrund. Ein Querschnitt (unten) zeigt die verschiedenen Ebenen und den Garten rechts im Bild.

Autre vue intérieure du bar avec le jardin à l'arrière-plan. Ci-dessous, plan en coupe des différents niveaux avec le jardin à droite.

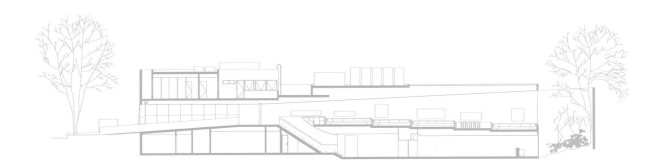

FASANO RESTAURANT

Punta del Este, Uruguay, 2010–11

Address: Hotel Fasano Las Piedras, Cno. Cerro Egusquiza y Paso del Barranco, La Barra 20400,
Punta del Este, Uruguay, tel: + 598 4267 0000, fax: + 598 4267 0707, www.laspiedrasfasano.com
Area: 390 m². Client: JHSF/Fasano Group. Cost: not disclosed

The simple wooden canopy design of the terrace overlooks a broad open countryside view.

Die Terrasse mit ihrem schlichten Holzdach bietet Ausblick auf die weite, offene Landschaft.

Le design simple de la terrasse couverte en bois ouvre largement sur un vaste panorama.

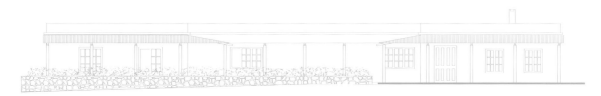

Located six kilometers inland from the coastal resort of La Barra, the Hotel Fasano Las Piedras, designed by Isay Weinfeld, overlooks Maldonado, in a beautiful natural setting near the Uruguayan coast. It is a boutique hotel with 20 modern bungalows all designed by Isay Weinfeld. Built in an old farmhouse, the **FASANO RESTAURANT** serves Italian food. This hilltop restaurant is located a short drive from the reception area on the 480-hectare site, in a rough, stacked-stone structure with dark wood paneling and glass walls that face the hilly environment. An outdoor lounge has a fireplace and there is an indoor café with counter-style seating. Isay Weinfeld was also the author of the Fasano Restaurant and Hotel in São Paulo.

Das Hotel Fasano Las Piedras von Isay Weinfeld liegt 6 km landeinwärts vom Küstenort La Barra mit Blick auf Maldonado vor einer beeindruckenden landschaftlichen Kulisse unweit der uruguayischen Küste. Das Boutiquehotel mit 20 modernen Bungalows wurde vollständig von Weinfeld entworfen. Das in einem alten Bauernhaus untergebrachte **FASANO RESTAURANT** bietet italienische Küche. Auf einem Hügel gelegen, ist es nur eine kurze Fahrt vom Empfangsbereich auf dem 480 ha großen Grundstück entfernt und in einem unverputzten Feldsteinbau mit dunkler Holzvertäfelung und Fensterfront zur Hügellandschaft untergebracht. Es gibt eine Outdoor-Lounge mit Kamin sowie einen Cafébereich mit Sitzgelegenheiten am Tresen. Isay Weinfeld gestaltete auch das Fasano Restaurant und Hotel in São Paulo.

Situé à 6 km à l'intérieur des terres de la station balnéaire La Barra, l'hôtel Fasano Las Piedras a vue sur Maldonado depuis un superbe décor naturel à proximité de la côte uruguayenne. Les 20 bungalows modernes du boutique hôtel ont tous été conçus par Isay Weinfeld. Aménagé dans une vieille ferme, le **RESTAURANT FASANO** sert des plats italiens. Situé en haut d'une colline, à un court trajet de la réception, sur un site de 480 ha, la structure brute de pierres empilées aux panneaux de bois sombre et baies vitrées fait face au paysage vallonné. Un salon extérieur est pourvu d'une cheminée et le café intérieur présente des sièges de style comptoir. Isay Weinfeld est aussi l'auteur du restaurant et hôtel Fasano de São Paulo.

Rough wood floors and ceilings are
set up on wood poles for the outdoor
terrace (left) and on stone columns
inside (above).

Auf der Terrasse ruhen die rustikalen
Holzdecken auf Holzstützen (links), im
Innern auf Mauerwerk (oben).

Les sols et plafonds de bois brut
reposent sur des piliers en bois sur la
terrasse (à gauche) et des colonnes
en pierre à l'intérieur (ci-dessus).

The outdoor dining terrace retains a somewhat rustic appearance with its wood surfaces.

Mit seinen Holzoberflächen bewahrt der Speisebereich auf der Terrasse ein gewisses rustikales Flair.

Avec ses surfaces de bois, la terrasse du restaurant conserve un aspect quelque peu rustique.

Right, a plan of the essentially
square structure. Below, the cave-
like entrance to the restaurant.

Rechts ein Grundriss des annähernd
quadratischen Baus. Unten der höh-
lenartige Eingangsbereich des Restaurants.

À droite, un plan de l'ensemble
presque carré. Ci-dessous, l'entrée
du restaurant fait penser à celle
d'une grotte.

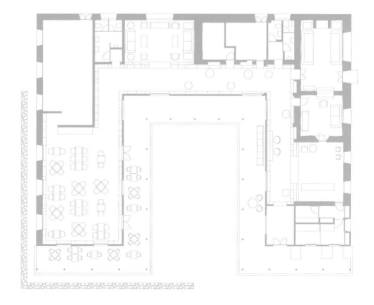

WONDERWALL / MASAMICHI KATAYAMA

Wonderwall Inc.
3–4–10 Sendagaya, Shibuya-ku
Tokyo 151–0051
Japan

Tel: +81 3 6438 1715
E-mail: contact@wonder-wall.com
Web: www.wonder-wall.com

MASAMICHI KATAYAMA was born in Okayama in 1966 and set up the firm H. Design Associates (1992–99) before creating Wonderwall in 2000. As his firm description has it: "While respecting conventional and traditional aspects of architecture, he believes in breaking boundaries... Hence the name, Wonderwall: a continuous endless journey. Each project is conceived from scratch, rarely repeating details and ideas used in past projects. When designing retail spaces, not only does Katayama address all the elements of the interior, such as lighting, materials, and proportions, he also considers the actual experience of shopping." His work includes Pierre Hermé Paris Aoyama (Tokyo, Japan, 2005); A Bathing Ape, Busy Work Shop (Hong Kong, China, 2006); Uniqlo Soho New York (New York, USA, 2006); A.P.C. Daikanyama Homme (Tokyo, Japan, 2007); Uniqlo 311 Oxford Street (London, UK, 2007); Tokyo Towers / Sky Lounge and Guest Suites (Kachidoki, Tokyo, Japan, 2008); and Colette (Paris, France, 2008). More recent work includes Nike Harajuku (Harajuku, Tokyo, Japan, 2009); Pass The Baton Omotesando (Tokyo, Japan, 2010); Mackintosh London (London, UK, 2010); Uniqlo New York 5th Avenue (New York, USA, 2011); Yoyogi Village / Code Kurkku (Tokyo, Japan, 2011); Westfield Sydney (Sydney, Australia, 2011); and Ozone in the Ritz-Carlton (Hong Kong, China, 2011, published here).

MASAMICHI KATAYAMA wurde 1966 in Okayama geboren und gründete zunächst H. Design Associates (1992–99), bevor er 2000 sein Büro Wonderwall eröffnete. In seiner Firmenbeschreibung heißt es: „Wenngleich er konventionelle und traditionelle Aspekte der Architektur respektiert, glaubt Katayama an das Überwinden bestehender Grenzen ... Darum auch der Name Wonderwall: eine kontinuierliche, nicht enden wollende Reise. Jedes Projekt wird von Grund auf neu entwickelt, Details und Ideen früherer Projekte wiederholen sich nur selten. Wenn Katayama Ladenräume entwirft, befasst er sich nicht nur mit sämtlichen innenarchitektonischen Elementen wie Beleuchtung, Materialien und Proportionen, er berücksichtigt auch das Einkaufserlebnis an sich." Zu seinen Projekten zählen: Filiale von Pierre Hermé Paris in Aoyama (Tokio, 2005), A Bathing Ape, Busy Work Shop (Hongkong, China, 2006), Uniqlo Soho New York (2006), A.P.C. Homme in Daikanyama (Tokio, 2007), Uniqlo Oxford Street 311 (London, 2007), Tokyo Towers/Sky Lounge und Gästesuiten (Kachidoki, Tokio, 2008) und Colette (Paris, 2008). Weitere jüngere Projekte sind u. a. Nike Harajuku (Tokio, 2009), Pass The Baton Omotesando (Tokio, 2010), Mackintosh London (2010), Uniqlo New York 5th Avenue (2011), Yoyogi Village/Code Kurkku (Tokio, 2011), Westfield Sydney (Sydney, 2011) und das Ozone im Ritz-Carlton (Hongkong, China, 2011, hier vorgestellt).

MASAMICHI KATAYAMA est né à Okayama en 1966 et a fondé la société H. Design Associates (1992–99) avant de créer Wonderwall en 2000. Comme le souligne la description de son agence : « Tout en respectant les aspects conventionnels et traditionnels de l'architecture, il croit en la transgression des frontières... D'où son nom, Wonderwall : un voyage permanent sans fin. Chaque projet est conçu à partir de zéro et répète rarement des détails ou idées de projets antérieurs. Lorsqu'il crée des espaces commerciaux, Katayama aborde tous les éléments intérieurs tels qu'éclairage, tissus et proportions, mais il tient aussi compte de l'expérience et du vécu des acheteurs. » Ses réalisations comprennent : la boutique Pierre Hermé Paris d'Aoyama (Tokyo, 2005) ; le Busy Work Shop d'A Bathing Ape (Hong Kong, 2006) ; Uniqlo Soho New York (New York, 2006) ; A.P.C. Daikanyama Homme (Tokyo, 2007) ; Uniqlo 311 Oxford Street (Londres, 2007) ; Tokyo Towers/Sky Lounge et suites (Kachidoki, Tokyo, 2008) et le magasin Colette (Paris, 2008). Ses projets plus récents comprennent Nike Harajuku (Harajuku, Tokyo, Japon, 2009); la boutique Pass The Baton d'Omotesando (Tokyo, 2010); Mackintosh London (Londres, 2010) ; Uniqlo New York 5th Avenue (New York, 2011) ; le restaurant Yoyogi Village/Code Kurkku (Tokyo, 2011) ; Westfield Sydney (Sydney, 2011) ; et le bar Ozone du Ritz-Carlton (Hong Kong, 2011, publié ici).

OZONE, RITZ-CARLTON
Hong Kong, China, 2011

Address: The Ritz-Carlton, International Commerce Centre, 1 Austin Road,
West Kowloon, Hong Kong, China, +852 2263 2263, www.ritzcarlton.com. Area: 755 m²
Client: Sun Hung Kai Properties Ltd. Cost: not disclosed

Completed in May 2011, this bar and lounge, which includes a dining room, is located on the 118th floor of the International Commerce Centre (ICC) in Kowloon. It is part of the Ritz-Carlton Hong Kong, which now has the distinction of being the "world's tallest hotel." The hotel occupies floors 102 to 118 in the tower that was designed by the American firm Kohn Pederson Fox (KPF). According to Wonderwall, **OZONE** was "designed around the theme of an 'Edenic Experiment'—a manmade environment of nature in an imaginary world. The spatial composition, the line of motion, and every material and finishing were carefully considered."

Die im Mai 2011 fertiggestellte Bar und Lounge, zu der auch ein Speisebereich gehört, liegt im 118. Stock des International Commerce Center (ICC) in Kowloon. Die Bar gehört zum Ritz-Carlton Hongkong, das inzwischen als „höchstes Hotel der Welt" gilt. Das Hotel in den Etagen 102 bis 188 des Hochhauses ist ein Entwurf des amerikanischen Büros Kohn Pederson Fox (KPF). Wonderwall zufolge entstand der Entwurf von **OZONE** „rund um das Thema eines ‚Paradies-Experiments' – als künstlich geschaffene Natur in einer fiktiven Welt. Die räumliche Komposition, die dynamische Linienführung und sämtliche Materialien wurden aufs Sorgfältigste ausgewählt."

Terminé en mai 2011, ce bar lounge avec salle de restaurant est situé au 118ᵉ étage du Centre international de commerce (ICC) de Kowloon. Il fait partie du Ritz-Carlton Hong Kong connu comme « l'hôtel le plus haut du monde » qui occupe les étages 102 à 118 de la tour créée par l'agence américaine Kohn Pederson Fox (KPF). Selon les termes de Wonderwall, **OZONE** a été « imaginé autour du thème d'une "expérience édénique" – un environnement naturel créé par l'homme dans un monde imaginaire. La composition spatiale, la ligne, le mouvement et le moindre matériau ou finition ont été soigneusement pensés ».

The International Commerce Centre, designed by KPF, stands out against the Kowloon skyline.

Das von KPF entworfene International Commerce Center hebt sich von der Skyline von Kowloon ab.

Le Centre international de commerce créé par KPF se détache sur la ligne d'horizon de Kowloon.

The corner plan of the bar is seen below. Above, the angular, brightly colored main bar.

Unten der Eckgrundriss der Bar. Oben die schiefwinklige, intensiv farbige Hauptbar.

Ci-dessous, plan du bar en coin. Ci-dessus, le comptoir anguleux principal très coloré.

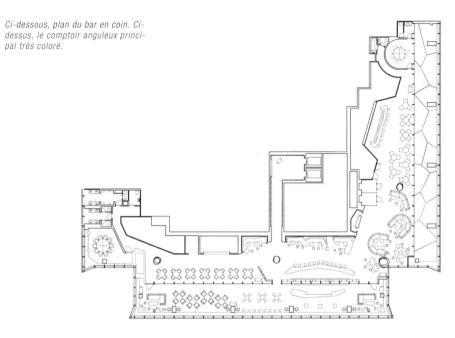

Wonderwall's design is intended in some sense to create a sort of artificial nature perched at the top of one of the world's tallest buildings.

Das Design von Wonderwall versteht sich in gewisser Weise als eine Art künstlicher Natur an der Spitze eines der höchsten Gebäude der Welt.

Le design de Wonderwall cherche pour ainsi dire à créer une nature artificielle perchée en haut de l'un des immeubles les plus hauts du monde.

A dining area in Ozone makes use of a spectacular chandelier and an abstract wood design on the neighboring wall.

Dieser Speiseraum im Ozone profitiert von einem spektakulären Kristalllüster und dem abstrakten Holzmuster auf der Wand.

Espace dînatoire d'Ozone, avec son extraordinaire lustre et le motif abstrait de bois sur le mur.

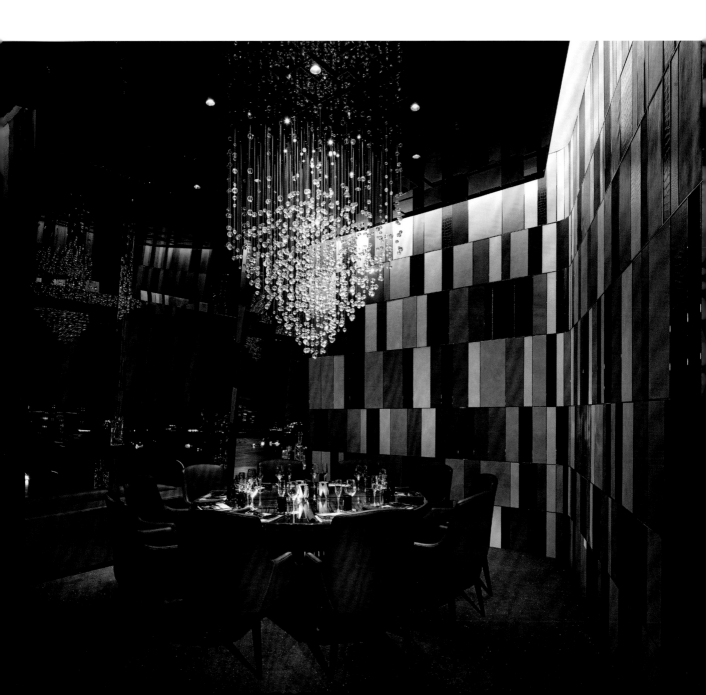

The hanging globe light fixtures light the tables and an irregular stone floor pattern that looks out onto the Hong Kong night.

Die hängenden Glaskugelleuchten werfen ihr Licht auf die Tische und das asymmetrische Muster des Steinbodens.

Les globes lumineux suspendus éclairent les tables et le motif irrégulier du sol de pierre qui fait face à la nuit de Hong Kong.

TOKUJIN YOSHIOKA

TOKUJIN YOSHIOKA INC.
9–1 Daikanyama-cho
Shibuva-ku
Tokyo 150–0034
Japan

Tel: +81 3 5428 0830 / Fax: +81 3 5428 0835
E-mail: yoshioka@tokujin.com / Web: www.tokujin.com

TOKUJIN YOSHIOKA was born in 1967 in Saga, Japan. He graduated from the Kuwasawa Design School and worked under the celebrated designer Shiro Kuramata (1987), and then with Issey Miyake beginning in 1988. He established his own studio, Tokujin Yoshioka Design, in 2000 in Tokyo. His work for Issey Miyake over a period of 20 years included extensive shop design and installations. His work is represented at the Museum of Modern Art (MoMA) in New York, the Centre Pompidou in Paris, the Victoria and Albert Museum in London, Cooper Hewitt National Design Museum in New York, and Vitra Design Museum in Germany. He has collaborated with companies such as Hermès, BMW, and Toyota. Among other objects, he designed Yamagiwa's lighting ToFU (2000); the paper chair Honey-pop (2000–01); Driade's Tokyo-pop (2002); Water Block, a representative work of optical glass projects (2002); Media Skin cell phone (2005); Stardust chandelier for the Swarovski Crystal Palace (2005); PANE Chair (2003–06); Waterfall (Tokyo, Japan, 2005–06); the Swarovski Flagship Store in Ginza (Tokyo, Japan, 2006–08); and VENUS–Natural crystal chair (2008). Yoshioka recently completed PLEATS PLEASE Issey Miyake Aoyama (Tokyo, Japan, 2009); Camper To&ether (London, UK, 2009); "The Invisibles" (Milan, Italy, 14–19 April, 2010, published here); 132 5. Issey Miyake (Minami-Aoyama, Tokyo, 2010, also published here); the Rainbow Church, MUSEUM Beyondmuseum (Seoul, South Korea, 2010); and "Twilight" (Milan, Italy, 12–17 April, 2011, also published here).

TOKUJIN YOSHIOKA wurde 1967 in Saga, Japan, geboren. Sein Studium schloss er an der Kuwasawa Design School ab. Er arbeitete für den bekannten Designer Shiro Kuramata (1987) und ab 1988 für Issey Miyake. Sein eigenes Studio, Tokujin Yoshioka Design, gründete er 2000 in Tokio. Zu seinen im Lauf von rund 20 Jahren entstandenen Arbeiten für Issey Miyake zählen zahlreiche Ladengestaltungen und Installationen. Zu sehen ist sein Werk auch im Museum of Modern Art (MoMA) in New York, dem Centre Pompidou in Paris, dem Victoria and Albert Museum in London, dem Cooper Hewitt National Design Museum in New York sowie dem Vitra Design Museum in Deutschland. Tokujin kooperierte mit Firmen wie Hermès, BMW und Toyota. Er gestaltete u. a. die Leuchte ToFU für Yamagiwa (2000), die Stühle Honey-pop aus Papier (2000–01), Tokyo-pop für Driade (2002), Water Block, eines von mehreren Projekten aus optischem Glas (2002), das Media Skin Mobiltelefon (2005), den Kronleuchter Stardust für den Swarovski Crystal Palace (2005), den PANE Chair (2003–06), Waterfall (Tokio, 2005–06), den Swarovski-Flagshipstore im Ginza-Viertel (Tokio, 2006–08) und den Stuhl VENUS aus Kristall (2008). In jüngster Zeit realisierte Yoshioka die Boutique PLEATS PLEASE von Issey Miyake in Aoyama (Tokio, 2009), Camper To&ether (London, 2009), *The Invisibles* (Mailand, 14.–19. April, 2010, hier vorgestellt), 132 5. Issey Miyake (Minami-Aoyama, Tokio, 2010, ebenfalls hier vorgestellt), die Rainbow Church, MUSEUM Beyondmuseum (Seoul, Südkorea, 2010) und *Twilight* (Mailand, 12.–17. April, 2011, ebenfalls hier vorgestellt).

TOKUJIN YOSHIOKA est né en 1967 à Saga, Japon. Il est diplômé de l'école de design Kuwasawa et a travaillé pour le célèbre designer Shiro Kuramata (1987), puis avec Issey Miyake à partir de 1988. Il ouvre son propre studio, Tokujin Yoshioka Design, en 2000 à Tokyo. Son travail avec Issey Miyake pendant 20 ans comprend de nombreuses boutiques et installations. Ses œuvres sont exposées au Musée d'art moderne (MoMA) de New York, au Centre Pompidou de Paris, au Victoria and Albert Museum de Londres, au Musée national de design Cooper Hewitt de New York et au Musée de design Vitra en Allemagne. Il a collaboré avec des entreprises telles qu'Hermès, BMW et Toyota et a créé, parmi d'autres objets : la lampe Yamagiwa ToFU (2000) ; la chaise en papier Honey-pop (2000–01) ; la ligne Tokyo-pop de Driade (2002) ; Water Block, un travail représentatif de projets en verre optique (2002) ; le téléphone cellulaire Media Skin (2005) ; la suspension Stardust pour le Swarovski Crystal Palace (2005) ; la PANE Chair (2003–06) ; la Cascade (Tokyo, 2005–06) ; le magasin-phare Swarovski de Ginza (Tokyo, 2006–08) et la chaise en cristal naturel VENUS (2008). Yoshioka a récemment achevé la boutique Issey Miyake PLEATS PLEASE d'Aoyama (Tokyo, 2009) ; le magasin Camper Together (Londres, 2009) ; *Les Invisibles* (Milan, 14–19 avril 2010, publié ici) ; la boutique 132 5. d'Issey Miyake (Minami-Aoyama, Tokyo, 2010, publié ici) ; l'Église arc-en-ciel au MUSEUM Beyondmuseum (Séoul, 2010) ; et *Twilight* (Milan, 12–17 avril 2011, publié ici).

"THE INVISIBLES"

Milan, Italy, 14–19 April, 2010

Address: n/a. Area: 56 m²
Client: Kartell. Cost: not disclosed

Created for a five-day period in 2010 during the Milan Furniture Fair, this installation in Kartell's Milan flagship store involved a development of Tokujin Yoshioka's earlier work on a bar made with optical glass to create seating in acrylic that would be almost invisible, generating an image of a "sitter floating in the air." Tokujin Yoshioka states: "I am drawn by things that do not have forms but leave an emotional effect on people. At a glance, such material is invisible and its existence is erased. Through the interaction with light, however, the form suddenly emerges. I am fascinated not only with such phenomena, but also elements that can stir and stimulate our imagination. I also like the idea of light, which is the form of design itself." His "snowflake" installation for the store's windows was made up of transparent plastic "prism" sticks, giving visitors the impression of "stepping into a snowflake."

Die fünftägige Installation zur Mailänder Möbelmesse 2010 im Flagshipstore von Kartell ist eine Weiterentwicklung früherer Entwürfe Yoshiokas, darunter einer Bar aus optischem Glas: Der Designer hatte Sitzmöbel aus Acryl entworfen, auf denen „der Sitzende in der Luft zu schweben" schien. Yoshioka erklärt: „Mich faszinieren Dinge, die im Grunde keine Form, aber dennoch eine emotionale Wirkung auf Menschen haben. Auf den ersten Blick sind solche Materialien unsichtbar, ihre Existenz scheint ausgelöscht. Doch durch das Zusammenspiel mit Licht tritt die Form unerwartet hervor. Nicht nur solche Dinge faszinieren mich, dasselbe gilt für Elemente, die unsere Fantasie berühren und anregen. Auch Licht als Konzept fasziniert mich; es ist die Gestalt von Design schlechthin." Die „Schneeflocken"-Installation für die Schaufenster des Ladens bestand aus transparenten „Prismenstäben" aus Kunststoff und ließ bei den Besuchern den Eindruck entstehen, „in eine Schneeflocke einzutreten".

Créée pour 5 jours pendant le Salon du meuble de Milan 2010, cette installation dans le magasin milanais de Kartell constitue la suite d'un travail antérieur de Tokujin Yoshioka, un bar en verre optique, sous la forme d'une chaise en acrylique quasi invisible, donnant l'impression que la personne assise « flotte dans les airs ». Tokujin Yoshioka déclare : « Je suis attiré par des choses qui n'ont pas de forme mais qui laissent une impression émotionnelle. À première vue, la matière est invisible et son existence effacée. Mais l'interaction avec la lumière fait brusquement apparaître la forme. Je trouve ce phénomène fascinant, de même que les éléments à même d'éveiller et de stimuler notre imagination. J'aime aussi l'idée de la lumière, c'est la forme même du design. » Son installation *Flocon de neige* dans la vitrine du magasin, faite de bâtonnets « prismatiques » de plastique transparent donne aux visiteurs l'impression de « pénétrer dans un flocon de neige ».

The frozen appearance of Yoshioka's "snowflake" design fills the windows of the Kartell flagship store in Milan.

Die scheinbar eiskalte „Schneeflocken"-Installation von Yoshioka füllt die Fenster von Kartells Flagshipstore in Mailand.

Le « Flocon de neige » de Yoshioka à l'aspect givré emplit la vitrine du magasin milanais de Kartell.

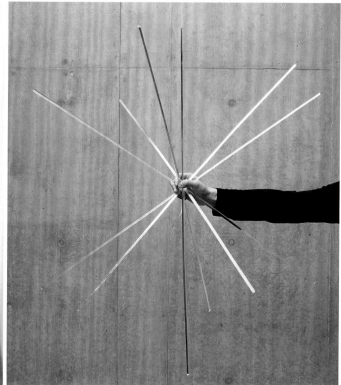

An individual transparent plastic
prism used to form the more complex
"snowflake" design. Right, a completed window leaves an opening in
the snowflake pattern to display
objects.

Ein einzelnes der Kunststoffprismen,
aus denen die komplexe „Schneeflocken"-Installation besteht. Rechts
ein fertiges Schaufenster mit einer
Öffnung, hinter der sich Objekte präsentieren lassen.

L'un des prismes en plastique transparent utilisés pour former la structure complexe du « Flocon de neige ».
À droite, une vitrine achevée ménage
une ouverture dans le « Flocon de
neige » pour y présenter des objets.

"TWILIGHT"

Milan, Italy, 12–17 April, 2011

Address: n/a. Area: 241.4 m²
Client: Moroso. Cost: not disclosed

Describing this project, Tokujin Yoshioka stated that he was seeking to "create space with light and an aura" for the display of a new series of chairs called MOON. "MOON," he said, "is a chair that appears as though it had been sculpted from the beautiful rounded shape of the moon. In this exhibition, light reflects on the surface of the chairs and reveals the beauty of the various textures that exist in the different white materials employed, such as plastics and unique fabrics." Occupying the Moroso showroom with little more than modulated light, the MOON chair appeared as an ethereal white presence, solid enough to be seated on. "The space," said Yoshioka, "would remind people of the natural phenomenon, known as the angel's ladder, and will bring visitors the celestial experience as if embraced by the natural world."

Bei der Beschreibung dieses Projekts spricht Tokujin Yoshioka davon, dass er versucht habe, einen „Raum mit Licht und einer Aura zu schaffen", um die neue Stuhlserie MOON zu präsentieren. „MOON", so der Designer, „ist ein Stuhl, der wirkt, als habe man ihn unmittelbar aus der wunderbaren Rundung des Mondes herausge-schlagen. Bei dieser Präsentation reflektiert das Licht auf den Oberflächen der Stühle und lässt die Texturen der unterschiedlichen verwendeten weißen Materialien, wie Kunststoffe und einzigartige Stoffe, hervortreten". Der Stuhl MOON gab sich im Moroso-Showroom, der von kaum mehr als moduliertem Licht erfüllt war, als ätherische weiße Erscheinung und war doch körperhaft genug, um sich darauf zu setzen. „Der Raum", so Yoshioka, „erinnert an Licht, das durch Wolken bricht, und beschert den Besuchern eine geradezu himmlische Erfahrung, als würden sie in eine übernatürliche Sphäre treten."

Pour décrire ce projet, Tokujin Yoshioka a déclaré avoir cherché à « créer un espace en lumière avec une aura » pour la présentation d'une nouvelle série de sièges appelée MOON. « MOON, déclare-t-il, est un fauteuil qui semble découpé dans les rondeurs si belles de la lune. Dans cette exposition, la lumière se reflète à la surface des fauteuils et révèle la beauté des diverses textures que présentent les différents matériaux blancs utilisés, comme le plastique ou les tissus spécifiquement créés. » Occupant l'espace d'exposition Moroso avec une lumière à peine modulée, le fauteuil MOON a pris l'apparence d'une présence blanche éthérée, suffisamment solide pour s'asseoir dessus. « L'espace, dit Yoshioka, rappelle le phénomène naturel connu sous le nom d'échelle de l'ange et apporte aux visiteurs l'expérience céleste d'être enlacés par le monde naturel. »

The misty, mysterious atmosphere created by the designer makes the MOON chairs and visitors appear in a ghostlike way. Below, right, the store seen from the exterior during the installation.

Der Designer schuf eine nebelhafte, geheimnisvolle Stimmung, in der die MOON-Sessel und die Besucher wie geisterhafte Wesen schienen. Unten rechts das Geschäft von außen während der Installation.

L'atmosphère mystérieuse et embrumée créée par le designer donne une présence fantomatique aux fauteuils MOON et aux visiteurs. Ci-dessous, le magasin vu de l'extérieur pendant l'installation.

132 5. ISSEY MIYAKE

Minami-Aoyama, Tokyo, Japan, 2010

Address: 1F 5–3–10 Minami-Aoyama, Minato-ku, Tokyo, Japan, +81 3 3499 6476, www.isseymiyake.co.jp
Area: 254 m² (installation space 219 m²). Client: Issey Miyake
Cost: not disclosed

Located in the Minami-Aoyama area of Tokyo where the designer Issey Miyake has long been present through various stores, **132 5. ISSEY MIYAKE** was the first space for a new label based on "regeneration and recreation." Tokujin Yoshioka focused here on a "way of selling" as opposed to "superficial interior design." As he further explains: "The clothes are displayed on five transparent torsos, which are strung down from the ceiling. Customers can freely access the computer graphic images of the complicated process on the iPad installed in the store. The display of the process from 2D to 3D…" is reminiscent of a typical Japanese kimono store.

Im Tokioter Viertel Minami-Aoyama, in dem Issey Miyake schon lange mit mehreren Boutiquen vertreten ist, war **132 5. ISSEY MIYAKE** der erste Laden für ein neues Label, das auf „Freizeit und Erholung" zugeschnitten ist. Tokujin Yoshioka konzentrierte sich hier auf eine „Verkaufsstrategie" statt auf eine „oberflächliche Innenarchitektur". Er erklärt weiter: „Die Mode wird auf fünf von der Decke hängenden, transparenten Torsos präsentiert. Die Kunden haben freien Zugang zu iPads, die im Laden installiert wurden, und auf denen Computergrafiken des komplizierten Designprozesses zu sehen sind. Die Visualisierung des Verwandlungsprozesses von 2-D zu 3-D …" erinnert an ein typisches japanisches Kimonogeschäft.

Situé dans le quartier Minami-Aoyama de Tokyo où le designer Issey Miyake est présent depuis longtemps avec plusieurs magasins, **132 5. ISSEY MIYAKE** est le premier espace dédié à un nouveau label basé sur la « régénération et recréation ». Tokujin Yoshioka s'y est concentré sur un « mode de vente », et non sur une « architecture intérieure superficielle ». Il explique encore que : « Les vêtements sont présentés sur cinq bustes transparents suspendus au plafond. Les clients ont librement accès aux images graphiques des processus complexes sur l'iPad installé dans le magasin. La présentation du processus de passage de la bidimensionnalité à la tridimensionnalité… » rappelle une boutique de kimonos japonaise typique.

In the case of this Issey Miyake store, the designer has chosen a sober white-on-white display where clothes and objects stand out whether seen from outside, or from the interior.

Bei diesem Issey Miyake Store entschied sich der Designer für ein strenges, vollkommen weißes Dekor, in dem Mode und Objekte von außen wie von innen auffallen.

Pour ce magasin Issey Miyake, le designer a opté pour une présentation sobre blanc sur blanc où vêtements et accessoires ressortent, qu'ils soient vus de l'extérieur ou de l'intérieur.

Tokujin Yoshioka uses extremely simple presentation to highlight the fashion—in this image, including an iPad-type screen.

Tokujin Yoshioka nutzt ausgesprochen einfache Mittel, um die Mode eindrucksvoll zu präsentieren – auf diesem Bild u. a. ein iPad.

Tokujin Yoshioka a recours à une présentation simplifiée à l'extrême pour mettre la mode en valeur – ici un écran de type iPad.

The display in this instance focuses
on a stark contrast between black
and white. Transparency dominates,
with white surfaces or transparent
mannequins used to highlight Issey
Miyake's still trendsetting designs.

Hier konzentriert sich die Präsentation auf den starken Kontrast von
Schwarz und Weiß. Transparenz dominiert. Besonders zur Geltung kommen
Issey Miyakes noch immer trendset-
zende Entwürfe auf weißen Flächen
oder transparenten Puppen.

La présentation se concentre ici sur
le contraste fort entre le noir et le
blanc. La transparence domine, les
surfaces blanches et les mannequins
transparents mettent en valeur les
créations toujours novatrices d'Issey
Miyake.

INDEX OF BUILDINGS, NAMES AND PLACES

INDEX OF BUILDINGS, NAMES AND PLACES

CREDITS

PHOTO CREDITS — 2, 7 © Tokujin Yoshioka Inc. / **8** © Jesús Granada/Bisimages / **11** © Bo Stranden / **12** © Roland Halbe / **13** © Neil Bedford / **14** © Peganaute / **15** © UNStudio / **16** © Leonardo Finotti / **17** © Hiroyuki Hirai / **19** © Hakuhodo Inc. / **21** © Tokujin Yoshioka Inc. / **23** © Actescollectifs Architectes SA / **24** © Louis Baquiast / **26** © Ewout Huibers / **27** © Michael Moran / **28** © Roland Halbe / **30** © Moreno Maggi / **31** © Leonardo Finotti / **33** © Daici Ano / **35** © Nacása & Partners Inc. / **37** © Roland Halbe / **38** © Toshiyuki Yano / **41** © Hélène Hilaire / **42** © Patrick Reynolds / **43** © GRAFT – Gesellschaft von Architekten / **45** © Roland Halbe / **46-47** © Fernando Guerra / **48** © 2G Arquitectos / **49-53** © Jesús Granada/Bisimages / **54, 56-59** © Actescollectifs Architectes SA / **55, 60-61** © Thomas Jantscher / **62** © Alt-Q Arquitectura / **63-67** © Jesús Granada/Bisimages / **68** © Architektur 6H / **69-73** © Antje Quiram / **74, 76-77** © Artek oy ab / **75, 78-79** © Bo Stranden / **80** © Auer+Weber+Assoziierte / **81-85** © Roland Halbe / **86** © Frank Tielemans / **87-89** © Marten de Leeuw / **90** © Basiches Architects / **91-95** © Leonardo Finotti / **96** © BCMF Arquitetos / **97, 99 bottom-101** © Leonardo Finotti / **99 top** © Jomar Bragança / **102** © BIG – Bjarke Ingels Group / **103, 105-107** © Leif Orkelbog Andresen / **104** © Iwan Baan / **108** © Campaign / **109-113** © Hufton + Crow / **114** © Tom Bunning / **115-119** © Neil Bedford / **120** © Ingrid von Kruse / **121, 123, 126-129** © Ute Zscharnt for David Chipperfield Architects / **122, 124** © Hiepler & Brunier / **125** © Andreas Fechner / **130** © Concrete / **131-149** © Ewout Huibers / **150** © Ivan Cotado / **151-155** © Héctor Santos Díez/Bisimages / **156** © Markus Deutschmann / **157-163** © Roland Halbe / **164-167** © Tom Dixon / **168** © Evan Douglis Studio / **169-171** © Michael Moran / **172** © Maurice Haas / **173-179** © Antje Quiram / **180** © Estudio Nómada / **181-185** © Héctor Santos Díez/Bisimages / **186-191** © Patrick Reynolds / **192** © Studio Fuksas / **193-194** © Maurizio Marcato / **195-197** © Moreno Maggi / **198-203** © GRAFT – Gesellschaft von Architekten / **204-207** © Bébé Branss / **208-213** © Hakuhodo Inc. / **214** © Benoit Linero / **215-221** © Hélène Hilaire / **222** © Architekturbüro Kergassner / **223-227** © Roland Halbe / **228** © Waro Kishi + K. Associates/Architects / **229-233** © Hiroyuki Hirai / **234** © studio mk27 / **235-239** © Sousa Cunhal, Tourismo, SA. / **240** © Nikolas Koenig / **241-243** © Danny Bright / **244** © David Lynch / **245-247** © Alexandre Guirkinger / **248** © March Studio / **249-251** © Louis Baquiast / **252** © Manolo Yllera / **253-263** © Paul Warchol / **264** © Miralles Tagliabue EMBT / **265-267** © Marcela Veronica Grassi / **268-275** © Nicolas Buisson / **276** © Yuko Nagayama & Associates / **277-279** © Daici Ano / **280** © Ninom / **281-287** © Jesús Granada/Bisimages / **288** © Ateliers Jean Nouvel / **289-293** © Roland Halbe / **294-297** © Philippe Ruault / **298** © Muti Randolph / **299-303** © Leonardo Finotti / **304** © Stefano Riva / **305-307** © Leonardo Finotti / **308** © Rizoma / **309-317** © Leonardo Finotti / **318** © Rojkind Arquitectos / **319-325** © Rojkind Arquitectos, photos by Paúl Rivera / **326-331** © SAQ / **332** © Chikara Ohno/sinato / **333-337** © Toshiyuki Yano / **338** © Sotero Arquitetos / **339-343** © Leonardo Finotti / **344** © Suppose Design Office / **345-353** © Toshiyuki Yano / **354** © Caterina Tiazzoldi/Nueva Ordentra / **355, 357** © Luca Campigotto / **356** © Frederico Rizzo / **358** © Alfons Tost Interiorisme / **359-363** © Eugeni Pons Fotografía / **364** © Triptyque / **365-369** © Leonardo Finotti / **370** © Inga Powilleit / **371-377** © UNStudio / **378** © Isay Weinfeld / **379-383** © Leonardo Finotti / **384-389** © Fernando Guerra / **390-397** © Nacása & Partners Inc. / **398-407** © Tokujin Yoshioka Inc. / **408, 411 top** © Yoshinaga Yasuaki / **409-410, 411 bottom** © Nacása & Partners Inc.

CREDITS FOR PLANS / DRAWINGS / CAD DOCUMENTS — 51, 53 © 2G Arquitectos / **57, 61** © Actescollectifs Architectes SA / **66-67** © Alt-Q Arquitectura / **73** © Architektur 6H / **77** © Artek oy ab / **85** © Auer+Weber+Assoziierte / **94** © Basiches Architects / **98, 100-101** © BCMF Arquitetos / **111, 113** © Campaign / **116-117, 119** © Gary Card / **123, 125-126, 129** © David Chipperfield Architects / **133, 135, 147, 149** © Concrete / **158, 162** © Odile Decq & Benoît Cornette / **175, 177, 179** © EM2N / **183** © Estudio Nómada / **189-190** © Fearon Hay / **196** © Studio Fuksas / **203, 206** © GRAFT – Gesellschaft von Architekten / **211** © Hakuhodo Inc. / **216, 219, 221** © Agence Jouin Manku / **224** © Architekturbüro Kergassner / **231** © Waro Kishi + K. Associates/Architects / **243** © LOT-EK / **251** © March Studio / **256, 261** © Courtesy of Peter Marino Architect PLLC / **266** © Miralles Tagliabue EMBT / **270-271, 273** © Agence Moatti-Rivière / **285, 287** © Ninom / **293-294, 297** © Ateliers Jean Nouvel / **301, 303** © Muti Randolph / **307** © Stefano Riva / **311-313** © Rizoma / **321-322** © Rojkind Arquitectos / **331** © SAQ / **335** © Chikara Ohno/sinato / **349, 351, 353** © Suppose Design Office / **357** © Caterina Tiazzoldi/Nueva Ordentra / **362-363** © Alfons Tost Interiorisme / **367** © Triptyque / **373-374, 376** © UNStudio / **381, 385, 389** © Isay Weinfeld / **393** © Wonderwall Inc. / **400-401, 407** © Tokujin Yoshioka Inc.